URBAN GOVERNMENT AND POLITICS

McGRAW-HILL SERIES IN POLITICAL SCIENCE

Adrian · State and Local Governments

Adrian and Press · Governing Urban America

Bone · American Politics and the Party System

Christenson and McWilliams · Voice of the People: Readings in Public
Opinion and Propaganda

Easton and Dennis · Children in the Political System: Origins of Political
Legitimacy

Gerberding · United States Foreign Policy

Harmon · Political Thought: From Plato to the Present

McCandless · Urban Government and Politics

McClosky and Turner · The Soviet Dictatorship

Millett · Government and Public Administration

Millett · Management in the Public Service

Neumann · European Government

Pool · Contemporary Political Science: Toward Empirical Theory

Pritchett · The American Constitution

Pritchett · American Constitutional Issues

Schuman · International Politics

Wilson · Police Administration

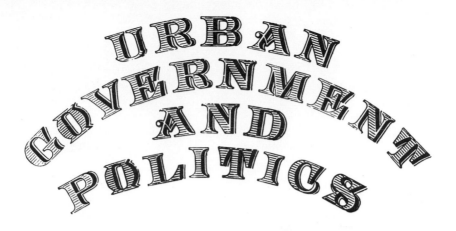

URBAN GOVERNMENT AND POLITICS

CARL A. MC CANDLESS

PROFESSOR OF POLITICAL SCIENCE
WASHINGTON UNIVERSITY, ST. LOUIS

McGRAW-HILL BOOK COMPANY

New York   St. Louis   San Francisco
Düsseldorf   London   Mexico   Panama
Sydney   Toronto

This book was set in News Gothic by Monotype
Composition Company, Inc., and printed on permanent
paper and bound by The Maple Press Company. The
designer was Paula Tuerk; the drawings were done by
John Cordes, J. & R. Technical Services, Inc. The
editors were Ronald Kissack and Timothy Yohn. Sally
R. Ellyson supervised the production.

Engravings courtesy of the Picture Collection
New York Public Library

PREFACE

This book is designed for use as a text in an introductory course in urban government and politics. The frame of reference used and the materials included were chosen to help the college student who wants to know more about how cities are governed and who may think he would like to do further study and research in the politics of urban and metropolitan areas. A conscious effort is made to relate the substantative and descriptive materials to what the author understands to be the nature of the discipline of political science.

No attempt is made to set forth value premises about city politics or to beat the drums for reforms in city government. Throughout the book the student is urged to understand politics as competition among groups seeking different results from the political process. Attention is focused on the nature of conflicts that arise in urban societies and on the manner in which existing institutions and legal systems make it easier for some groups and harder for others to control decisions flowing from the system. The book does not instruct the student as to what is *good* and what is *bad* about governmental institutions and policies, for what is good for some groups may very well be bad for others. It assumes that existing institutions and legal systems are never neutral; they operate to the advantage of some and the disadvantage of others. Therefore, city political institutions are described as dynamic, with interest groups constantly seeking changes they think will produce decisions more nearly in congruence with their values and desires.

Although the book was prepared primarily for college students, citizens interested in urban government may find the approach useful in understanding why politicians behave as they do and why numerous so-called reforms fall by the way as they are processed through the political system. The author has had a number of years of experience as a teacher of municipal government and politics, as a technical consultant to city-charter commissions, and as a city official, and he is convinced that the approach to the subject taken in this text is far more practical than would be an attempt to argue for specific governmental forms or processes so often offered as remedies to cure the ills of cities or to explain how city functions can be administered more efficiently.

During the process of teaching local politics over a number of years, the author has read numerous textbooks, analytical essays, and research reports. All these have most certainly added to his knowledge and understanding of the subject and have influenced the substance and the method of presentation of the material in this book. Where specific references are made to material from other sources, the author has sought to give proper credit, but at this point he wishes, in a general way, to acknowledge the contributions of the many students of local government and politics whose works have helped make the book possible but for whom no specific credit lines are included.

Carl A. McCandless

CONTENTS

PART 1

INTRODUCTION

1

ANALYZING CITY GOVERNMENT AND POLITICS

The purpose of this book is to present a description and analysis of one of the levels of government in which significant decisions are made in the American political system. The specific unit for study is the municipal corporation or, as it is more commonly referred to, the city. Although attention will be primarily concentrated on the city as a political arena in which important kinds of decisions are made, the relationships between the city and other local units of government, the state, and the nation will also be examined.

The systematic examination of any governmental unit requires that some frame of reference be established which will provide organization and unity to the entire study. The assumption is made in this text that the municipal corporation as a political institution plays a role or performs a function within the total political system of which it is a part and that the best way to learn about city politics is to center attention upon this role or function. Such seemingly diverse subjects as municipal taxation, land-use planning, waste collection and disposal, and law enforcement can be tied together if they are examined in relation to the accomplishment of a major function which the city is created to perform.

Certainly, students of politics are not in agreement on a single scheme of analysis which serves best as an orienting concept around which all facets of city government can be made to revolve, but most of them will agree that clarity and unity require that one of several possible alternatives be adopted. Obviously, the adoption of a single unifying concept about the function of the city places certain limits on the kinds of material that are relevant and on the manner in which it can be presented, but such a limitation is not as serious a handicap as would be the inclusion of a wide variety of descriptive material about cities without supplying any central theme which would give unity to the entire work.

THE CITY AS A SERVICE INSTITUTION

One possible approach is to view the city as a service institution created and utilized to supply certain services to its inhabitants which are unlikely to be performed by any other governmental agency or by private utility corporations. If this vision of the city is to be the focal point of analysis, attention will be centered on problems related to police administration, fire protection, mass transit, local public health, and similar activities commonly accepted as functions of cities. This concept of the function of cities dominated most of the literature of reform during the first quarter of the twentieth century, and it still is often an implied assumption in books whose major concern is municipal administration. This approach to the study of cities suggests that, as in private corporations, operating efficiency is the ultimate goal for which to strive. The implication is clear that the major outputs of city operation can be measured in terms of units of service rendered to the citizens and that inputs consist of units of money and manpower required to produce the services. The major problems, then, relate to ways and means of maximizing services and minimizing expenditures of manpower and money.

A FOURFOLD CLASSIFICATION

Williams and Adrian, in their study of four cities, identified four types of cities based on the function or role of the city as perceived by dominant groups within it. The assumption is made that the operations of a city government will be determined by the image the policy makers have of the purpose for which the city exists. Their classification, based on the purposes of cities, is (1) promoting economic growth, (2) providing life's amenities, (3) maintaining traditional services, and (4) arbitrating among conflicting interests.[1] Items (2) and (3) are not far different from the functional approach

[1] Oliver P. Williams and Charles R. Adrian, *Four Cities*, University of Pennsylvania Press, Philadelphia, 1963, pp. 21–39.

just described, and item (4) comes close to reflecting the view which will be used in this text and will be discussed at greater length later.

THE CITY AS THE GUARDIAN OF ORDER

Henry Schmandt suggests that the city be conceptualized "as the guardian of order."[2] His contention is that the city functions as an institutional control to produce conformity of individual and group behavior to the culturally established norms of the community. The idea of maintenance of order in the metropolis also pervades Scott Greer's analysis in *Governing the Metropolis*, as he finds that "one basic export of the city is order"; his topic heads include, "The City as the Center of Societal Order," "The City as a Problem of Social Order," and "Solutions to the Problem of Order."[3] If this concept of the role of the city is accepted as a unifying theme for study, discussion will necessarily concentrate on forms of social control available to local policy makers whose aim is to discover and promulgate the cultural norms and to institutionalize means of ensuring maximum compliance with them. Since "order" is much less susceptible to quantification and measurement than are "units of service," the notion of efficiency in terms of maximum output in relation to costs will be less central to the discussion than it would be if the city were conceived of as a service institution.

THE CITY AS A SOURCE OF SELF-SATISFACTION

Schmandt also suggests that there is within the social system "the individual who perceives the local polity as a source for satisfying his personal esteem and self-actualization needs."[4] He suggests that the political behavior of emigrant groups, particularly the Irish, who viewed local political offices as symbolic rewards, can be understood in terms of the thesis that they considered local government as an avenue for self-realization and, therefore, established control over the decision-making machinery in Eastern cities. Adoption of this view of the function of the city might well explain the emergence and political power of big-city bosses in the late nineteenth century. This concept, if adopted, would lead the writer to place great emphasis

[2] Henry J. Schmandt, "Order in the Urban Community: The Role of Local Government," paper prepared for the annual meeting of the Midwest Conference of Political Scientists, Bloomington, Ind., Apr. 22–24, 1965.
[3] Scott Greer, *Governing the Metropolis*, John Wiley & Sons, Inc., New York, 1962, pp. 4, 36, 37.
[4] Schmandt, *op. cit.*, p. 13.

on participation in politics, individual and group influence in elections, and political leadership, but it seems too narrow to include all the facets of city politics that should be presented in an introductory text.

THE CITY AS A POLITICAL ARENA

The central theme which will be utilized throughout this book is that the city may be viewed as an arena in which certain kinds of human conflicts arise, are debated, and are resolved through established political institutions under generally accepted rules and procedures. The adoption of this image of the major role of the city is prompted by the fact that the author wants to fit municipal politics into its proper place in the broad discipline of political science. If the author's purpose were to search out what is bad about cities and propose solutions for general reform, the approach adopted here would be entirely unsatisfactory. Since some readers will not have pursued a course of study which has provided them with a systematic analysis of the discipline of political science, a brief discussion of the author's concept of the discipline will make it easier for them to follow the presentation in the following chapters.

POLITICS AS CONFLICT

When the expression "political science" is used it implies two facts: first, that there are some kinds of phenomena that are political in character and, second, that such phenomena can be studied in a scientific way. Most students of politics will accept this statement, but not all will agree upon just what is to be considered *political* or what constitutes *scientific* analysis.

The essence of politics is conflict; therefore, the student of politics must be involved in analyzing conflicts. Human conflict arises when people who are in a position to react to each other disagree on some possible course of action. More often than not, the disagreement arises over the manner in which scarce resources are to be distributed within some kind of human association.[5] The behavior of persons involved in the conflict, the institutional arrangements available for its resolution, the generally accepted rules under

[5] This position is similar to that taken by David Easton when he describes political science as "the study of the authoritative allocation of values for a society" (David Easton, *The Political System*, Alfred A. Knopf, Inc., New York, 1953, p. 129). See also Francis J. Sorauf, *Political Science, An Informed Overview*, Charles E. Merrill Books, Inc., Columbus, Ohio, 1956, pp. 1–8; and Robert A. Dahl, *Modern Political Analysis*, Prentice-Hall, Inc., Englewood Cliffs, N.J., 1963, chaps. 1, 2.

which the competition is carried on, and the nature of the settlement all are the substance of politics.

Although, as indicated above, Greer emphasizes the concept of order maintenance, he recognizes that conflict is central to the study of political institutions, when, in speaking of the political nature of order, he says:

> Its function is the adjustment of conflict among the corporate citizens and the social categories of the area. The conflict is real, the stakes may be very high, and the first question is no less than this: Who is a first class citizen, and whose interests shall prevail in this area? Such questions are not answered by simple administrative routine; they cannot be answered in a laboratory or with an electronic computer. They can be answered only through a political process which is accepted as legitimate, and which can make binding decisions enforceable by the police power and the public treasury of society.[6]

Many who study politics as defined here are willing to accept such a broad image of what is political and therefore of concern to the political scientist. They are, therefore, concerned with conflicts which arise within all kinds of social organizations. They may study conflicts arising within a church congregation over the selection of a new minister or over construction of a new church building in a new location. Conflicts within labor unions over jurisdictional issues or demands to be included in new contracts might very well be studied as political phenomena. In fact, some researchers are convinced that factors and forces producing conflicts within social organizations and variables affecting the manner in which they are resolved are very much the same in all human organizations and that what is learned in one setting is transferable to another.

A narrower view may also be taken as to the kind of conflicts which should be the primary concern of students of politics and this is the one adopted for use here.[7] Conflicts are political when they are presented for resolution within the political institutions of a society. Such institutions are distinguished from religious, educational, fraternal, and professional institutions in two respects: (1) Political institutions include within their clientele the whole of the society. Individuals may elect membership in most social organizations or they may elect to be nonmembers, but when a government is created within fixed boundaries, all persons within these boundaries are subject to institutional decisions whether they like it or not. (2) Political organizations have at their

---

[6] Greer, op. cit., p. 41.
[7] See Haywood R. Alker, Jr., Mathematics and Politics, The Macmillan Company, New York, 1965, p. 15.

command sanctions with which to ensure compliance that are not available to other forms of social organization.[8] Churches, fraternities, labor unions, educational institutions, and social clubs may expel members and refuse certain benefits generally available to members, but only political organizations can incarcerate offenders in penal institutions or exact the death penalty. The term "legitimacy" is often used to describe the concept of mass acceptability of the authority of political organizations.

The use of the idea of conflict as the common element of political phenomena does not deny the fact that political institutions operating through their officers and employees do many things where there is no conflict or where any conflict that is present is of a very low order. City physicians in a municipally owned hospital go about their professional duties in much the same way as they would in a church-operated hospital. Professionals in many fields render public services as employees of political institutions, but since their tasks require the application of methods and techniques that are widely accepted as proper, their actions are not considered to be political. Research to improve surgical and engineering techniques may be sponsored and carried on in political institutions by public employees, but if no conflicts arise in such activity, it is not of general interest to the student of politics. At some point or another, however, even this activity is caught up in politics. One of the most universal conflicts that arises in a political organization concerns the allocation of public funds to the various activities of the organization. Hence, demands made for money to support research or to care for patients in a public hospital must compete with demands made by other units within the government which seek support for other activities. To this extent professionals must engage in the political process to secure financial support for their projects.

POLITICAL CONFLICT INVOLVES GROUPS

The kinds of conflict which merit the attention of political scientists are those in which groups of people with similar views seek to achieve some desired results through political institutions and are opposed by other groups which are not in sympathy with such demands. Although conflicts between individuals may shed some light on the nature of conflict, they are not likely to become political unless the participants are able to rally significant numbers

[8] Sorauf, *op. cit.,* p. 3.

of others to support their cause. An important part of the study of politics is, therefore, devoted to a study of the behavior of groups that participate actively in the political process.

The adoption of the concept of conflict as the focal point for the study of municipal politics does not imply that the established services performed by cities will not be subjects for discussion. The point to be remembered is that elements of conflict that arise in the determination of the range of services to be undertaken, the manner in which they will be financed, and the intensity with which they will be rendered are of primary concern to political scientists. A single illustration may clarify this point. If a given city has not supplied its householders with any kind of garbage and rubbish collection and disposal, the assumption is that private arrangements have been made between householders and some private persons to make collections at a fee stated in the contract. Each householder, however, is free to provide for his own disposal if he chooses to do so. Waste disposal becomes a political issue only when some householders, dissatisfied with the existing system, make demands upon city officials to include this service as a city responsibility. When this issue is on the agenda of a city council for debate, some citizens will appear to support the changes and others will insist on continuation of the existing system. But once the decision is made for the city to assume the collection function, other political conflicts arise. Shall this function be financed by a general tax on property or by service charges collected by the city from each householder? Shall collections be every day or twice each week? Shall householders be required to place kitchen refuse in one kind of container and rubbish in another? Various citizen groups want these questions decided in different ways. Therefore, in this text discussion of city functions will appear but attention will be centered on the nature of conflicts that arise in their performance, rather than upon the technical procedures required to perform the service.

SCIENCE AND THE STUDY OF POLITICS

If politics is viewed as groups of people competing with each other to secure decisions favorable to them through established political institutions, the student of politics must be interested in the end product of the conflict, the decision that is finally made, as well as in the procedure by which the final decision is arrived at. Can such a process be studied scientifically? On this issue there is no general agreement among those who profess to be political scientists. There are those who believe that the study of politics is more philosophy than science.[9] Historically, writers about politics, from Plato down to the twentieth century, seemed to be concerned with discovering the essentials of the *good life* and with the construction of governmental institutions which would make such a good life possible. Although the study of political philosophy is still an important part of the curricula of most college departments of political science, there is a definite trend toward making the discipline more scientific. Although there is no general agreement on what the term "scientific" means when used in this context, two elements seem to occur regularly in the literature on the subject.

Scientific Attitude

Most researchers in the field of politics are agreed that one who observes the political process in order to describe it accurately and to analyze it needs to acquire what may be called a scientific attitude. This implies that he approach his subject intellectually rather than emotionally. He is trying to understand the process, rather than praise or condemn it. Observations are made objectively, and no attempt is made to screen out of the observations that which is objectionable and to play up prominently that which is pleasing to the observer. Description portrays "what is" in the political process, not what the observer thinks it "ought to be." In short, the scientific observer seeks to submerge his own values about the merits of competing groups in a political conflict and to explain, not pass judgment on, the process by which settlement was reached.

This discussion is not intended to imply that a political scientist does not or should not have his own set of values by which to judge right and wrong in political conflicts, but it is important that when he writes as a scientist, his own value premises not be permitted to color the analysis he propounds. Nor is it to be implied that political scientists cannot or should not participate actively in the political process, but it is important that political activity not be permitted to distort objectivity in description. Objectivity is often made difficult by the common use of such terms as the "public welfare," the "general welfare," the "public good," and, on a larger scale, the "national interest." These terms are used by all groups which seek to make the position they espouse prevail in the political process. They are often used to

[9] For a good presentation of this point of view, see Herbert J. Storing (ed.), *Essays on the Scientific Study of Politics*, Holt, Rinehart and Winston, Inc., New York, 1962.

imply that anyone opposed to a given point of view is serving "selfish" interests or is opposed to what is good for all. If politics is viewed as resolution of interest conflict, obviously there is no single decision on any political question that is equally good for every interest group. Therefore, the student of politics needs to be alerted when he hears that a proposed course of action is "good," to ask himself: good for whom? John Kautsky states this point of view effectively when, in discussing the "national interest," he says:

> The national interest, then, always turns out to reflect the interest, i.e., the values and attitudes, of the individual who employs the concept and the group he speaks for (the group here being defined simply as those who share a common interest). These interests are then ascribed to the "nation," but since different individuals and groups ascribe different interest to it, the nation does not, in fact, have any interests on any matter on which there is disagreement within it, that is, on any matter involved in politics. The national interest exists subjectively for those involved in politics; it does not exist objectively for those who wish to analyze politics. It ought to follow that the political scientist should leave the concept to the politician and the policy maker.[10]

Scientific Method

A skilled and intelligent observer who maintains a sense of objectivity can supply a useful description of a particular conflict that has developed and has been resolved in the political arena. He can describe the issues in the conflict, the groups which participated, those who occupied positions of leadership, and the nature of the decision that, at least temporarily, resolved the conflict. This is what is accomplished by the typical case study in politics. If the student reads such case studies, he can learn a great deal about the techniques of the participants in a political conflict, and the procedures by which decisions are arrived at, but such descriptions do not meet all the requirements of scientific method demanded by many members of the discipline. This group seeks to apply to political phenomena the rigid methods used by the physical and biological scientists. They hope to make statements about social conflict that identify and evaluate the factors and forces operating in any conflict situation that account for the manner in which it is settled. This approach focuses attention on decisions as the output of the political system, then seeks specific answers to the question of why a particular decision was adopted rather than an alternative.

[10] Reprinted from John H. Kautsky, "The National Interest: The Entomologist and the Beetle," *Midwest Journal of Political Science*, vol. 10, p. 224, May, 1966, by permission of Wayne State University Press.

The scientific approach is in reality a search for regularities in the political process which can be observed in all political conflicts and which explain the outputs of the process. The assumption is implied that if the researcher can identify the factors and forces which produce political decisions, he can predict solutions to future conflicts. An example drawn from the natural sciences will illustrate this point. If the physicist observes that a confined gas increases the pressure in its container when heat is applied, he knows that heat is the force which accounts for the increase in pressure. He can by successive experiments determine with exactitude the increase in pressure that will result from each degree of increase in temperature. Specific general statements can then be made which describe the effects on confined gases resulting from temperature changes. Such statements are predictive and have general applicability in all locations regardless of who performs the experiments. An application of this method to politics might be found in an attempt to predict the voting behavior of a legislator. If a series of observations about his voting can be made, the observer may identify the forces which operate to determine his vote, and if these observations are correct, future voting behavior may be predicted.

At least two factors operate to make the methods of the natural sciences difficult to apply in the study of politics: first, the political scientist is dealing with human beings whose behavior is much more complicated than is the behavior of inorganic substances and of plants and lower animals; second, the type of laboratory in which controlled experiments can be set up is not available to the social scientist. The complicated nature of man and the difficulty of understanding his responses need no argument here, but something may be said about laboratories for observing political conflict.

THE CITY AS A POLITICAL LABORATORY

Although controlled experimental laboratories may be set up to study responses of individuals to different stimuli and even for the observation of problem solving in small groups, this method is impossible for the study of political parties or large interest groups as they campaign for the passage or defeat of a legislative proposal. The only laboratory available to the political observer is the actual life-sized political process as it operates to provide solutions to complicated and often emotionally charged conflicts. The success or failure of political institutions and processes may be measured by the extent to which they settle disputes peacefully; insurrection and revolution are grim evidences of the failure of many existing political processes to accomplish this purpose. There is no lack of operating laboratories in which the political process can be observed, and enough conflicts pass through these laboratories to satisfy all the political observers that our educational system can train.

International conflicts can be studied in such arenas as the United Nations, NATO-type alliances, and regular patterns of international diplomacy. Within the United States, national conflicts are waged in Congress, in the federal courts, and before federal administrative agencies. Each of the 50 states furnishes a wide range of conflict issues and a number of arenas in which decisions are made. The city also furnishes a useful arena for observing the political process. The kind of issues over which group conflicts arise are easily identified and access to those directly involved is not too difficult. Most political scientists can, without too much trouble, interview and in many cases work with participants in a conflict and with those who ultimately make the decision.

The number of cities available for observation makes them particularly useful for comparative studies. The number and variety of cities make it possible to concentrate on some variables operating in a political system when other variables are fairly constant; i.e., certain cities can be selected for study which have many factors in common but which differ in other respects. The selection can be made along one of many lines, such as population size, economic base, or political party composition. If the selected cities are similar with respect to these characteristics but very different with respect to racial characteristics, we may, after observing differences in the political process, speculate on the causes of the observed differences. Political scientists who stress the comparative approach to the study of politics and political systems should find cities excellent laboratories to test their assumptions.

A MODEL OF THE POLITICAL PROCESS

Politics has been defined as the resolution of group conflicts that arise within a society when the conflict is resolved within generally accepted institutions which possess power to enforce decisions. The institutions within which the decisions are made and enforced may be referred to as government; the procedures through which conflicts are brought into governmental machinery for resolution and the ways and means by which a decision is finally arrived at within this machinery may be called the political process. Those who operate within the process to influence the final outcome are the political actors, and those who, at the end of the process, must produce and enforce a decision are the decision makers. Needless to say, the political process is complex and it differs widely from one society to another and from one city to another, but the student will be better prepared to observe and understand the process in a specific city on a single conflict issue if he has some general pattern which suggests to him what he may expect to find and some indication of what the process may be like. The simple model suggested here consists of the enumeration of a series of events which should be useful when one tries to observe with understanding the political process.

1. Conflicts arise among groups and are presented to some part of the governmental machinery of the city for action. At some decision-making center in the city, a group presents its desires and finds one or more other groups opposing its demands. The decision-making center is often the city council, but it may also be the mayor's office, an administrative board or commission, or the municipal court.

2. Since the demands made upon decision makers are so diverse and since many group demands are in opposition to demands of other groups, a final and definitive decision is seldom possible. The best that can be expected to result from most conflicts in the political arena is that some kind of compromise can be hammered out which, at least for the present, will be accepted by participants so that other items on the political agenda can be brought up for consideration.[11]

3. Although opposing groups who have been participating in the conflict appear willing to accept, peacefully, the compromise worked out, they may not give up on the possibility of ultimate victory in the long run. Acceptance of less than complete victory comes from a feeling that something is better than nothing at all, from a sense of frustration, or from lack of money to continue the fight at the time; seldom does it come from the feeling that the war has been won or lost. Therefore groups who are not completely satisfied with results will seek other avenues to achieve their ends.

Each of the steps in the political process as outlined above needs some elaboration.

Nature of Conflict in Cities

Those who live in cities have images of what they expect from the local political system, but the expectations of some are quite different from the expectations of others. Therefore, when some citizens collectively try to get city officials to do what they expect of them, other citizens, who do not want this kind of response, organize to prevent the action. In this way conflicts enter

[11] See Charles R. Adrian, *State and Local Governments*, McGraw-Hill Book Company, New York, 1960, pp. 1, 2.

the political process.[12] What are the major sources or bases from which these conflicts arise in cities? Some of the most significant sources can be identified.

Scope of Government Activity   A significant source of conflict arises out of the different images people have about the proper scope of government activity. Disputes arise because honest people hold different opinions about which activities should be within the scope of private business activity and which should be the responsibility of government. Few cities that have operated as much as twenty years have not witnessed bitter political battles over public versus private ownership of electric power distribution, government garbage and refuse collection versus private sanitary companies, government versus private housing, and similar issues. These conflicts often divide citizens along what may be described roughly as conservative and liberal lines and often along established political party lines.

Sources of Financial Support   Since each possible method of financing governmental activities falls upon citizens in different ways, any proposal to raise money is a source of group conflict. Perhaps the broadest conflict in this category revolves around the issue of support of governmental programs by general taxation or by service charges. In the first instance, payment is related in some way to ability to pay without reference to service received, while in the second, payment is related directly to service received. For example, rapid transit systems may be supported partly from general taxation or wholly by charges against riders. Water may be supplied by the city at a flat rate per householder, it may be metered so that charges are based on amount used, or the system may be tax-supported. For those city services that have for years been supported from general taxation, the kind of tax to be levied becomes a significant political issue.

Allocation of Tax Money among Various Types of Government Activities These conflicts are often referred to as conflicts over budget allocations. Each kind of service rendered by a city has its supporters, often organized into associations, whose chief concern is support for their specific pet service. One fact of life in city politics is that total resources are never sufficient to allocate to each group all it would like; therefore each group feels that it must exert maximum pressure to be assured of its fair share.

Control of Land Use   Some years ago a major conflict revolved around the issue of whether or not a city government should by ordinance determine

[12] For a good discussion of the types of conflicts that arise, see James S. Coleman, *Community Conflict,* The Free Press, Glencoe, Ill., 1957, pp. 3–9.

the uses to which private owners could put their land. This issue has now been resolved in most places, and government action to control land use has wide acceptability. But the kinds of controls and the kinds of uses to be permitted continue to be sources of major conflicts. Homeowners consistently oppose city action which would permit the encroachment of commercial and industrial uses in their areas, while landowners and developers seek to use land in such a way that it will produce maximum return on investment. A public hearing to discuss a change of zoning applied to any given piece of land in the city is sure to produce heated discussions.

Civil Rights   In recent years attention has been focused on minority rights at all levels of government, but the issues are of direct concern at the local level. The city has become an arena for conflict in relation to city jobs for minority groups, right to purchase and rent housing in all areas of the city, access to private accommodations in hotels, restaurants, and places of entertainment, and access to all places of public accommodation such as parks, playgrounds, and swimming pools. These issues may seem remote to the city dweller when they are debated in Congress or even at the state capital, but they come close to home when group support for civil rights is dramatized by violent demonstrations.

Service Conflicts   Although there is a high degree of consensus that the city should provide a wide range of public services such as street construction, repair and maintenance, public health and sanitation, police and fire protection, and social welfare, the actual performance of these public services provides ample room for divergent views. A few examples will serve to illustrate the nature of such conflicts. Police regulations which provide parking restrictions seem necessary to ensure free flow of traffic, but the manner in which such restrictions are drafted determines who is helped and who is hurt. Numerous area and district shopping centers are clustered around major streets that lead to the main downtown section. Therefore, those with interests in the downtown area seek to limit parking along major streets. On the other hand, the local shopping interests have no desire to make it easier for people to drive through their shopping centers so that they can spend money in the downtown shops. The economic interest of the merchants in the district shopping areas forces them to fight attempts to limit parking on streets bordering their establishments.

Location of new streets or widening and improvement of old ones raises similar conflicts. All citizens willingly support efforts to improve roadways and traffic flow, but when planning reaches the stage at which location of new streets or widening of old ones becomes specific, consensus ends. Everyone wants easy access to major trafficways, but no one wants them so close as to disturb his own residential living area.

City officials find very little difficulty in getting general agreement that garbage and refuse should be disposed of in modern incinerators, but first-rate disputes break out when the engineers present proposed locations for the needed installations. These examples serve only to indicate that regardless of the type of service which city governments seek to provide, there is within each the potential for politics—i.e., for the resolution of conflict. Any notion that service functions can by some means be turned over to professional engineers, public health specialists, or traffic control experts is an illusion. It may well be that city councilmen, mayors, and other political decision makers would like to turn conflict issues over to the experts in order to avoid making political enemies, but their voting publics will never let them get by with it. There is too much at stake for some groups in every decision made by city government to expect that political officers can avoid making hard decisions by simply proclaiming that the conflicts are a matter for the experts.

Political Decisions as Compromises

Those in decision-making positions, particularly legislators and administrators, discover that almost every decision with which they are faced involves so many diverse groups making differing demands that final disposition of the issue is impossible. The best that can be expected is that some kind of compromise can be arranged which will work, at least for the present, so that other conflicts can be resolved. Since each decision is a compromise solution and no group receives what is really wanted, each decision has within it the seeds of future conflict. Politics is, then, a continuing process, partly because changing conditions produce new issues in the arena, but also because most of the old issues are never settled; they are only compromised in such a way as to leave potential for future conflict.

The compromise nature of political settlements is what produces the host of persons often called politicians. These persons serve as brokers and mediators to bring opponents closer together so that peaceful solutions can be worked out to settle issues which produce profound differences of opinion. Often, these politicians have very little personal stake in the issues which produce group conflict, and hence they do not worry too much about "principles"; they are far more concerned with reducing the heat of conflict and ensuring stability and continuity in the established political order. When any society consisting of persons with diverse economic, social, and religious views fails to produce political types who can serve this mediating function, established institutional procedures will be seriously threatened by revolutionary processes.

The role of the politician as compromiser was stated clearly by T. V. Smith:

> So difficult to adjust are the conflicts of interests that furnish the problems for democratic politicians that dictatorship has again become in many erstwhile democratic lands the standardized method of dealing with them.
>
> It is precisely that outcome of intergroup conflicts which the politicians shield us from. . . . People elsewhere get killed in the conflicts of interests over which our politicians preside with vices short of crimes and with virtues not wholly unkin to magnanimity. . . . The presence among us of these generalized specialists in conciliation is our firmest basis of concrete hope that community can be made to survive the process of specialization which gives us good men who would like, but find it baffling, to be also good citizens.[13]

Reactions to Compromise Solutions

One feature of the American political process at all levels has been its remarkable flexibility. Although many political conflicts have deep roots in economic, cultural, racial, and religious differences, except for the war between the states, the system has produced compromises sufficiently acceptable to all contestants to maintain the stability of the process, at least until the 1960s. Serious riots and disorders in such large cities as Los Angeles, Detroit, Philadelphia, and Chicago, accompanied with considerable bloodshed, indicate that the political process is under a strain greater than at any time since the Civil War. Dissatisfaction among Negro populations with the inability of the system to provide more and better employment opportunities, decent housing, and a more significant role in the decision-making process has led them to resort to methods of protest that have generally been considered beyond the accepted norms of political action. No one can predict with certainty that the existing system will meet the demands of these militant groups sufficiently to prevent even more violent demonstrations.

The apparent stability of American political systems in the past may be accounted for by the fact that the range of conflicts has not been great. Rapid urbanization has increased the differences between the "haves" and the "have-nots" and has, therefore, intensified the nature of conflict for scarce

---

[13] T. V. Smith, *The Promise of American Politics*, The University of Chicago Press, Chicago, 1936, pp. 248, 249.

resources the system has to offer. A feature of the system that tends to give it stability is that it offers to groups a number of avenues through which they can seek to achieve their goals. This pluralistic character of the decision-making machinery can be understood by more careful examination.

A fair assumption is that most issues arising within a city will be first fought out in the legislative arena. The form of the encounter is likely to be a proposed ordinance introduced by one or more of the city councilmen at the request of an organization which has decided to push for the program embodied in the proposed ordinance. According to the model presented here, this proposed course of action will arouse organizations who seek to block passage of the ordinance. Although a coalition can be put together sufficient to secure passage of an ordinance, some groups will not be happy with the results. Their leaders, therefore, search for some other arena to which the conflict can be transferred, which, they hope, may produce different results. The possibilities for this sort of strategy are almost unlimited.

Administration   The nature of legislation is such that the output takes the form of lengthy legally phrased documents with numerous provisions that mean different things to different persons. In fact, the legislators who vote for any given ordinance often differ significantly on the meaning they attach to certain parts of the document. Therefore, groups with a stake in the contents of the ordinance turn their attention to its administration. Ordinances affect citizens only when city officials put them into effect; i.e., an ordinance to control air pollution does not affect an industry until specific action is taken to require compliance. The administrative institutions, therefore, become another arena in which the original legislative conflict can be renewed. A series of administrative policy decisions under which city inspectors will work must be formulated into rules and regulations, and the effects of the original ordinance on people will depend significantly upon these operating rules. Since those who promulgate these rules are different persons from those who enacted the original ordinance, they may be guided by different sets of values and be influenced by different political groups. It is quite possible that a group which lost its point at the ordinance-making stage may win it in the administrative arena. Administrators gain and lose their jobs in different ways from which the legislators gain and lose theirs. Groups have different weights in seeking to influence a mayor who is elected at large than they have with legislators, who are more likely to reflect the interests of small geographic areas of city. The important point to note is that the administrative machine of a city is another political decision-making center to which competing groups can carry their conflict.

The Judiciary   In the complex legal machinery which has developed within the American political system, the courts become another arena in which political conflicts can be waged. It is difficult to conceive of an instance in which a group within a city, feeling itself injured by an ordinance and the manner in which the ordinance is being enforced under administrative rules and regulations, cannot find a way to bring the dispute into the judicial arena. A claim can be made that the ordinance is beyond the scope of power of the legislature, that the rules and regulations are not in accord with the ordinance, that enforcement is arbitrary or does not comply with due process of the law. When specific cases are brought into the courts for adjudication, judges are in a position to make decisions on the issues which have previously been decided by either legislators or administrators. Since the legal background of judges tends to give them certain sets of values and since they are likely to respond to different kinds of pressures, they may produce decisions which affect groups in very different ways from that originally intended by those who voted on the ordinance or those who sought to enforce it.

Transfer to a Different Level of Government   The pluralistic character of the American federal system provides different levels of government which can deal with many given political issues. Therefore, when a political action group is dissatisfied with the compromise solution to a conflict that has been worked out in all available institutions of the city government, it simply seeks a different kind of decision at the state level. All that is necessary to change the effects of a city ordinance is an act of the state legislature; the state supreme court, likewise, may change the decisions made by courts at the local level; and, in some instances, the governor may change actions of local administrators. This means that groups which were unable to control the kind of decisions coming out of the local political system may have greater success in influencing state officeholders. The dominant political group which determines the selection of city officers may not be able to determine the selection of state officeholders. The wing of the dominant party in a state that controls city elections may be a minority wing of the party on a statewide basis, and in some states the party that controls the largest city is the minority party in the state capital. But even if party policy is not evident in a given issue, the factors and forces acting upon state officers may be very different from those that influence local decision makers.

The same line of analysis will also explain why many groups prefer to have issues which vitally affect them transferred to the national arena. Nationally organized policy groups feel they have better access to decision makers in

Washington than they have at either the state or local level. The extent to which those who seek major reforms in cities place their demands before Congress and federal administrative agencies indicates that they feel decisions coming out of that arena will be more favorable to the city than would decisions that come from state officials.

Changes within the Local Arena   Each of the reactions discussed above implies a change in the arena in which a decision is made. Local interest groups may, however, choose to keep the dispute at home and seek a more favorable decision by other means. They may feel that time is on their side and seek to postpone final action. They may feel that the next election will produce changes in personnel and thereby changes in the ultimate decision. Hence they may choose to concentrate their efforts on influencing the oncoming local election process.

Since the institutional structures through which the conflict is processed and a decision is reached seem to produce results unfavorable to some groups, they may seek changes in these structures. When political groups become reformers, it usually means that they have concluded that they can no longer control the output of the system under existing structures and operating rules. The reforms of the first quarter of the twentieth century are cases in point. When the decision-making structures in large cities were dominated by political machines and reform groups sought to change the character of decisions emanating from the system, they sought to do so by structural reform. The direct primary, initiative and referendum, nonpartisan elections, and the short ballot were introduced to change the locus of decision making and to place control of decisions in the hands of different people. The movement for reapportionment of legislative bodies that has proceeded since *Baker v. Carr* is either supported or opposed by groups who perceive change as producing decisions favorable or unfavorable to them.

No doubt there are some who support structural change simply because they value certain kinds of organization and certain procedures for their own sake. But most often the motives behind those who support or oppose structural reform can be best understood in terms of the expected results of such change, i.e., in the kinds of decisions that are expected to follow from the change. The types of structural reform that are common to local government will be discussed at appropriate places in this text, but emphasis will be placed not on whether such alterations are good or bad but rather on how the change may affect the political process and which groups are likely to benefit from the changes or find them disadvantageous.

BIBLIOGRAPHY

Books

Banfield, Edward C., and James Q. Wilson: *City Politics,* Vintage Books, Random House, Inc., New York, 1963, chap. 1.

Charlesworth, James R. (ed.)·: *The Limits of Behavioralism in Political Science,* American Academy of Political and Social Science, Philadelphia, 1962.

Coleman, James S.: *Community Conflict,* The Free Press, Glencoe, Ill., 1957.

Dahl, Robert A.: *Modern Political Analysis,* Prentice-Hall, Inc., Englewood Cliffs, N.J., 1963, particularly the first three chapters.

Easton, David: *The Political System: An Inquiry into the State of Political Science,* Alfred A. Knopf, Inc., New York, 1953, particularly chaps. 2 to 4.

Eulau, Heinz: *The Behavioral Persuasion in Politics,* University of Illinois Press, Urbana, 1962.

Greer, Scott: *Governing the Metropolis,* John Wiley & Sons, Inc., New York, 1962, chap. 2.

Hyneman, Charles S.: *The Study of Politics,* University of Illinois Press, Urbana, 1959.

Lasswell, Harold: *Politics: Who Gets What, When and How,* The McGraw-Hill Book Company, New York, 1936.

Sorauf, Francis J.: *Political Science: An Informal Overview,* Charles E. Merrill Books, Inc., Columbus, Ohio, 1965, particularly the first five chapters.

Storing, Herbert J. (ed.): *Essays on the Scientific Study of Politics,* Holt, Rinehart and Winston, Inc., New York, 1962.

Van Dyke, Vernon: *Political Science: A Philosophic Analysis,* Stanford University Press, Stanford, Calif., 1960.

Articles

Almond, Gabriel A.: "Political Theory and Political Science," *American Political Science Review,* vol. 60, pp. 869–879, December, 1966.

Dahl, Robert: "The Behavioral Approach," *American Political Science Review,* vol. 55, pp. 763–772, December, 1961.

Easton, David: "Traditional and Behavioral Research in American Political Science," *Administrative Science Quarterly,* vol. 2, pp. 110–115, June, 1957.

Editorial: *PROD* (now *American Behavioral Scientist*), vol. 1, pp. 42–43, July, 1958.

Harris, J. P., et al.: "The Relations of Political Scientists with Public Officials: A Report of a Committee to the American Political Science Association," *American Political Science Review,* vol. 35, pp. 333–343, April, 1941.

2

THE NATURE OF CITIES AND THEIR POLITICS

Reference has been made to the fact that the city may be viewed as a political arena in which the political process can be observed in action. In order to use this political laboratory effectively, one must acquire some knowledge of the nature of the city as a social entity.

URBAN GROWTH

In a recent publication outlining recommendations for modernizing local governments the Committee for Economic Development says:

> This country has shared in the world-wide population "explosion" doubling in number from 1870 to 1900, redoubling by 1950, and reaching toward the 300,000,000 mark before the end of the century. But while total population is rising, most of the nation's countryside is the scene of continuing depopulation. For 200 years the proportion of "rural population" has fallen, from 95 per cent in 1910 to about 25 per cent by 1970. Since 1950 the decline has been *absolute* as well *as relative*.[1]

In 1790 there were only 24 urban places in the United States and they included only 5 percent of the total population. By 1910 the number of urban

[1] Committee for Economic Development, *Modernizing Local Government*, New York, 1966, p. 20.

TABLE 2.1   Changes in Rural and Urban Population, 1910–1960 (000 omitted)

	1910	1920	1930	1940	1950	1960
No. of urban places	2,262	2,722	3,165	3,464	4,741	6,041
Total population	91,972	105,711	122,775	131,669	150,697	179,323
Total urban	41,999	54,158	68,955	74,424	96,468	125,269
Percent urban	45.7	51.2	56.2	56.5	64.0	69.9
Total rural	49,973	51,553	53,820	57,246	54,230	54,054
Percent rural	54.3	48.8	43.8	43.5	36.0	30.1

Source: From U.S. Bureau of the Census, *Statistical Abstract*, 1962, p. 21.

places had increased to 2,262 which contained 45.7 percent of the total population. Table 2.1 shows the population growth from 1910 to 1960.

Since 1910 the percentage of the total population living in urban areas has increased steadily except for the decade from 1930 to 1940, when the increase in urban and rural areas was approximately equal. This was the period of the great depression when jobs were unavailable in cities and a "back-to-the-farm" movement was officially encouraged. In 1920 for the first time urban population exceeded rural population, and by 1960 approximately 70 percent of the people of this nation were living in urban areas. Figure 2.1 depicts graphically the changes in urban and rural population in each census period.

Although accurate figures are not available on population trends since 1960, there is substantial evidence that the trend toward urban living has continued. The gain in total population of the United States to 1965 is estimated at 7.6 percent, but the estimated rate of increase in metropolitan areas is 10.1 percent and in suburbs of metropolitan areas it is estimated at 13.9 percent. *The Municipal Year Book,* in discussing these trends from 1960 to 1965, states:

> Metropolitan areas, with just over three-fifths of the 1965 population, accounted for practically four-fifths of the increase. All in all, the data indicate continued concentration in Metropolitan areas, and particularly in their suburban parts; less impressive increase in non-metropolitan cities; and relative deconcentration from central cities and the non-metropolitan remainder of the nation.[2]

The change from a rural to an urban society in the last few years has not been evenly spread over the entire country. The older industrial sections of

[2] International City Managers Association, *The Municipal Year Book,* Chicago, 1966, p. 34.

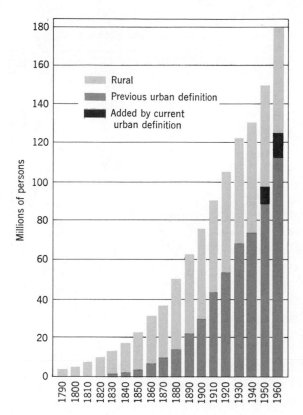

Figure 2.1   Urban and rural population: 1790–1960. (Source: U.S. Bureau of the Census, *Characteristics of the Population*, 1960, Vol. I, Part I, p. 524)

the Northeast have experienced slightly more population growth in urban areas than in rural areas. The percentage increase in urban areas from 1950 to 1960 was 14.2, while the increase in rural areas was 9.0. The greatest increase in urban areas has been in the West, where the increase was 55.3 percent against 1.7 percent for rural areas. The South, where industrialization has proceeded at a rapid rate, had a 40.1 percent increase in urban population, while its rural population declined by 5.9 percent. The North Central states increased their total urban population by 24.5 percent, while the rural population was increasing by only 1.1 percent.[3]

The map in Figure 2.2 shows by states the distribution of rural and urban population in 1960, and Figure 2.3 shows the percentage increase in urban population by states from 1950 to 1960.

[3] *Ibid.*, p. 19.

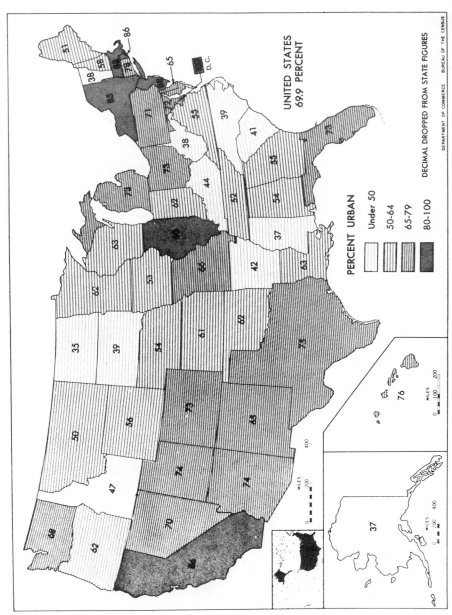

Figure 2.2   Percent of urban population, by states: 1960. (Source: U.S. Bureau of the Census, *Characteristics of the Population*, 1960, Vol. I, Part I, p. 254)

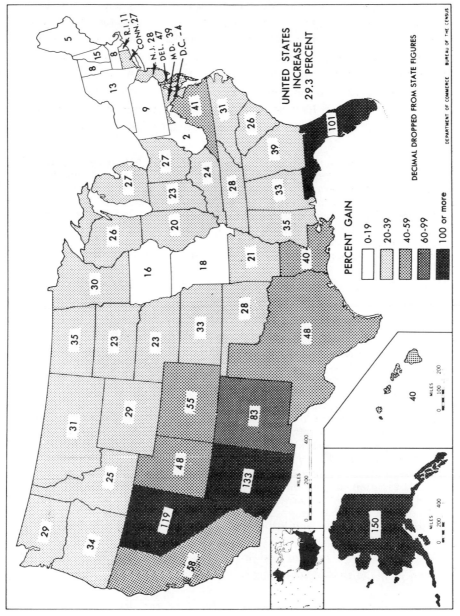

Figure 2.3   Percent change in urban population, by states: 1950–1960. (Source: U.S. Bureau of the Census, *Characteristics of the Population*, 1960, Vol. I, Part I, p. 524)

CHARACTERISTICS OF URBAN LIFE

Urban sociologists have used different schemes to identify the characteristics of social life that distinguish urban living from rural living. Regardless of the analytic scheme used, the results indicate significant differences in patterns of group behavior which are of consequence to the student who seeks to understand politics in urbanized areas. The following quotations from two sociologists are used to indicate the extreme poles of rural and urban life. The first is from Robert Redfield's description of what he refers to as an ideal type of folk society as contrasted with modern urbanized society.

> Such a society is small, isolated, nonliterate, and homogeneous, with a strong sense of group solidarity. The ways of living are conventional-ized into that coherent system which we call "a culture." Behavior is traditional, spontaneous, uncritical, and personal; there is no legislation or habit of experiment and reflection for intellectual ends. Kinship, its relationships and institutions, are the type categories of experience and the familiar group is the unit of action. The sacred prevails over the secular; the economy is one of status rather than of the market.[4]

Louis Wirth pictures the other end of the spectrum in his description of urban society.

> Urbanism. . . . refers also to that cumulative accentuation of the char-acteristics distinctive of the mode of life which is associated with the growth of cities. . . . The bonds of kinship, of neighborliness, and the sentiments arising out of living together for generations under a common folk tradition are likely to be absent or, at best, relatively weak. . . . Under such circumstances competition and formal control mechanisms furnish the substitute for the bonds of solidarity that are relied upon to hold a folk society together. . . . The city is characterized by secondary rather than primary contacts. The contacts of the city may indeed be face to face, but they are nevertheless impersonal, superficial, transitory, and segmental. . . . Whereas, therefore, the individual gains, on the one hand, a certain degree of emancipation or freedom from the personal and emotional controls of intimate groups, he loses, on the other hand, the spontaneous self-expression, the morale, and the sense of par-ticipation that comes with living in an integrated society.[5]

Gist and Halbert, in their text in urban sociology, also deal with these differences in life style at some length.

[4] Robert Redfield, "The Folk Society," *The American Journal of Sociology*, vol. 52, abstract p. 293, January, 1947.
[5] Louis Wirth, "Urbanism as a Way of Life," *The American Journal of Sociology*, vol. 47, pp. 5, 11–13, July, 1938.

In so far as the urban environment involves a type of social contact and interaction that differs widely in many respects from interaction in a rural area it becomes a special laboratory for social investigation and analysis. The city by its very nature offers a vast complex of stimuli that become conditioning factors in development of personality traits. On the one hand, are the mechanised aspects of urban culture that touch the lives of metropolites at every point; on the other hand, are the manifold forms of social organization that are a constant source of psychic stimulation. Out of the interaction between the individual and the environment in which he lives come behavior patterns that, to some degree, are peculiar to the city.[6]

The terminology used in the following discussion to identify specific characteristics of urban life that are significant for the student of politics is adapted from a single text in urban sociology, but examination of other texts reveals striking similarity.[7]

Impersonalization of Social Relations

In rural societies the interactions one person has with others in regular day-to-day activities are generally with the same people, and such contacts become quite personal in that each of the participants soon knows the other on a fairly intimate basis. On the other hand, in cities very few such personal relationships exist. A resident shops in supermarkets and department stores, his children go to a school in a building with thousands of others, and he attends a sporting event without recognizing a single spectator as someone he knows. In part, this impersonality in human relations may be due to the nature of our money economy. Individuals must purchase everything they use, and human labor is just another commodity to be bought and sold in the marketplace. Since the buyer and the seller may have no other personal contacts, hard-hearted bargaining becomes the general rule.

Since the urbanite cannot know personally the vast number of persons he sees in the buses, on the streets, and in the marketplaces, he tends to form mental images of classes of people in terms of the one or two persons whom he happens to know more intimately. For example, as far as he is concerned all politicians are like the one he happens to know in his block, and all Jews are the same as his landlord who comes each month to collect the rent.

The reactions of urban dwellers to candidates seeking office or to office-holders in city government can be understood, in part, if one knows the kind

[6] Noel P. Gist and L. A. Halbert, *Urban Society*, 3d ed., Thomas Y. Crowell, New York, 1950, p. 263.
[7] *Ibid.*, chap. 3.

of mental image the urbanite has of the class to which the candidate or officeholder belongs. In the same manner candidates seeking office or public relations firms trying to sell a program to the electorate capitalize on their knowledge of the stereotypes which the voter has developed, and they key their campaigns so as to identify with the favorable image of the group to which they are making their appeal.

Human contacts in cities tend to be secondary rather than primary in nature. Many of these contacts are mechanical, by telephone, radio, or public address system, rather than personal. When the urbanite deals with a clerk in the supermarket or with an employee at the welfare office, he takes a number and waits his turns with others whom he does not know, and at each visit he may be waited on by a different clerk or social worker. In such an impersonal environment social controls that are so effective in conditioning social behavior in rural communities are not operative. Therefore, formal control through ordinances, administrative regulations, and institutional rules becomes more significant in conditioning behavior in urban areas.

What sociologists refer to as "social distance" is much greater among urban dwellers than among small-town and rural residents. That is, for each city resident there are very few persons with whom he feels he has anything in common or with whom he can join in a common cause. Some of this lack of intimacy may be due to social prejudices that exist in the American culture and to the fact that it is in the urban environment that significant numbers of racial and nationality groups are found.

Since most contacts in an urban society are of a formal or business nature, the image a person projects is determined to a large extent by outward appearance. If a man dresses well, drives a good car, lives and works at "good" addresses, he will be typed by these external appearances, and very few will know anything about his home life, his debts, or his moral values. Although ruralites may have the urge to "put on the dog," the nature of their society is such that they cannot hide their financial status or their social life behind a front put on for business and social purposes. The anonymity of city life produces a freedom in moral codes not found in rural societies. The church leader in the city who is faithful in his ritualistic practices may, on weekdays, frequent gambling houses or engage in illicit sexual relations without his church associates being aware of these extracurricular activities, but such behavior would be most difficult in a small-town community. A society in which an individual can pursue such conflicting standards of conduct may produce internal stress which affects personality as well as patterns of behavior.

Mobility

The population in urban areas consists of persons on the move. Families establish a home within an area where rents are within their means, but they have plans to move as soon as increased income makes it possible for them to afford a higher-prestige address. Single workingmen and some women move frequently from one hotel or boarding house to another. Businesses find it advantageous to transfer their employees from one plant or office to another, and members of the armed services in both civilian and noncivilian capacities find it almost impossible to settle down at one address. This pattern of mobility makes it difficult to develop a sense of community or neighborhood, and the type of social control that comes from social communities is lost. People on the move do not find time or sufficient interest to become politically active, nor do they become sufficiently involved in political conflicts to exercise political initiative.

The nature of urban living "has been more successful in creating human desires than in satisfying them."[8] Those who take satisfaction in following the crowd in clothing styles and in social conduct find their needs met in urban life. Innovations in wearing apparel and in modes of entertainment soon catch on in the city and collective behavior changes the novel to the commonplace. But the city is also the place of group unrest. Those who cannot or do not choose to follow collective behavior patterns find others ready to join them in protests against social norms, political restrictions, and current life styles. The large number of organizations found in every large urban area bears witness to the feeling of alienation that pulls urbanites into groups either for self-satisfaction or for the purpose of seeking change. Labor unions, political organizations, and civic reform groups depend largely on urban population for their membership strength.

A note of caution is required as one tries to evaluate the political significance of the social characteristics of urban life that set it apart from rural life style. Improved means of transportation, human mobility, and systems of mass communication have tended to bridge the gap between the two life styles. Advertisements from the large city stores reach into rural homes, and the drive from farm to city is short when measured by time rather than distance. Large business corporations are decentralizing their operations, and management personnel are moving from the big centers of population into the less-urban communities. Labor organizers follow industry as plants are relocated. Reorganization of school districts has resulted in the bussing of

[8] *Ibid.*, p. 275.

rural students into urban areas where the larger school plants are located, and ruralites are depending more and more on the cities for recreational facilities such as parks, theaters, and professional sports. All this points to the fact that important changes are taking place in rural life style, and the direction of the change makes it more and more like that found in urban places.[9]

MYTHS ABOUT CITIES

Within any human association there arise and flourish certain ideas which become so generally accepted that they condition the behavior of those within the society; such ideas are referred to as myths. These myths are passed down from one generation to another and give continuity to thought patterns of a society. Whether these myths are true or false is of little concern to the student of politics as long as members of society permit them to affect their actions. The particular myth which has profoundly affected the pattern of American life is the one that identifies cities as the spawning ground for all kinds of evil. The notion is widespread that crime, graft, and corruption flourish in the cities while the rural setting produces the good community life. This image of the evil city is particularly significant to the student who seeks to understand the political relationships between state legislatures and cities. The typical image the ruralite has of the city politician is of a cigar-smoking city boss who, with his corrupt henchmen, dominates the decision-making machinery of the city for the purpose of private gain. The attitudes of rural legislators who are required to pass judgment on proposed legislation affecting the cities are conditioned by this persistent image.

Nor is this image of the city confined to rural dwellers. Many of those whose home is within the cities because their job is there harbor the same image about the evils of city society. This is particularly true in very large cities where the relationships between citizens and officeholders are on an impersonal basis. Reform movements which are common in most cities base their popular appeal on the assumption that graft and corruption are the order of the day around city hall and that periodically the rascals must be thrown out. Another evidence of the prevalence of this myth among city

[9] See Wirth, *op. cit.*, p. 5. For further discussion of the nature and effects of urbanization see Philip M. Hauser, "Urbanization: An Overview," and Kingsley Davis, "The Urbanization of the Human Population," in Jeffrey K. Hadden, Louis H. Masotti, and Calvin J. Larson (eds.), *Metropolis in Crisis*, F. E. Peacock Publishers, Inc., Itasca, Ill., 1967, pp. 55–106.

dwellers is the back-to-the-farm movements that arise whenever jobs become scarce, as well as the flight to the suburbs of upper- and middle-class families. To many inhabitants of the city it is only the place where they earn a living and they look forward to the day when they can retire from a regular job and live peacefully in the country or a small town. Scott Greer has effectively described the attitude of many American city dwellers.

> Though Americans have, willy nilly, become a preponderantly urban people, they have refused to accept an image of the megalopolis as their true home. Instead, they have endeavored to transform the conditions of the great city into "garden towns"—and have, in the suburbs, come close to achieving their aims. The American middle class in trying to make itself at home in the urban area, has solved many problems by developing suburban neighborhoods separated from the central city by governmental walls.[10]

Source of Anticity Attitude

James M. Beshers, in his discussion of the public image of the city that has grown up in America, identifies three kinds of hostility and tries to account for each in terms of historical incidents.[11] The first he calls "distaste for mobs and masses." He attributes this attitude to a reaction against the events of the French Revolution, which fixed in the minds of Americans an association between mob violence and cities. The second he refers to as the "return to nature theme." This attitude he ascribes to American literature which tends to emphasize the wholesomeness of rural life in which the family group extracts a living from the soil and in which man is close to his creator. The third expression of hostility towards the city takes the form of emphasizing the virtues of small-town living where rich and poor intermingle and each citizen knows and is known by most other citizens of the community. These small towns became the preserves of the "Protestant ethic," which places hard work and thrift high on the scale of values and where such virtues are properly rewarded.

Regardless of the sources from which these negative attitudes toward cities arise, ample evidence of their existence is found in legislation which places restrictions upon cities as political institutions and limits their power

[10] Scott Greer, *Metropolitics: A Study of Political Culture*, John Wiley & Sons, Inc., New York, 1963, pp. 6, 7.
[11] James M. Beshers, *Urban Social Structure*, The Free Press, Glencoe, Ill., 1962, pp. 3–5.

to act independently, in the literature of social reform, and in federal government programs which until very recently, were almost entirely intended to encourage agriculture and rural life.

Some Positive Attitudes

Not all the evidence indicates a negative attitude toward city life. The need for cities in an industrialized society is now taken for granted. Some evidence of this may be found in the interest that is shown in the role of the city in emerging nations which are seeking to industrialize their economies without going through a long evolutionary period from an extractive to an industrialized society. Many exponents of city life are stressing the cultural advantages of the city by emphasizing the growth of creative art, music, literature, and drama in the large metropolitan centers. They point to the city as the spawning places of liberal philosophy, since they provide an environment in which talented persons can break with the traditional mores of society and expect to be rewarded for their originality rather than for their conformity. Furthermore, cities can be singled out as centers of recreation, health research, medical care, and of higher education.

No attempt is made here to pass judgment on which image of the city is correct; rather, the discussion is included to show that very definite ideas about cities have developed in this country and the behavior of those who make decisions about them can be understood better if one is familiar with the attitudes of the actors.

DEFINITION OF TERMS

For purposes of clarity a distinction must be made between the terms "urban areas" and "cities." The expression "urban area" as used here will have the broadest meaning of all the terms employed. It will be used to refer to any given area where people live in high density (as measured in terms of persons per square mile), depend on outside sources for agricultural products, and exhibit a high degree of social and economic interaction. In describing an urban area we are concerned with general patterns of living, not with fixed geographic boundaries. All such areas will have some form of political organization, but there is no assumption that a single governmental unit will encompass all of an urban area. Urban areas may depend wholly on the state and the county to perform the political function, but in many urban areas, separate local government machinery may be created to perform at least some political activities. Sociologists are likely to call urbanized areas cities since they are interested primarily in life style rather than political institutions and processes, but political scientists reserve the term "city" for a more definite type of community.

The term "city" will be used to refer to areas in which the inhabitants have acquired, through established legal procedures, the right to exercise local governmental powers within fixed boundaries and have created a municipal corporation. Although this term is also broad, it is narrow enough to leave out all those urbanized areas which have not elected to form local governments of their own. Usually, municipal corporations are also urban areas but occasionally a municipal corporation will be formed to include almost wholly industrial areas or area designated for industrial purposes only. In such cases very few people will live within the corporation boundaries. Most municipal corporations are designated as cities by state law, but many smaller ones are classified as towns or villages. The distinguishing characteristics of a municipal corporation are fixed boundaries, a charter of incorporation from the state, and local governmental institutions performing within these fixed boundaries according to powers granted in the charter. Any large urbanized area generally includes a number of both large and small municipal corporations as well as a number of unincorporated areas.

WHY ARE MUNICIPAL CORPORATIONS NECESSARY?

Cities cannot exercise any power unless that power is within the scope of powers reserved to states in the federal system. States can legally exercise any power which a city can exercise, either directly or through delegation to counties. Since each city is either a county itself or is within one or more counties, why cannot the demands of urbanized areas be met adequately from the state through county government without the creation of municipal corporations? A hypothetical case may serve to answer this question.

Suppose that a large industrial corporation decides to locate a processing facility in a Midwestern state and, through real estate agents, purchases a 25-square-mile area of marginal land which has only a few small farmers living on it at the time of purchase. Assume further that the area for the new plant is too far away from any existing city to make commuting attractive to workers. The corporation officers will recognize that they must provide facilities for workers if they are to be able to staff their plant. They, therefore, employ planners, an architectural firm, and building contractors to design and construct housing for thousands of persons who will be employed.

The corporation may elect to sell some houses, rent others, and provide apartments on a rental basis. As families move into the new homes, demands for other kinds of facilities are created. Supermarket operators will lease land for their markets, service establishments of all kinds will seek the business the new community offers. Lawyers, doctors, dentists, and other professionals will move into the area as demands for their services arise. Recreational establishments such as theaters, taverns, bowling alleys, and pool rooms will soon be ready to attract the new residents. Within a very few years an urban area will have been created in and around the 25 square miles purchased by the corporation; the total population may easily reach 50,000 or 100,000.

The creation of such an urban community produces social problems. Conflicts arise over the location of certain kinds of establishments, with some residents objecting to the location of commercial buildings in the residential areas, or poolrooms adjacent to the public schools. Demands for regular garbage and rubbish collection are voiced at local PTA and church meetings. Traffic control to halt the "hot rodders" and fire protection sufficient to reduce fire insurance rates become regular topics of conversation when groups get together. These are fit subjects for governmental agencies to deal with, but what agency is competent to deal with them in such a new community? Since the area is wholly within a county, delegations may go to the county sheriff and petition for police service, but his reply will not be very satisfactory. The number of deputies he can employ is fixed by state law, and salaries are such that he cannot employ the professional peace officers that are needed in such a community. Visits to county health officers will produce even less satisfactory answers to demands for sanitary services. The point is that county governments as they are structured by state statutes are not equipped, nor were they intended to be equipped, to render the kind and intensity of governmental services required by large highly urbanized areas.

Citizen leaders in such a community will soon learn that the only road open to them if they want city services is to petition to become a municipal corporation. The new corporation will then be granted through its charter the governmental powers to meet the collective demands of the citizens of the community. They will also learn that such incorporation can come about only through specific procedures laid down by the state.

The lesson to be learned here is that the mere existence of a highly urbanized area which needs and demands governmental services does not of itself create governmental authority, and counties and single-purpose special districts are generally not adequate to meet public demands in such areas. The only governmental unit available to do the job required is the city or, more exactly, the municipal corporation.[12] The discussion thus far has assumed a fairly high degree of consensus within the community as to the need for public services at a high level of intensity; the real political issues arise when the incorporation has been achieved and decisions must be made with respect to how services will be paid for and the manner in which the services will be provided.

THE DETERMINANTS OF CITY POLITICS

Since a major purpose of this text is to describe city politics and since politics has been defined as the process of resolving conflicting group demands through governmental institutions, some attention must be given to the characteristics of cities which produce varying and often conflicting group demands upon their political institutions. These same characteristics may make it possible to understand why decisions which flow from the political process in a given city seem regularly to be advantageous to some groups and unsatisfactory to others.

Although cities may be defined formally in terms of law, area, and structural form, their political character derives from the fact that they are full of people and these people are different in many ways. Since they are different, they have different wants and needs as well as different images of how their desires should be fulfilled. The assumption can be made that the wider the differences among the residents of a city the greater will be the conflicts fought out through its political process. If one could conceive of a city in which all citizens thought alike, had similar interests, and accepted the same philosophy about the proper role of government in their society, he could imagine a community without conflicting demands and without politics. But although there are no such cities in existence, there are great differences among cities in the character of their populations, which make the nature of politics differ from one city to another.

The purpose of the discussion that follows is to seek to identify the characteristics of city populations that may account for differences in their politics. Put more specifically, what facts would you need to know about a given city if you wanted to understand its politics? That is, what kind of group

[12] In some instances large highly urbanized counties have been given power by the state to perform municipal-type services through the regular county government structure; such counties are often referred to as municipal counties, and they are frequently given authority to draft their own form of government under a county home rule charter.

demands are likely to be made upon its political institutions, and which groups will speak with the loudest voice in influencing the decisions that are made?

The nature of the demands made upon the political system in a city will depend, in part, upon the kinds of people who make up its population; therefore some means of classifying masses of people is necessary if meaningful comparisons among cities are to be possible, and the basis of the classification scheme used must represent factors that are relevant to political interests. An enumeration of factors which might be politically relevant are age, education, occupation, race, religion, income, and family status. Information about many of these factors for large cities is available in the regular decennial census of population.

One of the most widely used indexes for analyzing and classifying city populations is the Shevky-Bell index.[13] The application of this index for social-area analysis in any one city is particularly useful since comparisons with other cities which have been analyzed by the same index are then possible. Furthermore the components of the index appear to have a high degree of relevance to political behavior. This system of analysis employs three indexes to indicate social differentiation: social rank, urbanization, and segregation. Social rank is determined by a composite scale which includes educational level and occupation. Rank at the lowest end of the scale denotes unskilled laborers and factory workers and adults with no more than an eighth-grade education. At the upper end of the scale are professionals, business executives, and white-collar workers who have finished high school or college.

The index of urbanization is designed to measure the life style of a community. Rank on the scale is determined by three components: (1) the ratio of children under five years of age to women of child-bearing age, (2) the proportion of women with jobs outside the home, and (3) the proportion of dwelling units that are detached single-family residences. High rank on the index of urbanization would mean apartment and rooming-house dwellers, single men and women, and childless couples with both husband and wife working outside the home. Low rank on this urbanization scale would mean families living in single-family homes, couples with children, and wives staying at home rather than working.

The third index is a measure of the ethnic character of a community. Its

[13] For a more complete discussion of this index see Eshref Shevky and Wendell Bell, *Social Area Analysis*, Stanford University Press, Stanford, 1954. Other methods of analysis are found in Stuart Alfred Queen and David Bailey Carpenter, *The American City*, McGraw-Hill Book Company, New York, 1953, chap. 8; Joseph A. Kahl and James H. Davis, "A Comparison of Indexes of Socio-economic Status," *American Sociological Review*, vol. 20, pp. 317–325, June, 1955.

purpose is to locate concentrations of minority groups, e.g., Negroes in Mid-western cities, Puerto Ricans in New York, and Orientals in West Coast cities. The specific measure used is the proportion of segregated populations (e.g., Negroes) in any given area compared with the proportion the same segregated group bears to the total population of the city or metropolitan areas being analyzed.[14]

These indexes are designed to measure differences in given populations and to supply tools for understanding the patterns of political behavior that may correlate with these differences. Sufficient evidence is now available, for example, to justify conclusions about the relation between participation in elections and educational level and income level. Such indexes are useful in showing how different classes are dispersed within a given urban area, and they are indispensable if comparative studies of a number of large cities are to produce meaningful results.

URBAN ECOLOGY

Attention has thus far been directed toward characteristics of populations that may explain patterns of political behavior. It is not enough, however, to learn the percentages of a population in terms of race, socioeconomic level, religion, and other characteristics that may be relevant to an understanding of the politics of a city; the manner in which the population is distributed spatially over the area under study is also significant. A 20 percent Negro population, for example, may have a certain political consequence if the Negroes are concentrated in a single geographic area, another if they are grouped to-gether in a half-dozen widely scattered pockets, and still another if they are integrated in a random fashion over the entire area. Many of the practical problems related to drawing lines for representative districts arise because of the manner in which certain groups are spatially distributed within a given area.

When considering boundaries for wards in a city, one is not concerned about how people with red hair, or tall people, or fat people are distributed over the area because there is no assumption that these characteristics correlate with political behavior. There is great concern, on the other hand, among political leaders about how racial and nationality groups, religious groups, and socioeconomic groups are included within ward boundaries, since there are strong evidences that these characteristics do affect political views

[14] For an application of the Shevky-Bell index to a single metropolitan area, see Metropolitan St. Louis Survey, *Background for Action*, St. Louis, 1957, chap. 1.

as well as political participation. One of the major factors that make it difficult to consolidate into a single governmental unit the numerous small cities which make up our large metropolitan areas is the fact that not all classes of the population are distributed equally over the entire metropolitan area. If some of these small cities are predominantly upper-class suburbs, some are predominantly Negro, while others are clusters of union laborers, as long as each remains a decision-making unit in itself, decisions will conform to the social class norms of its residents, but if decision making is changed to a larger area, the mix of interests involved is changed and the nature of decisions can no longer be predicted with assurance.

Patterns of Spatial Distribution

Sociologists and geographers have for years been studying the distribution of populations in large urban centers, seeking to discover regularities that apply generally to all such areas. Obviously, no two areas are alike. Historical events account for the high proportion of certain nationality groups in some urbanized areas, location of certain natural resources accounts for the development of industries which require large numbers of unskilled labor, and governmental decisions to locate research centers in a given area ensure a large population of scientists, engineers, and skilled workers. But population studies have tended to confirm the belief that, in spite of individual differences, valid generalizations about areal distribution can be made about urbanized areas generally, and evidences indicate that these distribution patterns have significance for the student of urban politics.

Scott Greer, in discussing the "map of the metropolis," says, "Where you live tells those persons with information about a city such things as your general income level, the kind of people you live among, your probable prestige or social honor, and a number of less basic matters."[15] He might have added that it also tells something about your values, way of looking at political issues, and degree of participation in politics.

One of the earliest attempts to generalize about spatial distribution of population in cities was the concentric-ring model suggested by Ernest W. Burgess.[16] He visualized the development of the city in terms of concentric rings around a central core, with the areas between the rings differentiated

[15] Scott Greer, *Governing the Metropolis*, John Wiley & Sons, Inc., New York, 1962, p. 3.
[16] Ernest W. Burgess, "Urban Areas," in T. V. Smith and Leonard D. White (eds.), *An Experiment in Social Science Research*, University of Chicago Press, Chicago, 1929, pp. 113–138.

by distinctive land-use patterns. The core area contained the central business district with its large department stores and adjacent industrial areas. Surrounding this core is an area of transition, usually marked by vacant stores and housing units, marginal businesses, and unkept streets and flats. The circles beyond the transitional zone are primarily residential, with differences among the zones being the value and quality of the dwelling units. The typical pattern is for the value and quality to increase as the distance from the core increases.

The implications from this model are that there are similarities among the people living within each concentric ring and significant differences between those living in the different rings. These social, economic, and cultural differences result in different sets of values that motivate thought and action within the sectors. Political action, in particular, is affected by the variations of life style spatially distributed throughout an urban area. Different demands are made upon the political system by the residents of these discrete areas, degree of participation is different, and the recruitment of decision makers is not evenly distributed over the whole of the political subdivision.

Homer Hoyt proposed what is referred to as the sector theory to describe in a general way the spatial distribution of people and business in urban areas.[17] According to this model, urban growth follows main transportation routes—rail, highway, or water—and similar types of land use develop along each transportation axis. This theory also assumes a circular development from a central core area, but similar types of land use are not grouped in concentric rings. Rather, a specific type of land use starts near the center, then grows outward along some transportation axis, creating a fan-shaped sector as it expands outward. For example in high-class residential areas, land use tends to move from its original central location outward along lines of fastest transportation and on land with the highest elevation. Similarly, low-quality housing tends to expand outward from its original location along a fixed axis, forming another sector of similar land use. The significant point of this model is that the kind of land use that develops originally in sections of the city determines the areas of similar land use as the urban area expands. Therefore if the southeast section of a city develops as a low-rent area, housing low-income groups, the southeastern sector of the city as it expands will continue to have this same social characteristic.

Another model which seeks to generalize about urban growth rejects the idea of the city developing from a single central core, which is implied in both

[17] Homer Hoyt, "The Structure of American Cities in the Post-War Era," *American Journal of Sociology*, vol. 48, pp. 476–477, January, 1943.

the models just described. It assumes that any large urban area is organized spatially around a number of central places or nuclei, some of which may have existed as separate independent urban places before the expansion of population brought them together to form a common urbanized area. The assumption is that certain types of activities tend to cluster because they profit by being together. This multiple-nuclei model seems to fit the pattern of large shopping centers now so popular in this country. Industrial parks may also constitute nuclei around which land-use patterns will develop.[18] These three models are represented in Figure 2.4.

Observers of the urbanization process can see evidences of each of these models of development in different cities, and evidences of each may be seen in most any single large urban area, yet none of them alone seems to fit exactly a single urbanized area. The student of politics will find them useful as general statements about urban growth, rather than as explanations of the growth pattern of a particular area. They may have greatest significance for those who seek to plan in a formal way the physical growth pattern of a city. The subject of city planning will be considered later, but a word here may be useful. If there is a development theory that can explain the economic and social forces that operate to determine what might be called the "natural" growth pattern of urban areas, to what extent can city officials intervene by land-use controls to alter this natural growth pattern? City planning is grounded in the assumption that a planning authority composed of qualified citizens can decide the growth pattern they would like the city to follow and then by control ordinances assure this development. It may well be that such planned development will result only if the planners have accurately gauged the economic and social forces acting to affect such development.[19]

Dynamics of Urban Growth

Regardless of the theory one accepts to explain the pattern of urban growth, he must recognize that these areas are in a constant state of change. Within any zone of the city, intrazone changes are being made as shops move from one location to another and as smaller businesses expand into larger quarters. But the most significant changes are interzonal in character, i.e., the shifting of businesses and populations from one zone to another. Urban

[18] Chauncy D. Harris and Edward L. Ullman, "The Nature of Cities," *Annals of the American Academy of Political and Social Science*, vol. 242, pp. 7–17, November, 1945.

[19] See Harry W. Zorbaugh, "The Natural Areas of the City," in George A. Theodorson (ed.), *Studies in Human Ecology*, Harper & Row, Publishers, Incorporated, New York, 1961, pp. 45–49.

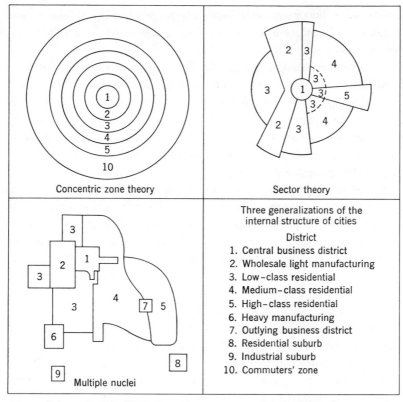

Concentric zone theory

Sector theory

Multiple nuclei

Three generalizations of the
internal structure of cities

District
1. Central business district
2. Wholesale light manufacturing
3. Low–class residential
4. Medium–class residential
5. High–class residential
6. Heavy manufacturing
7. Outlying business district
8. Residential suburb
9. Industrial suburb
10. Commuters' zone

Figure 2.4   Spatial distribution of population in cities (generalizations of internal structure of cities). The concentric-zone theory is a generalization for all cities. The arrangement of the sectors in the sector theory varies from city to city. The diagram for multiple nuclei represents one possible pattern among innumerable variations. (Source: Annals of the American Academy of Political and Social Science, Vol. 242, p. 13)

geographers are agreed that the most significant movements within urban areas are either from center outward or from periphery toward the center, rather than from one section to another within a single ring of development. An excellent discussion of the play of the two forces constantly operating to produce interzone changes within a given urban area is supplied by Charles C. Colby.[20] His studies lead him to believe that two sets of forces are continually operating in an urbanized area. Centrifugal forces tending to spin functions outwardly to the periphery of the area are a combination of uprooting impulses in the central zone and attractive qualities of the outlying

[20] Charles C. Colby, "Centrifugal and Centripetal Forces in Urban Geography," *Annals of the Association of American Geographers*, vol. 23, pp. 1–20, March, 1933.

fringe. At the same time centripetal forces are in operation which tend to hold existing functions in the central zone and make it a center of gravity which draws new functions toward it.

Dynamic forces for change are constantly altering the form and land-use patterns of all urban areas. A study of any single urban area will reveal the forces described by Colby; the balance of these forces will be different from one area to another, accounting for variations in developmental patterns from city to city, and the balance will be different from one time period to another in the same area, causing the central area to experience surges of growth spaced by periods of decline.

For the student of politics, knowledge of growth patterns in urban areas and forces producing change have special significance, since many of the conflicts that reach the political arena are the result of conscious efforts of individuals and groups to intervene, through the political process, in this dynamic process of growth. In fact the issue as to whether or not the governmental agencies operating in an urban area should attempt to intervene in the developmental pattern of an area or should permit the interplay of economic and social forces to have free reign is itself a burning political issue. Certainly, present governmental programs of urban renewal, public housing, and public improvements are conscious efforts to use the political process to shape the pattern of development that seemed destined to result in a decline in the core areas of the city and to produce slums and blighted areas in what were once the most attractive parts of the city.

If the decision to intervene in the process is made, the number of political conflicts which will arise are legion. Landowners will be affected differently from nonlandowners in any attempt to legislate growth patterns, large corporations will be affected differently from smaller business interests, and labor's interests will not coincide with those of management. Hence, the seeds for political conflict are sown by any proposal to alter what seems to some the natural play of social and economic forces in urban change.

BIBLIOGRAPHY

Books

Adrian, Charles R.: *Governing Urban America*, The McGraw-Hill Book Company, New York, 1962, chap. 1.

Anderson, Nels: *The Urban Community*, Henry Holt and Company, Inc., New York, 1959, chaps. 1, 2, 5.

Bergel, Egon Ernest: *Urban Sociology*, The McGraw-Hill Book Company, New York, 1955, chaps. 5, 6, 9–11.

Beshers, James M.: *Urban Social Structure*, The Free Press, Glencoe, Ill., 1962.

Bollens, John C., and Henry J. Schmandt: *The Metropolis: Its People, Politics and Economic Life*, Harper & Row, Publishers, Incorporated, New York, 1961, chaps. 2, 4.

Davis, Kingsley: *Human Society*, The Macmillan Company, New York, 1949, chap. 12.

Gist, Noel P., and L. A. Halbert: *Urban Society*, Thomas Y. Crowell Company, New York, 1950, chaps. 5–8.

Greer, Scott: *Governing the Metropolis*, John Wiley & Sons, Inc., New York, 1962, chaps. 1, 2.

Hatt, Paul K., and Albert J. Reiss, Jr. (eds.): *Cities and Society*, The Free Press, Glencoe, Ill., 1957.

Hawley, Amos: *Human Ecology*, The Ronald Press Company, New York, 1950.

Kahl, Joseph A.: *The American Class Structure*, Holt, Rinehart and Winston, Inc., New York, 1957.

Mayer, Harold M., and Clyde F. Kohn (eds.): *Readings in Urban Geography*, University of Chicago Press, Chicago, 1959, sec. 10.

Peterson, William: *Population*, The Macmillan Company, New York, 1961, chap. 8.

Queen, Stuart Alfred, and David Bailey Carpenter: *The American City*, McGraw-Hill Book Company, New York, 1953, chaps. 4, 7–10.

Shevky, Eshref, and Wendell Bell: *Social Area Analysis*, Stanford University Press, Stanford, Calif., 1955.

Smith, T. V., and Leonard D. White (eds.): *An Experiment in Social Science*, University of Chicago Press, Chicago, 1929, chaps. 1, 5, 8.

Theodorson, George A. (ed.): *Urban Ecology*, Harper & Row, Publishers, Incorporated, New York, 1961.

Articles

Colby, Charles C.: "Centrifugal and Centripetal Forces in Urban Geography," *Annals of the Association of American Geographers*, vol. 23, pp. 1–20, March, 1933.

Form, William H.: "The Place of Social Structure in the Determination of Land Use," *Social Forces*, vol. 32, pp. 317–324, May, 1954.

Harris, Chauncy D., and Edward L. Ullman: "The Nature of Cities," *Annals of the American Academy of Political and Social Science*, pp. 7–17, November, 1945.

Hoyt, Homer: "The Structure of American Cities in the Post-War Era," *American Journal of Sociology*, vol. 48, pp. 475–481, January, 1943.

Redfield, Robert: "The Folk Society," *The American Journal of Sociology*, vol. 52, abstract p. 293. January, 1947.

Wirth, Louis: "Urbanism as a Way of Life," *The American Journal of Sociology*, vol. 47, pp. 293–308, July, 1938.

PART 2

THE LEGAL FRAMEWORK WITHIN WHICH CITIES ARE GOVERNED

3

THE LEGAL SYSTEM WITHIN WHICH LOCAL GOVERNMENTS FUNCTION

The author is aware of the limitations inherent in approaching the study of urban politics from an examination of formal documents such as constitutions, statutes, and charters, but he is also convinced that one important variable affecting political behavior within local governments is the legal system within which the actors are forced to operate. This legal system supplies the rules of the game, and although the political actors may seek to stretch the law in the fashion which is most advantageous to them, there are limits beyond which they dare not go. Acceptance of the idea of written constitutions and the "rule of law" is firmly implanted in the American political culture, and this belief in adherence to law is a conditioning factor that must be considered in analyzing individual and group behavior in political situations.

Ever present in the deliberations of city councils and administrative agencies is the question of the limits of their legal authority to act. Few local government officials will proceed with a proposed course of action if they are convinced that such action is beyond the limits of their authority in law, regardless of how committed they are to the desirability of the contemplated action. Operating within the legal framework is a value taken seriously by those who are entrusted with local decision-making power. Furthermore, city officials do not like to have their actions overruled by courts, and since state courts have consistently maintained a narrow interpretation of the powers of cities, decisions of city officials are often restricted in order to stay within approved limits. Since custom prescribes that local officials rely on legal advice whenever a question of limits of authority is raised, the lawyer becomes a significant actor on the local scene, even though he may be no more than a professional employee of the government. By training and experience he is oriented to think in legalistic terms, and his interpretation of the limits of available action open to decision makers will give a prominent place to the legal rules of the game. His decision is more likely to depend on his answer to the question "Is the action legal?" than on his reply to the question "Is it a useful action to take?" We must remember also that American lawyers have an affinity for politics, and therefore, more lawyers than members of any other calling or profession may be found among government decision makers.[1]

Another factor which adds weight to the notion that many decisions of local officials are conditioned by the formal legal system in which they perform their duties is the acceptance of the idea of judicial review. In the American system of government at all levels, one finds it difficult to isolate any important decision which cannot be made a matter for court action. Council actions can be challenged in the courts on the grounds that they are not in conformity with the city charter or state statutes. Administrative decisions are, in addition to being subject to challenge on the above grounds, liable to challenge simply because they are unreasonable or arbitrary. This means that many of the decisions made by legislative officers will finally end up before judicial tribunals. Judges, even more than practicing lawyers, are apt to be legalistically minded and permit questions of legal interpretation to weigh heavily in reaching a final conclusion.

LEGAL BASIS FOR THE MUNICIPAL CORPORATION

The American legal system does not recognize any right of the inhabitants of an urban area to create a municipal government and perform functions generally associated with local government on their own volition. That is, no inherent right exists for a community to exercise local government powers

---

[1] For an excellent discussion of the convergence of the professions of politician and lawyer, see Heinz Eulau and John D. Sprague, *Lawyers in Politics: A Study in Professional Convergence,* The Bobbs-Merrill Company, Incorporated, Indianapolis, 1964.

until such right has been conferred upon it by a higher governmental agency. Although municipal corporations existed before the present United States Constitution was drafted in 1787, this document did not provide specifically for future incorporation of municipalities or for city government. Under the accepted notion of American federalism, it is assumed that, since this power was not lodged with the federal government and not specifically prohibited to the states, it was, by the Tenth Amendment, left to the states. The doctrine that cities are the creatures of the state and are therefore completely subject to action of the state has become firmly fixed as a part of our legal heritage. Every attempt to break it down has failed. Judge Dillon's statement of the legal position of the city is a classic.[2]

> Municipal corporations owe their origin to, and derive their powers and rights wholly from, the legislature. It breathes into them the breath of life, without which they cannot exist. As it creates, so it may destroy. If it may destroy, it may abridge and control. Unless there is some constitutional limitation on the right, the legislature might, by a single act, if we can suppose it capable of so great a folly and so great a wrong, sweep from existence all the municipal corporations in the State, and the corporation could not prevent it. We know of no limitation on the right so far as the corporations themselves are concerned. They are, so to phrase it, the mere *tenants at will* of the legislature.

An attempt to provide a basis in law for a degree of independence for cities can be found in a few judicial decisions, notably the Cooley doctrine,[3] that cities have certain inherent powers of self-government and that such rights cannot be destroyed by state action. This line was not generally followed by other courts, and the principle of *stare decisis* has given ascendancy to the so-called Dillon's rule, which holds that cities are creatures of the state and subject, without recourse, to action of the state.

Practical application of this legal formality means that cities can be chartered only by state action, their form of government can be provided by the state, the limits of their power can be determined by state legislation, and their continued existence as a municipal corporation is dependent upon the state. Some explanation is necessary here as to the meaning of "the state" as it is used in the discussion above. The legal doctrine is that all powers left to the states by terms of the federal constitution reside in the legislative body of the state unless the state's own constitution decrees to the

---

[2] *City of Clinton v. Cedar Rapids and Missouri River R. R. Co.,* 24 Iowa 455 (1868).

[3] *People ex rel. LeRoy v. Hurlbut,* 24 Michigan 44 (1871).

contrary. The constituent (constitution-making) power of most states resides in the electorate. This power may be lodged in a constitutional convention at a given time, but even the acts of such a body are usually submitted to the voters for ratification. Provisions of state constitutions can, therefore, assign the residual powers of the state to agencies other than the legislature or can specifically deny certain of these powers to the state legislature although such powers may be clearly within the scope of the state's constitutional authority. This means, then, that in the absence of limitations in the state constitution, all powers the state has with respect to municipal corporations are lodged in the legislature, but the people can, and often do, curtail this legislative power by constitutional provisions. In fact, a significant trend over the last fifty years in state government has been the tendency to limit freedom of legislative action severely and to increase the authority and responsibility of the governor.

Numerous specific limitations on legislative action which might affect cities are found in the basic law of many states. Perhaps the most significant of these is one which requires legislatures to deal with local units of government by general rather than specific statutes. Evidence of state action designed to punish a single city by an act applicable to that city only are not difficult to find. These actions include such provisions as abolishing existing governmental agencies, state selection of important city officers, and state control of certain budget items of cities. The requirement that state legislatures act only by general law was designed to prevent the legislature from singling out a specific city for special punitive action.

The most important constitutional provisions which limit the control of state legislatures over cities are constitutional *home rule* provisions. These are designed to permit cities of certain sizes to write and adopt their own charters and to give to such cities limited freedom of action from legislative interference. Although such provisions have not, in practice, offered complete political independence to cities, they have created a different legal relationship between the state legislature and constitutional home rule cities from the relationship existing between the state legislature and non-home rule cities. The nature of home rule charters will be considered at greater length later.

INCORPORATION OF CITIES

As has been described earlier, urbanized areas become municipal corporations only after some formal process has been consummated. The legal fiction is that the power to grant incorporation to the inhabitants of an urban area is legislative in character and therefore cannot be delegated to any other authority. This fiction is still adhered to in many instances even though practice hardly coincides with principle.

For many years specific requests for municipal incorporation were few in number and were addressed directly to the state legislature where they were acted upon at regular legislative sessions. As the work load of state legislatures expanded and the number of requests for incorporation increased, the legislatures assigned at least part of their job to other government agencies. In most states the assignment was made to the chief legislative and administrative agency of the county. This agency usually consists of from three to seven members who are locally elected and are known by such names as county council, board of supervisors, county trustees, or county courts.

The legal fiction that incorporation is a legislative act is maintained by the assumption that the county legislative body is performing only an administrative or ministerial rather than a legislative act. That is, the state legislature, by general act, specifies the conditions and procedures under which incorporation can take place, and the county agency merely determines whether or not these conditions have been met. If it is determined that all conditions have been met, the local agency has no choice but to grant the incorporation. If this is the case, no discretion can be exercised by the county agency to determine whether or not the incorporation is in the public interest. As a matter of practice some such discretion may be exercised by the county agency simply by postponing actions on petitions about which the board has definitely negative opinions. Petitioners have access to the courts in such cases to force action by the local agency, but such action takes time.

In a few instances court decisions have in the past recognized as municipalities urban areas which have not complied fully with the laws governing incorporation. Such cities are referred to as de facto (in fact) corporations rather than de jure (in law) corporations. The most likely case of this kind is one in which a group of residents followed, to the best of their knowledge, the requirements of the law and some authorized governmental agency actually granted incorporation, but, at a later date, examination revealed that an error, undetected at the time, had occurred in the proceedings. Although, strictly speaking, the city was not legally incorporated, the courts have held that the city is a de facto corporation and its official actions are as binding as if the city were a de jure corporation.[4]

4 Tulare Irrigation District v. Shepard, 185 U.S. 1 (1901).

Procedures for Incorporation

Specific procedures for incorporation of cities are determined by the laws of the states. The major steps in a typical process are:

1. Some official evidence must be presented to show popular support for the incorporation. This may require signatures on a petition of a certain percentage of the voters or landowners in the area, or it may require that a popular vote be taken in the area to be incorporated.

2. The petition for incorporation must specify the exact boundaries of the area to be incorporated. No area which is already within an incorporated municipality can be included in a request for creation of a new municipal corporation.

3. Some states require that the area include a minimum number of residents, but this is not universal.

4. If the petition is approved by the proper authority, that authority appoints a set of officials to assume the powers of government for a limited period of time or provides for the first elections to select a set of officials.

5. The incorporation is made a matter of public record and no part of the territory so incorporated can, without its consent, be included as a part of a future petition for incorporation.

The actual incorporation is generally evidenced by the granting of a charter, which for all intents and purposes becomes the constitution for the city. Various kinds of charters have been developed over the years.

Charters of incorporation for cities are not granted for specific periods of time; they are granted without time limitations and continue until formal action is taken to end their existence. The mining towns of the West which flourished a few years ago and are now ghost towns may still be legal corporations, since courts, in the absence of specific legislation to the contrary, usually hold that the mere fact that a city has ceased to exercise its charter powers for a period of time is not enough to dissolve the corporation.[5] Usual procedure requires that a petition for disincorporation must be filed with a governmental agency designated by state law (usually a county or state court). If the petition is granted, orders are issued under which corporate property is to be disposed of and debts are to be paid. Trustees are then appointed to carry out these orders.

CLASSES OF CITY CHARTERS

Except for home rule cities, all city charters are drafted by state legislatures; they are often simply part of the statutes of the state and are of general applicability. The following classification of statutory charters indicates how legislatures have provided for the government of cities.

[5] *Hill v. Anderson*, 122 Ky. 87 (1906).

Special Charters

The standard practice for granting charters of incorporation to cities prior to the middle of the nineteenth century was for the state legislature to pass a special act for this purpose. Each community seeking incorporation appealed to the state legislature, and, if that body was in sympathy with the request, a special act, designating the city by name, indicating its boundaries, establishing city offices, and designating its powers, was passed. To all intents and purposes these charters were state statutes, but they were applicable only to the city named in the act. Although under this practice each city had an individual charter supposedly adapted to its special needs, there was considerable similarity among these special charters, since each new one was patterned after those issued previously. It was true, however, that powers or limitations applicable to one city and not to others could be written into these special charters. The press of business faced by state legislatures, the increasing number of requests for corporate charters, and public demand for greater uniformity brought an end to this practice in most states. Although some state legislatures can still grant special charters, the constitutions of many of them now require that cities be incorporated under general laws.

General Charters

If the practice of granting to each city a special charter is at one extreme, the general charter is at the other. Under this plan the state legislature adopts a single charter of incorporation to be granted to all urban areas seeking incorporation. This practice emphasizes uniformity, since each new city would have identical powers, be subject to the same limitations, and operate under the same type of governmental institutions as existing cities. Since urbanized areas petitioning for incorporation ranged from rural crossroads communities to large industrialized complexes, a single charter proved to be inadequate for all areas seeking incorporation.

Classified Charters

Classified charters occupy a place somewhere between the special and the general charter. Under this system the legislature classifies cities and adopts a single charter applicable to all cities within a single class. The most common basis for classification is population, although total assessed value of taxable property may be an adequate basis for differentiating between the needs of various sizes of cities. A newly created city begins operating under the charter for the class of city to which it belongs. Since a charter is granted at a specific period in time, it may become unrealistic if the city grows sufficiently to place it within a different class. The general rule has prevailed that a city does not automatically pass from one class to another simply by changes in its population or assessed property value. If a city, when its population entitles it to be in a different class, wants to change to the charter applicable to its new class, it must follow some formal procedure to make the change. The process required varies from state to state, but a popular election to approve the change is a common one. The author has known cities to operate for years under a charter for one class of cities when their population clearly qualified them to move to a higher classification. Peculiarities in the charters often cause city leaders to prefer the charter applicable to one class of cities over the charter applicable to cities of a higher class.

Optional Charters

Many states have adopted a practice of permitting cities to choose one from among two or more charters available to them. This is in line with the trend to extend greater freedom for cities to decide their own form of government. No doubt, the appearance of different forms of government at the city level added to the pressure for optional charters. A common practice is for the state legislature to draft three charters, one with a mayor-council form of government, one with a commission form, and another with a council-manager form and permit each city to select the one it wants. The selection is usually by popular vote within the city.

The optional charter system can be used in combination with a system of classification. For example, the legislature may divide cities of the state into four classes on the basis of population, and provide optional charters for cities within one or more of the classes. A single charter may be adequate for all cities of a class which does not include any city with a population of more than 2,500, but for a class that includes cities ranging from 25,000 to 100,000 optional charters may prove very popular.

Special note must be made of the fact that all the types of charters discussed above are statutory, i.e., they have been passed as a regular piece of legislation by the state lawmaking body. Therefore, any legislature at any time can amend or abolish an existing charter or adopt a totally new one, and all cities operating under the charter thus changed will be affected thereby. The only recourse a city has if it learns of a proposed charter change is to appeal to the legislature either to support or oppose the change. This fact is the most significant difference between the charters discussed above and home rule charters, which are discussed below.

HOME RULE

The term "home rule" has been assigned many different meanings by different writers, and its implications have been the subject of numerous court cases. A simple definition of home rule is that it is the right of a city to draft and adopt a charter for its own government. For some purposes this is a satisfactory definition, but it fails to take into account the source from which this right is derived. In fact, the first cases of home rule under this definition were in Iowa, where this right was given to cities by action of the state legislature.[6] This type of home rule is often referred to as legislative home rule, to distinguish it from constitutional home rule which is a constitutional grant. The difficulty inherent in home rule which is derived from the state legislature is that it is constantly subject to withdrawal by the same source. Since the doctrine that the acts of one legislature are not binding on its successor is fairly well established, a city operating under a charter which has been adopted by virtue of an act of the state legislature may still find itself subject to future legislative interference with no legal recourse available. Experience with this kind of home rule, however, reveals that cities have enjoyed a high degree of independence over a long period of years. This may or may not be because a home rule clause is on the statute book; it may simply reflect a reluctance on the part of the legislature to interfere with the internal affairs of cities in the state, or the political pressures brought upon legislatures to allow cities freedom of action.

Constitutional home rule may be defined as the right of cities to prepare and adopt their own charters when such right is granted by specific provisions of the state constitution. These constitutional provisions may be interpreted as direct limitations upon the power of the legislature to prescribe for cities the form of government which they shall have. Under constitutional home rule a city may adopt a charter which its voters think is adequate to meet its needs, without regard to what the legislature may think. If, in such cities, the legislature attempts to dictate the structural form of government the city shall employ, legal recourse is available through the courts to block such interference.

Historically, constitutional home rule dates from 1875 when the con-

[6] Russell M. Ross and Kenneth F. Millsap, *State and Local Government and Administration,* The Ronald Press Company, New York, 1966, p. 51.

stitution of Missouri made home rule available to all cities in the state with a population of 100,000 or more (Kansas City and St. Louis). The historical background out of which this provision came illustrates the purpose such a political concept was designed to serve. The appeal for constitutional home rule came from St. Louis and was designed to afford a degree of protection from the vindictiveness of the legislature growing out of the Civil War. An example of this conflict was the act of the legislature which removed control of the St. Louis police from city officials and gave it to a board appointed by the governor.

Each state provides by law the procedures under which home rule is achieved, but the following steps are fairly representative.

1. The electorate first indicates a desire for home rule. The issue is usually presented to the voters of the city either by a resolution of the existing city council or by an initiative petition to be signed by the required number of qualified voters.

2. If the voters, usually by a simple majority, vote for home rule, a charter commission is created to prepare a charter draft. Although the manner of selection of such a commission varies from state to state, popular election at large is a common method.

3. When the commission has agreed on a proposed charter, it is submitted to popular vote for approval or rejection. A simple majority of those voting on the proposed charter is usually sufficient for its adoption.

4. Some states may require that the charter be submitted to the state legislature for approval, but others require only that it be filed with the secretary of state, after which all courts are required to take judicial notice of its existence. This procedure requires the voters to pass judgment on home rule as an issue, the commissioners who are to write the charter, and the charter itself, but it is not uncommon that the first two steps will be submitted at a single election.

Constitutional home rule does not give cities a position of complete independence from state action, nor does it create a city-state which is no longer subject to the general acts of the state legislature. It authorizes a city to draft its own charter, and with respect to some subjects that are assumed to be proper parts of a charter, it affords protection from legislative interference. One may say with some degree of assurance that the general form of government can be determined by the home rule charter and that its provisions will be given preference by the courts over any contrary acts of the state legislature. Kinds of city officers, their terms, and their manner of selection and salary are certainly areas for local discretion. For example, a state law which provides that no mayor in a city in the state shall be given a term longer than two years would not prevent a home rule city from providing a four-year term for its mayor in the charter, or a state law requiring city managers to be residents of the state at the time of their selection would not prevent a home rule charter from permitting the city council to employ a manager who lived in another state. Generally, home rule charters will take precedence over contradictory state statutes in purely procedural matters. Although courts may require that home rule charter provisions relative to procedures for notification of elections, notice of zoning changes, and hearings on condemnation proceedings meet certain requirements of "due process," they are not likely to require them to conform in detail to state laws on these subjects.

In dealing with questions relating to the powers which cities can exercise, the line between the application of state general laws and home rule charters is much less clear. Practically all home rule charters contain extensive lists of powers which the city can exercise or they contain broad general statements designed to give the city all power not expressly denied by the federal or state constitution. The statement of powers of the city in the *Model City Charter* is an example of a broad general grant: "The city shall have all powers possible for a city to have under the constitution and laws of this state as fully and completely as though they were specifically enumerated in this charter."[7] In most states general laws exist which place limits on the power of all cities or of cities within certain population ranges. These limits often refer either to kinds of taxes which can be levied, maximum tax rates, power to take private property for public purposes, or power of police officers to make arrests and hold suspects for certain periods without filing charges before a magistrate. No entirely satisfactory statement can be made which shows accurately where the powers of home rule cities begin and those of the state legislature end. Attempts have been made to list certain powers supposedly of purely local concern and others which are matters of general concern to the state at large, and then to generalize that in matters of purely local concern, the provisions of a home rule charter take precedence over general state laws, while in matters of statewide concern, the charter provision must give way to state law when a conflict occurs. The real difficulty comes when an attempt is made to enumerate the specific powers which are included in each list. Decisions of the courts of the various states are not uniform, and a careful student will find that even within a single state a definite pattern is difficult to discover.[8]

---

[7] National Municipal League, *Model City Charter*, 6th ed., 1964, p. 1.
[8] An excellent discussion of this problem in a single state is found in Henry J. Schmandt, "Municipal Home Rule in Missouri," *Washington University Law Quarterly*, vol. 53, pp. 385–412, December, 1953.

Even with respect to officers who perform functions within the city, conflicts between state law and city charters have developed, although it is generally assumed that this is an area in which the state cannot interfere with provisions of a home rule charter. Again, the dispute hinges not on the soundness of the principle but on its practical application. The argument is made, and often accepted by the courts, that some officials who appear to be city officers are in fact state officers performing state functions within the boundaries of the city. A case in point is the treasurer of the City of St. Louis. The city home rule charter provides that he be appointed by the mayor. A state law, however, provides that all county treasurers be popularly elected. Now, since the city treasurer collects the kinds of taxes within the limits of the city that county treasurers collect in other areas of the state, the courts have held that the state law must be applied, and, although the specific provision in the city charter has never been changed, the treasurer is, in fact, popularly elected. State statutes have also been upheld when they prescribe controls over city police on the grounds that these officers are really state officers since they are obligated to enforce state statutes as well as city ordinances within the limits of the city.

One may not be far wrong to conclude that state judges have been trained in an environment which tends to support the position that cities, being mere agencies of the state, are subject to its legislative pronouncements, and unless the evidence is extremely strong in support of the position of independence for the city, decisions will generally give precedence to general laws of the state over city charters, even though the charters have been written under authority of a constitutional home rule grant. The burden of proof to justify the independence of the city is usually upon those who seek to support city independence against state laws.

If, in the final analysis, the most important thing home rule gives to a city is the right to mold the structure and form of its government, what incentive is there for city officials to adopt home rule rather than accept an optional charter provided by the state legislature, particularly if the optional plans offer the three most widely used forms of government (mayor-council, commissioner, and council-manager)? Home rule may still have special appeal for two reasons.

1. Home rule charters offer a wider choice of alternatives within any of the three structural forms. For example, a statutory charter which provides the mayor-council form of government may provide for the selection of city councilmen from representative districts or wards, for the election of 10 councilmen all at a single election, and for two-year terms for them. No variation of this pattern is possible if a city chooses this option as a charter for the city. But

if a city writing its own charter also chooses the mayor-council as the basic form for its government, it still has a wide latitude of choice as to the composition of its council. It can, for instance, provide for the election of all councilmen at large, limit the number to six, and give them overlapping terms of four years.

2. If a city elects to adopt an optional statutory charter, it cannot, through any action of its own, make even the slightest change which might be dictated by experience. Likewise, it may find some change made in its charter by the legislature without its consent, or in some cases, even its knowledge. If a single city operating under an optional charter should through its representatives in the legislature secure the passage of a bill amending the optional charter, this amendment would actually apply to every other city operating under the same charter. On the other hand, a city which has drafted its own charter can by its own action adopt amendments from time to time to correct defects which have become apparent through practice or which are required to meet new city problems. Although constitutional home rule has not produced the degree of independence of action its supporters expected of it, it still offers certain attractions which ensure its continued existence in state legal systems.

Recent criticisms of constitutional home rule for cities have emerged as a result of attempts to restructure the political system in large metropolitan areas.[9] Those who support proposals to reassign certain local powers or functions from individual cities to larger units of government through action of the state legislature, find that constitutional grants to home rule cities located in metropolitan areas are often legal barriers to the accomplishment of their objectives. The Advisory Commission on Intergovernmental Relations in its report suggested that states modify the traditional home rule concept:

> Local home rule for strictly local problems; metropolitan home rule for areawide problems but with the State free to legislate and otherwise act with respect to problems which transcend county boundaries and which are not soluble through interlocal cooperation. The Commission believes that the States would be well advised to lose no opportunities in the normal processes of constitutional change to make sure that constitutional home rule provisions are so modified as to insure that the authority of the State with respect to its metropolitan areas is not unduly restricted.[10]

EVALUATION OF HOME RULE

How is the model for understanding politics suggested earlier in this text useful in understanding the position of those who support home rule for cities

[9] Eugene C. Lee, "Home Rule Appraised," *National Civic Review*, vol. 51, pp. 486–488, October, 1962.
[10] Advisory Commission on Intergovernmental Relations, *Governmental Structure, Organization and Planning in Metropolitan Areas*, July, 1961, p. 20.

and those who maintain that cities should be subject to control by the state legislature? When any conflict arises over a specific course of action which city officers propose to pursue, some groups will view the action as favorable to their interests and others will oppose the action as contrary to their interest. Each group is likely to prefer to have the decision made in the political arena in which it feels its chances for a favorable result are best. If the participants in the process are to be limited to those persons within the city (home rule), then one set of interests will prevail. But, on the other hand, if the decision can be taken to the state legislature in which an entirely different mix of interests exists, the interests which were in the minority within the city may often emerge victorious. For example, in an industrial city, organized labor may be sufficiently strong politically to dominate actions of local officials. Therefore, such an organized group is likely to support a policy of maximum home rule. On the other hand an organization of business and professional men who are consistently in the minority when conflict issues are decided locally, may find strong support for their position from rural representatives in the state legislature. Such a group is, then, led by self-interest to favor state legislative action rather than greater home rule.

Political party leaders may often be found supporting continued legislative control over cities rather than clamoring for greater home rule. Historically, home rule has often ridden the crest of reform movements. As a result, home rule charters are apt to provide nonpartisan elections, replace job patronage with a merit system for the selection of city employees, and in other ways make the influence of political party officers less significant in locally made decisions. These conditions are less likely to be found at the state level. Legislators are elected on a party basis, and state jobs are more likely to be dispensed as political patronage. Therefore, party influence in local decisions is likely to be more significant when the decision is made in the state legislature than when it is made in the local political arena. Although much of the support for and opposition to the home rule concept can be explained in terms of interest representation, the concept has in some areas become a sort of status symbol. When some cities within a geographic area adopt home rule charters, other cities may feel compelled to follow the same pattern simply to "keep up with the trend."

CHANGES AFTER INCORPORATION

A rather simple change which a municipal corporation can make after its original incorporation is to change from its original charter to another. This can be accomplished by becoming a home rule city under procedures outlined earlier. For cities which have classified statutory charters, this can be accomplished by moving into another class as population increases. Since these changes involve only a single city, a popular vote within the city affected is usually all that is required for the change.

Processes which result in changes in existing boundaries of cities become somewhat more complicated. Two such processes, *annexation* and *consolidation,* are available to most cities. The term annexation is generally used to designate a boundary extension which brings contiguous unincorporated areas within the limits of an existing city; consolidation combines into a single city two or more existing municipal corporations. Some states in their legal system have a procedure whereby a given city can annex parts of existing cities, but such actions are uncommon. The annexation laws of the 50 states are so varied that generalization becomes very difficult. Perhaps the following classification will serve to given an overview of the process in general.

1. Some states permit annexation of adjacent unincorporated areas by action of the annexing city only. In some cases the proposal to annex must be approved by a majority of the qualified voters of the city, but in other cases, action of the city council is sufficient. State statutes prescribe the procedure which applies to non-home rule cities, but home rule cities are permitted to include in their charters specific procedures for annexation. This simple procedure was provided in Texas law, and her cities have made extensive additions to their territory in recent years.[11]

2. A number of states permit annexations by joint action of the city doing the annexation and the residents of the area to be annexed. Although the city may act through its council, approval by the voters of the area to be annexed is required. Since opposition to proposed annexations often comes from residents of the area to be annexed, this requirement is an important factor limiting annexation.

3. Some states, notably Virginia and Missouri, make the judicial branch a part of the annexation process. In Virginia a special three-judge court hears arguments on proposed annexation and, under criteria contained in the state statutes, decides what annexations shall be accomplished and the specific procedures under which the change shall take place. Of special interest in the Virginia process is the fact that a proposed annexation plan may be presented to the court by the governing board of the county in which the affected area is located.[12] In most states action for annexation must originate in the annexing city or in the area to be annexed.

[11] See O. A. Spain, "Politics of Municipal Annexation in Texas," *Southwestern Social Science Quarterly,* vol. 30, pp. 18–28, June, 1949.

[12] See Chester W. Bain, "Annexation: Virginia's Not-so-judicial System," *Public Administration Review,* vol. 15, pp. 251–262, Autumn, 1955; and "Terms and Conditions of Annexation under the 1952 Statute," *Virginia Law Review,* vol. 41, pp. 1129–1158, December, 1955.

The Missouri practice presents an interesting variation. When a city proposes to annex adjacent territory, it must present its case to the regular trial court of the county (circuit court) and seek a declaratory judgment permitting it to hold an election on the proposed annexation. In determining whether or not to issue the declaratory judgment the court is required by law to determine:

1. That such annexation is reasonable and necessary to the proper development of said city; and

2. The ability of said city to furnish normal municipal services of said city to said unincorporated area within a reasonable time after said annexation is to become effective.[13]

Decisions of the lower courts in these cases are subject to review in higher courts, and even in states where the judicial branch does not participate in the original annexation process, courts have accepted suits filed by parties in interest which claim that the action is unreasonable and arbitrary. A single case in St. Louis will serve as an illustration of the legal complexities involved in the annexation process. The case was in the courts for four years, and was finally decided by the state supreme court in 1963.

The City of Olivette sought to annex a strip of land which was adjacent to its western border and which was not within the corporate limits of any city. The strip extended from the Olivette boundary westward to a four-lane highway. The city asked the circuit court for a declaratory judgment to permit an election within the city on the proposed annexation. The judge granted the request, and an election date was set. On a request for rehearing, however, opposition lawyers argued that under Missouri law the area sought for annexation was no longer subject to annexation. St. Louis County is a home rule county with a charter adopted locally under provisions of the state constitution. The argument presented was that the adoption of a home rule charter which specifically refers to the county as a "body politic and corporate" had the effect of making all of the county "incorporated territory" and as such no longer subject to annexation. The judge accepted this argument, reversed his original decision, and enjoined the city from proceeding with the election.

On appeal, the state supreme court overruled the circuit court and held that a home rule charter did not make the entire area of a county "incorporated" within the meaning of the annexation statutes. But in this opinion, the court held that the act (quoted above) which required a declaratory judgment implied that in considering the reasonableness of the proposed annex-

---

[13] R. S. Mo. 1959, Art. 71.015.

ation, the circuit court must determine its reasonableness for (1) the annex-ing city, (2) the area being annexed, and (3) the county as a whole. The case was then returned to be retired under the new instructions.[14] After prolonged hearings, the circuit court ruled that the annexation was reasonable on all three counts and issued an order permitting the city to hold an election on the issue. This decision was also appealed to the state supreme court, which finally decided that the judgment of the local circuit court was in error, that the annexation was not reasonable from the standpoint of the county as a whole, and therefore no election could be held.[15]

This case not only demonstrates the complexities which may arise in an annexation attempt, but also shows how the time factor alone may affect the issues in conflict so as to make the original issues insignificant. As long as the strip of land involved was unincorporated, the land-use pattern could legally be determined by the county zoning board and the county council. If it were annexed by the City of Olivette, however, the land-use pattern would be determined by the city zoning commission and the city council. County authorities had zoned a large section of the land for industrial use; the chances are very good that the city would have limited all of it to residential use. As long as the annexation issue was before the courts, the county's au-thority over the area was in effect. During this four-year period industrial construction had proceeded to the point where the city could not have changed the land-use pattern even if it had won the case in the supreme court. In fact, passage of time, not political agencies, had determined the real issue (zoning) in conflict.

LEGAL LIABILITY OF MUNICIPAL CORPORATIONS

Since a city is a municipal corporation which, like a private corporation, can sue and be sued, plead and be impleaded, the question of its liability for the acts of its agents is a matter of some concern. The doctrine of *respondent superior* (the superior is responsible for the acts of his servants) is well established as the ruling doctrine in cases where private corporations are held to be responsible for the acts of their agents. The law with respect to mu-nicipal liability, however, is not nearly so clear.

Although municipal corporations are artificial persons in the eyes of the law, they can act only through real persons. Legislators, administrators, and employees act in behalf of the corporation. When do acts of these agents

[14] *City of Olivette v. Graeler*, 338 S.W. 2d 827 (1960).
[15] *City of Olivette v. Graeler*, 369 S.W. 2d 85 (1963).

create a legal liability on the part of the city—i.e., when will their acts create a situation in which the taxpayers may be forced to pay money damages? Conflicts occur when actions of city agents do not comply with all legal formalities, when these agents are accused of failure to act when they should have acted, or when their actions produce personal injuries or property damage.

Liability for Contracts

Many activities of cities are accomplished through contractual obligations. Public works of all kinds are constructed under contracts with construction firms, certain municipal services, such as garbage collection and disposal, are let out on contract to private bidders, and contracts for the purchase of supplies and materials are regular procedures. In general a public corporation will be held liable on its contracts, just as are private corporations. Certainly, a change in political officeholders will not alter contractual liability; i.e., if a duly elected mayor and city council enter into a contract the terms of which are clearly within the powers of the city and they follow faithfully procedures required by law, the city will be obligated by its terms even though a new mayor and council, whose members are wholly opposed to the contract, are elected before its time limit expires. To that extent duly elected officers of a city can bind a city by contract even though it may be clear that they will be defeated at the next election.

Cities are not, however, required to meet the terms of contracts which call for action beyond the legal limits of their power. Such contracts are *ultra vires,* and courts will relieve the city from the liability they are intended to create. Lack of familiarity on the part of the contractor will not be a defense to prevent loss sustained if a city does not accept its obligations under such contracts.

Cities are not responsible for contracts unless the persons who negotiated the contract had legal authority to do so. Some city charters require that all contracts for public works be approved by ordinance. If a director of public works for the city without council approval enters into a contract for construction of a sewage disposal plant, the contract may be voided by the city. Likewise a contract does not bind the city if it is negotiated and signed by an employee of the city who represents himself as the officer legally qualified to sign contracts but who actually does not have such authority. Again the burden is upon those who deal with the city to make sure the persons with whom they deal are legally competent to bind the city by contract.

Liability for Torts

Torts are generally defined as civil wrongs (other than failure to meet terms of a contract) which result in injury to another. The rule of law is that individuals are liable in damages for their own torts and corporations are liable for the torts of their agents. The question that arises with respect to cities is the extent to which cities, as corporations, are liable for the torts of their employees. The most common tort that arises is negligence of an employee which results in injury to persons or property.

Common law rules have given the municipal corporation a dual personality, i.e., it may perform functions which are considered public or governmental in character (police, fire, health, education), and it may perform acts which are essentially private or proprietary in character (supplying electricity, gas, and water or operating a transit system). In the performance of the public functions, courts have held that cities are not liable for the negligent acts of its employees, but in the performance of proprietary functions the city must assume the same liability that private corporations have.

Criticism of the rule which protects a city from liability for the torts of its employees who are performing governmental services has been voiced by students of government, lawyers, and judges, and changes in both the rule and the manner of its application have been increasing. Changes in the rule can, of course, be made by acts of the state legislature which specifically remove the present immunity now enjoyed by cities. Perhaps the Federal Tort Claims Act of 1946, which in substance made the federal government financially liable for torts of its agents and provided that damage suits arising from the law can be tried in regular federal courts, has stimulated action on this subject in states. New York has a statute similar to that of the federal law.

The old rule is also undergoing substantial change through changes in court decisions. Judges are more likely to interpret the law in such a way as to make cities liable, and in some instances they have completely abolished the old common law rule of legal immunity for cities. The following statement from the Illinois Supreme Court in a case involving an injury on a school bus serves to show the attitude of that court toward the common law rule.

> We are of the opinion that none of the reasons advanced in support of school district immunity have any true validity today. Further we believe that abolition of such immunity may tend to decrease the frequency of school bus accidents by coupling the power to transport pupils with the responsibility of exercising care in the selection and supervision of the drivers. . . .

We conclude that the rule of school district tort immunity is unjust, unsupported by any valid reason and has no rightful place in modern day society.[16]

The whole question of municipal liability is as much political as judicial, and this fact is being recognized by both judges and city officeholders.[17] Obviously there still is difference of opinion as to the wisdom of maintaining a legal principle which protects the taxpayer from paying claims for damages sustained by negligence of city employees, and the question will ultimately be resolved by the play of political forces which are concerned with the issue. City officials fear that the effectiveness of police and fire departments will be impaired if the city must face lawsuits every time someone is injured or property is destroyed by action of a fire department company as it fights a fire or by police officers as they raid a tavern where illegal gambling is suspected. Taxpayer groups fear that lowering the immunity bar will produce such a large number of damage claims that governmental costs will be forced upward. They claim juries in such damage suits will be sympathetic and award excessive amounts as payment for damages, since they know payment will come out of the public treasury. On the other hand, some argue that there is no good reason why a citizen who is injured by the carelessness of a driver should not receive damage payments merely because the vehicle happened to be city-owned and operated by a city employee. In fact they maintain that the city administration would be improved by elimination of the immunity rule, since greater care would be exercised in selecting, training, and supervising city employees in order to reduce accidents to a minimum.

The real issue today is not what the legal rule of liability is or which functions are governmental and which are proprietary, but, under modern conditions, to what extent the decision makers in our cities want the city government to be financially liable for the tortious acts of city personnel. Legislative action to change the common law rules which have clothed cities with immunity will be forthcoming when politically active groups make demands on their elected representatives.

SUMMARY

The legal system within which municipal corporations are required to operate constitutes one of the forces which determine the kinds of decisions which

---

[16] *Molitor v. Kaneland Community Unit District No.* 302, 163 N.E. 2d 89 (1960).
[17] In Florida the state supreme court has eliminated the distinction between governmental and proprietary functions and has held cities liable for the torts of its agents. *Hargrove v. Town of Coco Beach,* 96 So. (2d) 139 (1957). New York by law has abolished the tort immunity of cities.

are made by city officials. Likewise, the nature of the legal system determines the strategies adopted by those who seek some favorable decision from the political system. The legal system constitutes the rules of the game, and these rules are seldom neutral; as they operate at any given time they work to the advantage of some and the disadvantage of others. Therefore part of the total political conflict takes the form of attempts to change existing rules. The coach of a basketball team knows that the rules of the game as they exist at any given time may work either to his advantage or to his disadvantage. If he has an exceptionally tall group of players, he may profit by keeping the basket 10 feet from the floor, but if his opponent has tall players and he has small, fast players, he may be the strongest supporter of a proposal to raise the basket to a position 12 feet from the floor. Parties to conflicts in the political arena behave in much the same way; they support existing legal forms when they seem to work to their advantage and become proponents of modernizing the legal system when it no longer serves their ends.

BIBLIOGRAPHY

Books

Adrian, Charles R.: *Governing Urban America,* 2d ed., The McGraw-Hill Book Company, New York, 1961, chap. 7.

Bain, Chester W.: *Annexation in Virginia: The Use of the Judicial Process for Readjusting City-County Boundaries,* The University Press of Virginia, Charlottesville, Va., 1966.

David, Leon T.: *The Tort Liability of Public Officers,* Public Administration Service, Chicago, 1940.

Dillon, John F.: *Commentaries on the Law of Municipal Corporations,* 5th ed., Little, Brown and Company, Boston, 1911.

Eulau, Heinz, and John D. Sprague: *Lawyers in Politics: A Study in Professional Convergence,* Bobbs-Merrill Company, Inc., Indianapolis, 1964.

Fordham, J. B.: *Local Government Law—Text, Cases, and Other Materials,* Foundation Press, Brooklyn, 1949.

Kneier, Charles M., and Guy Fox: *Readings in Municipal Government,* Rinehart and Company, Inc., New York, 1953, pp. 25–112.

McBain, H. L.: *The Law and Practice of Municipal Home Rule,* Columbia University Press, New York, 1916.

McGoldrick, J. D.: *Law and Practice of Municipal Home Rule,* Columbia University Press, New York, 1933.

Mandelker, Daniel R.: *Managing Our Urban Environment,* The Bobbs-Merrill Company, Inc., Indianapolis, 1963, particularly chaps. 1, 2.

Mott, Rodney L.: *Home Rule for American Cities,* American Municipal Association, Chicago, 1949.

National Municipal Association: *Model City Charter,* 6th ed., New York, 1964.

Rhyne, C. S.: *Municipal Law,* National Institute of Municipal Law Officers, Washington, 1957.

Articles

Agger, Robert E.: "Lawyers in Politics: A Starting Point for a New Research Program," *Temple Law Quarterly,* vol. 29, pp. 434–452, summer, 1956.

Bain, Chester W.: "Annexation: Virginia's Not-so-judicial System," *Public Administration Review,* vol. 15, pp. 251–262, autumn, 1955.

Baker, Benjamin: "Cities on Their Own," *National Municipal Review, Public Administration Review,* vol. 44, pp. 193–197, April, 1955.

Derge, David R.: "The Lawyer in the Indiana Legislature," *Midwest Journal of Political Science,* vol. 6, pp. 19–53, February, 1962.

Lee, Eugene C.: "Home Rule Appraised," *National Civic Review,* vol. 51, pp. 486–488, October, 1962.

Schlesinger, Joseph A.: "Lawyers and American Politics: A Clarified View," *Midwest Journal of Political Science,* vol. 1, pp. 26–39, May, 1957.

Schmandt, Henry J.: "Municipal Home Rule in Missouri," *Washington University Law Quarterly,* vol. 53, pp. 385–412, December, 1953.

Spain, O. A.: "Politics of Municipal Annexation in Texas," *Southwestern Social Science Quarterly,* vol. 30, pp. 18–28, June, 1949.

Warp, George A.: "Can the 'King' Do No Wrong?" *National Municipal Review,* vol. 21, pp. 311–315, June, 1942.

The legal relationship between the state and its cities has already been discussed; all that needs to be repeated here is that the doctrine of state supremacy has never been altered substantially. The legal authority of the state to deal with cities in any way it wants through its lawmaking procedure is subject only to limits contained in the state's own constitution. Legal authority, however, is not always the same as political power, and although a state legislature may possess legal authority to pass certain restrictive legislation relating to cities, the play of political forces may make such action most unlikely.

The movement for municipal home rule which gives to cities a measure of independence in their governmental affairs can be explained, in part, by the atittude of city civic and political leaders that existing relations between cities and states are unsatisfactory. Although in some instances specific actions taken by states which adversely affected one or more cities have produced a reaction against state interference in local affairs, most criticism results from inaction on the part of the state to take positive steps to help their cities meet the problems thrust upon them by rapid social and economic changes. Political and civic leaders in the large cities have recognized that under existing legal and institutional structures the locus of power at the state level has been in the outstate areas rather than in the cities. It is, therefore, not difficult to understand why political leaders in cities who recognized the need for positive action at the state level which will enable them to do their jobs locally became severe critics of the established role of the state in local affairs.

EVIDENCES OF CHANGE

Most significant changes that have occurred in intergovernmental relations have been preceded by study commissions which produce packages of recommendations for reform supported by a series of reports made available to interested citizens. Since 1950 the problems associated with intergovernmental relations have received their share of study, evaluation, and recommendations for solution. Congress in 1953 created the Commission on Intergovernmental Relations (commonly referred to as the Kestubaum Commission from its chairman Meyer Kestubaum), composed of members appointed by the President, the President of the Senate, and the Speaker of the House. Reports of this Commission were published in 1955, and some of them dealt with local government and the impact of federal grants-in-aid on the structure of state and local government. Two points stand out in these recommendations that relate to state-city relations: (1) states had not, as they should have, assumed leadership in attacking problems in their metropolitan areas, and (2) the federal government should stimulate states to take more effective action and seek better coordination of national and state policies in seeking solutions to metropolitan problems.[1]

In 1956 the Council of State Governments published the results of a study conducted for it by John Bollens at the direction of the Governors' Conference. This study focused attention on the responsibilities of states in solving the problems of their metropolitan areas. After firmly asserting that states should assume leadership in dealing with metropolitan areas, the report made the following recommendations: (1) States should adopt constitutional and legal provisions authorizing the establishing of metropolitan units of government. This recommendation was designed to provide a legal framework within which the areas themselves could work out some of their structural problems. (2) States should appraise the adequacy of local governments. After listing a number of inadequacies of local units of government, the report suggests that the "states should seek to develop units that can efficiently perform their functions and that can provide opportunities for broad citizen participation in

[1] Commission on Intergovernmental Relations, *A Report to the President for Transmittal to Congress*, Washington, 1955, pp. 52, 53.

local affairs."[2] (3) States should create agencies to analyze on a continuing basis the needs of metropolitan areas and make recommendations for their solution. Discussion of this specific recommendation indicated that a single state agency was expected to assume this responsibility.

In 1959 Congress created the Advisory Commission on Intergovernmental Relations as a permanent body. This commission has among its members persons appointed by the President from lists recommended by organizations of state and local governmental officials, members of both houses of Congress, and administrators from federal agencies that deal with cities and metropolitan areas. This Commission has also emphasized the central role states should play in attempts to improve metropolitan areas. In order to concentrate state attention on metropolitan problems, the Commission repeated the position taken by the Council of State Governments that states should create an agency of the state government for continuing attention, review, and assistance with respect to the metropolitan areas of the state and associated problems of local government, planning, structure, organization, and finance.[3]

In a report prepared by the Advisory Commission in cooperation with the Subcommittee on Intergovernmental Relations of the Committee on Governmental Operations of the United States Senate, the following recommendation, which would further strengthen the position of the state, was made.

> The Commission recommends that the States assume their proper responsibilities for assisting and facilitating urban development; to this end it is recommended that Federal grants-in-aid to local governments for urban development be channeled through the States in cases where a State (a) provides appropriate administrative machinery to carry out relevant responsibilities, and (b) provides significant financial contributions, and when appropriate, technical assistance to local governments concerned.[4]

It will lay the groundwork for a discussion of the political nature of the issues presented by this recommendation to note that Robert C. Weaver, Mayors Hummel, Tucker, Blaisdell, and Naftalin, as well as Senator Muskie lodged strong protests against the recommendation. The statement made by Mayors Tucker, Blaisdell, and Naftalin, in dissenting from the above recom-

[2] John C. Bollens, *The States and the Metropolitan Problem,* Council of State Governments, Chicago, 1956, p. 132.
[3] Advisory Commission on Intergovernmental Relations, *Governmental Structure, Organization and Planning in Metropolitan Areas,* Washington, 1961, p. 35.
[4] Committee on Governmental Operations, U.S. Senate, *Impact of Federal Urban Development Programs on Local Government Organizations and Planning,* Washington, 1964, p. 30.

mendation, says, "It ignores the success of current federal and city co-operation in present urban development programs and would threaten the substance of the programs to gain an arbitrarily preferred form in inter-governmental structure."[5]

The fact that these conflicts of opinion exist on the question of routing all federal aid to metropolitan areas through the state rather than by means of direct contacts between federal agencies and the cities reveals that the issues involved are primarily political in character, although inferentially some ques-tions of organization and procedure may be involved. The statement just quoted implies that existing federal-city relations on federally aided urban development programs were viewed by mayors as successful. Although the statement did not say so directly, one may assume the mayors were not con-vinced that state-city relations would be as satisfactory for them. To say it another way, the mayors felt that the responses of the federal government to the needs of cities more nearly conformed to their own ideas than would the responses of the state agencies. The Advisory Commission recognized this political reality in one of its reports,

> It is a much more satisfying endeavor for a publicly elected official to push for a Federal grant with the Congressmen and Senators concerned than it is to push a bill at the State House for authorization to levy a new type of local tax or to raise an existing limitation on property taxes or borrowing. . . . Consequently, mayors and other local government officials from metropolitan areas receive careful attention from the U.S. Congress. . . .[6]

The political reality just described cannot be accounted for in terms of formal organizational structure or in the legal nature of the federal system; it must be sought in political terms. Why do mayors of large cities so often go to the state capital with a legislative package which they feel is vital to the development of their city and so often not only come away empty-handed but with the feeling that they have not been treated with respect? Although there are other factors operating to account for the situation, a significant one has been the prorural and anticity attitude of a majority of state legislators. In part, this is a function of the way the representation systems have operated in the Congress and in state legislatures.

Urban interests are generally better represented in the Congress than they are at state legislatures. One might assume that since small states have

[5] *Ibid.*, footnote, p. 30.
[6] *Ibid.*, pp. 8–10.

representation in the Senate equal to that of large states, rural interests would exert a dominant influence there, but this is not necessarily the case. As total population increases and industry expands in size but decentralizes geographically, more and more states become urban. On the basis of 1960 census figures, 39 states are more urban than rural; 60 percent or more of their population is classed as urban.[7] Since senators are chosen from states in at-large elections, urban voters have a preponderance of voting strength in these 39 states. If mayors and the parties they represent can exert influence on the electorates of their cities in the selection of senators, these senators may be expected to give some deference to them when they come seeking aid for their cities.

In the House of Representatives there is some overrepresentation by rural areas but not to the extent found in many states. A *Congressional Quarterly* study reported that, contrary to popular belief, strictly urban areas were only slightly underrepresented in the 1960 Congress. These figures show that predominantly urban districts have 29.7 percent of the total population and have 27.5 percent of the total seats, and rural districts include 56.2 percent of the total population and have 62.8 percent of the seats. Suburban areas were the most underrepresented, having 14.1 percent of the population and only 9.3 percent of the seats. In the Eastern states and the Western states the urban areas were slightly overrepresented.[8]

CITY REPRESENTATION AT THE STATE LEVEL

Representation of cities in state legislatures had, prior to 1962, consistently failed to keep pace with the population expansion of urban areas. Various measures have been formulated to show mathematically the extent of inequality of city representation in state legislatures. Paul T. David and Ralph Eisenberg developed a measure of the relative values of the right to vote in terms of the extent to which population size of legislative districts deviates from what the size would be if all districts in a state were equal. Table 4.1 shows this measure for the smallest and largest counties in each state for 1910, 1930, 1950, and 1960. A figure of 100 indicates equality in which a vote value is the same in the smallest and in the largest counties; a figure of 50 indicates that the vote value is half of the statewide average, and a

---

[7] Gordon E. Baker, "The United States Senate and Urbanism," in Glendon Schubert, *Reapportionment*, Charles Scribner's Sons, New York, 1965, p. 167.

[8] Congressional Quarterly Weekly Report, "Suburban Areas Most Underrepresented in the House," in Schubert, *op. cit.*, pp. 191–192.

TABLE 4.1 Relative Values of the Right to Vote for Representation in State Legislatures in the Smallest and Largest Categories of Counties, as Percentages of the Statewide Average, by States, 1910, 1930, 1950, and 1960

State	1910		1930		1950		1960	
	S	L	S	L	S	L	S	L
Alabama	104	45	146	37	194	26	216	25
Alaska							163	51
Arizona	109	82	126	68	217	64	533	53
Arkansas	106	90	109	85	104	81	123	61
California	119	91	333	48	419	59	562	63
Colorado	130	72	123	70	141	78	211	70
Connecticut	169	77	239	79	230	75	216	75
Delaware	148	69	179	62	186	61	187	61
Florida	129	47	177	29	276	36	476	16
Georgia	116	24	129	21	153	29	182	12
Hawaii							228	67
Idaho	98	54	119	53	137	46	167	48
Illinois	112	87	151	71	131	89	151	91
Indiana	89	111	108	85	120	85	133	69
Iowa	116	39	128	35	139	40	150	36
Kansas	115	42	125	34	142	33	176	30
Kentucky	108	81	126	68	122	76	131	60
Louisiana	104	105	129	88	158	95	177	105
Maine	113	94	122	83	127	83	133	81
Maryland	220	45	260	52	334	62	445	83
Massachusetts	262	102	273	96	273	100	277	102
Michigan	113	79	200	55	179	72	205	74
Minnesota	111	86	124	68	136	60	156	55
Mississippi	108	92	119	84	129	49	139	34
Missouri	130	70	154	67	151	73	174	69
Montana	115	51	114	54	128	56	146	53
Nebraska	108	55	103	96	115	77	130	66
Nevada	100	100	122	48	192	43	287	28
New Hampshire	102	97	102	98	133	98	147	99
New Jersey	397	60	255	61	253	69	356	76
New Mexico	100	100	108	62	151	40	237	30
New York	216	77	303	80	319	84	348	86
North Carolina	116	89	145	67	173	67	204	61
North Dakota	101	98	103	90	111	71	122	60
Ohio	144	85	177	85	204	86	242	87
Oklahoma	102	98	121	54	150	35	175	27
Oregon	121	66	139	65	127	86	137	85
Pennsylvania	192	89	252	88	246	88	317	85
Rhode Island	263	70	199	73	154	80	154	88
South Carolina	136	92	154	65	185	65	215	59
South Dakota	100	102	101	99	105	82	113	66
Tennessee	97	95	115	70	137	60	162	49
Texas	94	82	104	70	126	49	156	45
Utah	124	70	130	82	173	71	232	68
Vermont	127	89	132	88	132	84	149	83
Virginia	108	81	109	87	112	89	124	73
Washington	135	85	128	93	130	94	141	88
West Virginia	103	97	115	81	130	78	130	69
Wisconsin	115	100	130	84	104	96	119	92
Wyoming	100	100	103	76	113	67	132	55

Source: Paul T. David and Ralph Eisenberg, *Devaluation of the Urban and Suburban Vote.* Bureau of Public Administration, New Institute of Government, University of Virginia, Charlottesville, Va., p. 15.

figure of 200 indicates a vote value twice that of the average. For all states the average vote value of counties with a population under 25,000 rose from 113 in 1910 to 171 in 1960, while the average vote value for counties of 500,000 or more fell from 81 to 76. In a single state, New Mexico, where the vote value for the largest and the smallest counties were equal (100) in 1910, the value in the largest county was 30 and of the smallest 237 in 1960.[9]

Causes of Inequality

The major cause of the inequalities is the much more rapid growth of population in urban areas than in rural areas without corresponding changes in representative districts. The political implications involved are discovered when one seeks an answer to why district changes have not been made. In short, those who stood to lose most by a change in districts were the ones who legally controlled redistricting machinery. Legislatures have traditionally been given power to control the allocation of legislative seats and the drawing of district lines. Since the maintenance of the status quo served the interests of the existing membership, changes were very difficult. Malcolm Jewell has pointed out that one "of the most widely accepted norms in the politics of reapportionment is that sitting congressmen should be disturbed as little as possible."[10] Since it is difficult to add representatives to the urban areas to compensate for their increased growth without reducing the number from rural areas, there are strong political pressures within the state legislature to maintain the existing pattern. The rural representatives who prefer to keep their high ratio of representatives often find welcome support from some interest groups within the cities.

Since rural areas are generally more Republican than are the cities, city Republicans may join forces with rural legislatures to keep city representation to a minimum. Since organized labor is strongest in the cities, business interests there may support rural interests in maintaining rural dominance; therefore chambers of commerce are often found in opposition to reapportionment. Since the Negro population is more and more concentrated in the cities, white segregationists may give aid to rural legislators as they try to keep city representation low.

Because the institutional arrangements for redistricting are often found in state constitutions, change has not been easy. Even though cities have gen-

[9] For other indexes see *ibid.*, pp. 62–79.
[10] Malcolm E. Jewell, "Political Patterns in Apportionment," in Schubert, *op. cit.*, p. 35.

erally been more equally represented in constitutional conventions than they have been in legislatures, urban equality has never been written into new state constitutions. Two factors may have operated to account for the willingness of city delegates to accept inequitable systems of representation. First, convention delegates are less likely to be politicians in the regular sense of the word. Business and professional men, who would not be found in races for legislative seats, often are willing to try for convention seats. Therefore, city delegations in constitutional conventions may be less committed to equality for cities than would be a city legislative delegation. In the second place, constitutions are constructed by series of compromises. City delegates may accept some inequality in legislative representation in order to win the support of rural delegates for some other constitutional provision in which they are particularly interested, e.g., some method of selecting judges other than by popular election.

Movement for Reapportionment

The inequalities in representation shown above provided a potential force for change if some event could provide a breakthrough in the long-established barrier to reapportionment. This breakthrough came as a result of the decision of the United States Supreme Court in *Baker v. Carr* which resulted from a suit commenced in Tennessee.[11] Since the House of Representatives of the State of Tennessee had not been reapportioned after 1901, the areas of the state with the largest net increases in population were grossly underrepresented. City officials of the four metropolitan centers took the initiative to achieve reapportionment. Attempts to secure action in the state courts were unsuccessful, and a group of lawyers in Knoxville brought suit in the federal district court, seeking a declaratory judgment and an injunction to prevent state officials from enforcing the 1901 apportionment act. Among other things the complaint stipulated that citizens living in the underrepresented areas were being deprived of "equal protection of the law" guaranteed by the Fourteenth Amendment of the United States Constitution. The district court in Tennessee, relying largely on *Colegrove v. Green,*[12] dismissed the suit on the grounds of lack of jurisdiction. The decision in *Baker v. Carr* resulted from an appeal of this case to the United States Supreme Court.

The issue in the Colegrove case involved the problem of inequality of congressional districts in Illinois. The Court had in this case refused to intervene

[11] *Baker v. Carr*, 369 U.S. 186 (1962).
[12] *Colegrove v. Green*, 328 U.S. 549 (1946).

to compel legislative reapportionment. The general assumption has been that reapportionment cases involved what are considered to be political issues and therefore are within the province of legislatures and executives rather than the courts. Although Justice Brennon, in delivering the opinion in the Baker case, stated that the decision did not overrule the Colegrove case, it had that effect. The *Baker v. Carr* case decided:

1. That the federal courts possessed jurisdiction to decide cases involving apportionment of state legislatures
2. That action can be brought to the courts under the "equal protection of the law" clause
3. That citizens who claim that their rights under the Fourteenth Amendment have been denied have standing to challenge state apportionment practices

The Supreme Court made no judgment on the Tennessee act in question but simply remanded the case to the federal district court with instructions to hear the case on its merits. The district court was given no guidelines by which to decide when apportionment was in violation of the "equal protection" clause.

This case, which opened the doors of the federal court to cases involving apportionment of state legislature, produced a rash of cases involving most of the states in the union; on June 15, 1964, the Court announced decisions in eight such cases. One of these is of special importance. Justice Warren, speaking for the Supreme Court in *Reynolds v. Sims*,[13] set forth some guidelines for deciding apportionment cases. The Court gave official recognition to the principle of equality. "The fundamental principle of representative government in this country is one of equal representation for equal numbers of people, without regard to race, sex, economic status, or place of residence within a state. . . . Legislators represent people, not trees or acres. Legislators are elected by voters, not farms, or cities or economic interests." This is, stated simply, the "one man, one vote" principle.

The decision also specified that this principle of equality must be applied to both houses of a state legislature.

We hold that, as a basic constitutional standard, the Equal Protection Clause requires that seats in both houses of a bicameral state legislature must be apportioned on a population basis. Simply stated, an individual's right to vote for state legislators is unconstitutionally impaired when its weight is in a substantial fashion diluted when compared with votes of citizens living in other parts of the State.

[13] *Reynolds v. Sims*, 377 U.S. 533 (1964).

None of these cases has set forth a measure of unrepresentativeness that will be unacceptable. Obviously, it is impossible to draw district lines with a high degree of compactness that will include exactly the same number of voters or persons in each district. Some legislatures like to follow county lines or natural boundaries (rivers or major transportation routes) in creating a district map. The question still remains as to what extent districts which follow such boundaries can be unequal; can districts, for example, vary by as much as 10 percent and still meet the test of "equal protection"?

It should be mentioned here that the position of cities in the lower house in Congress will also be strengthened by Supreme Court apportionment decisions. In *Wesberry v. Sanders*[14] the Court applied the principle of equality of population to Congressional districts in the states, just as it did to state legislatures in the Sims case.

Nongeographic Inequality

Thus far, the cases which have made history in regard to legislative reapportionment have dealt with the issue in terms of numbers of persons or of voters in legislative districts defined in terms of geographic area. Representation in this country has traditionally been based on areal representation, but the issue may certainly arise as to whether such districts, even though they contain equal numbers of voters, actually provide equal representation. If one thinks in terms of equal representation for Negroes, lower-income groups, social classes, or occupational groups, there is no reason to assume that equality of districts affords equality of representation to these groups. In fact, equal districts may be drawn so as to deny a minority group a representative even though their number justifies one. The economic and social facts of life have produced a pattern of urban living in which various groups are congregated in fairly discrete sections of the city. Negroes, Orientals, blue-collar workers, professionals, and management people are by no means dispersed evenly within the boundaries of a city. At first glance, it may appear that geographic representation is peculiarly suited to this kind of spatial distribution, since each group can be included in one or more districts, depending on their size, and thereby can be assured representation according to their numbers. But, on the other hand, such a distribution of population makes it easy for those who determine the location of district lines to deny equal representation if they choose to do so. This practice of constructing representative district lines so as to deny to some groups the representation

[14] *Wesberry v. Sanders,* 376 U.S. 1 (1963).

they deserve and to give overrepresentation to others is familiar to students of politics and is referred to as "gerrymandering." The simple charts shown in Figure 4.1 indicate how districting on a geographic basis can cut up a group with common interests so that they constitute only a minority in a number of districts rather than a majority in any single district and still comply with the existing legal requirement of equality of voters in the districts.

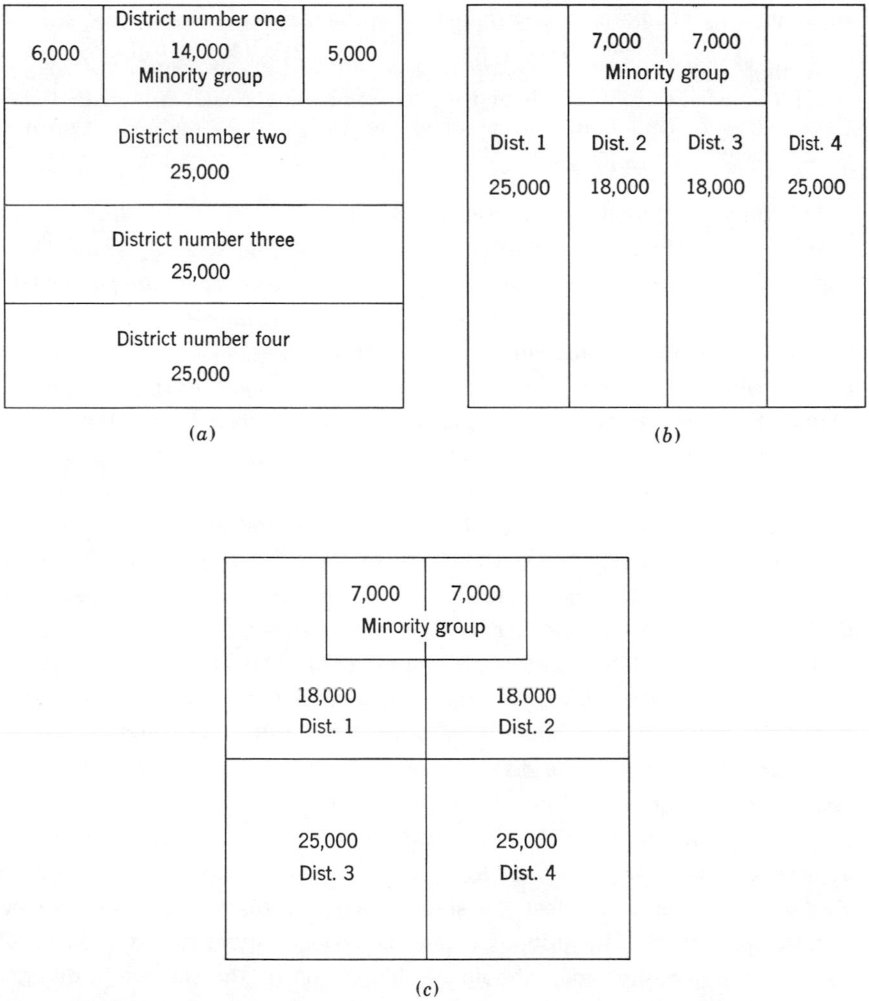

(a)

(b)

(c)

Figure 4.1   Effect on minority group of three ways of drawing legislative districts. Total populations are equal in *a*, *b*, and *c*; districts are compact and contiguous in *a*, *b*, and *c*; but only in *a* does the minority have a chance of electing a representative.

There is now some evidence that courts are recognizing this problem and are trying to include within the sweep of "equal protection" more than merely equal numbers of persons in each district. A good example is found in a recent decision of a three-judge federal district court in Hawaii.

> While it is a fundamental factor under the decision of the court [the United States Supreme Court], population is not the sole definitive measure for setting up either representative or senatorial districts. Compactness and contiguity of the territory are admittedly also factors, but community of interests, community of problems, socio-economic status, political and racial factors—each and all must be laid out with the totality of those factors having been taken into consideration but even more, the sum total of all of the districting must result in substantial equality of meaningful representation to each and all of the voters of the state.[15]

If "equal protection" is interpreted to mean that geographic districts not only must contain substantially equal numbers of voters but also must have substantial equality of representation for groups with common political interests, the real problems may be that of devising electoral machinery or devices which will accomplish these objectives; certainly the single-member district which operates on a winner-take-all basis does not meet these demands. Perhaps proportional representation, which is described in the chapter on elections, may receive greater attention in this country than it has in the past.

In the light of the recent court decisions requiring apportionment wholly on a population basis, a word should be said about the use of multimember districts to select representatives to state legislatures from urban areas. This device, as it is generally used, may meet the Court's requirement for equality and still serve to dilute the strength of a minority political party or substantial minority groups who are active politically. If we assume that a city is apportioned five seats in one house of a state legislature, one could be elected from each of five legislative districts, or all five could be elected at large with each party supporting a slate of five candidates. In the first case, it would be difficult to draw five districts so as to prevent a minority party from getting at least one representative, but in the second case, the party with one more vote than its rival could elect the slate of five. The same is true with respect to a substantial minority group. Unless an obvious gerrymander is forced upon the city, the minority group should be able to control the election in one district, but in an at-large election their strength will be dissipated so that they

---

[15] *National Civic Review*, vol. 54, pp. 318, 319, June, 1965.

may not elect any representatives. The courts have not yet declared that at-large elections violate equality of representation, but they have indicated that they would look at each case that comes to them to see if any substantial inequality is inherent in the scheme.

EVALUATION OF CITY APPORTIONMENT

Only limited information is now available upon which to judge the effects, in terms of legislative output, of the court-enforced reapportionment of state legislatures. It is clear, however, that more legislators will be coming from urban and suburban centers than has been true in the past. If the size of the houses are not increased, this will mean there will be fewer coming from the rural areas. This mere change in relative numbers may result in some satisfaction on the part of city dwellers, but the important question is: will the voting pattern be changed in such a way as to alter the output of legislative sessions? At this time, the answer is not available; however, examination of legislative results from reapportioned legislatures when they are available will be more meaningful if some possible consequences are kept in mind.

Since the significant change produced by current reapportionments is in the relative strength of urban and outstate delegations, changes should be expected in those areas of conflict on which legislators have historically divided on a rural-urban basis. If conflict issues are such that no pattern of urban solidarity or outstate unity emerges, it is safe to predict that reapportionment will produce little change in decision making. Examination of studies of roll-call data in state legislatures does not reveal any substantial pattern of rural-urban split on most roll calls.[16] Thomas Dye reports that there is no noticeable difference in the policy outcomes of well-apportioned and malapportioned legislators.[17] Gordon Baker suggests that restrictive labor legislation in many states reveals the influence of rural legislators and that other conflict issues that have a rural-urban base are "regulation of wages and hours, protection of migrant workers, distribution of certain tax revenues (especially from gasoline), daylight saving time, and state aid to roads and education."[18] He recognizes, however, that on some of these issues coalitions of rural and business-oriented city legislators are formed to determine the final outcome.

[16] David R. Derge, "Metropolitan and Outstate Alignments in Illinois and Missouri," *American Political Science Review*, vol. 52, pp. 1051–1065, December, 1956.

[17] Thomas R. Dye, "Malapportionment and Public Policy in the States," *Journal of Politics*, vol. 27, pp. 586–601, August, 1965.

[18] Gordon E. Baker, *The Reapportionment Revolution*, Random House, Inc., New York, 1965, p. 50.

A few generalizations may help the student who desires to follow legislative action and to assess the results of increasing the ratio of urban to rural representation.

1. If the urban vote in a state is predominantly Democratic and the rural vote tends to be Republican, the Democratic party platform should fare better since reapportionment. This, of course, assumes party solidarity on conflict issues. This will be counterbalanced to some extent by increased representation in Republican suburbs.

2. If union labor is concentrated in urban areas and rural areas are predominantly antiunion, issues supported by union labor should now receive greater support. This should be true for issues such as the closed shop and minimum wages.

3. If issues arise on which central city and suburban legislators take opposing positions, reapportion should work to the advantage of suburban areas, since they have grown much faster than have central cities. Such issues as annexation procedures and city consolidation should fall into this class.

4. The effects of reapportionment on the fate of proposals which have regularly been presented to state legislatures by the mayors of large cities cannot be predicted with accuracy. These issues include requests for more city power to handle local issues, e.g., power to construct off-street parking by issuing revenue bonds to be funded from parking meter receipts, and authority to levy new kinds of taxes. The difficulty with these kinds of proposals is that, although they may be supported by a strong mayor who was elected from the city at large, there is no assurance that city representatives in the state legislature, who are elected at different times and from small districts, will support the mayor's proposal. If they do not, his bills will not be ensured passage simply by increasing the number of city legislators.

A number of factors are operating which seem to indicate that reapportionment may not change legislative attitude toward cities as much as has often been predicted. Many issues do not divide legislators on a rural versus urban basis, and city legislators are by no means a solid block on issues affecting the city. If, before reapportionment, the city legislators split 8 to 7 on an issue, doubling city representation will probably simply produce a 16 to 14 split. Increases in number of suburban representatives who oppose city-sponsored measures may more than offset any advantage reapportionment may give to the large core cities. Coalitions between some rural interests and some urban interests may be as effective as before in defeating certain kinds of legislation sponsored by liberal interests from core-city areas.

ADMINISTRATIVE RELATIONS

Attention thus far has been concentrated on legislative relations between cities and states; operationally, the relations between cities and state administrative agencies may be more important than are relations with the legislature. In most instances the jurisdiction of state administrative agencies extends to cities the same as it does to rural areas, but in many instances the cities have administrative agencies whose work parallels that of state agencies. The working relations between these two become a matter of some concern.

In general, these relations are on a decentralized basis, i.e., the city deals with a state department or agency on a functional basis, rather than with a single state agency which centralizes all state-city relations. In matters of public health the cities deal directly with the state department of health, and in matters of streets and highways the relationships are directly with the state highway department. This pattern applies to most functions the performance of which necessitates state-city cooperation. The existing arrangements, however, may be subject to change as states experiment with the creation of central departments of urban affairs. The creation of the Department of Housing and Urban Development at the national level will certainly promote a debate within the states on the issues involved in centralizing the states' relations with their cities. The recommendations of the Council of State Governments and the Advisory Commission on Intergovernmental Relations for a single state agency have been referred to earlier. Some states have already created such a centralized agency.

The attempt to set up state departments of urban affairs will produce conflicts which will have to be resolved in the state legislature or by changing state constitutions. Although in some quarters it will be viewed as evidence that states are ready to face up to their obligations to come to the aid of their cities, others will view it as an attempt on the part of the state to exercise more effectively the legal control it now has over cities and to forestall further direct relations between the cities and the federal government. Smaller cities which recognize their inability to employ professional staff locally to handle their problems may willingly look to centralized state agencies for technical help, while larger cities may feel that their own professional administrators are more competent than are those who would be attached to a state agency. States often have notoriously low salary scales for professional staff, and they are often selected on a patronage basis without assurance of tenure. Large cities are much more likely to have a career service and a higher salary level. Therefore, large cities may feel that the state centralized office will have little to offer them. The vital decisions which may determine the extent to which states move toward the unified department will probably be made in Washington. If national legislation and administration practice emphasizes direct relations between the national government and cities, the need for a state department will not be great. But if Congress and the national administration decide to channel all their urban aid programs through the state, pressure for a central state agency will be overwhelming. In fact, federal law now requires that certain kinds of federal aid for cities (e.g., planning) must be channeled through a state administrative agency. The Council of State Governments and, in particular, the Governors' Conference constitute a strong pressure group to assign a more significant role to the state in federal programs designed to aid large metropolitan centers. The National Council of Mayors is likely to constitute a strong counterforce seeking to maintain direct contact between cities and the federal government.

NATURE OF ADMINISTRATIVE RELATIONS

The relationships between cities and state administrations vary so much from one state to another that a general discussion is very difficult.[19] The best approach to a general discussion of this subject is to identify and classify types of state controls or influences available to state administrators in terms of institutional devices through which state control can be exercised.

The classification of administrative devices by which state influence is felt in city government developed by Schuyler Wallace many years ago supplies categories that are still useful.[20] The changes that have occurred since the appearance of the Wallace study are in the relative extent to which the various categories are used, rather than in the nature of the control devices. The order of listing was intended to represent the order of their effectiveness. (1) requiring reports, (2) inspections, (3) giving advice, (4) grants-in-aid, (5) requiring state approval, (6) state review of action, (7) orders from state to local officials, (8) enactment of ordinances applicable to a single city, (9) removal of local officials, (10) appointment of local officials, and (11) substituting state for local action.

The Council of State Governments in its report on state-local relations recommends restraint on the part of states in using the devices available to it to exercise control over municipalities. In general the report suggests that coercive devices (orders, appointment, substitute administration) be used only to establish minimum standards of performance or to meet emergency situations.[21]

---

[19] For a discussion of relations between New York City and the State of New York see Sayre and Kaufman, *Governing New York City: Politics in the Metropolis,* Russell Sage Foundation, New York, 1960, pp. 564–584.

[20] Schuyler Wallace, *State Administrative Supervision over Cities in the United States,* Columbia University Press, New York, 1928, p. 39.

[21] Council of State Governments, *State-Local Relations,* Chicago, 1946, pp. 41, 42.

COUNTERINFLUENCES

Obviously, countervailing influences operate within the political system to protect cities from arbitrary and capricious action on the part of state administrators. Although the legal structure which sets out the official rules of the game recognizes the power of states to use all the devices mentioned above, strong political influences restrain precipitate action. The philosophy embodied in the concept of home rule is strongly entrenched in the value scales of local as well as many state politically influential persons, and raising the cry of state interference with home rule will rally a wide assortment of group support to the side of the city.[22]

State officials are aware of the strength of city political organizations in statewide elections. Top state administrators who are elected from the state at large depend on city support for election, and they have no desire to commit political suicide by supporting arbitrary and unreasonable action against city officials. City delegations in state legislature, although they have been small in relation to the city's population, are not without power to limit the freedom of action of administrators. This is particularly true if the state action is sufficiently distasteful that the city delegation will oppose it as a bloc. Rural legislatures often justify their refusal to support legislative programs sponsored by big-city mayors on the grounds that the proposals are not backed solidly by the city's legislators, but if there is unanimity in the city delegation, rural support can be expected.

City administrators can also put together an effective lobby to defend their interests when they feel threatened. Political officers and city officials are, of course, ready to appear before legislative committees or at hearings held by state administrative agencies, but, more than this, some of the most important business and civic leaders can be persuaded to use the influence of their names and positions to defend the city against what they are persuaded to believe is a threat. The influence that can be wielded by the big-city press must also be considered a potential force to protect the independence of the city.

Changes in the legal structure have also operated to reduce the freedom of states to deal with cities in a punitive manner. Constitutional grants of home rule have helped, but more specific are the requirements that states must deal with cities on a general rather than a specific basis.

[22] A good discussion of these influences in New York is found in Sayre and Kaufman, *op. cit.*, pp. 584–592.

VOLUNTARY COOPERATION

One of the important changes in the relations between states and cities is the growing awareness on the part of governors and other high state officials that state governments have an obligation to promote city development and a tendency on the part of city officers to recognize that they need assistance from the state. State officers recognize that cities are the major sources of state revenues and that the condition of the state treasury is in large measure dependent on the economic health of the cities. And, on the other hand, city leaders recognize that to meet the demands for services made by their citizens they must have assistance from the state. This assistance may come from state sharing of revenue or from authority for the city to experiment with new revenue-producing measures.

At the levels of administrative operations a broad range of cooperative efforts exists between city and state personnel. City police cooperate with the state police and with state bureaus of criminal identification and detection, and local school administrators cooperate with their counterparts on the state level through jointly sponsored institutes and in-service training programs. State civil service agencies and city personnel departments interchange examinations and conduct examinations for each other. City and state health departments may jointly plan immunization programs, jointly draw up standards for restaurant inspections, and cooperate to sponsor health education programs. Much cooperative effort goes unnoticed since it is not formalized in law or administrative regulations or institutionalized in the formal pattern of bureaucracy, but it is, none the less, effective.

UNIVERSITY EXTENSION EFFORTS

When state-city relations are the subject of examination, emphasis has generally centered on the relations between cities and the regular state government agencies with central offices in the state capital, but the efforts of state universities in the last few years to play a role in urban growth and development deserve some attention. The Morrill Act, passed during President Lincoln's administration, laid the groundwork for the land-grant state institutions of higher education to develop programs of research and teaching in the fields of agriculture and mechanic arts. Agricultural experiment stations were integral parts of state colleges of agriculture. In 1914 Congress passed the Smith-Lever Act, which created the so-called agricultural extension service. Under this program the state agricultural colleges sponsored agricultural agents in the agricultural counties of the state to act as the medium through which research results could be introduced to the farmer. Home economics agents and 4-H Club agents worked with the county agents but concentrated on working with young people.

The success which was achieved by the agricultural extension service in translating academic research into farm practice through local agents led some of those familiar with the service to recommend that the plan be extended to include urban extension programs. J. Martin Klotsche, chancellor of the University of Wisconsin, in his book, *The City and the University*, states the case for urban extension.

> The University should do for the urbanized areas what the land grant colleges have done for the nation's farm population, taking the knowledge of a scholar into the community and extending the outreach of its influence to all phases of urban life. . . . Neither the complexity nor the controversial nature of many of our urban problems should deter universities from developing new techniques and approaches. Creative innovation, rather than the performance of routine services, is the special role of the university in urban extension.[23]

Beginning in 1959 the Ford Foundation made grants to eight universities for experimental programs in urban extension. By the Higher Education Act of 1965 Congress authorized a program of community service and continuing education in colleges throughout the nation. The law provides for, among other programs, "a research program and a university extension or continuing education offerings, which is designed to assist in the solution of community problems in rural, urban or suburban areas. . . ."[24]

The Ford Foundation grants were made only to land-grant colleges and state universities and were administered primarily through the agricultural extension service; the new grants under the 1965 act are available to any institution of higher education. The federal funds are to be in the form of grants to states to be administered by the Division of Adult Education Programs in the Bureau of Adult and Vocational Education, U.S. Office of Education. Grants will be made to support plans drawn up by an appropriate agency in the state. Final approval must be by the Federal Commissioner of Education. If the trend toward a unified state department of urban affairs continues, a federally financed urban extension service may present some hard political problems for state decision makers. If a state governor chooses to concentrate the state's relations with its urban areas in a single department of urban affairs,

[23] *Urban Extension: A Report on Experimental Programs Assisted by the Ford Foundation,* The Ford Foundation, New York, 1966, p. 1.
[24] *Ibid.,* p. 4.

he will prefer to have the extension work operating out of such a department. The established extension service of the university may seek to serve urban areas by expansion of the existing extension service. But the state department of education may also lay claim to at least some of the services the federal program is supposed to offer, since it is already involved in programs of continuing education and vocational training.

SIGNIFICANCE OF POLITICAL DIFFERENCES

One cannot understand fully the conflicts that develop between political decision makers in the city and at the state capital without reference to the political party struggle. Although this factor does not apply to all states, there is a good chance that at least one large city in a state will be controlled by one political party and the state capital will be dominated by its rival. Even if the same political party controls both city and state offices, there often exists an internal struggle within the party which sets the city party organization against the rural courthouse rings. Sayre and Kaufman point out how Republicans at the state capital in New York State seek to harass and embarrass New York City Democrats in order to assist Republican candidates in the city, and city Democrats seek to blame the ills of the city upon Republican state officeholders in order to defeat Republican candidates.[25]

In Missouri, St. Louis County (not including St. Louis City) has the largest concentration of population in the state, having surpassed the city some time ago. The election of 1966 has given this urbanized county a Republican administration. Since the state government is firmly in control of the Democrats, considerable sparring for political advantage between the county and state may be expected. In the county election campaigns the Democrats in their appeal emphasized the need for electing a Democratic county administration to ensure cooperation with the Democratic state administration in solving the county's problems of rapid urbanization, while the Republican candidates blamed the state for the county's ills.

Recognition of the built-in difficulty of securing cooperation between cities and states in meeting the urgent needs of cities because of differences in party control accounts, in part, for the organization of so-called nonpartisan citizen committees to represent the city in seeking favorable action at the state level either from the legislature or from administrative agencies.

The issues inherent in problems of intergovernmental relations must be considered as political in character. Cities will prefer to deal directly with

[25] Sayre and Kaufman, *op. cit.*, p. 562.

agencies most likely to represent their own views of what major urban problems are and how they can best be solved. Since from past experience mayors have had better receptions in Washington than they have at state capitals, they tend to favor direct dealings with the federal government. If federal aid is to be made available to cities indirectly through the state, the practical political problem will be to determine if a single state department will dispense all such aid or if a decentralized structure based on functional programs will be adopted. The play of political forces in the state will work out the solution to these questions if the decision is left to the states, but if cities are unhappy with the solution, they may pressure the federal government not only to supply the funds but also to prescribe the state structure through which the state will administer the programs.

BIBLIOGRAPHY

Books

Adrian, Charles R.: *State and Local Governments*, 2d ed., McGraw-Hill Book Company, New York, 1967, pp. 99–110.

Advisory Commission on Intergovernmental Relations: *Governmental Structure, Organization and Planning in Metropolitan Areas*, Washington, 1961.

Baker, Gordon E.: *The Reapportionment Revolution*, Random House, Inc., New York, 1965.

————: *Rural versus Urban Political Power*, Random House, Inc., New York, 1955.

Banfield, Edward C., and James Q. Wilson: *City Politics*, Vantage Books, Random House, Inc., New York, 1963, chap. 5.

Bollens, John C.: *The States and the Metropolitan Problem*, Council of State Governments, Chicago, 1956.

———— and Henry J. Schmandt: *The Metropolis*, Harper & Row, Publishers, Incorporated, New York, 1965, chap. 17.

Committee on Governmental Operations, U.S. Senate: *Impact of Federal Urban Development Programs on Local Government Organizations and Planning*, Washington, 1964.

Council of State Governments: *State-Local Relations*, Chicago, 1946.

Elazar, Daniel J.: *American Federalism: A View from the States*, Thomas Y. Crowell Company, New York, 1966, chap. 7.

Hamilton, Howard D. (ed.): *Legislative Apportionment*, Harper & Row, Publishers, Incorporated, New York, 1964.

Jewell, Malcolm E. (ed.): *The Politics of Reapportionment*, Atherton Press, Inc., New York, 1962.

Larson, James E.: *Reapportionment and the Courts*, Bureau of Public Administration, Washington, 1962.

McKay, Robert B.: *Reapportionment: The Law and Politics of Equal Representation*, The Twentieth Century Fund, New York, 1965.

Schubert, Glendon (ed.): *Reapportionment*, Charles Scribner's Sons, New York, 1965.

Wallace, Schuyler: *State Administrative Supervision over Cities in the United States*, Columbia University Press, New York, 1928.

Articles

Derge, David R.: "Metropolitan and Outstate Alignments in Illinois and Missouri," *American Political Science Review*, vol. 52, pp. 1051–1065, December, 1958.

Dye, Thomas R.: "Malapportionment and Public Policy in the State," *Journal of Politics*, vol. 27, pp. 586–600, August, 1965.

Engle, Robert H.: "Weighting Legislators' Votes to Equalize Representation," *Western Political Quarterly*, vol. 12, pp. 442–448, June, 1959.

Schaller, Lyle E.: "Home Rule—A Critical Appraisal," *Political Science Quarterly*, vol. 76, pp. 402–415, September, 1961.

Tollenaar, Kenneth C.: "A Home Rule Puzzle," *National Civic Review*, vol. 50, pp. 411–416, September, 1961.

Vickery, William: "On the Prevention of Gerrymandering," *Political Science Quarterly*, vol. 76, p. 105, March, 1961.

President Johnson, referring to the plight of American cities in a commencement address at the University of Michigan in 1964, concluded that the problems with which they are faced "require us to create new concepts of cooperation—a creative federalism—between the National capital and the leaders of local communities."[1] This statement, in the first place, highlights the need for increased attention to the problems facing the cities but in the second places raises the question of whether or not the American federal system—considering all the folklore that has grown up around its legal structure—is flexible enough to cope with the needs of a population that is rapidly becoming urbanized.

THE LEGAL FICTION

The legal structure of the federal system needs little elaboration. The only two governments constitutionally recognized in the system are the federal government and the states, and the spheres of authority within which each operates are supposedly defined by the specific grants of power made to the

---

[1] Quoted in Roscoe C. Martin, *The Cities and the Federal System*, Atherton Press, Inc., New York, 1965, p. 42.

federal government in Article I of the United States Constitution and the powers reserved to the state by the Tenth Amendment. No place was reserved for the city as a participant in the system; hence by established practices and court pronouncements cities have been relegated to a position of dependence upon the state government. The status of cities in the total pattern of American government caused very little concern until changes in the economic structure produced profound changes in both the relative size of urban areas in terms of population and the socioeconomic character of city population. No serious efforts were made to restructure the bipolar theory of federalism until problems of urban poverty, housing, education, transportation, and physical deterioration reached such proportions that leaders of all political persuasion recognized that existing political structures and precedents were inadequate to meet current needs. Historians may conclude, when they evaluate the forces which produced profound changes in the character of intergovernmental relations in this country after 1930, that it took the most severe economic depression the country has experienced to produce any significant change.

Although there is little doubt that the facts demonstrate that the position of cities (particularly the large ones) in the federal system has been elevated to one of greater importance, it is interesting to note that this has occurred with almost no alteration in the formal legal structure which defines the nature of the federal system. The significant change, obviously, is the extent to which the large city is becoming a third partner in the system.

This situation has been produced by the increasing number of instances in which the federal government has dealt directly with cities as viable political units competent of themselves to enter into cooperative relations with federal agencies. This does not mean that the issues of "state rights" and federal usurpation of power have not been raised by opponents of federally sponsored programs; what it does mean is that the political leaders of cities have recognized that they had needs which could not be met without external assistance, and that this need was recognized by decision makers in the federal government long before it was admitted by state decision makers. And, more importantly, practical assistance was made available by Congress at a time when the state legislature had nothing to offer. Some of the large American cities produced mayors who were sensitive to the needs of their urban residents and who were ready and willing to initiate and carry through reform programs if they could find help in terms of technical assistance and money. When both these resources were made available by the federal government while the mayors were being rebuffed in their own state capitals, it is not difficult to see why these mayors established firm control lines to Washington. The drowning swimmer does not care whether the life-guard who throws him a line is the one formally assigned to his beach area; he is happy to accept assistance from the one available with the resources when they are needed. There may be times to debate organizational jurisdictions and proper lines of authority after the most pressing demands are met and when the cities have a choice, but when the federal government offers some resource to meet existing needs and the state offers practically none, niceties of legal myths about the nature of federalism will not deter mayors from reaching out for federal help. Roscoe Martin put the point very well when, in contemplating the possible directions and extent of change, he asked:

> What are the interests of the national government, the states, and the city in the problems of a metropolitan society? What resources—leadership, vigorous and effective organization, skilled and experienced manpower, demonstrated success in governing, money—is each prepared to plough into the war to make American cities livable? How deep, how firm, and how effective is any commitment that may be undertaken likely to prove? These are the kinds of questions that are relevant to the President's call for creative federalism. They are most pertinent and most timely when asked of the states.[2]

The foregoing discussion has rather loosely referred to state, city, and federal attitudes and actions within the framework of American federalism; the fact is, however, that each of these governmental entities acts only through individuals who occupy positions institutionalized in constitution and law. Whether or not the state or the national government adopts policies designed to assist cities depends on the values and behavior of officeholders at these levels of government. There can be no question about the existence of ample legal authority for either states or the federal government to adopt policies which are designed as solutions to what they perceive to be the most pressing problems of cities. The significant question is why the national policy makers have moved faster than have state decision makers in presenting programs of aid to city officials.

The literature seems to stress that the federal government has acted because it is the only government with financial resources adequate to the enormity of the task at hand. The assumption is that the kinds of taxes used by the federal government produce much larger revenues than are available to states from the sources available to them. It is well known that the greatest

[2] *Ibid.*, p. 43. Reprinted by permission of the publishers, Atherton Press, Inc. Copyright © 1965, Atherton Press, Inc., New York, all rights reserved.

revenue producer for the federal government is the individual and corporate income tax. But the income tax has always been available to the states if their legislatures had chosen to make use of it. The fact is that an amendment to the United States Constitution was required to confer the power to levy such a tax upon the federal government. One may conjecture that if the states had moved into the income tax field to secure the revenues needed to cope with problems of their cities, the federal government would not have chosen to depend so heavily on this tax source. When the states began to levy general retail sales taxes, which have now become a big revenue producer, the federal government refrained from duplicating this form of taxation. About the only form of taxation now used to produce federal revenue not available to states are import duties and levies on interstate commerce. State legislatures have never moved actively to raise revenues in the degree of magnitude necessary to meet the needs of the large cities, nor is there any substantial evidence that they would do so even if the federal government should significantly lower its income tax rates in order to make more revenue available for state and local purposes.

Operating to restrain state decision makers from greater use of the corporate and personal income tax is the fact that businesses and individuals can move from a state with a high tax rate to one with lower rates. There is no such easy means for taxpayers to escape federal income taxes since they operate uniformly in all states.

If one seeks to explain growing city-federal involvement in the governmental process in terms of financial resources, the power to contract debt is probably more important than is the taxing power. Constitutional restrictions on the procedure by which states can contract indebtedness, the upper limits on total indebtedness, and the requirements for operating on balanced budgets which hinder state action do not exist at the national level. Congress can, without popular approval, contract any debt the economic system will absorb, and it can consistently appropriate for spending more than the total revenue available to meet the obligation and make up the difference by borrowing in the open market. But there is little past experience to justify a prediction that state legislatures would use such flexible debt limits to come to the aid of cities even if there were no constitutional inhibitions to deter them.

The evidence available seems to indicate that those who have occupied the seats of power in the state government have either failed to recognize the problems faced by cities during the period of their rapid growth or were not sufficiently sympathetic to urban areas to initiate programs of city improvement. The failure of legislatures to respond may be accounted for, in part, by the overrepresentation of rural areas; this may also have been a factor in the governor's apathy since he needs legislative cooperation to secure other programs to which he may be committed. A large part of the behavior of state officials can be explained simply by the fact that urban residents and ruralites have different sets of values, view the functions of government very differently, and are influenced by quite different myths and stereotypes, particularly with respect to the needs for states to commit resources to the cities. Martin, in discussing these differences, remarks:

> In terms of racial origins, mobility, religious affiliation, inherent personal attributes, outlooks on life, education, school enrollment, composition of the labor force, income, and color composition the urban dwellers of industrial America are so completely different from their agrarian counterparts as to constitute virtually a new and radically different people.[3]

This difference, in a sense, is also reflected in differences between state government officials and those at the national level.

The entire administrative structure of many state governments is stacked with rural-oriented personnel. Since legislators are often in control of patronage, they secure jobs for leaders in their own constituencies. Since the constituencies have been predominantly rural, the appointments reflect rural values. State salaries are often lower than salaries in cities for comparable work; therefore state departments would find it difficult to recruit administrators from the cities even if they chose to do so.

The federal government presents a different picture. Not only do the houses of Congress better represent urban interests, but the administrative departments are staffed with top personnel who more nearly represent the culture of American cities. City officials may resent what they consider to be an excessive amount of red tape, lack of coordination, and excessive waste of time involved in city-national relations, but they recognize that in Washington they can deal with people who understand what city life is like and are intent on helping, within the limits of their means, to solve the problems of the cities. It will take nothing less than a complete restructuring of the political philosophy of the officials of many of the states to create a relationship between states and cities which will offer any hope for attacking the major problems of urban areas. Although lack of resources available to state governments may be a factor, the lack of understanding and desire on the part

---

[3] *Ibid.*, p. 12. Reprinted by permission of the publishers, Atherton Press, Inc. Copyright © 1965, Atherton Press, Inc., New York, all rights reserved.

of state officialdom is of more importance in encouraging cities to look toward Washington for help.

FEDERAL GRANTS-IN-AID

The most significant relationships that have developed between cities and the national government are those created by federal programs offering financial aid. In some instances the aid is made available directly to city governments, in some the aid available to cities is channeled through some state agency, and in others the aid is granted to semipublic agencies for programs in cities. Although federal grant-in-aid programs were started in the nineteenth century, the growth of their number and importance was greatly accelerated by the great economic depression of the 1930s and the social and economic problems which accompanied the rapid growth of large cities and metropolitan areas following the Second World War. Martin reports that as late as 1932 the total of federal grants that went directly to cities was no more than $10 million and most of this was for the District of Columbia; this amount had risen to $941 million in 1963. This means that federal payments direct to local governments rose by 94 times; during the same period state payments to local governments were going up 14 times and federal payments to states were increased 34 times.[4] Federal aid in urban areas in 1968 is estimated at $10,329 million, including both budget and trust accounts.

Early federal aid programs to cities during the 1930s were of an emergency nature and were probably viewed as short-range measures not ordained to make lasting changes in the established pattern of American federalism. The Public Works Administration and the Works Progress Administration were two of the most publicized agencies that administered federal aid during the early years of the depression. Their main purpose was to put more people to work in order to pump new life into the economy. At the same time these programs were expected to provide much-needed public facilities. More recent programs have been devised to make the financial resources of the national government available to cities to improve physical facilities, abolish slums, provide better housing for low-income families, eliminate poverty, improve mass transit facilities, and improve educational opportunities.

OTHER PHASES OF FEDERAL AID

Federal aid may be extended to cities primarily to make available to them the money required to accomplish objectives which are considered to be of na-

[4] *Ibid.,* see Table 4, p. 112.

tional concern, but through this device federal officials may seek to accomplish other objectives which they consider worthwhile. Obviously grants-in-aid are accompanied by some controls. Congress, in the laws which authorize the aid, determines the purpose for which the money is to be spent and designates the federal agency which is charged with the responsibility of making sure expenditures conform with the intended purpose. Controls are also established which prescribe adequate accounting and reporting procedures to ensure accuracy and honesty in local expenditures. Although these controls may at times seem overcomplicated to local officials, they are recognized as essential parts of the grant-in-aid system. Greater conflict is generated when federal officials seek to accomplish certain kinds of local reforms through their power to grant or withhold aid funds.

Area-wide Planning

Section 701 of the Housing Act of 1954 specifically provides federal aid for comprehensive planning for urban development. Cities can secure grants of from two-thirds to three-fourths of the costs involved in preparing these comprehensive plans. This is direct aid for physical planning, but through other aid programs federal agencies may encourage or even require some type of comprehensive planning. Although most federally aided programs require some kind of planning, it is often special-purpose planning designed to coordinate a single program rather than comprehensive planning on an area-wide basis. Some programs are designed, however, to stimulate broad-gauge planning. The open-space program requires that each proposed land acquisition for which federal aid is sought must "be important to the execution of a comprehensive plan for the urban area."[5] The urban renewal, community renewal, and public housing programs can be carried out only if workable programs and development plans have been prepared. The Highway Act of 1962 provided that after 1965 no federal aid would be made available for highway construction in metropolitan areas unless a comprehensive planning process was established for the entire metropolitan area.[6] As metropolitan planning agencies have been established to meet this requirement, they are being used by federal agencies in other aid programs. City plans for local parks, for example, must be approved by these area-wide planning agencies before the city will be eligible for grants to purchase land for park

---

[5] Subcommittee on Intergovernmental Relations of the Committee on Government Operations, United States Senate, *Impact of Federal Urban Development Programs on Local Government Organization and Planning*, Washington, 1964, p. 17.

[6] *Ibid.*, p. 106.

use. Likewise, the Area Redevelopment Act of 1961 provides that each re-development program must be consistent with an overall economic develop-ment program prepared and adopted by the local redevelopment organization. In addition it specifically suggests that the community "develop a compre-hensive land use and highway plan to guide community and area develop-ment."[7]

Although by no means all federal aid programs require local comprehensive planning, it is obvious that some of those of first importance to large urban areas are clearly designed not merely to assist the area to solve a functional problem but also to force the areas to undertake planning on a comprehensive scale. Insofar as a federal administrative agency can determine the adequacy of such plans, the judgment of federal officers may take precedence over that of local officials. This provides the substance for conflict which may reach beyond the immediate local and federal officials involved, since political officials at the city level have access to congressmen, senators, and admin-istrative officials above those who at the operational level participate in actual negotiations. Mayors of such cities as New York, Chicago, and St. Louis often head local party organizations that play an important role in national elections, and they often prefer to fight any battles they have with federal bureaucrats over federal aid at a higher level of decision making.

Restructuring of Local Governments

For many years students of local government and many civic reform groups have condemned the fragmentation of government in large metropolitan areas. Numerous attempts have been made in specific metropolitan areas to con-solidate the numerous governmental subdivisions into a single large area-wide government or at least to provide a structure through which a single function could be administered on an area-wide basis. Most of the plans for reform have been rejected when submitted to popular vote. The defeat of such plans has prompted some reformers to suggest that restructuring of local govern-ments will come about only when an outside force intervenes to force struc-tural change. One such outside force could be the federal government, and the urban grant-in-aid program could serve as the vehicle by which such force could be exerted. The federal government would need only to prescribe that certain kinds of aid to metropolitan areas be withheld until a government with area-wide jurisdiction to administer the grant was established.

[7] *Ibid.*, p. 111.

A recent study sponsored by the Advisory Commission on Intergovernmental Relations and made by the Subcommittee on Intergovernmental Relations of the Senate Committee on Government Operations addressed itself to two important issues related to the effects of federal aid programs on local governmental structures: (1) the extent to which these programs encourage the use of special-purpose districts rather than general governmental agencies to carry out federally aided programs, and (2) the extent to which federally aided programs tend to perpetuate existing fragmentation of government or encourage consolidation of local political subdivisions.

With respect to the encouragement of special-purpose units of government rather than the strengthening of general-purpose units, the report states:

> A relatively new type of Federal Aid recipient has arisen in recent years—the special purpose units of government with independent or semi-independent status. These new units, actually induced and sometimes even required by about a quarter of all Federal programs, include public housing and urban renewal authorities, State and local planning agencies, local area redevelopment organizations, industrial development authorities, State and county rural area development committees, irrigation districts, water users associations, soil conservation districts, State and county agricultural stabilization and conservation committees, and State and local Farmers Home Administration committee.
>
> Despite the fact that most Federal aid is available to both general purpose and special purpose units of local government, several programs show a strong tendency to bypass general purpose units. Except for shared revenue (Federal Power Act, Flood Control Act, etc.) programs, general purpose units are not designated as exclusive recipients for any urban development programs.[8]

This feature of federal aid is significant for those who either favor the wider use of special-purpose districts or those who insist that the functions of such districts should be transferred to regular governmental subdivisions which are responsible for a wide spectrum of public services. The political implications are fairly obvious.[9] To a large extent federal preference for special districts shifts the decision on types of local government structure from the local decision-making arena to the federal arena. Politically active groups may be found that differ on the wisdom of such a transfer; the unbiased observer need only comment that the nature of the official decision will be determined, in large part, by the arena in which it is made. It is

[8] *Ibid.,* p. 15.
[9] For a discussion of the semi-independent Chicago Housing Authority, see Myerson and Banfield, *Politics, Planning and the Public Interest,* The Free Press, New York, 1964, pp. 36–59.

interesting to note the value judgment expressed by the above report in its recommendations.

> The Commission recommends that the Congress and appropriate executive agencies take legislative and administrative action to remove from Federal aid programs for urban development all organizational limitations which require or promote special-purpose units of local government to the disadvantage of general-purpose units of local government (i.e., municipalities, towns, and counties). Other factors being equal, general-purpose units of government should be favored as federal aid recipients. Special-purpose recipients should be required to coordinate their aided activities with general-purpose governments.[10]

Obviously, some counterforces were operating in the political process or the special-purpose districts would have received less recognition in the original statutes and in administrative practices. Many of these same forces still exist to oppose the committee's recommendations. Special-purpose districts provide a decision-making arena in which there is consensus, at least, on the importance of the function being performed and on the broad purposes to be achieved. Conflict is reduced to less important procedural matters. Usually this type of agency does not have to compete for limited resources with other functions of government and has a fairly low degree of involvement in regular political disputes and election contests that more directly affect general-purpose governments. These characteristics are appealing to many civic-minded persons who want to see more federal-local cooperation to achieve specific goals and who do not want to get involved in what they refer to as politics.

On the other hand there are those who will support the commission's position since they feel they can exercise greater influence with the officeholders in regular municipal governments. They prefer to let the functions often performed by special-purpose districts compete in the open political market for limited community resources. The issue is not a technical or professional one; it is by its nature political, and competing forces which in the past have fought out their conflict at the state and local levels will find that, because of the impact federal aid can have on the outcome, they must wage their battles on the federal level as well.

Federal grant-in-aid programs can be an effective external force to produce governmental consolidation or, at least, intergovernmental cooperation within a large metropolitan area. In assessing the existing aid programs on this score, the committee's report indicated that most federal aid programs

[10] Subcommittee report, *op. cit.*, p. 23.

do not serve to encourage area wide jurisdiction over planning and administration of urban development programs. On the contrary, nearly two-thirds of the surveyed physical development programs either accept whatever areas of jurisdiction (usually strictly local) the states and localities make available for administration of the aided function, or actually prefer or require limited local jurisdiction.[11]

What pressure federal aid has produced upon local units of government has been in the area of joint or comprehensive planning, discussed earlier, rather than in structural reform or even cooperative administrative efforts.

On this issue the report did not take as strong a stand as it did on the special-district issue. "The Commission recommends that the Congress and appropriate executive agencies authorize and encourage responsible joint participation by local governmental units having common program objectives affecting the development of an urban area overlapping existing political boundaries."[12]

The political difficulties involved in achieving any major change in governmental structure of metropolitan areas will be considered in a later chapter; the question that arises here concerns the extent to which federal decision makers should use grants-in-aid purposely to pressure reluctant local subdivisions into some kind of area-wide organization. If it is decided to use such pressure, a number of means are available to achieve this objective. Aid could be withheld from any governmental unit below a certain size, aid could be extended on condition that governmental units provide a structure so that the granting unit can deal with a single decision center, or grants can be made only to the governmental unit whose territorial jurisdiction most nearly covers the entire area. If no positive federal policy is adopted, grants may have the effect of making local action more difficult. The one important force that might push local officials toward some form of consolidation of units of government is the financial inability of small units to support services demanded by residents. To the extent that federal grants erase this disability they constitute a force for maintenance of the status quo.

Politically, decision makers in Washington are in a much better position to opt for governmental reform than are those in the local areas. The pressures on local officers are close, vocal, and persistent, while any similar pressure on national officials is remote and far less effective. There is reason to believe that many local officials are convinced that urban development is impeded by the existence of many small independent governments in the

[11] *Ibid.*, p. 15.
[12] *Ibid.*, p. 27.

area and that they would welcome external pressure for reform which would make it possible for them to shift the political blame for reform from their own shoulders.

The broad general recommendations made by the subcommittee report are of interest in this respect.

> In summary, then, the criteria for judging the adequacy of organization and planning requirements imposed on local jurisdictions by Federal programs of financial aid to urban development are in terms of the extent to which the programs promote (1) policy coordination at the Federal level, (2) local planning for comprehensive urban development, (3) local planning for each aided function, (4) joint planning and performance of work by localities to meet common needs within governmentally fragmented urban areas, (5) general purpose units of local government rather than special purpose units, and (6) organizational flexibility within general purpose units of local government receiving aid.[13]

COORDINATION AT THE FEDERAL LEVEL

A policy of federal assistance to urban areas is now well established, and indications are that the relationships between cities and the national government will continue on an increasing scale. This prediction can be justified in part by the reactions of city leaders who have had direct experience in dealing with national agencies. Martin, in his study of cities in the federal system, reports on interviews with about 100 officials and states:

> For one thing, they are all but unanimous in their support of the federal-city programs. . . . Virtually all city spokesmen, whether political leaders or administrators, find the direct channel from city hall to national capital agreeable; like Mayor Taft [quoted below], they would rather "do business" with the Washington agencies than with their state governments. This view is so generally held that it is not necessary to explore it further.[14]

As Martin points out, however, there are significant criticisms of national-city relations in practice, even though there is general acceptance of the principle. One problem that has plagued national-city relations concerns the

---

[13] *Ibid.,* p. 10.
[14] Martin, *op. cit.,* p. 146. The quotation referred to was a part of a dialogue between a committee member and Charles Taft, Mayor of Cincinnati. Mr. Dawson: You would rather do business with the Federal Government? Mr. Taft: I would rather do business with Washington and don't tell me I am a New Dealer when I say that. *Ibid.,* p. 167.

adequacy of coordination among the numerous national programs which directly affect cities. Robert H. Connery and Richard H. Leach, in their study of the federal government and metropolitan areas, comment on this point.

> Urban programs are created as isolated units and are administered in isolation from one another. The result is a jungle of disconnected programs and projects, strewn among a variety of administrative agencies. A typical example of the way Congress failed to see the metropolitan forest in its hurried selection of urban trees is the new highway program. As noted above, in establishing that program Congress gave no consideration at all to the impact of highway construction on metropolitan areas. It did not, for example, require any coordination between the highway program and the urban renewal program in the areas affected.[15]

Connery and Leach suggest that the problem of coordination at the legislative level is complicated by the practice of dividing responsibility for a single function among numerous committees and by the lack of any institutional means of correlating their efforts.[16] This, however, is only one part of a much larger problem. In the operation of federally aided urban programs, city officials must deal with federal administrators who have authority within limited functional areas. Two difficulties have been identified in these administrative relationships. The first is the dispersal of federal authority among a number of administrative agencies without any central clearinghouse for ensuring unity of federal policy; the second arises from the internal relations between the Washington office and the regional officer of a single agency involved in extensive urban aid programs.

The Advisory Commission on Intergovernmental Relations, commenting on federal programs for urban development, noted:

> The fragmented and conflicting impact at the State and local level of disparate Federal programs concerning urban highways, urban renewal, housing, airport and sewage facility construction, and so on, are well known. If improvements in governmental structure and metropolitan area planning are to be made by the State and local level as recommended in earlier chapters of this report, there must be corresponding improvements at the national level.[17]

[15] Reprinted by permission of the publisher from Robert H. Connery and Richard H. Leach, *The Federal Government and Metropolitan Areas*, Harvard University Press, Cambridge, Mass., copyright © 1960, pp. 98, 99 by the President and Fellows of Harvard College.

[16] *Ibid.*, p. 101.

[17] Advisory Commission on Intergovernmental Relations, *Governmental Structure, Organization and Planning*, Washington, 1961, p. 52.

The report maintained that federal responses to metropolitan problems had been on a single-purpose basis without adequate planning on a comprehensive basis. Though large amounts have been spent by the federal government on individual projects, "little attention has been given to developing a coordinated plan of action at the national level to overcome the conflicts and gaps in their impact upon particular metropolitan areas."[18] The variety of federal agencies which deal with urban areas and the size of their contributions are summarized in Table 5.1. Expenditures of such magnitude have a profound effect on the decisions which must be made at the local level; it seems obvious that some means should be established to ensure that federal agencies involved do not work at cross purposes and that all combine to achieve predetermined goals. Local officials are aware of the serious consequences that can result from lack of coordination in administering federal programs; Mayor Dilworth made the point when he commented to a Senate committee:

> If people are given no help in relocating from the path of highways this obviously augments the housing problems which the renewal program is trying to solve. And renewal activities must be closely related to the programming of highways if we are to avoid on the one hand the creation of new blight along new highways and, on the other hand, the clearing up of a newly renewed area to make way for a new highway.[19]

FEDERAL DEPARTMENT OF HOUSING AND URBAN DEVELOPMENT

Reference has already been made to recommendations for the creation of a single department in the national government to deal with urban affairs. Prior to the establishment of the present Department of Housing and Urban Development, some attempt at achieving coordination had been indicated.[20] During the 1930s the National Resources Committee (later the National Resources Planning Board) recommended the creation of a unit in an appropriate federal agency to perform functions for urban areas similar to those performed by the Department of Agriculture for rural areas, and this agency had set up regional offices to deal with planning on a regional basis before its life was ended by Congress in 1943. Prior to the inauguration of President Kennedy an Ad Hoc Interagency Committee on Metropolitan Area Problems called attention to problems of interagency coordination and urged that greater attention be given to a means of eliminating these defects in the federal government's

[18] *Ibid.*, p. 52.
[19] Quoted in Connery and Leach, *op. cit.*, p. 19.
[20] For a brief summary see Advisory Committee on Intergovernmental Relations, *op. cit.*, pp. 53, 54.

TABLE 5.1 Federal Aid Payments in Urban Areas (budget and trust accounts in millions of dollars)*

Function and program	1961 actual	1966 actual	1968 estimate
National defense (civil defense and National Guard centers)	10	20	26
Agriculture and agricultural resources	155	149	235
Natural resources	54	105	200
Commerce and transportation:			
Highways	1,398	2,138	2,176
Economic development		2	36
Airports	36	30	33
Other	1	52	6
Housing and community development:			
Public housing	105	169	208
Water and sewer facilities			61
Urban renewal	106	235	336
Model cities			132
Urban transportation		14	98
District of Columbia	25	44	71
Other	2	23	100
Health, labor, and welfare:			
Office of Economic Opportunity		449	1,010
School lunch, special milk, food stamp	131	196	290
Hospital construction	48	75	95
Community health	33	127	450
Public assistance (including medical care)	1,170	1,905	2,243
Vocational rehabilitation	37	108	211
Employment security and manpower training	303	417	501
Other	21	47	101
Education:			
Elementary and secondary	222	895	1,292
Higher education	5	37	172
Vocational education	28	90	160
Other	3	27	80
Other functions		(†)	6
Total aids to urban areas	3,893	7,354	10,329

* Excludes loans and repayable advances.
† Less than $0.05 million.

Source: Office of the Vice President, *Handbook for Local Officials.* Washington, 1967, p. 259.

program. President Kennedy abolished this ad hoc committee in 1961 and assigned its functions to a special assistant to the President for urban affairs.

In 1965 Congress by law established the Department of Housing and Urban Development to be headed by a secretary with cabinet rank. The core of the new department was created by assigning to it "all of the functions, powers, and duties of the Housing and Home Finance Agency (including the Community Facilities Administration and the Urban Renewal Administration) of the Federal Housing Administration and the Public Housing Administration and the heads and other officers and offices of those agencies."[21] The Federal Mortgage Association was also transferred to the department. Robert C. Weaver, formerly the Housing Administrator, was named as the first secretary of the new department, and Robert C. Wood, an established authority in the metropolitan field, was made undersecretary.

The department has been in operation for too short a time to make any evaluation of its impact on federal-city relations, in general, or on internal federal coordination, in particular. From the nature of the agencies assigned to it, it appears that the major thrust of the department will be in the areas of housing and planning. Some important federal-city relations, such as highways, education, airports, and defense activities, will continue to be handled through individual departments as before. It is interesting to note that the organizational format of the department includes an Office of Intergovernmental Relations and Urban Program Coordination headed by a director with the rank of deputy assistant secretary. In the formal statement of the duties of this office one can see prospects for some interagency coordination if the duties are pursued vigorously.[22]

> The Office, headed by a Director, conducts studies and analyses and provides staff assistance to the Assistant Secretary and Deputy Assistant Secretary in matters of intergovernmental relations and urban program coordination, including representing the Department in the development of effective working relationships with other Federal agencies that have a major impact on community development. . . .[23]

Certain situations make cooperation difficult even when institutional arrangements for such cooperation are available. Federal agency personnel have over the years established working relations with the persons in local agencies with whom they must work. Both these local officers and the national officers are reluctant to make changes in structures or lines of communication which might upset the established order. These officers constitute little internal pressure points which make change politically difficult. Some national agen-

---

[21] Office of the Federal Register, National Archives and Record Service, General Services Administration: *United States Government Organization Manual,* Washington, 1966–1967, p. 388.

[22] For a critical view of the work of HUD since its establishment, see James E. Wilson, "The War on Cities," in Robert A. Goldwin (ed.), *A Nation of Cities,* Rand, McNally & Company, Chicago, 1968, pp. 17, 36.

[23] *Ibid.,* p. 393.

cies whose activities make a profound impact on city development deal almost wholly with the state rather than with local agencies, while others deal almost exclusively with city officials. The Bureau of Roads deals with state highway departments, and the Office of Education deals with state departments of education, but the federal housing programs and urban renewal are handled on a direct basis with cities. This difference in clientele produces differences in attitude and approach and introduces a third partner into any dialogue about general program coordination.

CENTRAL OFFICE–FIELD OFFICE RELATIONS

All governmental agencies which administer programs over a large geographic area are faced with the problem of working relations between the central office and the field offices which must be located long distances away. In programs involving grants-in-aid to urban areas this problem has been critical. One phase of the problem is related to the amount of discretionary authority that will be delegated to regional directors; the other arises out of the urge of local mayors and other policy officers to go to the top when they are working on important projects.

Martin reports "almost universal criticism of federal agencies on the ground of delay."[24] Although there is no substantial evidence to place the blame for undue delay on field offices, there is reason to believe that the problems inherent in central-field office operations contribute to delays. Although manuals and central office directives help to clarify the ranges of freedom of choice open to regional directors, they can never cover all the contingencies that arise. Central offices hesitate to delegate too much decision-making authority since they know the criticism that will arise if cities in one region are being treated differently from those in other regions. Therefore, to ensure national uniformity central offices may require clearance procedures in all cases not clearly covered by the manual. Regional officers are much less likely to deviate from the "book" in order to give flexibility when specific cities face unusual situations; hence city officials may have to delay projects while an appeal to the central office is made.

Political leaders in cities think they know something about how decisions are made in the political world, and they often seek to use all the political leverage they can to get approval for their projects. Although they may follow the formalities of going to the regional offices first, they really expect to plead their case in Washington. Since city officials feel that their state senators and

[24] Martin, op. cit., p. 156.

local congressmen can be helpful, the central office seems to be the best place for them to put on the pressure.

FEDERAL CONTROLS

Federal grants-in-aid to cities are, of course, accompanied by certain kinds of federal controls relating to the use of aid funds. The most obvious type of control relates to programs to be undertaken. Since federal decision makers authorize the extension of financial aid, they determine the kinds of local programs that are to qualify for aid funds. In some instances federal judgment about the most pressing needs of cities may not conform to the image local officials have of their needs. In such cases decisions at the national level may have significant effect on budget decisions made locally. Most federally aided programs require some kind of expenditures from local resources; hence budget makers in the city tend to allocate available funds to those programs for which federal grants are available, whether or not they think these programs deserve highest priority in their own communities. But since city lobbies are very influential in determining congressional action on such matters, this problem is not generally serious.

Setting Standards

More significant are controls exerted through the imposition of standards with which cities must comply in order to qualify for federal aid. Such controls may range from technical standards relating to construction of buildings, roads, or sewers to procedural standards prescribing how contracts are to be let, what wages are to be paid, and the kinds of relations that will be maintained with labor unions. In order to ensure compliance with established standards, numerous kinds of reports are required on a continuous basis, and regular inspections are made by federal agency personnel. Since funds are allocated at fixed times as the program progresses, failure to comply with standards can result in withholding of aid funds. These kinds of controls constitute means by which racial integration may be stimulated, prevailing wage scales maintained, and certain kinds of planning concepts incorporated into urban workable programs.

Audits

Federal agencies established auditing procedures to ensure that expenditures on federally aided projects are spent in conformity with plans previously approved. Although the need for some kind of financial audit is generally recognized and accepted, the auditing practices of federal agencies have come in for considerable criticism from local officials, who maintain that they are used to centralize control rather than to check on honesty and integrity of handling funds.[25] In addition to regular agency audits, the General Accounting Office makes spot checks of local programs which are supported by federal funds. The reports of the GAO, if critical of such projects, may influence congressional attitudes toward aid projects.

COOPERATIVE RELATIONS

Attention has thus far been concentrated on national-city relations that result from attempts of the national government to come to the aid of cities by sharing financial resources. No doubt, these grant-in-aid programs will continue to dominate such relationships, but significant cooperative arrangements, many of which were started long before large aid programs became fashionable, will continue to play a useful role in intergovernmental relations. A few examples will serve to indicate the nature of this cooperative effort. The federal government has engaged in many activities which have brought together a great deal of expertise not available to most cities, and these agencies render technical assistance to cities. The FBI fingerprint service, its training program for city police, and its uniform crime-reporting system are cases in point. The United States Civil Service Commission cooperates with local agencies in the preparation of standard tests, in giving examinations, and in the collection of statistical material. The United States Bureau of Standards compiles standard specifications for numerous products used by cities and makes them available to local governments that want to purchase materials by means of competitive bids.

Federal agencies constitute a valuable source of information from which cities can draw. The various kinds of censuses supply information about population, business, housing, and governmental spending that are used by cities as well as by private organizations. Such functional agencies as the Office of Education, the Commerce Department, and the Federal Reserve System are central sources of information to cities.

Regional agencies like the Tennessee Valley Authority, because of the nature of their functions, are brought into close relations with municipal governments. The TVA, for example, sells electricity to cities and can, by its control over the sale, encourage municipal ownership of such utilities. The agency also actively works with city officials in planning for recreational facilities and expanding regular public services.

[25] *Ibid.*, pp. 159, 160.

The TVA and numerous other agencies acquire in the local areas where they have offices a large amount of property which goes off the tax rolls as soon as title passes to the government. Since cities depend heavily on the general property tax for revenue, federal acquisition of property often poses a serious threat to city revenue sources. To compensate for such losses many federal agencies are authorized to make payments to local governments in lieu of taxes. This is particularly true where extensive defense installations have been constructed in municipalities and school districts.

METROPOLITAN PRESSURE GROUPS

Connery and Leach made a point of the absence of a single interest group to lobby for metropolitan areas comparable to the unified voice through which farmers have been able to influence congressional action.[26] This can be explained, in part, by the fact that cities do not have a common interest which will arouse united support to the same extent that farmers have. In fact, in some instances cities compete with one another in their lobbying efforts. Interests of large cities are not the same as those of small cities, and suburban cities often fail to recognize the needs of central cities or to support them in seeking relief when the needs are identified. But as national-city relations have increased, so have lobbying activities. Smaller cities are represented through the American Municipal Association; the larger ones through the United States Conference of Mayors. County governments concentrate their Washington efforts through the National Association of County Officials. The Council of Metropolitan Regional Organizations was organized to provide a voice for metropolitan planning groups and public authorities which often operate in geographic areas larger than single cities. In addition the very large cities have their own spokesmen to carry the message to Washington. Mayors make frequent trips to Washington to appear before congressional committees, to enlist the aid of their senators and representatives, and to appeal to national administrators.

Although Connery and Leach maintain that "since individual lobbying continues to yield a high return on the investment of municipal time and energy, it will probably continue to be relied on," they deplore the fact that "urban lobbying has not presented a united front."[27] Until the piecemeal approach is replaced by a strong and united voice, an orderly and coherent federal program for metropolitan growth will not be developed, and the metropolitan area problem will not be solved.

[26] Connery and Leach, op. cit., pp. 63–93.
[27] Ibid., p. 93.

SUMMARY AND EVALUATION

Banfield and Wilson, in the closing chapter of their excellent book, *City Politics*, predict, "If the control over cities is taken from the states it will be taken by the federal government, not the cities."[28] This statement emphasizes the unmistakable trend toward more direct relationships between cities and the national government. The legal nature of the American federal system focuses attention on state-city relations. But in practice, relations between states and cities have been negative rather than positive, so that state action was generally viewed by cities as restrictive rather than constructive. Officials of large cities distrusted state legislatures, partly because they were rurally dominated, and when they found they could receive a more sympathetic hearing in Congress, they turned to Washington for help.

The federal government has recognized the needs of large cities and has developed numerous programs which were expected to relieve some of the most pressing problems. The most significant device to accomplish this purpose has been the federal grant-in-aid. Numerous grants were made available to help cities attack such problems as housing, slums, highways, health, and education. In some instances the federal government worked directly with cities; in other programs, aid was channeled through the states. The number of programs and the speed with which they were developed produced difficulties. Coordination on the local level was difficult because of the large number of local units of government with which the national government had to deal directly. Coordination on the national level was complicated because there was no single national agency through which programs were coordinated. The creation of the Department of Housing and Urban Development with cabinet rank may provide the instrumentality through which federal action to help cities meet their needs can be marshaled.

Political implications of direct federal-state relations are obvious. The willingness of city officials to accept federal aid with its accompanying controls indicates that they are convinced their influence in the national decision-making process in Washington is greater than it is at the state capitals. Time will tell whether or not state reapportionment will change this image. Even if a shift in balance of power from the rural areas to the cities in state legislatures should become a reality, there would still exist strong pressure for federal aid as an equalizing force to "collect revenue where it is found and to spend it where it is most needed."

[28] Edward C. Banfield and James Q. Wilson, *City Politics*, Vintage Books, Random House, Inc., New York, 1963, p. 344.

BIBLIOGRAPHY

Books

Adrian, Charles R.: *Governing Urban America*, McGraw-Hill Book Company, New York, 1961, pp. 299–304.

Advisory Commission on Intergovernmental Relations: *The Role of Equalization in Federal Grants*, January, 1964.

————: *Statutory and Administrative Controls Associated with Federal Grants for Public Assistance*, May, 1964.

————: *State Legislature Program of the Advisory Commission on Intergovernmental Relations*, October, 1964.

————: *Government Structure, Organization and Planning*, July, 1961.

Anderson, William: *The Nation and the States, Rivals or Partners?* University of Minnesota Press, Minneapolis, 1955.

Banfield, Edward C., and James Q. Wilson: *City Politics*, Vintage Books, Random House, Inc., New York, 1963, chap. 5.

Benson, George C. S.: *The New Centralization*, Farrar and Rinehart, Inc., New York, 1941.

The Commission on Intergovernmental Relations: *A Report to the President for Transmittal to Congress*, June, 1955.

Committee on Government Operations, United States Senate: *Impact of Federal Urban Development Programs on Local Government Organization and Planning*, Washington, 1964.

Connery, Robert H., and Richard H. Leach: *The Federal Government and Metropolitan Areas*, Harvard University Press, Cambridge, Mass., 1960.

Graves, W. Brooke: *American Intergovernmental Relations*, Charles Scribner's Sons, New York, 1964, chaps. 19, 24 to 26.

Martin, Roscoe C.: *The Cities and the Federal System*, Atherton Press, Inc., New York, 1965.

National Institute of Law Officers: *Federal-City Relations*, Washington, 1953.

Articles

Cleveland, F. N.: "Congress and Urban Problems," *Journal of Politics*, vol. 28, pp. 289–307, May, 1966.

Connery, Robert H., and Richard H. Leach: "U.S. Needs a New Program," *National Municipal Review*, vol. 46, pp. 394–400, September, 1957.

Grant, Daniel R.: "Federal-Municipal Relationships and Metropolitan Integration," *Public Administration Review*, vol. 14, pp. 259–267, autumn, 1954.

Hanks, D. W.: "Neglected Cities Turn to U.S.," *National Municipal Review*, vol. 35, pp. 172–173, April, 1946.

Zimmerman, F. L., and Mitchell Wendell: "No Positive Barriers," *National Civic Review*, vol. 47, pp. 522–525, 554, November, 1959.

6

THE METROPOLIS AND ITS SUBURBS

Few areas of politics in the United States have received as much attention from students of government, popular journals, and the daily press as have metropolitan areas. Although some work has attempted to do no more than describe specific features or characteristics of such areas, the burden of most literature on the subject has clearly carried normative connotations. Some metropolitan studies have dealt with the growth trend in these areas, the characteristics of metropolitan populations, mobility within single areas, and voting behavior of residents of the metropolis. But studies financed by foundation grants and most of the articles in the popular press have concentrated on the "problems of metropolitan areas" and have proposed to solve these problems through realignment of governmental boundaries and alterations in governmental forms and structures. The purpose of this chapter is to provide information in summary form about the characteristics of metropolitan areas in this country, to identify the nature of internal conflicts that arise in such areas, describe the existing political machinery within which these conflicts are resolved, and analyze the political implications inherent in the schemes that have been proposed for solving metropolitan problems.

NATURE OF METROPOLITAN AREAS

The term "metropolitan area" is used loosely to designate a large concentration of urban population in which there is a high degree of economic interdependence and social interaction. This use of the term disregards governmental boundaries and emphasizes the social and economic characteristics of such concentrations of population. If comparative research is to be possible, some standard definition of what constitutes a metropolitan area is necessary. Since most extensive information about metropolitan areas is contained in the United States census reports, the definition prepared by the U.S. Bureau of the Budget and used by the U.S. Census Bureau is probably the most useful one available. The census figures have been compiled for areas designated as metropolitan since 1910, but the specific names and definitions applied to such areas have changed a number of times. A formal definition of a "Standard Metropolitan Area" was prepared in 1949 and used in the 1950 census. In 1958 some minor revisions were made, and the term "Standard Metropolitan Statistical Area" was adopted for use in the 1960 census.[1] The general concept of a metropolitan area is one of an integrated economic and social unit with a recognized large population nucleus. The minimum size for a city which can constitute such a nucleus is 50,000. The simplest SMSA would be a city (or town, in New England) of 50,000 and the county in which it is located. Other surrounding counties are included in the SMSA if they meet specific criteria of *metropolitan character* and *integration.*

Geographic Distribution of SMSAs

The number of SMSAs is constantly increasing as the Bureau of the Budget announces that population changes have brought additional areas within the scope of the definition. The 1960 census reported 212 SMSAs in the United States. The 1964 *Standard Metropolitan Statistical Areas* bulletin of the Bureau of the Budget reported 219 such areas; 14 additional areas were added through July, 1968, making a total of 233. Population figures available for metropolitan areas are, however, based on the 1960 census tabulations. Figure 6.1 shows the location of metropolitan areas in the United States.

Only 3 states—Alaska, Vermont, and Wyoming—have no SMSAs, 11 states have only one, 5 states have two, and 10 states have three. Texas, with 23

[1] The entire definition may be found in Bureau of the Budget, *Standard Metropolitan Statistical Areas*, Washington, 1964, pp. 1–3.

SMSAs, is far ahead of other states, Ohio with 14 is second, California is third with 14, and Pennsylvania is fourth with 12.[2] The number of metropolitan areas in a state is, of course, no indication of the population density of the state. A small New England state might ultimately become so uniformly dense in population that it would constitute a single SMSA, while a large state like Texas may have many of them and still have a low density overall.

Population in SMSAs

Although in terms of total land coverage metropolitan areas cover only a small part of the land area of the United States, they include a large part of its total population. Of the latest population of 179,323,000 in 1960, 112,885,000 persons (approximately 63 percent) lived in one of the 212 metropolitan areas. Since the trend toward greater concentration of population was pronounced from 1950 to 1960, one can assume that the percentage of population in metropolitan areas has increased since 1960. While total population in the United States increased only 18.5 percent from 1950 to 1960, the increase in metropolitan areas was 26.4 percent.

It is interesting to note the population changes taking place within the metropolitan areas themselves. Population in the 212 metropolitan areas increased 26.4 percent from 1950 to 1960, but the areas outside the central cities showed an increase of 48.6 percent. The increase in central cities was only 10.7 percent, and in many of the larger cities there was an absolute decline.[3] Table 6.1 shows the changes in central city and suburbs for the 23 largest metropolitan areas; Figure 6.2 shows these changes graphically for various sizes of classification.

Some of the extreme cases may be noted. In the Boston area the central city lost 13 percent between 1950 and 1960 while its suburbs gained 17.6 percent. New York City lost at the rate of 1.4 percent while the suburban area in New York State increased 75 percent. The central city of St. Louis lost 12.5 percent, and its Missouri suburbs increased by 73.5 percent. Any attempt to compare population changes in metropolitan areas will be misleading unless each area is examined in terms of its boundaries. Some cities, e.g., Houston and San Diego, show large percentage increases in the central cities; others show either declines or small increases. This can be accounted for, in part, by the fact that city boundaries either have been extended since 1950 or, if they were extended before 1950, have included large areas of

[2] From data in *ibid.*, pp. 51–54.
[3] U.S. Bureau of the Census, *Census of Population: 1960*, p. XXXIV.

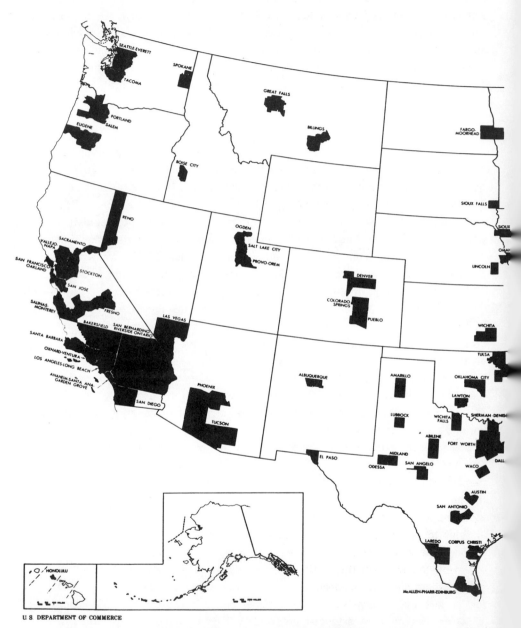

U.S. DEPARTMENT OF COMMERCE

Figure 6.1   Standard metropolitan statistical areas as defined by the U.S. Bureau of the Budget to March, 1967. (Source: Bureau of the Budget, *Standard Metropolitan Statistical Areas*, Washington, 1967)

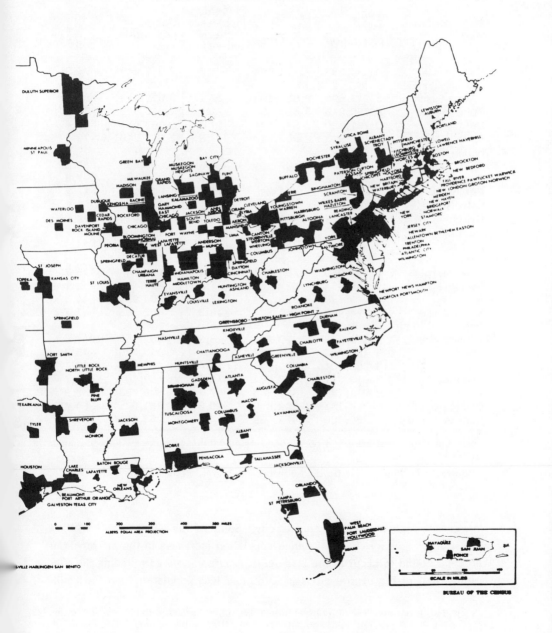

BUREAU OF THE CENSUS

TABLE 6.1   Population of 23 Largest Metropolitan Areas, 1960, with percentage of Change from 1950

Metropolitan area	1960 total population	Central-city population	Percentage increase or decrease since 1950	Suburban population	Percentage increase since 1950
New York City	10,694,633*	7,781,984	−1.4	2,912,649*	+75.0*
Los Angeles- Long Beach	6,742,696	2,823,183	+27.1	3,919,513	+82.6
Chicago	6,220,913*	3,550,404	−1.9	2,670,509*	+71.5
Detroit	3,761,360	1,670,144	−9.7	1,589,011*	+48.4
Philadelphia	3,591,523*	2,002,512	−3.3	2,092,216	+79.3
San Francisco- Oakland	1,783,359	1,107,864	−4.5	1,675,495	+55.0
Boston	2,589,301	697,197	−13.0	1,892,104	+17.6
Pittsburgh	2,405,435	604,332	−10.7	1,801,103	+17.2
Cleveland	1,796,595	876,050	−4.2	920,545	+67.2
Baltimore	1,727,023	939,024	−1.1	787,999	+72.9
Newark	1,689,420	405,220	−7.6	1,284,200	+24.7
St. Louis	1,572,905*	750,026	−12.5	822,879*	+73.5
Minneapolis- St. Paul	1,482,030	796,283	−4.4	685,747	+115.7
Buffalo	1,306,957	532,759	−8.2	774,198	+52.1
Houston	1,243,158	938,219	+57.4	304,939	+44.8
Milwaukee	1,194,290	741,324	+16.3	452,966	+41.7
Paterson-Clifton- Passaic	1,186,873	279,710	+6.9	907,163	+47.6
Seattle	1,107,213	557,087	+19.1	550,126	+45.9
Dallas	1,083,601	679,684	+56.4	403,917	+30.7
San Diego	1,033,011	573,224	+71.4	459,787	+108.7
Atlanta	1,017,188	487,455	+47.1	529,733	+33.9
Cincinnati	864,121*	502,550	−0.3	361,671*	+64.4*
Kansas City, Mo.	730,206*	475,539	+4.1	254,667*	+96.5*

* Includes only that suburban population located within the same state as the major central city (or cities).

Source: From William J. D. Boyd, "Suburbia Takes Over," *National Civic Review,* vol. 54, p. 295, June, 1965.

low-density land around the central city.[4] Some of the older cities have had few if any boundary changes; hence population increases in the metropolitan area are bound to occur in the less-dense suburban area surrounding the city. Almost half of the central cities in 1960 had less population than their sub-

[4] If 1950 boundaries of central cities are used, areas outside central cities showed a 61.7 percent increase and central cities showed only 1.5 percent increase.

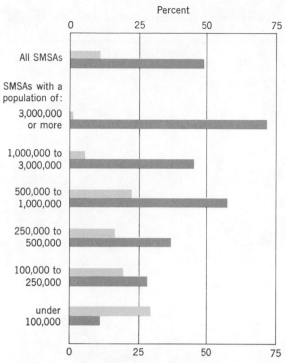

Figure 6.2   Percent change in population in and outside central cities by size of metropolitan statistical areas, 1950–1960. (Source: U.S. Bureau of the Census, Census of Population, vol. I, part I, p. 29, 1960)

urbs, and if the trend has continued since 1960, the number is now greater.[5]

Since there has been a relative, and often an absolute, decline in number of rural dwellers, the proportion of the population of each state living in metropolitan areas is increasing. Twenty-six states had more than half their total population in metropolitan areas in 1960, and in 10 states over 75 percent of the total population was in these areas. Figure 6.3 shows the percentage of total population living in metropolitan areas in 1960, by states. Disregarding the states with no metropolitan areas, the range is from 8.6 percent in Mississippi to 86.5 percent in California.[6]

There is wide variation in the size of metropolitan areas, and any attempt

[5] See William J. D. Boyd, "Suburbia Takes Over," National Civic Review, vol. 54, pp. 294–298, June, 1965.

[6] See John C. Bollens and Henry J. Schmandt, The Metropolis: Its People and Economic Life, Harper & Row, Publishers, Incorporated, New York, 1965, p. 16.

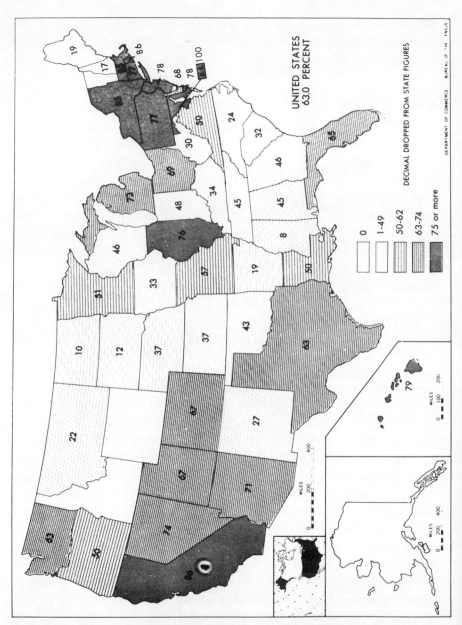

Figure 6.3   Percent of population in standard metropolitan statistical areas by states, 1960. (Source: U.S. Bureau of the Census, *Census of Population*, vol. I, part I, p. 29, 1960)

at comparative analysis will have to take this variation into account. The range in 1960 was from Meriden, Connecticut, with 51,850, to New York with 10,694,633.

Political Organization in Metropolitan Areas

One characteristic that most metropolitan areas have in common is that they do not have a single governmental entity which functions for the entire area. Most governmental units functioning in metropolitan areas are limited in terms of both the geographic area of their jurisdiction and the subject matter within their competence. In the very small SMSAs (those with populations of less than 100,000), a single county government may have territorial jurisdiction over the entire area but the subject matter within its jurisdiction will be very limited. Most of the municipal corporations and special districts which operate within metropolitan areas have territorial authority in only a small portion of the entire area. Table 6.2 gives some gross figures to show the number of governmental units that were functioning in the 227 metropolitan areas of the United States for which information was available.

These governmental units range from villages of fewer than 100 persons to cities the size of New York. In all cases they have authority to raise money either by service charges, taxes, or both, and they make decisions which affect not only their own residents but their neighbors as well. Within a single metropolitan area the governmental pattern is complicated by the fact that the territorial boundaries of political units overlap. For example, parts of a municipal corporation may lie in two or more school districts and, in some

TABLE 6.2   Number of Local Governments in Metropolitan Areas, 1967

Size of SMSA	No. of SMSAs	No. of local governments
All SMSAs	227	20,703
1,000,000 or more	24	7,367
500,000–1,000,000	32	3,878
300,000–500,000	30	2,734
200,000–300,000	40	2,919
100,000–200,000	74	3,123
50,000–100,000	27	682

Source: U.S. Bureau of the Census, *Census of Governments: 1967.* vol. I, *Governmental Organization*, Washington, 1968, p. 11.

instances, in more than one fire protection district. It may not be uncommon for a single resident of a municipality to pay taxes or service fees for the support of a county, a city, a fire protection district, a sewer district, a public school district, a junior college district, and a bistate authority.

The governmental pattern is further complicated because many SMSAs cross county and state lines. Of the 212 SMSAs in 1960, 79 included more than one county, and the range was from two to eight counties; see Table 6.3. Twenty-four SMSAs, not including New York and Chicago, included territory in more than one state. These two areas are interstate only if the definition for Standard Consolidated Areas is applied to them. Table 6.4 shows the SMSAs that are interstate.

METROPOLITAN PROBLEMS

There has been no scarcity of literature about metropolitan areas in the last 20 years, and much of what has appeared has discussed what is called "the metropolitan problem." Everyone seems to know that there is a metropolitan problem, but when one seeks to identify this problem so that it can be more carefully analyzed, it becomes very illusive. Perhaps the metropolitan problem is not unlike the story of the blind men who sought to describe an elephant;

TABLE 6.3   Metropolitan Areas by Number of Counties They Contain, 1960

No. of counties in SMSA*	No. of SMSAs	Population, 1960		
		No. (in millions)	Percent of SMSA population	Percent of U.S. population
1	133	32.4	28.7	18.1
2	39	22.8	20.2	12.7
3	22	15.2	13.5	8.5
4	5	5.2	4.6	2.9
5	5	15.9	14.0	8.8
6	5	14.2	12.6	7.9
7	1	2.0	1.8	1.1
8	2	5.1	4.6	2.9
Total	212	112.9	100.0	62.9

* Counting for New England, counties of which any portion is within an SMSA. New York City is counted here as a single area, rather than in terms of its five component county areas. Because of rounding, detail may not add to totals.

Source: Advisory Commission on Intergovernmental Relations, *Governmental Structure, Organization and Planning in Metropolitan Areas,* Washington, 1961, p. 12.

TABLE 6.4   Interstate Metropolitan Areas, 1960

Metropolitan area	States with part of territory*	No. of county areas	1960 population
New York-northeastern New Jersey†	New York-New Jersey	13‡	14,759,429
Chicago, Ill.-northwestern Indiana§	Illinois-Indiana	8	6,794,461
Philadelphia	Pennsylvania-New Jersey	8	4,342,897
St. Louis	Missouri-Illinois	6	2,060,103
Washington	District of Columbia-Maryland-Virginia	7	2,001,897
Cincinnati	Ohio-Kentucky	3	1,071,624
Kansas City	Missouri-Kansas	4	1,039,493
Portland	Oregon-Washington	4	821,897
Providence-Pawtucket	Rhode Island-Massachusetts	8	816,148
Louisville	Kentucky-Indiana	3	725,139
Allentown-Bethlehem-Easton	Pennsylvania-New Jersey	3	492,168
Omaha	Nebraska-Iowa	3	457,873
Wilmington	Delaware-New Jersey	2	366,157
Chattanooga	Tennessee-Georgia	2	283,169
Duluth-Superior	Minnesota-Wisconsin	2	276,596
Davenport-Rock Island-Moline	Iowa-Illinois	2	270,058
Huntington-Ashland	West Virginia-Kentucky-Ohio	4	254,780
Columbus	Georgia-Alabama	3	217,985
Augusta	Georgia-South Carolina	2	216,639
Evansville	Indiana-Kentucky	2	199,313
Wheeling	West Virginia-Ohio	3	190,342
Lawrence-Haverhill	Massachusetts-New Hampshire	2	187,601
Steubenville-Weirton	Ohio-West Virginia	3	167,756
Fall River	Massachusetts-Rhode Island	2	138,156
Fargo-Moorhead	North Dakota-Minnesota	2	106,027
Texarkana	Texas-Arkansas	2	91,657

* The State containing the central city (or the more populous one when there are two central cities) is listed first.

† A "standard consolidated area," consisting of four standard metropolitan statistical areas (New York, Newark, Jersey City, and Paterson-Clifton-Passaic) plus Middlesex and Somerset Counties, N.J.

‡ Counting New York City as a single area, rather than in terms of its five component "counties."

§ A "standard consolidated area," consisting of two standard metropolitan statistical areas (Chicago and Gary-Hammond-East Chicago).

Source: Advisory Commission on Intergovernmental Relations, *Governmental Structure, Organization and Planning in Metropolitan Areas*, Washington, 1961, p. 13.

the description given by each man depended on whether he felt the trunk, side, or leg. Some observers whose training conditions them to look at governmental form and structure are astounded that as many as 100 governments with independent authority seek to perform the governmental function within an area which in many ways is a social and economic unit. Such observers tend to assume that if the governmental machinery of metropolitan areas could be restructured in such a way as to eliminate the small, overlapping, and competing jurisdictions that exist, other problems that plague such areas would be solved with dispatch. No attempt will be made to justify the political arrangements found at the present time in metropolitan areas of the United States, but the reader is cautioned that changes in governmental form and structure will not, of themselves, alter the nature of conflicts that arise in these urban complexes. Reorganized patterns of government may change the balance of power among various groups, thereby affecting decisions in the political system and perhaps removing certain formal and procedural roadblocks in the decision process, but they will not automatically alter the racial distribution, disparities in income, differences in educational opportunities, and psychological and emotional forces which condition group behavior; these are the factors which produce a large part of the so-called metropolitan problem.

To others the metropolitan problem is perceived in terms of communication and circulation. They are concerned about the barriers and bottlenecks that impede the free flow of people and goods within the urban complex, and they seek to remedy the problem by origin and destination studies which will reveal where people want to go. They maintain that when better highways are constructed and more rapid mass transit systems are devised, the metropolitan problem will be solved.

Others view the problem in terms of racial integration, slum clearance, adequate housing, or attracting more industry to locate in the area. The fact is that no one can define the metropolitan problem in the singular; what passes in public dialogue as the metropolitan problem is a mass of many problems which are social, economic, and political in character. Anyone who attempts to make our metropolitan areas more attractive places for family living must recognize the complex and interrelated character of problems faced by these areas and must seek solutions on a broad front. Attention here will be concerned with politics and government and will be focused on the solution of problems through the political process, although private industry, labor unions, churches, and social service organizations have significant roles to play in determining what life in the metropolis will be like.

In order to give greater definition to the nature of metropolitan problems which are directly related to the political process, a fourfold classification will be used. The metropolitan problem may be perceived as (1) a public-service problem, (2) a problem in public finance, (3) a problem in public decision making, and (4) a problem in governmental structure. Physical planning might be considered as a separate category, but since it is so intricately tied up with the four classes listed above, it will not be treated separately here. A later chapter will deal with the politics of planning in urban areas.

The Problem of Metropolitan Services

In the introduction to this text it was suggested that some students view local governments as primarily service institutions; i.e., they exist to supply certain public services which private utility corporations are unlikely to per-form. Certainly in large metropolitan areas with diverse racial groups, wide ranges of income levels, and complex commercial and industrial structures, some means must be found to perform public services. Political issues do not arise with respect to the need for local governments to perform what are widely accepted as governmental functions; conflict is generated only when some group suggests that a service which is being performed by private agencies be transferred to the local government. The discussion here will relate to those functions which are so widely accepted as falling within the proper range of local government authority that their performance raises no conflict in the political arena. Many different lists of functions of local governments are available, but their major differences are in the manner in which they are classified, not in the overall or total group of services involved. The classification used by the U.S. Census Bureau in reporting local government expenditures will serve as well as any for purposes of this discussion. The services it comprises are (1) education, (2) utilities, (3) highways, (4) public welfare, (5) hospitals and health, (6) sanitation, (7) police protection, (8) housing and urban renewal, (9) fire protection, (10) parks and recreation, and (11) all others.[7]

Within any single local government the performance of each of these func-tions produces a host of political problems, i.e., group conflicts over how they should be performed. Within a single school district conflict will develop over the location of new buildings, the emphasis to be given to competitive sports,

[7] U.S. Bureau of the Census, *Census of Governments*, Washington, 1962, p. 13.

new math, the role of foreign languages, and the degree of emphasis to be given to liberal arts and to semivocational subjects. The same is true within any single municipal corporation with respect to the performance of any single service. Sanitation may be used as an example; the location of incinerators, the stringency of air pollution regulations, the frequency of garbage collection, and the kinds of restaurant inspection required are matters over which groups disagree, and therefore they present conflicts which must be resolved by municipal decision makers. But these kinds of service conflicts are not peculiarly metropolitan in character. They occur regularly within each political subdivision that operates within a metropolitan area; as long as they are confined within the boundaries of a single governmental unit, they are no different from the conflicts that take place in local governments outside metropolitan areas.

The dimension of the service problem that concerns the student of metropolitan politics is: What local government services will be performed individually by each of the multitude of governmental units, and which, if any, should be assigned to governmental units with area-wide or near-area-wide jurisdiction? The question is extended a step further if the metropolitan area is so large that no existing local government has territorial jurisdiction over the entire area. If the simplest metropolitan area is used as an example, it would be a single county in which there is one city of 50,000 and a number of small cities, some school districts, and perhaps one or more other special-purpose districts. Since the county has jurisdiction over the entire area, it is possible to argue that some services are of such a character that they should be performed uniformly and therefore should be assigned to the county government, but on the other hand, there will be those who insist that the functions of the county be held to a minimum so that other local services can be performed by smaller governmental units. The larger and more complex the metropolitan area becomes, the more interdependent local units of government become and the more the issue of centralization of functions produces group conflict. The service conflict in metropolitan areas is really not so much one of how the services should be performed, but rather what kind of governmental unit should perform them.

One way to discuss the service problem in metropolitan areas is to try to view service functions as either (1) of primarily local concern, or (2) of area-wide concern. The implication is, then, that small local governmental units can be permitted to perform the first, but that the second should properly be delegated to a governmental unit with area-wide jurisdiction. A second way to view the metropolitan service problem is to assume that matters of local concern will continue to be handled independently by smaller local governments and that even the matters of area-wide concern will continue to be handled by these same units but with sufficient supervision from an area-wide government to ensure their performance at a level of intensity prescribed by the larger unit. Numerous examples of this attempt to dichotomize service functions as either of primarily local concern or of areawide concern are available. A 1966 report of the Committee for Economic Development recommended: "In situations where a single county contains an entire metropolitan area, . . . a reconstituted county government [should] be used as the basic framework for handling *areawide* problems."[8] The report suggests that in metropolitan areas composed of a number of counties, some kind of multicounty federation should be created to plan and enforce solutions for area-wide problems. This particular report fails to provide lists of functions that should be considered as area-wide, but other sources have supplied such lists or, at least, have suggested criteria for the preparation of such lists.

Victor Jones, who has been concerned with problems of metropolitan government as long as any political scientist, suggested that an overall metropolitan area government is desirable under the following circumstances:

(1) When co-ordination of functions over the whole area is essential to effective service or control in any part of the area;
(2) when it is desired to apply the ability-to-pay theory of taxation to the area as a whole instead of allowing each part to support its own activities at whatever level its own economic base will allow;
(3) when services can be supplied more efficiently through large-scale operations and when the advantages of large-scale operations are desired; and
(4) when it is necessary in order to assure citizens a voice in decisions that affect them at their places of work and recreation as well as at their places of residence.[9]

The Advisory Commission on Intergovernmental Relations in a 1962 study suggested a set of seven standards for determining whether a local government function should be considered as local or area-wide:

(1) The unit of government responsible for providing a particular service should have territorial jurisdiction large enough to enable the benefits from that service to be consumed primarily within the jurisdiction;

[8] Committee for Economic Development, *Modernizing Local Governments*, New York, July, 1966, p. 45.
[9] Victor Jones, "Local Government Organization in Metropolitan Areas: Its Relation to Urban Development," in Coleman Woodbury (ed.), *The Future of Cities and Urban Development*, University of Chicago Press, Chicago, 1953, p. 508.

(2) it should be large enough to permit realization of the economics of scale;

(3) it should have a geographical area of jurisdiction adequate for effective performance;

(4) it should have the legal and administrative ability to perform the service;

(5) it should be responsible for a sufficient number of functions so that it provides a forum for resolution of conflicting interests and is able to balance governmental needs and resources;

(6) it should be so organized that the performance of its functions remains controllable by and accessible to its residents; and

(7) it should be able to maximize the conditions and opportunities for active citizen participation, while still permitting adequate performance.[10]

This list has resulted from the deliberations of a group of persons who probably had conflicting opinions about what specific functions should be considered area-wide, since it appears to be a compromise to resolve specific conflicts in such a way as to present a show of unity where none really would exist if the generalities were reduced to specifics. But this is typical of the political process when real conflict issues are considered. The difficulty of using the above standards to judge when a specific issue is to be considered of area-wide concern can be seen if items 2 and 7 be considered together; the first is an economic standard, while the second is political. At what point should consideration of economies of scale, which seems to prescribe big governmental units, give way to active citizen performance, which seems to require smaller units?

The commission did, however, in the same report seek to identify, on the basis of these criteria, which functions were most local and which were most area-wide. It considered typical local government services and arranged them in a continuum, ranking each in the order of its local or area-wide concern. The rank order is shown in Table 6.5. Obviously, this ranking is based on the combined value judgments of the commission members and is not supported by any empirical research. Other equally competent observers might prefer a different order, but the use of a rank-order method of presenting the local character of selected services has much to recommend it.

Casting the metropolitan service problem in terms of local versus area-wide control highlights the significance of the politics involved in any attempt to alter the existing governmental arrangements. If the political facet of metropolitan life is pushed aside, technicians and engineers can produce reasonable

[10] Advisory Commission on Intergovernmental Relations, *Performance of Urban Functions: Local and Areawide,* Washington, September, 1963, pp. 41–60.

TABLE 6.5   Suggested Rank Order of Urban Functions on the Basis of Local Area-wide Character*

Function	Rank
Fire protection	1
Public education	2
Refuse collection and disposal	3
Libraries	4
Police	5
Health	6
Urban renewal	7
Housing	8
Parks and recreation	9
Public welfare	10
Hospitals and medical care facilities	11
Transportation	12
Planning	13
Water supply and sewage disposal	14
Air pollution control	15

* A rank of 1 indicates that the function is *most local* and *least area-wide;* a rank of 15 indicates that the function is *least local* and *most area-wide.*

Source: From Advisory Commission on Intergovernmental Relations, *Performance of Urban Functions: Local and Areawide*, September, 1963, pp. 9–23.

solutions to many of the specific problems that have developed in large urbanized areas. A couple of examples will serve to illustrate the significance of the political conflict in providing the standard municipal services within a complex metropolitan area.

The term "environmental sanitation" is used to designate certain kinds of public health services that municipal corporations can be expected to supply for their residents; they include, among other services, mosquito control and air pollution abatement. If one starts with the value premise that mosquitoes are a threat to the health of people living in an urbanized community, he readily accepts the idea that these insects should be eradicated. Public health specialists and sanitary engineers can, with the knowledge and experience available to them, prepare a program which will destroy these pests in their breeding places and give assurance that any health threat which they pose will be minimized. One element of such a program will, however, be based on the assumption that the control measures proposed will be applied uniformly over a geographic area determined by scientific tests and based on the range of mobility of the mosquito. So far, the attack on the problem poses few questions; the difficulty comes when the politicians must secure legitimate regulations backed by the force of government to make the program effective. If a single decision-making center is legally competent to pass the ordinances required to put the plan into effect, the problem is not metropolitan in character and can be worked out by the play of forces in a single political arena with the assurance that whatever control scheme is decided upon will be uniformly applied in all areas where it is needed. On the other hand, if the control measures must be debated and worked out in 100 separate and independent political jurisdictions, the probability of arriving at any uniform program is slim indeed. And the critical feature of the dispersion of authority is that the failure of one or two of the jurisdictions involved to adopt and enforce control measures will nullify any attempts to the others to achieve results. Breeding places in the uncontrolled areas can produce enough mosquitoes to infest the entire metropolitan area.

The problems involved in moving traffic in a metropolitan area are very similar. Certain thoroughfares or throughways constitute about the only routes over which traffic can move from one part of the area to another. Although the technology of traffic movement and control has not reached the stage of sophistication that public health engineering has, traffic engineers can prepare a viable plan which will both increase the flow of through traffic and make it safer. But desired results depend entirely on the uniform adoption of the control plan over the entire area involved. The failure of one or two small municipalities to accept their responsibility to give effect to the plan will make it ineffective, not just for their own small area, but for the entire area as well.

This is not to deny that local decision makers have some good reasons why they are unwilling to go along with the overall plan; they are responding to their constituents when they make their decisions. The point to be emphasized is that the nature of the decentralization of decision making in existing metropolitan areas permits a small constituency to nullify programs which would have strong majority support if the issues were decided in an arena in which the entire area participated. It may well be that only a few services are like the two just discussed; there may well be many issues which can be dealt with by fairly small communities and the way they are decided will affect only slightly, if at all, the people living in other sections of the area. Such issues would then be considered local in character. The order of rank shown in Table 6.5 was an attempt to show the relative degree of local and area-wide concern involved in standard public services.

The Metropolitan Finance Problem

Even if the voluntary actions of all governmental units in a metropolitan area resulted in the acceptance of area-wide and uniform plans for major services, the existing patterns of decentralization would present a problem in financing public services. Anyone who has lived in a major metropolitan area can, without making any statistical analyses, observe that different socio-economic groups are not dispersed randomly throughout the area. Economically, the high-income groups tend to be clustered in a few areas, the middle-income groups are in others, and the lowest-income groups are concentrated in areas with the poorest housing. Industrial plants are grouped together where transportation is available and a stream or river can be used to carry away industrial wastes. Large shopping areas and tall office buildings tend to be concentrated in a few spots within the area. In some instances the spatial distribution of homes, apartments, industrial plants, and commercial centers has been determined by governmental action through planning and zoning techniques, but in many cases the distribution has resulted from unrelated decisions of land developers, industrial managers, and real estate speculators. Probably the one factor which has been considered least in the spatial distribution of physical facilities has been the problem of financing public services required in metropolitan areas.

The financial problem results from the fact that existing tax arrangements relate tax collections to specific political subdivisions within the metropolitan area, rather than to the area as a whole. The tax on real estate is an excellent example to reveal the nature of the problem. Real estate is always taxed at the location of the property, without regard to the residence of the owner. Some kinds of property yield very high tax returns without making heavy demands for public services from the community in which they are located. An industrial park, for example, often contains large warehouse facilities with showrooms for a manufacturer's products. These buildings are usually low, of fireproof construction, and on streets that are either private or require minimum maintenance since they carry little through traffic. Employment in these parks is usually limited, since no fabrication takes place and no assembly lines are in operation. The point is that the tax income from such property is high and the public expenditures to provide public services is relatively light. The same is generally true for high-rise office buildings and luxury apartments, which cater to single persons or married people with few or no children. If the tax structure of a large urbanized area is such that tax income from these high-income-producing sources goes into a central treasury so that it can be used to supply services throughout the area, the spatial distribution of such developments will not be of great concern. But since the governmental structure of metropolitan areas is highly decentralized, the income from such developments goes into the treasury of the small political subdivision in which it is located and none of it is available to help supply services to other parts of the metropolitan area.

A specific example will show the dimensions of the problem. In a large, highly urbanized county containing a large number of municipal corporations, one of them will be the county seat, the place where all county offices are located and where the courts hold their sessions. Lawyers, real estate brokers, land title companies, and other professionals seek office space around the courthouse, and the demand for such space is very high. To meet this need developers construct high-rise office buildings in the city which has the courthouse. The concentration of officeworkers attracts other commercial enterprises, and soon the value of the property for tax purposes in the county seat town is extremely high. The resident population has, however, not increased and may have declined as those who sold their homes to the developers moved to other areas. The result is that the county seat town has a tax base that produces large amounts of revenue and the service needs are no more, and perhaps less, than they are in other areas with much smaller tax bases. Public education also illustrates the nature of this problem. The office buildings, commercial establishments, and luxury high-rise apartments place little drain on the public schools since the apartment dwellers have few children and some of those who have children send them to private schools; furthermore, the daytime occupants of the commercial establishments and office buildings live in other school districts which must pay for the education of their children. A more structurally integrated urban area would be able to spread the tax resources of the area around the courthouse over a wider geographic area to meet service needs. The capital investment for the construction has, in many cases, come from persons who do not live in the county seat town and do not share in the high level of services the high tax base makes possible; therefore, they would have little reason to object to reforms aimed at spreading the tax resources over a wider area.

The example used above may present an exceptional case, but many similar situations can be found in any of the large metropolitan areas of the United States. A recent location of a huge auto assembly plant is another case in point. The site finally chosen for the plant was in a single school district and in the corporate boundaries of a very small town. The tax base of these two political subdivisions was increased tremendously, and the facility placed a minimum of additional service load on them. However, many of the families of those who worked in the plant moved into towns and school districts surrounding the area of the plant. These towns and school districts felt the financial pressure imposed by the influx of new families without being able to benefit from the tax base created by the new plant.

Recognition of the public-finance consequences of the location of certain kinds of physical facilities within the boundaries of political subdivisions has produced keen competition among them. These subdivisions do all they can within the law to persuade certain kinds of land development within their borders. If there are advantages in planning the use of land in a metropolitan area so as to locate the different kinds of housing, commerce, and industry in the places where natural terrain, availability of transportation, and compatibility are given major consideration, the kind of competition which governmental decentralization generates is dysfunctional. If the tax base created by any new land development is dispersed over an entire area rather than concentrated within the boundaries of a small political subdivision, the considerations which finally determine location are completely changed.

Financial implications inherent in existing metropolitan governmental patterns are probably more serious for areas which for one reason or another include the lowest-income groups and minority racial groups. The play of economic forces and real estate marketing practices have resulted in very uneven distribution of these groups over the metropolitan area. Without central control or planning of the boundary lines of municipal corporations and school districts, these low-income and minority areas have been omitted from municipal corporations and school districts which have substantial tax bases. Any annexations, consolidations, or reorganizations that have taken place have left these areas as isolated pockets. Limited as they are to revenues derived from their inadequate tax bases, they are able to provide services at only a minimal level even though the residents pay a property tax rate higher than that of some other communities. Unless metropolitan areas find a way of spreading the tax base so that these isolated communities can have more public revenue, they will have no other choice than to look for state or federal aid.

If the boundary lines of the various political subdivisions in any large metropolitan area are examined, one can find little justification for their present location. In very few cases do boundaries represent natural barriers. Occasionally, a major river will divide an area, but in most cases boundaries of municipal corporations represent nothing but historical accident and present-day residents cannot give any reasons why they are located where they are. If these boundaries represented only emotional attachments, they would present no problem, but since their location has profound consequences for the kind of public services that can be supported, they are one phase of the total metropolitan problem.

The Problem of Governmental Structure

A recent report of the Committee for Economic Development deals largely with recommendations designed to alter the structure of local governments in this country. In discussing metropolitan areas the report states, "The most pressing problem of local government in metropolitan areas may be stated simply. The bewildering multiplicity of small, piecemeal, duplicative, overlapping local jurisdictions cannot cope with the staggering difficulties encountered in managing modern urban affairs."[11] Although one may maintain that the solution of all the ills of metropolitan areas cannot be subsumed under a study of governmental structure, he must admit that the existing structure is hard to justify and that the metropolitan problem may be perceived as one that can be solved only if some structural reform is possible. An examination of many metropolitan area studies will reveal that for the most part they focused on the size and kinds of governmental units that existed in the area. And if the studies produced a package of recommended reforms, as most of them did, governmental restructuring received top priority. Although the studies included some social and economic analysis, the results of such analyses were used primarily to support recommendations for governmental change.

The generalizations most commonly made about governments in metropolitan areas are that there are too many of them, they are too small, their jurisdictions overlap one another, and their performance is inadequate. If these charges are true, one may very well say that a useful way to examine the metropolitan area is to examine its governmental structure. Table 6.2, page 123, shows that there were a total of 20,703 local governments in 227 metropolitan areas in 1967—an average of 91 per area. Even the small metropolitan areas with populations from 50,000 to 100,000 had an average of 25 local governments for each area; the Chicago area had 1,060; Philadelphia, 806; New York, 555; and St. Louis, 439. In very few instances does any single unit include the entire metropolitan area. In the smaller areas a single county encompasses the entire metropolitan area, but the scope of

---

[11] Committee for Economic Development, *op. cit.*, p. 44.

its authority is generally severely limited by state constitutions and statutes. The largest governments, territorially, are likely to be special-purpose districts which have a very narrow range of service functions. Municipal corporations in one single metropolitan area, for example, range from a village with a population of 13 to a core city of 700,000. The complex and varied character of governmental units in metropolitan areas and the way such a pattern may affect governmental performance may be considered under three headings: (1) size, (2) jurisdictional conflicts, and (3) service interdependence.

Implications of Size

If the assumption is made that the purpose for which municipal corporations are chartered is to create a legitimate governmental agency to provide public services at a level of intensity not available from other governmental units, it seems reasonable to insist that the newly chartered corporation be large enough to perform such responsibilities effectively. Although no study has determined empirically an ideal size for cities, some observations can be made which cast doubt on the capacity of very small cities to justify their existence in metropolitan areas. In a metropolitan area which depends on a large water source (river, lake, or ocean) to dispose of its liquid wastes, accessibility to the source is a necessity. With a single large municipality in the area, part of the city boundary will lie along the river, but with a pattern of multiplicity of small cities at least some of them will be cut off from the water source. These small cities must depend on contractual arrangements with cities which lie between them and the river to secure a sewer outlet. The facts of life have forced some small cities in metropolitan areas to support a consolidated government for supplying sewer service even though they oppose vigorously consolidation for other purposes.

A case can be made for the elimination of very small cities as suppliers of police and fire protection. These services require twenty-four-hour service by qualified personnel, dispatching facilities, special arson squads, qualified crime detection service, and expensive mechanical equipment. Size alone makes it impossible for small cities, by themselves, to supply these services at a high level of intensity. Small cities cannot maintain public hospitals or intensive public health programs, parks, or public schools with a wide range of curricula and adequately trained teachers. There is ample evidence to demonstrate that officials of small cities are aware of their inability to provide a full range of municipal services. They seek to contract with other governments for some services and support collective arrangements with other cities for centralized crime laboratories, police and fire dispatching service, and special detective squads.

Insofar as modern municipal government requires the services of professional career civil servants, very small cities are unable to meet current needs. The establishment of careers in local public service requires recruitment programs, opportunities to move up in the system by promotion, adequate salary with fringe benefits, and an attractive retirement program. Only fairly large cities can have an employment force large enough to justify such a professional career program.

Although statistical support to show economics of scale is hard to come by, many observers of city government are convinced that the unit costs for some city services decrease as cities increase in size, at least up to a certain point. Sewer systems, water systems, garbage and rubbish collection probably fall in this class. Reference has been made previously to the fact that available cost figures show that per capita expenditures in cities increase as the size of cities increase. This relationship may be accounted for by the fact that larger cities supply more services at a more intense level than do smaller ones; or by the greater demands made upon governments in large cities by the high density of population and the number of low-income families. The evidence available does not prove that overall unit costs could not be reduced if a group of neighboring cities united to form a single large city and kept public services at the same level as before the consolidation.

Functional Conflicts   The functional conflicts referred to here result from the different kinds of governmental units operating in metropolitan areas rather than conflicts that arise because of the number of cities that exist within a single area. These conflicts arise because more than one governmental unit performs functions in the same geographic area. For example, within a given area a municipal corporation will perform a fairly broad range of services, including police protection, street maintenance, land-use zoning, and regulation and inspection of new building construction. Within the same geographic area a school district furnishes education, a special fire protection district supplies fire protection, a sewer district is responsible for the maintenance of a sewer system, and the county may render certain kinds of health services. The number and variety of governments which function within a given geographic area may confuse the citizen when he wants to communicate with the governmental officials responsible for a specific problem, but more significant are jurisdictional problems that the system produces.

Examples of jurisdictional problems will indicate the nature of the confusion. School districts are regularly involved in the construction of new buildings and the renovation of old ones. Architects are hired by boards of education, and construction contracts are awarded by them. Within the school district, however, a special fire district board is responsible for the protection of these buildings against the hazards of fire. The fire district may have regulations relating to the use of fireproof materials, installation of sprinkler systems, use of fire doors, and related matters. Questions continually arise as to the extent to which a fire district can dictate to a school district in matters related to building construction and maintenance. What, for example, could a fire district do if its inspectors decided a school building did not comply with the fire district code? Inspections of school lunch facilities have presented similar conflicts. The regulations of a school board relating to lunchrooms in the public schools may be quite different from the regulations of a city health department respecting all public eating facilities within the city. To what extent can city officials force their standards upon schools located within the city? The problem is further complicated by the fact that a single school district may operate schools located in two or more cities. If each city has its own set of health regulations and they differ in some respects, the school district cannot have uniform rules in all its schools if the district is required to comply with each set of regulations.

Similar conflicts arise between city officials and special sewer district officials over planning and construction of sewers within city boundaries. City officials seek to make decisions about location and size of sewer mains and to require that certain water drainage courses be enclosed. Often the demands made by city officials are not in conformity with regulations adopted by sewer district officials, resulting in such heated conflict that city police will halt sewer construction projects. Numerous similar conflicts arise over police protection for schools, police assistance at fires, and the location of physical facilities of special district governments within city boundaries when zoning is controlled by the city.

Conflict may arise between firemen and police or between the health department and the school superintendent even if a single government controls all public functions within a metropolitan area, but such conflicts can be resolved within the system by action of either a chief executive or a single legislative body. In an area where the units of government which are parties to the conflicts are independent of each other, however, the disputes must be settled outside the system. Often the state, through either its courts or its legislature, will have to sit in judgment in these disputes.

Service Interdependence   Reference has been made to the fact that in many metropolitan areas some governmental units are too small to provide urban-type services at a high degree of intensity. This inability of some cities to provide services for its own residents is serious enough, but the more serious fact is that the inability or refusal of some cities to perform certain services makes it impossible for others to secure desired results. The problem of smoke abatement and air pollution, which is now receiving so much attention, is a case in point. Air pollution can be effectively controlled only at its source. If industrial plants that contribute heavily to the pollution problem are located within one city, action by that city is necessary to alleviate the problem. Even if all adjoining cities adopt model air pollution—control ordinances, they will be ineffective unless the city in which the industries are located takes similar action.

THE METROPOLITAN PROBLEM AS A PROBLEM IN DECISION MAKING

Firmly implanted in most of the literature about American government is the philosophy that decisions made by governments should have direct or indirect approval of the people who are to be affected by the decisions. This is the philosophy contained in the popular phrase "consent of the governed." Although few would wish to debate the wisdom of a system of government in which decisions are legitimized by public approval, examination of governmental decision making in a large metropolitan area will reveal that application of the principle presents a number of difficulties. The first question one must ask is, "Who are the governed from whom consent is to be secured?" If consent is to be secured only from persons living within small political areas, decision making in a large metropolitan area will be fragmented, parochial, and often conflicting. If, on the other hand, consent is to be secured on the basis of the social and economic community, as distinguished from the political community, decision making will proceed on a more uniform basis and each decision will have area-wide applicability. If consent of the governed implies that all those who will be affected by public decisions shall have an opportunity to participate in making them, the decision-making process in most metropolitan areas will not meet the test. A few examples will illustrate the point of view of those who maintain that the existing multiplicity of governments denies participation to many who are very directly affected by decisions which flow from the system.

A number of cities now levy a tax on the earnings of persons who work in the city regardless of where they live. Such taxes are usually approved by a vote. But voting is determined by place of residence; therefore all those who live outside the city limits but whose job is in the city are not given an opportunity to participate in a decision that affects them very directly. One city may, by its zoning powers, permit the construction of industrial establishments on its border, even though along this same border but in an adjoining city there are only single-family residences. Although these homeowners will feel that the decision affects them very directly, they can have no voice in making it. A very small city may adopt very stringent traffic laws and permit parking on both sides of a street that serves as a major traffic artery from one part of a metropolitan area to another, thereby affecting the flow of traffic along the trafficway well beyond the boundaries of the city in question. Although the number of persons affected by the traffic rules may be greater than the total population of the city that made them, they have no legal way to make their influence felt. It is not uncommon for investors to have property holdings and business enterprises in a number of locations within a metropolitan area. They, therefore, have an interest in the governmental decisions that affect their investments and businesses, but since they can have a voting residence in only one city, they cannot vote on decisions made in other political subdivisions.

In the above cases the situation would be different if the decisions were made in a political arena which included the whole of the area. The earnings-tax decision would come before a legislative body in which all parts of the area would be represented, or it would be submitted to a referendum in which all voters of the area without regard to their specific residence could exercise their right to vote. Land-use zoning would be determined not alone by small groups living within limited boundaries but by all who might be affected by zoning ordinances.

There is little question but that the kinds of decisions which are made within metropolitan areas are determined to a considerable extent by who is permitted to participate in making them. It is most unlikely, for example, that traffic rules that seriously retard traffic flow on a small section of a through street could be adopted if the larger community had a voice in making the decision. Nor is it likely that industry would be permitted to develop next to an existing residential community without adequate buffers if all affected by zoning decisions participated in making them. But there is another side to the decision-making coin.

Not all those living within a metropolitan area have the same degree of interest in or are affected equally by decisions made within the area. If the principle that those most directly affected by decisions should have the greatest voice in making them is followed, smaller decision-making units may be justified. Parents whose children must cross a major street going to and from school are much more interested in traffic regulations that ensure the safety of their children than they are in commuters who use the street to go to and from work. They also know that their only hope to secure the approval of such restrictive regulations is to maintain a local municipal corporation so that only those living in the immediate area can participate in making them. If a small community within the larger metropolitan community wants to maintain a strictly single-family residential area, they know that one way to do it is to maintain a structural system that does not permit persons living in other parts of the area to participate in zoning decisions.

This is all to say that the political arrangements for decision making in metropolitan areas pose conflicts and that the position taken by participants in the system will generally depend on how their own interests are affected. Very few will perceive the problem as one involving basic philosophies of governmental participation; they are much more likely to be influenced by whether or not they use a major street to commute to work and whether they live in one of the houses threatened by the encroachment of industry.

PROPOSALS FOR CHANGE IN METROPOLITAN AREAS

Just how serious the problem of governing metropolitan areas is depends on who is asked to judge it. The rather consistent defeat of proposals to alter existing governmental patterns would indicate that the residents of the areas do not think it is very serious, but the amount of literature that has been published about metropolitan areas would indicate that the problems must be worse than the residents are willing to admit. Hardly any large metropolitan area has not been subjected to at least one study which was designed to discover what was wrong with it and what should be done to improve it. The Council of State Governments has published a volume on metropolitan areas, and at the national level the Advisory Commission on Intergovernmental Relations has produced reports dealing primarily with these areas. There have been so many suggested remedies for metropolitan areas that it is difficult to make a classification scheme that will include them all. The scheme used here is adopted from the extensive study of the metropolis by Bollens and Schmandt: (1) the cooperative approach, (2) the one-government approach, and (3) the two-level approach.[12]

[12] Bollens and Schmandt, *op. cit.*, pp. 13–15.

The Cooperative Approach

Practical problems faced by city officials as they try to cope with service problems in governmental units too small for the jobs to be done have forced these officials to improvise cooperative arrangements which, although they do not alter structure, provide some relief for their service problems. Many state constitutions and statutes now specifically provide the legal sanctions for intergovernmental cooperation. The wide variety of cooperative arrangements that have been introduced into metropolitan government may be grouped into three classes: (1) those in which one governmental unit contracts with another to perform services for it, (2) those in which two or more governmental units jointly operate some service facility under contractual arrangements, and (3) those in which two or more governmental units agree to assist one another when the need arises, usually in emergency situations.

Contracts for Specific Services   Perhaps the most extreme example of service by contract is the Lakewood Plan, so called because the city of Lakewood, California, contracts for the full range of municipal services from Los Angeles County.[13] The simplest form of service contract is one in which a city contracts with the county to collect its taxes on a fee basis. Between these two extremes there are many kinds of service contracts among governmental units within metropolitan areas. Public health services furnish an excellent example of the use of contractual arrangements to provide some unity in administration. Most counties maintain health departments, and in metropolitan areas these departments are staffed by professionals with a personal commitment to public health programs. Since their jurisdiction is often limited by the nature of metropolitan structure, they work within the limits the system imposes upon them. The county department lists the health service programs they are equipped to supply county-wide and establishes a formula by which charges to other governmental units will be computed. Cities within the county can, then, determine the services they wish to contract for. In St. Louis County, for example, some of the larger cities contract for the full range of health services, and to eliminate any question of legality, they appoint the Director of the County Health Department as their city health director or commissioner. Other smaller cities in the county contract only for the specific health services they feel are needed in their cities, and they pay accordingly.

Numerous examples may be cited to show the extent to which service contracts are used. City police departments contract for a central dispatching

[13] See Samuel K. Gove, *The Lakewood Plan*, University of Illinois Press, Urbana, 1961.

service, for care of prisoners, and for police training. Some smaller cities often contract for their total police protection, including routine patrol. Contracts for the uses of trunk sewers, for landfills for garbage disposal, for inspections of building construction, and for electrical and plumbing work are very common. Remember, the county in these cases is not rendering services on a county-wide basis, it is serving only those municipalities which seek the service and are willing and able to pay for it.

Joint Operation of Service Facilities   To ensure more efficient operation of expensive equipment, cities have entered into agreements for joint use of the equipment. Small cities have cooperative library arrangements whereby they jointly employ trained personnel and enlarge the book selections available to residents. Joint arrangements for erection and maintenance of traffic signals are common where city boundaries are major street intersections. The limited use made of this cooperation does not exhaust the possibilities. Joint construction and operation of incinerators for waste disposal, airports, and police radio stations are distinct possibilities.

Mutual Assistance Pacts   Most of the cities in metropolitan areas recognize their need for help in time of emergencies; therefore many of them have entered into agreements or associations which obligate each member to come to the assistance of the others. Fire protection is, perhaps, the best example of this kind of cooperation. A group of cities, each with its own professionally staffed fire department, agree to respond to the needs of the others. The arrangements are usually drawn up by a committee and passed in the form of identical ordinances by the councils of all cities involved. The fire alarm systems are integrated, and departments respond to calls close to them whether or not the scene of the fire is within its city boundaries.

Similar arrangements can be made for police cooperation by a system of deputizing the police of one city as peace officers in another or by deputizing city police officers as county police, which extends their jurisdiction throughout the county. Such mutual assistance pacts may be particularly valuable in civil defense work.

The Metropolitan Council Approach

Since the organization of the Supervisors Inter-county Committee in the Detroit area in 1954, 86 councils of government have been formed.[14] These

[14] For further discussion of this fairly recent movement see Bollens and Schmandt, *op. cit.*, pp. 392–395; Henry J. Schmandt, "The Areas Council— Approach to Metropolitan Government," *Public Management*, vol. 42, pp. 30–32, February, 1960; John K. Parker, "Cooperation in Metropolitan Areas through Councils of Government," *Public Management*, vol. 45, pp. 223–225, October, 1963.

councils generally consist of groups or committees of chief administrative officers of governmental units in the area. Their chief function is to provide a forum for the discussion of common problems and to seek some kind of voluntary and cooperative means of, at least, reducing the seriousness of the problems. These councils do not constitute any new formal governmental machinery, and they have no coercive powers. If any results come from council meetings, they will be limited to kinds of action upon which there is unanimity of opinion. Such a council in New York has dealt with problems of jet plane noise, in San Francisco with regional planning, and in St. Louis with air pollution.

The difficulty inherent in all types of cooperative arrangements is that the local units of government retain their independent decision-making power. Contracts can be canceled almost at will, and material aid agreements are likely to last only as long as no serious disagreement arises among the participants. There can be no doubt that, given the existing proliferation of governments in metropolitan areas ranging from very small ones to large ones, cooperative arrangements have resulted in improved services in some areas and have provided a useful dialogue among officials about common problems. There is a possibility, however, that such arrangements postpone a more realistic approach to metropolitan problems. The observer is often inclined to sense that the move for a metropolitan council or a series of cooperative arrangements is not really an attempt to seek rational solutions to recognizable problems but a conscious effort to prevent other solutions which will more seriously disturb existing power holders.

The selective character of cooperative arrangements also casts doubt on their ability to meet the needs for change in metropolitan areas. All metropolitan areas contain pockets of untouchables. Negro areas have often been excluded when a group of citizens seeks a municipal charter, they have been kept out of enlarged school districts, and they are by themselves unable to provide essential services at adequate levels. Cooperative arrangements are likely to leave these areas untouched, since the same kind of attitudes that isolated them in the first place will keep them out of the newer councils and joint agreements. Minority group communities are not the only ones that may be left out of cooperative arrangements.

The One-government Approach

The creation of a single municipal-type government for all of a metropolitan area appears, at first glance, to be the most rational approach to governmental problems in these highly urbanized areas. This approach seems particularly attractive if the entire area is within a single state; interstate metropolitan areas present special problems. The creation of a single government makes it possible to have an area-wide tax base and a uniform tax rate, and to allocate total revenues where the need is greatest, without regard to artificial political boundaries. Functions of government can be performed on an area-wide basis, ensuring a greater degree of coordination and uniformity. Insofar as the elimination of uneconomic small governments is accomplished and duplication and overlapping of services is minimized, a single government should be more efficient and economical. This approach has, however, met with great popular resistance and has had little opportunity to prove itself in practice. A number of avenues are available to a community which seeks to have a single metropolitan government. They may be summarized under two broad categories: (1) integration under a single large city, and (2) integration under an urban county government.

Integration under a Single City   In a metropolitan area where a core city includes a large majority of the total population in the area, this city may be used as the one government for the entire area. The processes of annexation or consolidation, used alone or in combination, could be the vehicle to accomplish this objective. In cities where population growth has been fairly recent and greater increases are expected, the city may annex large areas of surrounding territory before new municipalities have been incorporated around its borders. Oklahoma City, Phoenix, Houston, and Dallas have all annexed large areas of land on their borders. From 1950 to 1960 Oklahoma City increased its size from 5.8 square miles to 321.5 square miles, Phoenix expanded from 17.1 square miles to 187.4 square miles, Houston grew from 160.0 square miles to 328.1 square miles, and Dallas with 112.0 square miles in 1950 had increased to 179.9 square miles by 1960.[15]

Many older cities have not been able to expand so easily because numerous smaller cities have already been incorporated around their borders. Any attempt to expand the city to create a single government in these areas requires consolidation rather than annexation. This process has not produced as spectacular results as has annexation, since the legal restrictions are more severe. Whereas many cities can annex surrounding unincorporated territory without the consent of those living in the area to be annexed, this is not the case in consolidations. The usual procedure for consolidation is to require separate, favorable majorities within each city involved in the proposed consolidation; an unfavorable vote in any single city, regardless of how small it is,

---

[15] Bollens and Schmandt, *op. cit.*, pp. 412–414.

will defeat the proposal even though it is approved in the other cities. Many states, in order to encourage the consolidation of school districts, have provided that proposed consolidations need only a majority vote within the entire area involved; therefore favorable votes in some districts may cancel out unfavorable votes in others. Since this system has worked with considerable success for school districts in many states, it has been proposed as a way to achieve more integration in cities in metropolitan areas.

The Urban County   In 102 SMSAs a single county government has jurisdiction in the entire metropolitan area.[16] If the county government in these areas could be given adequate power and financial resources, it could constitute an area-wide metropolitan government. In some cases structural reorganization of the county government would be required to equip it to function effectively to perform municipal-type functions.[17] In order for the county to become the single government for the entire area, existing cities would have to be included in a county-city consolidation. In the two-level approach discussed later, the county could be the agent to handle all area-wide functions, and existing cities could continue to perform purely local functions.

In the larger metropolitan areas which include a number of counties, the single urban county approach offers less hope for successful integration. Jealousies among counties make change very difficult. State action, however, might either create a single new county for the entire area or consolidate all the area under one of the existing counties. If the days for governmental experimentation are not over, perhaps some state will come up with a new form of supermetropolitan corporation to assume responsibility for governing a single large complex metropolitan area.

The Two-level Approach   The practical difficulties involved in providing a single government for metropolitan areas have prompted many students of metropolitan politics to seek a compromise solution which provides a central government with territorial jurisdiction within the entire area but leaves existing governments to exercise local jurisdiction within their own boundaries.

[16] This does not include metropolitan areas in New England which are included in a single county, since these counties are not strong forms of government. See Committee for Economic Development, *op. cit.*, p. 44.

[17] For discussion of the urban county approach, see Victor Jones, "Urban and Metropolitan Counties," in International City Managers Association, *The Municipal Year Book*, Chicago, 1962, pp. 57–66, and *ibid.*, 1954, pp. 133–147; Stephen B. Sweeney and George S. Blair (eds.), *Metropolitan Analysis: Important Elements of Study and Action*, University of Pennsylvania Press, Philadelphia, 1958, pp. 99–122.

This is essentially the federal approach to metropolitan government. The major problems involved in developing federal systems are to determine what government shall be endowed with area-wide jurisdiction and to determine how total powers shall be allocated among the central government and the smaller units.

In some areas an existing county government may be revamped to constitute a central government, but this is extremely difficult in metropolitan areas which include two or more counties. Where a single very large city and a single county are within a metropolitan area, a city-county consolidated government might become the central government. A more practical solution may be to create a new multipurpose district government which includes the entire metropolitan area and assign to it area-wide functions. In any event the smaller units of government would continue to perform a limited number of local functions. One might hopefully assume that once such a federation is in operation, efforts would be made to reduce the number of governmental units within the area by annexation, consolidation, and disincorporation.

The problem of deciding which powers are to be delegated to the central government and which are to be left for local units is inherent in the nature of federalism. The rationale is, of course, that functions which can be described as area-wide will be within the province of the central unit and that the remaining, purely local functions will be retained by the other units. The difficulty is that, in practice, agreement on which functions of local government are area-wide in character is next to impossible. When federal schemes are drafted, the manner in which powers are distributed results from compromises among those involved in the process, rather than from the application of specific principles. Possible methods of identifying area-wide functions were discussed earlier in this chapter, but since each metropolitan area has its own myths, historical rivalries, and combinations of interests, a list acceptable in one area might be wholly unacceptable in another.[18]

The plan adopted for Dade County, Florida (Miami area), used an existing county government as the area-wide authority and kept existing municipalities for the performance of local functions. In addition to its responsibility for administering the wide range of area-wide functions, the county government was authorized to set minimum standards which municipal governments would be required to meet in performing their local services.[19]

[18] For a list of area-wide powers see *Proposed Charter for the City and County of St. Louis*, 1959, pp. 3–6.
[19] Bollens and Schmandt, *op. cit.*, pp. 460–463.

EVALUATION: POLITICS OF METROPOLITAN CHANGE

Considerable time, money, and physical and mental effort have been directed toward rearranging the governmental structure in America's large metropolitan areas, yet only minimum results have been achieved. Some success in Miami, Baton Rouge, and Nashville may be claimed, but a number of well-developed plans have gone down to defeat, as in Cleveland, St. Louis, Dayton, and Pittsburgh. Since most of the technical skill and expertise available have been called upon to devise rational schemes to integrate governments in metropolitan areas, why have these plans so often failed? The skill and attention which went into their preparation lead the observer to conclude that defeat was not due to defects in the organizational schemes devised nor to weaknesses in the specific charter document within which the schemes were incorporated. No doubt, with popular support and a little time to work out the bugs that would appear in making a paper plan operational, any of the plans could have functioned effectively. Many of them did not have an opportunity to prove themselves because (1) the rank-and-file metropolitan dweller does not see in the present operating patterns the problems which professional reformers and civic leaders discover and complain about, and (2) the nature of politics in metropolitan areas makes major changes very difficult.

The natural thing for an American citizen to do is to complain about his government and the service level it renders, but one should not conclude that because citizens complain about their city government, they are ready to give it up. The governmental expert can observe the morning and evening rush-hour traffic and prepare a pessimistic report about how the traffic problem is impeding the economic growth of the city. But what seems strange to many observers is the fact that those who commute in this heavy traffic twice a day do not think it is unbearable. Many of the ills of urban areas that receive great attention from urban planners, political scientists, and civic reformers are not perceived to be serious problems by the rank-and-file residents of these urban areas. As long as governmental functions are performed at the levels that are now common, no ground swell for governmental reform is likely to arise. Specific problems will arise in the system, and public indignation will demand some reform, but attention will focus narrowly on the specific problem involved and it will be taken care of by improvisation or by some minor change in the total governmental system. The point is, things do get done in metropolitan areas even though the arrangement of governmental agencies appears to be both inefficient and uneconomical. Streets are constructed and maintained, residents are supplied with pure water and other utilities, fires are put out, criminals are caught, and sewers carry away liquid wastes. The perfectionist can satisfy himself and some others that although things are getting done, they could be done better, but Mr. Average Citizen is not easily convinced that this is so. Empirical evidence that is available substantiates this conclusion. Studies in St. Louis and Dayton revealed no great public criticism with existing governmental services. A similar study in Cleveland revealed that only for bus and transit did the number "completely satisfied" fall below the 50 percent mark and for some services 89 and 90 percent expressed "complete satisfaction."[20] Perhaps it is merely a matter of poor communication, but nonetheless people living in metropolitan areas have not been convinced that their public services are so bad that they are willing to scrap the present governmental patterns to improve them.

Although, as indicated above, there has been no grass roots dissatisfaction with public services in large metropolitan areas, there have been expressions of dissatisfaction with existing governmental arrangements from many sources. Mayors of large core cities, students of politics and government, civic leaders in both the business and labor communities, and federal officials who administer grant-in-aid programs to urban areas have called for reassessment of the existing decentralized governmental system in metropolitan areas. Critics of the existing system have been people who command respect and have access to the mass media to make their positions known. Yet all the effort expended on metropolitan reform has produced little change. In fact, many of those who have worked for governmental reform in metropolitan areas have about abandoned hope that such reform is attainable through local action; they, therefore, hope that reform will be forced upon these areas through state or federal action. Why have reform attempts, even when supported by many of the leaders in the community, failed? There is probably no simple answer to this question, but some understanding of the problems involved can be found in the nature of the political system within which decisions in metropolitan areas must be made. The legal system which has permitted the creation of many small independent governmental units within metropolitan areas has produced local governments which are internally very much alike but which differ from one another in significant ways. Small monolithic communities have been created, to a large extent, by economic forces and by the nature of real estate development. New communities have often been created by action of a single group of real estate developers who have employed planners, architects, and engineers to lay out an entire com-

[20] *Ibid.*, pp. 495–496.

munity project. The kinds of housing constructed, the market price placed on dwelling units, the kind of commercial and recreational facilities provided, all have combined to determine the kinds of people attracted to the community.

As long as these communities were simply parts of larger governmental units they constituted only one of the many interest groups which influenced public policy decisions. When one of these communities felt that its voice was a minority one in the larger governmental arena, pressure developed to incorporate the community so that the important political decisions affecting its residents could be made locally where near-unanimity could be assured. Within a single county there may be many of these rather distinct communities, ranging from a Negro section where income levels are very low, through white working-class areas, upper-middle-class suburbs where professional people are the dominant group, to the residential areas of the very rich. In order to protect the character of these communities each has become a separate municipal corporation so that political decisions important to them can be made locally.

Some of the decisions most important to these individual communities relate to land-use control, the kind of housing that can be constructed, police service, and traffic regulation. Local control of decisions made in these policy areas can fairly well assure the future character of the community.

Once this system of local community autonomy has been established, any proposal to restructure the pattern of government constitutes a threat to these monolithic communities. Decisions which determine the future character of existing communities will, after reform, be made in a larger political arena composed of communities with differing images of how future development should proceed. The individual community which, as an independent government, can make its own decisions, will be able to to do no more than plead its case before a larger policy-making group which will be subject to pressures from other communities, some of which will have very different sets of values. Asking these communities to support a reform program which takes from them their power to make decisions on matters they think are very important and which transfers those powers to a government whose response to their desires cannot be predicted, may be too much to expect. Knowledge of this political reality forces many students to doubt the success of major reform efforts which require popular approval until the area in question changes its social and economic character. If existing social, economic, and racial groups are distributed more equally throughout the area so that one class can no longer dominate the decisions within a single city, much of the opposition to change may disappear. The mix of interests making decisions in a single city may then be not far different from the mix of interests that would be found if a single central government were given area-wide decision-making power. When this situation arrives, local approval for major change may be possible.

The kind of analysis applied above to areas where individual communities have common interests which they seek to protect by maintenance of the status quo may be used to account for opposition of other interest groups to metropolitan reform. Political party groups which can now dominate elections within existing governmental units may not be able to dominate elections that would be held in a much larger area created by a reform proposal. If we consider only a single large city and a single large county within a metropolitan area, the problem will become clear. Elections in the city may be dominated by a Democratic Party organization, while elections in the county may be won regularly by the Republicans; a consolidation will mean that one or the other is bound to lose its position of dominance. But even when the same political party dominates the large county and the core city, the committee organization in each of the areas may be as much in conflict as if control were in the hands of different parties. The city organization would fear integration that might give the county organization power within the entire area, and the county organization would fear that overall dominance would go to the city organization.

No analysis of the politics of metropolitan areas can be complete without a discussion of the position of Negroes. The core cities of metropolitan areas are increasingly becoming the residence of Negroes. Although there are Negro communities outside the core city, the number of residents in them is so small that their chances of influencing policy decisions outside the core city are slim indeed. As the proportion of Negroes in the central cities rises, the chances of their playing a major role in city politics increases. The number of Negro aldermen in central city legislatures has been increasing, and Negro political leaders can look forward hopefully to the time when they can elect mayors, as they have done in Cleveland, Ohio, and Gary, Indiana. If the central city government were to be abolished in favor of a new metropolitan government or if the existing central city government should become a government for the entire area, the strength of the Negro vote could be diluted to the point where they would elect a small minority of legislators and their chances of electing a chief executive would be reduced to zero. Given this outlook, it is not difficult to see why the large Negro vote in core cities will represent a potentially strong force in opposition to major change.

According to a similar line of reasoning, the large number of officers in the existing governmental units may constitute another obstacle for reformers to deal with. Although the number of officeholders does not itself represent a large bloc of votes, the fact that they can win elections within their political subdivisions or can be appointed to office indicates that they have some political influence with others. Therefore, whenever any reform proposal constitutes a threat to these local officials, they can rally a large vote to oppose it. Local officials who feel they have sufficient strength outside their local area to win election on an area-wide basis may see something to be gained by structural integration, but the majority will see only a possible dilution of their present power position.

This general analysis points up the difficulty of securing major metropolitan reform as long as the decision must be made within the local political system. If the decision can be transferred to a different arena, the negative pressures that exist on the local level will play a much less important role; i.e., if the decision to reform or not to reform is made at the state capital or in the United States Congress, the interest alignment is very different and change may be possible. The existing legal system makes it possible for reform to be accomplished by direct action at the state level, and it might well be accomplished indirectly by federal action through grant-in-aid programs.

BIBLIOGRAPHY

Books

Adrian, Charles R.: *Governing Urban America*, 2d ed., McGraw-Hill Book Company, New York, 1961, chap. 11.
Advisory Commission on Intergovernmental Relations: *Performance of Urban Functions: Local and Areawide*, Washington, September, 1963.
Bollens, John C.: *The States and the Metropolitan Problem*, Council of State Governments, Chicago, 1956.
———— (ed.): *Exploring the Metropolitan Community*, University of California Press, Berkeley, 1961.
———— and Henry J. Schmandt: *The Metropolis: Its People, Politics and Economic Life*, Harper & Row, Publishers, Incorporated, New York, 1965.
Committee for Economic Development: *Modernizing Local Governments*, New York, July, 1966.
Duncan, Otis D., and Albert J. Reiss, Jr.: *Social Characteristics of Urban and Rural Communities*, John Wiley & Sons, Inc., New York, 1956.
Fiser, Webb S.: *Mastery of the Metropolis*, Prentice-Hall, Inc., Englewood Cliffs, N.J., 1962.
Greer, Scott: *Governing the Metropolis*, John Wiley & Sons, Inc., New York, 1962.

————: *Metropolis: A Study in Political Culture,* John Wiley & Sons, Inc., New York, 1963.

Jones, Victor: *Metropolitan Government,* The University of Chicago Press, Chicago, 1942.

Sofen, Edward: *The Miami Metropolitan Experiment,* Anchor Books, Doubleday & Company, Inc., Garden City, N.Y., 1966.

Sweeney, Stephen B., and George S. Blair (eds.): *Metropolitan Analysis: Important Elements of Study and Action,* University of Pennsylvania Press, Philadelphia, 1958.

Vernon, Raymond: *Metropolis 1985,* Anchor Books, Doubleday & Company, Inc., Garden City, N.Y., 1963.

Warren, Robert O.: *Governments in Metropolitan Regions: A Reappraisal of Fractionated Political Organization,* Davis Institute of Government Studies, 1966.

Weaver, Robert C.: *The Urban Complex,* Anchor Books, Doubleday & Company, Inc., Garden City, N.Y., 1966.

Wood, Robert C.: *Suburbia: Its People and Their Politics,* Houghton-Mifflin, Boston, 1959.

————: *1400 Governments,* Harvard University Press, Cambridge, Mass., 1961.

Woodbury, Coleman (ed.): *The Future of Cities and Urban Development,* The University of Chicago Press, Chicago, 1953.

Articles

Banfield, Edward C.: "The Politics of Metropolitan Area Organization," *Midwest Journal of Political Science,* vol. 1, pp. 77–91, May, 1957.

Boyd, William J. D.: "Suburbia Takes Over," *National Civic Review,* vol. 54, pp. 294–298, June, 1965.

Grant, Daniel R.: "Urban and Suburban Nashville: A Case Study in Metropolitanism," *The Journal of Politics,* vol. 17, pp. 82–99, February, 1955.

Greenstein, Fred I., and Raymond E. Wolfinger, "The Suburbs and Shifting Party Loyalties," *The Public Opinion Quarterly,* vol. 11, pp. 473–482, winter, 1958–1959.

Meyerson, Martin, and Barbara Terrett: "Metropolis Lost, Metropolis Regained," *The Annals of the American Academy of Political and Social Science,* vol. 314, pp. 1–9, November, 1957.

Ostrom, Vincent, Charles M. Tubout, and Robert Warren: "The Organization of Government in Metropolitan Areas: A Theoretical Inquiry," *The American Political Science Review,* vol. 55, pp. 831–842, December, 1961.

Ylvisaker, Paul N.: "Innovation and Evolution: Bridge to the Future of Metropolis," *The Annals of the American Academy of Political and Social Science,* vol. 314, pp. 156–164, November, 1957.

PART 3

ORGANIZATIONAL STRUCTURE OF URBAN GOVERNMENT

7

GENERAL FORMS OF CITY GOVERNMENT

If there is any significance for political science in the different institutional patterns of government which have arisen in cities, it must be because these structural forms are variables which impinge on decision makers and affect the nature of decisions which flow from city government. No particular form of government is by its nature good or bad; each must be judged in terms of its effects on the process of resolving political conflict. If a pattern of government fairly consistently produces decisions which conform to the desires of an individual or a group, to them, it will be good, and their support for structural reform will be most difficult to get. A few who carry torches for governmental reform may actually think of form and structure as positive values in themselves, but if they rally any substantial organized support to the cause, it will be because organization leaders feel that the existing institutions tend to give preference to interests opposed to their own.

Form and structure do play a role in the decision-making process that is sufficiently significant to justify its examination, but they are only one of a number of factors operating within the political process to determine its output. When, after the turn of the century, a number of writers, led by Lincoln Steffens, focused attention on characteristics of city action that did not conform with the public norms of legitimate conduct, reform leaders arose to champion a holy crusade against the evils of city graft and corruption. Rightly or wrongly, the target of these attacks was the political boss and the political organizations through which he supported his position of power, and the remedies most often suggested to cure these evils were changes in governmental institutions. Many of the things which are considered in this text, such as the professional city manager, nonpartisan elections, direct primaries, permanent registration of voters, and the merit system of civil service, were responses of "good government" groups which felt compelled to strike a blow for decency and against government corruption. It probably did not occur to early reformers that as long as boss control produced governmental actions favorable to large groups of the city's population, more than structural change would be required to unseat him. Certainly the city manager form of government in Kansas City did not undermine the political strength of Boss Pendergast; he simply adjusted his mode of operation to the new structural arrangement.

Forms of government establish lines of access to those who are in positions of power; they make it easier for some and harder for others to influence decision makers and to get kinds of governmental action favorable to their interests. Forms of government may well be a significant factor in attracting or discouraging certain kinds of persons to seek elective office, and certainly the form which prescribes election of some officeholders rather than executive appointment affects the pool of available candidates for these offices. Americans tend to be constitutionally minded in their approach to government; therefore form and structures as prescribed in legal documents such as city charters may condition their behavior. The fact that a city charter specifically refers to the "strong mayor" or "weak mayor" may have significant psychologic impact on the incumbent of the office, since he is conditioned to follow what he considers to be the basic law.

Recent literature in political science has tended to seek factors other than form and structure of government to account for the output of the political system, but some fairly recent studies indicate that this variable cannot be neglected as one which helps account for political behavior in cities. Williams and Adrian, in a study of four Midwestern cities, observed:

> The authors felt prior to the study that minor structural differences were insignificant but the data have indicated that this was not so in all situations. Indeed, most structural features appeared to affect in some way the access or influence of particular groups.[1]

[1] Oliver P. Williams and Charles R. Adrian, *Four Cities: A Study in Comparative Policy Making*, University of Pennsylvania Press, Philadelphia, 1963, pp. 55, 58.

In particular, the study indicated that elections of councilmen by wards appeared to increase the influence of lower socioeconomic groups and the absence of direct primaries prior to general elections increased the chances of election of persons from higher socioeconomic groups.

Eugene Lee's study of 192 municipalities in California was concerned, primarily, with nonpartisan elections, and he indicates that the absence of formal political organizations tended to increase the influence of the professional, managerial, and sales classes in city policy making.[2]

Robert Salisbury, in observing the political process in St. Louis, concluded that peculiarities in the structure of government play a significant role "in shaping the nature and scope of political conflict in the city." The specific structural arrangement referred to is the existence of two sets of officers operating within the city. The state constitution of Missouri stipulates that St. Louis shall be both a city and a county; therefore it has a set of city officials as well as a full complement of county officers. Under the home rule charter, most city administrators are appointed by a strong mayor and their employees are covered by a merit system. County officers, on the other hand, are popularly elected, and they select their employees on a patronage basis. Business leaders depend on the mayor to support broad policies essential to create the kind of climate necessary to attract industry and to provide the city services necessary for economic growth, while lower-income interests, who seek specific favors rather than board policy implementation, find easy access to the elected county officers. He states his general conclusions as follows:

> If the data reviewed here permit one to offer a tentative statement about relationships between interests, party, and structure, it would appear that the interest group system, as Bentleyans argue it must be, is basic. At the same time, however, the governmental structure affects in critical ways the manner in which these interests will be articulated into political parties, and in so doing it plays an important role in determining the scope and intensity of political conflict in the community.[3]

The particular models of city governmental structure presented here are not intended to represent the exact patterns of government in any specific cities. In fact, few cities in America have identical governmental forms. The

[2] Eugene Lee, *The Politics of Nonpartisanship: A Study of California Elections*, University of California Press, Berkeley, 1960.

[3] Robert H. Salisbury, "St. Louis Politics: Relationships among Interests, Parties, and Governmental Structure," *Western Political Quarterly*, vol. 13, p. 506, June, 1960. Reprinted by permission of the University of Utah, copyright owners.

best that can be done is to make a reasonable scheme for classifying city governments that will bring within a single category cities which have significant characteristics in common. Examination of the government of any specific city will reveal certain characteristics which clearly place it in one of the classes that will be described, but certain elements of its form will not fit the model exactly.

MAYOR-COUNCIL GOVERNMENT

Prior to the twentieth century, when a few cities began to experiment with new governmental structures, the mayor-council form of government was the accepted pattern for all American cities. The identifying characteristics of this plan of city government are:

1. A mayor who is designated as the chief executive of the city and who is popularly elected for a fixed term of office.

2. A city legislative body, called either a council or board of aldermen, whose members are popularly elected. Although legislators are usually elected from representative districts called wards, this is not a distinguishing characteristic of the plan.

3. A number of major administrative officers who head the departments which are responsible for the day-to-day operations of the city government. These department heads may be popularly elected or appointed by the mayor, usually with approval of the council. In most cities operating under this plan some of the administrators are popularly elected while others are appointed by the mayor.

4. One or more municipal courts. In very small cities the mayor may act as the judge, but in the larger cities judges are either popularly elected or appointed by the mayor with council approval.

5. Numerous boards and commissions which play some role in the administration of the functions of the city. Although some such boards exist in cities with other forms of government, they are apt to play a less active role in administration of service activities than in the mayor-council form.

The idea of separation of powers and of checks and balances so much stressed by those who designed the structure of the national government is inherent in mayor-council government, particularly the strong-mayor variety. The powers of each branch are set forth specifically in the city charter, and access to the courts is readily available to keep the executive from encroaching upon the prerogatives of the legislature and vice versa. Likewise, the usual internal checks are firmly incorporated in the charter. The mayor has the veto power to hold as a threat over the council, and in some cities, he presides over council sessions. He addresses the council on matters that he thinks deserve their attention, and if he feels he is in a strong position of political leadership, he may use his political power to influence the actions of individual councilmen. On the other hand, the council controls the purse strings and thereby determines the amount of money available for public purposes, and the mayor cannot spend tax money until he receives council authorization through budget approval or appropriation ordinances. Generally, appointments by the mayor must be submitted to the council for approval, and many charters provide that the mayor can be removed by council action before his regular term expires.

Mayor-council government has evolved over a long period of time, and various political events have had their effect in altering its structure. Since there is such a wide variation in the character of the form in different cities, observers have, for purposes of analysis, divided mayor-council cities into two broad classes: the weak-mayor–council form and the strong-mayor–council form.

The Weak-mayor–Council Form

The major difference between the two variations of the mayor-council form of city government is in the position of the mayor and his relation to city administration (see Figure 7.1). Most city governments prior to 1880 operated with the weak-mayor structure. Although charters may have specified that the mayor shall take care that the ordinances of the city are faithfully executed, he was given few tools by which he could fulfill this responsibility. What administrative departments were created were administered either by a board or commission or by a department head who was popularly elected. Since the mayor had no legal means by which he could direct the activities of administrative heads, the council often assumed a direct role in administration. Council committees often bore the same names as the administrative departments, and administrative heads looked to these committees both for support and direction. Appropriations for support of administrative activities were sought directly through council committees, with little or no clearance through the mayor. In some cities operating under this form of government the chairman of the streets committee of the council, for example, actually exercised management control over the director of streets who was, in name, the head of the department. The head of the department felt that there was little the mayor could do for him, and he knew the chairman of the streets committee could be very influential in presenting his needs to the council.

With respect to the position of the mayor in relation to the council, there is little difference between the weak-mayor and the strong-mayor system. In

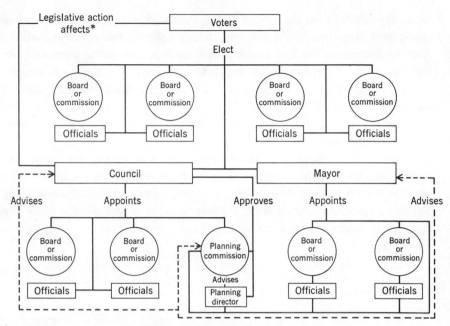

* Administrative action of mayor is usually subject to council. Planning commission may
  advise other boards, commissions or officials.

Figure 7.1   The weak-mayor–council form of government. (Source: Charles A. Joiner, *Organizational Analysis: Political, Sociological, and Administrative Processes of Local Government,* **The Michigan State University Press, East Lansing, 1964, p. 26)**

each the mayor may preside over council meetings, deliver messages, and exercise the veto power. The weak mayor may, in practice, lose some of the political pressure that can be exerted upon legislators by a strong mayor simply because he has little or no patronage which he can use to bargain with them.

The weak mayor has few or none of the tools usually given to the strong mayor by which unity of administration is achieved. Since he can neither appoint nor remove key administrative officers, he cannot direct any of them to fit their public statements and administrative actions into a single pattern designed to achieve broad policies worked out by the mayor in party conferences or in cabinet meetings.

The weak-mayor–council form reflects the impact of the Jeffersonian and Jacksonian philosophies on the American political system. These philosophies implied that the degree of democracy achieved may be measured roughly by the number of officers that are popularly elected, and that the character of governmental work was so simple that no special competence was required of administrative officials. The system also reflects the fear of a strong executive officer that can be traced to colonial opposition to the English colonial governors; this fear also influenced the nature of the office of state governor provided in early state constitutions.

The Strong-mayor—Council Form

Strong-mayor—council government evolved naturally by adapting the weak-mayor—council form to meet increasing demands upon city government around the turn of the twentieth century when increasing urbanization produced a need for more energetic leadership (see Figure 7.2). In many respects it may represent an attempt more nearly to implant the national model in city government. The identifying characteristics of the plan are:

1. A mayor, who is popularly elected, with formally assigned power to exercise control over and give direction to the major administrative departments of city government. This means that he appoints department heads (generally with council approval) and can remove them from office if they fail to meet the demands he makes upon them.

2. A legislative body, called either a council or board of aldermen, whose members are popularly elected either from wards or at large. The same forces which produced a strong mayor generally had some impact on the structure of legislatures; therefore elections at large are more probable in the strong-mayor cities than they are in cities with weak mayors, but this is not essential to the plan.

3. A number of major administrative officers who are appointed by the mayor. Usually council approval is required for these appointments, but this is often a matter of form, since the council, except in unusual circumstances, gives this approval. In most cases there will be one or more administrative officers popularly elected. City treasurers, comptrollers, and prosecuting officers may remain elective even in a strong-mayor system.

4. One or more municipal courts, with the judges either appointed by the mayor with the consent of the council or popularly elected. In general, the structure of the courts in cities is not significantly different in the various forms of city government.

5. Some semi-independent boards and commissions are found in the strong mayor-council cities, but they will probably not administer major city functions; often they are advisory in character and do not have direct administrative authority.

This outline shows that the major differences in the two forms is in the nature of the office of mayor. With the new position assigned to him, he is expected to assume control of the total administrative task of the city, and give to it coordination and unity of purpose. This change was often achieved by campaigns which directed attention to the waste, inefficiency, and over-

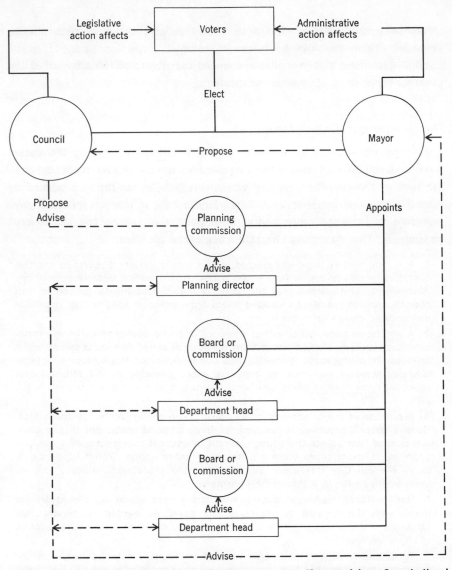

Figure 7.2   The strong-mayor form of local government. (Source: Joiner, *Organizational Analysis: Political, Sociological, and Administrative Processes of Local Government*, p. 27)

lapping of responsibility that could be found in the weak-mayor cities and which emphasized that a strong mayor could, by his central control, increase efficiency and economy by eliminating duplication, overlapping responsibility, and lack of departmental cooperation. At the same time the supporters of the strong mayor asserted that governmental administration would be more responsible to the people since they could hold one man responsible for the total administrative process.

Although the structure of the council is not necessarily altered in the strong-mayor form, in operation it may be significantly affected. The weak position of the mayor tended to swing council committees into the administrative process, and, as was noted earlier, committee chairmen maintained close relations with and exercised a great deal of influence over administrative heads. When the mayor assumes direct responsibility for administrative activities, department heads must look to him for advice and direction rather than to council committees. The end result may be for the council to concentrate more of its time on policy formulation and less on administrative control. As the mayor's executive position was strengthened, his political leadership stature increased and, as a consequence, his influence in the legislative process was enhanced. Councilmen sought his support for reelection, asked him to appoint certain political friends for office, and urged his public endorsement of bills which they were sponsoring. As a response to such favorable actions by the mayor, he expected a friendly response from them on legislative matters which were of interest to him.

Change from a weak to a strong mayor has produced a shorter ballot in terms of the number of officers popularly elected and has given the mayor tools which he can use to strengthen his position of leadership in the local political organization.

Examination of the governmental structure in any modern American city whose charter prescribes the mayor-council form of government will reveal that it includes certain aspects of both the weak- and the strong-mayor pattern. In fact, it may prove difficult to be sure whether some cities should be classified as weak- or strong-mayor cities.

The real strength of a mayor, however, cannot always be ascertained merely by reference to the list of powers formally ascribed to him in the city charter. The personality of the mayor, which may or may not make him a "leader type," his own image of the proper role for a chief executive, and the nature of the organization which produced his election are all factors that influence the position occupied by the mayor in the total political process. Meyerson and Banfield give an excellent account of a strong mayor who operates within the framework of a weak-mayor formal structure.

> In Chicago, political power was highly decentralized *formally* but highly centralized *informally*. The city had what textbooks in municipal government called a weak-mayor form of government to be sure, but it also had a powerful mayor, or, if not a powerful leader of the council.

This paradox of a "weak" government that was strong was to be explained by the presence of the Democratic machine, an organization parallel to the city government but outside of it, in which power sufficient to run the city was centralized. The weakness of the city government was offset by the strength of the party.[4]

Perhaps the most significant policy area in which the position of the mayor has been strengthened is in fiscal policy. A badge of the strong mayor is the executive budget. This implies that an overall spending program based on estimates of available income is prepared by the mayor and submitted to the council by him as his program. Along with this responsibility usually goes the authority of the mayor to veto specific items from the council's appropriations or even to reduce specific items without affecting other sections of appropriation bills. In many cities where a change from the weak- to the strong-mayor system has been accomplished, the mayor is given the added authority, through an appointed comptroller, to determine when a proposed expenditure is or is not within the intent of the appropriation.

The strong-mayor governmental structure has been given additional stature by the appearance in a number of our large cities of mayors who are effective, in terms of positive action secured. Examples such as DeLesseps Morrison of New Orleans, Raymond R. Tucker of St. Louis, Joseph Clark and Richardson Dilworth of Philadelphia, and Albert Cobo of Detroit have been cited as evidence of "New Strength in City Hall."[5]

COMMISSION FORM

The commission form of city government may be considered as the first major experiment in local government in this country. The mayor-council form and its variants can be traced to the English system, which was transmitted through the colonies to the new nation. Although those who have studied the history of the commission plan find similar patterns in Sacramento as early as 1863, and point out that New Orleans in 1870 and Memphis in 1873 had governmental structures similar in many ways to this plan, modern commis-

---

[4] Martin Meyerson and Edward C. Banfield, *Politics, Planning and the Public Interest*, The Free Press, The Macmillan Company, Glencoe, Ill., 1955, p. 287. Reprinted with permission of The Macmillan Company, copyright 1955 by The Free Press, a division of The Macmillan Company.

[5] Editors of Fortune, *The Exploding Metropolis*, Doubleday & Company, Inc., Garden City, N.Y., 1958, pp. 62–91.

sions are generally copied after the plans adopted in Galveston in 1901 and Des Moines in 1907.[6]

In 1900 parts of Galveston were severely damaged by a tremendous tidal wave. Besides the great destruction that was wrought upon private residences and commercial and industrial property, municipal facilities and public works were destroyed or so badly damaged that a complete reconstruction was recognized as imperative. Lack of public confidence in the existing political system to plan and execute such a reconstruction program with sufficient dispatch led an existing nongovernmental organization to take the lead in seeking new governmental devices. The Deepwater Committee had been created to improve the city's harbor facilities and was composed of representatives of the business community. After a subcommittee of the committee drafted a proposed new city charter, it was submitted to the Texas legislature for adoption, and was put into effect in 1901.

The original charter had provided for five city commissioners, three of whom were to be appointed by the Texas Governor and two of whom were to be elected by the Galveston voters. The section providing for appointive commissioners was successfully challenged in the courts as being in violation of the state constitution, and the legislature altered the charter to make all commissioners popularly elected.

Success stories of the results of the Galveston experiment reached other cities which were considering reforms in their governmental structure, and the system, with alterations, was copied in other cities. Action in Des Moines did much to add to the popularity of the plan. In the Des Moines experiment there were at least four significant new features: (1) nomination and election of commissioners was put on a nonpartisan basis, (2) through a recall procedure, the commissioners could be removed by a popular vote before the expiration of their regular terms, (3) through the initiative and referendum, a certain degree of popular control over legislative power was provided, and (4) most city employees were placed under a merit system which was designed to prevent commissioners from building political machines through the manipulation of job patronage.

The early years of the commission plan coincided with reform movements stimulated by the exposures of graft and corruption in various cities, and the

[6] For a more complete discussion, see T. S. Chang, *History and Analysis of the Commission and City Manager Plans of Municipal Government in the United States,* University of Iowa Ph.D. thesis, Iowa City, 1918; and Clinton R. Woodruff, *City Government by Commission,* D. Appleton & Company, Inc., New York, 1914.

plan spread rapidly. By 1917, 500 cities were operating under this form of city government. The decline in favor of the commission plan of municipal government in recent years can probably be accounted for by the rise in popularity of a new form (council-manager) which was catching the attention of efficiency-minded reformers rather than by specific dissatisfaction with the plan itself. Although the number of cities operating under the plan has decreased rather sharply, it still persists in enough cities to make it of more than merely historical importance.

Nature of the Plan

The most significant feature of the commission form is its complete break with the idea of separation of legislative and executive powers (see Figure 7.3). A group of commissioners (usually from three to seven) is delegated, by charter, both legislative and administrative authority. The commissioners meet regularly as a group and at such meetings enact ordinances setting tax rates, authorizing expenditures, planning bond issues, approving contracts for repair and maintenance of physical facilities, zoning land for particular uses, and, in fact, doing all the kinds of things a city council does in a mayor-council system. But each commissioner, as an individual officeholder, is head of one of the city's administrative departments. In this capacity he hires employees in his department, prepares estimates of his budget needs, decides matter of administrative policy, and in general, does the work that would be performed by a department head in any other form of government.

Another significant feature of the plan that sets it apart from any of the others discussed in this chapter is the absence of any single chief executive officer. The mayor performs this function under the mayor-council system and the manager is an administrative director in the council-manager system, but none of the commissioners is given similar authority. It is true that one of the commissioners is usually given the title of mayor, but charters generally assign to him no greater administrative authority than any of the other commissioners have. By virtue of his title, he sits as chairman at commission meetings and is the titular head of the city for ceremonial and legal purposes, but his executive power is not legally increased by his having the title of mayor.

Although the basic form of government is similar in all cities classed as commission-governed cities, there are many variations in the plan from city to city. A large majority of commissioners are elected on a nonpartisan ballot, but this is not true in all of them and is not considered an essential element

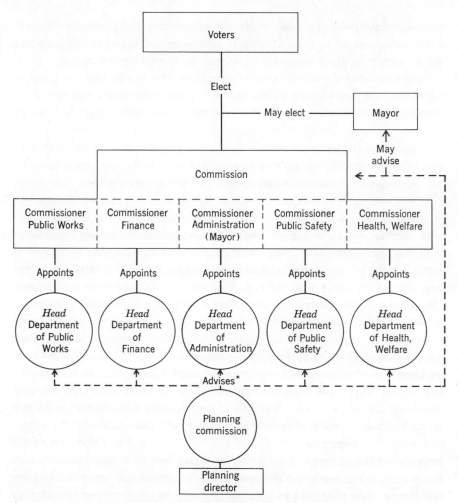

*May be in any one department. There may be no executive elected under the commission form.
Each commissioner is head of his department. The commissioners sit collectively as the council.

Figure 7.3   The commission form of government. (Source: Joiner, *Organizational Analysis: Political, Sociological, and Administrative Processes of Local Government*, p. 28)

of the plan. The method of selecting the chairman of the commission (who usually has the title of mayor) varies in different cities. Some charters provide that the commissioner elected to head one of the departments (i.e., public safety) shall be ex officio commission chairman. In other cities the chairman is selected by the commission after each election.

In some cities the commissioners are elected to head specific departments and the election ballot permits the voter to make a selection for each administrative department; in other cities the voters select the number of commissioners provided by the charter, and after their election, the commissioners assign each one of its members to a specific administrative duty.

Terms of office of commissioners vary from city to city, and in some all commissioners are elected at the same time while in others the terms are staggered so that only a part of the commission can change in a single election.

If one notices that each year a few cities abandon the commission plan and no new city adopts it, he may assume that in time the form will disappear, but more careful observation will reveal that it has already been abandoned in practice in some cities even though no formal charter change has occurred. In some cities which operate under a state statutory charter which clearly provides the structural pattern of the commission form, the actual practice conforms more nearly to the mayor-council system. The commissioner of public safety is automatically designated mayor, and he is often reelected term after term while no other commissioner has enjoyed such long tenure. The citizens of the community are, for the most part, unaware that their mayor is any different from the mayors of neighboring cities which operate under mayor-council charters. The voters look to him for leadership, and he plays out his public role just as mayors are expected to do. Moreover, other commissioners accept his leadership on policy matters, and although he does not appoint administrators as other mayors do, he certainly exercises influence over them. In fact, if an observer were to draw a chart to represent the pattern of government in some commission cities by actually observing the actors and without reference to formal charter provisions, he would come up with a diagram not far different from what he would find in a mayor-council city. Since such adjustments can be made informally within the commission structure, many cities may cling to their old commission charters even though they have ceased to follow some of its significant features.

Any attempt to judge the significance of institutional arrangements must take into account how they affect the nature of decisions that emanate from the system. Anyone who supports the commission form of goverment in a city, probably does so because he thinks it gives access to the decision-making process to individuals and groups predisposed to make decisions in conformance with his values. His judgment is apt to be arrived at from a knowledge of the kinds of people who have in the past been able to gain control of the city offices and the nature of the decisions they have made. There is very little empirical evidence to support generalizations about the specific effects of the form of government upon the nature of final decisions made in cities, but some observations can be made about commission government which might be tested by research techniques.[7]

1. Since the commission form of government abandons the familiar separation of powers and the checks-and-balances principle regularly associated with American governmental structures, it may facilitate decisive and positive action to solve pressing problems. It arose to prominence out of a crisis situation, and it may be most effective in such circumstances.

2. Since total legislative and executive power is concentrated in the hands of a small number of commissioners, internal friction and conflict may be minimized. The practice of electing all commissioners at the same time from the city at large and often on a single slate may also serve to keep conflict within the government at a low level since parochial interests are minimized.

3. The shortness of the ballot (in terms of number of officials to be elected) may affect both the nature of the candidates who present themselves for public office and the groups within the electorate who actually go to the polls. Observers have suggested that more business and professional men (therefore those in a higher socioeconomic bracket) are willing to seek office in commission cities. Empirical evidence is lacking to support it, but proponents of the short ballot claim it attracts more voters who are not active in regular political parties or in established political interest groups.

4. The commission form is not likely to receive strong support from regular party organizations. One reason for this is that most such cities generally operate with nonpartisan elections and job patronage is reduced through the use of a merit system, but perhaps a more important factor is that no city officials operate from a ward base. Party organizations are based on wards, with party representatives in each ward, and the success of party machines is determined by the ability of the central authority to have local leaders who can be counted on to deliver the ward. At least part of the ward leader's strength comes from his relationship with a popularly elected ward councilman. The establishment of close working relations between a ward party leader and a councilman elected at large is much more difficult to achieve. From this we may infer that civic reform groups may have less competition from party organizations in commission cities than in those with the mayor-council form of government.

COUNCIL-MANAGER GOVERNMENT

If one looks for an innovation in governmental structure that has caught on sufficiently in this country to become a dominant form, the council-manager model of city government is an excellent example. Not only have more cities with populations over 10,000 in this country adopted the plan than any other, but it has become well established in Canada, Ireland, and in some of the European countries.

[7] Views about the Commission Plan may be found in E. S. Bradford, *Commission Government in American Cities*, The Macmillan Company, New York, 1911, and in C. M. Fassett, "The Weaknesses of Commission Government," *National Municipal Review*, vol. 9, pp. 642–647, October, 1920.

Some disagreement exists as to the city in which the system started, but many students give credit to Staunton, Virginia, for having the first city manager in this country.[8] In 1907 a committee was created in Staunton to study ways and means for improving the efficiency of the city government. At that time considerable publicity was being given to the successes of the commission form in Galveston, but since the Virginia constitution required a mayor-council government in cities of Staunton's size, the committee had no choice but to retain that general form or seek an amendment to the state constitution. Rather than try for an amendment, the city council, by ordinance, provided for an office of general manager within the regular mayor-council structure. In 1908 the council appointed an engineer as the city's first general manager. Although the Staunton experiment did not receive widespread attention in the popular press, it was known to students of local government throughout the country.

Many students like to credit Lockport, New York, with having started the council-manager form of government. In 1911 Richard A. Childs, one of the best-known figures in local government reform movements, prepared a proposed charter for Lockport at the request of the board of trade of that city. The board sought action from the state legislature to put the charter into effect, but favorable action was never taken. The proposed charter was really a variation of the commission form with the addition to it of a chief executive officer to be known as a city manager, and the proposed plan was referred to at the time as a commission-manager plan. Although this charter never became effective in Lockport, it was widely publicized and certainly had an effect on those who were considering charters in other places. Mr. Childs, who is now generally acknowledged as the father of the council-manager system, was a leader in the short-ballot movement, and the organization interested in the short ballot endorsed the new plan since the only elected officers were councilmen.

The first city in the United States to operate under a council-manager charter was Sumter, South Carolina. A charter embodying the new form was granted to Sumter by the state legislature in 1912. The first city to adopt a council-manager plan under home rule was Dayton, Ohio, in 1913. Dayton was also the first city over 100,000 in population to adopt this form of government. Although the plan spread rapidly after the Dayton adoption, its greatest acceptance has been since the Second World War.

---

[8] For an early account of the council-manager plan see T. S. Chang, *op. cit.;* also Harold A. Stone et al., *City Manager Government in the United States,* Public Administration Service, Chicago, 1940, chap. 1; and National Municipal League, *The Story of the Council-Manager Plan,* New York, revised, 1959.

TABLE 7.1   Forms of Government in Cities of over 5,000 Population

Year	Council-Manager		Mayor-Council	
	No. of cities	Percent of total	No. of cities	Percent of total
1941	315	15.5	1,305	64.2
1951	593	25.6	1,389	59.9
1961	1,114	37.5	1,595	53.7
1966	1,245	40.3	1,600	51.8

Source: The *Municipal Year Books* of the years listed.

The above table gives some indication of the growth of the plan since 1941.

In 1912, 212 cities were operating under the council-manager plan, but this figure included cities of 1,000 or more in population; the totals above include only cities of 5,000 or more. It is interesting to notice that while the percentage of total cities with the council-manager form of government has increased from 15.5 to 40.3 percent from 1941 to 1966, the percentage of cities with the mayor-council form has dropped during the same period from 64.2 to 51.8 percent.[9]

Nature of the Plan

There is no such thing as a standard or typical council-manager plan. The *Model City Charter*, prepared by the National Municipal League, incorporates the council-manager form of government and has been used widely as a pattern by many charter commissions, but numerous variations are found in the charters of cities classified as having this form (see Figure 7.4). Certain features of the plan, however, are fairly uniform and are included in most council-manager cities.

1. A city council with legislative powers is popularly elected. Considerable variations exist among council-manager cities as to size and method of selection, but in general, the number of councilmen is small (usually nine or less), and they are more often elected at large than from wards.

[9] Of the 2,007 places in the continental United States that had council-manager government in 1965, the following states had the greatest numbers: California, 269; Texas, 162; Michigan, 151; Maine, 149; Pennsylvania, 136; Florida, 105; and North Carolina, 97.

According to the International City Managers Association, *The Municipal Year Book*, 1966, pp. 73, 74, a total of 86 places have abandoned the plan by vote of the people since 1908.

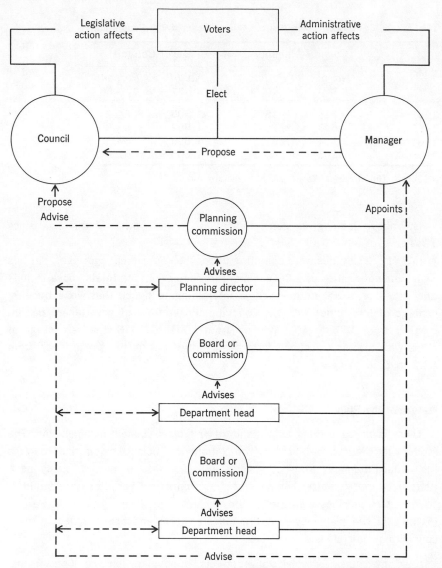

Figure 7.4   The council-manager form of government. (Source: Joiner, *Organizational Analysis: Political, Sociological, and Administrative Processes of Local Government*, p. 29)

2. A chief administrative officer, generally called a city manager, is chosen by the council. Although there are many exceptions, the general rule is that the manager is chosen on the basis of his professional training and experience and that he serves as long as a majority of the city council is satisfied with his work.

3. Major administrative officers (department heads) are appointed by the manager and serve as long as their performance is satisfactory to him.

4. A presiding officer of the city council, usually with the title of mayor, is the nominal head of the city. He is a regular voting member of the council but possesses no more administrative authority than any other council member. In the event that legal papers must be served on the city, they will be served upon the mayor, and if the city should need to call upon the governor for help from the national guard, the call would go in the name of the mayor.

More important than the structural arrangements that distinguish the council-manager form of government from other forms is the philosophy which undergirds the plan and conditions the behavior of those who function as officers under it, those who are decision leaders in it, and those who in a judicial capacity must pass judgments on its powers and its actions.

1. Proponents of the plan assume that a reasonably clear line can be drawn between functions of a city government that are policy-making in character and those that are administrative in nature. The first of these functions is delegated to the council, and the second is accepted as the prerogative of the manager. Council-manager charters specify in considerable detail the powers and duties of the city council and of the manager in order to identify those that are policy-making in nature and those that involve execution of policy. In practice, however, this dichotomy often breaks down, and many of the conflicts between managers and their councils arise over differences of opinion as to what is policy and what is administration.

2. Supporters of council-manager government maintain that the tasks involved in operating a modern city are technical in character and, therefore, require the services of a specially trained manager for their proper performance. This notion is consonant with the economy and efficiency movement that influenced many governmental reforms in the early part of the twentieth century. Much of the management philosophy stressed in schools of business administration is assumed to be relevant to city management as well as to business administration. Ability to coordinate the efforts of competent city workers and accomplish tasks with a minimum of expenditure of manpower and money, rather than ability to build and manage a political organization, is assumed to be the chief prerequisite of a city manager.

3. Council-manager government rests on the assumption that city management can become professionalized and that city managers merit the same kind of recognition accorded to business managers, school superintendents, lawyers, and doctors. Experience over fifty years produces some evidence to support this assumption. The International City Managers Association is well established, numbers among its membership most of the city managers in the country, and through its code of ethics exercises some influence over the development of the profession. Schools of public administration with special courses designed to train city managers are affiliated with some of the well-known universities in the country. The association, through its literature and annual meetings, serves as a reference group to influence the behavior of managers in the cities where they work. In fact, a city manager may prefer to risk dismissal from his job rather than compromise what he feels are the accepted standards of his professional colleagues.

4. Advocates of the council-manager form maintain that the public can assure responsible government through popular control of the legislature only. They

assume that the type of decisions which are of concern to people living in cities are within the province of the council rather than in that of the executive. Underlying this assumption is the notion that the city council will decide what is to be done and the chief administrator will simply see that it is accomplished effectively and with a minimum of expenditure. Some of the questions that have been raised about further extension of this form of government indicate that, at least in the minds of some observers, the public is as interested in how programs are carried out as they are in what programs should be undertaken. Therefore, in practice, managers do become directly involved in the conflict issues which arise within the political system of which they are a part, since the manner in which city functions are administered produces conflicts just as serious as are policy questions which arise in the council.

Advocates of the council-manager plan for cities have often, particularly during the early years of its development, compared it in a favorable way with the typical corporate structure of modern business organizations. The analogy implies that stockholders, as voters in the corporation, represent the electorate in the city, the corporate board of directors represents the city council as the policy-making body, and the general manager or president of the company is the counterpart of the city manager. This kind of comparison gives the plan a certain prestige with businessmen and those who contend that cities should be run like businesses, but it repels many citizens whose contacts with big-business *modus operandi* have been unpleasant. In fact, a much more likely comparison can be made of city-manager government with the structure of government which has developed in public school districts. Here the electorate is the same in each case; the voters of the school district choose a school board as the policy-making agency just as the voters of the city elect a council. The school board hires a professional superintendent as the chief executive officer of the board, and the council selects a city manager to be the chief executive. The superintendent appoints administrators, either assistant superintendents in large systems or principals in small systems, and the city managers appoint department heads. The similarities in these two governmental units indicate that the council-manager form of government is not an entirely new idea introduced into the American political system but is an adaptation from other governmental units which have received general acceptance.

The popularity of the council-manager form does not mean that mayor-council government is on its way out. While the percentage of cities with the council-manager form of government has declined from 59.9 percent in 1951 to 51.8 in 1966, the total number of cities over 5,000 classed as mayor-council cities has increased from 1,389 in 1951 to 1,600 in 1966. One may venture a guess that in the future the job of classifying cities as council-manager or as mayor-council may become increasingly difficult. Many competent observers see distinct advantages in each of the forms and at the same time find features in each of which they disapprove. Therefore, as new council-manager charters are authorized, their draftsmen may seek to incorporate into them what they think are the best features of the mayor-council system. Likewise, drafters of new mayor-council charters may seek to include what they think are the best features of mayor-council government but weave into them features of the council-manager system which they find attractive. The result may tend to erase some of the sharp differences now found in the two forms, and a comparison of the actual operations of two cities classed with different structural forms may well reveal that their differences are more in name than in reality. Some evidence is already available to demonstrate this trend. The short-ballot idea, which was an important consideration in sparking interest in council-manager government, has found its way into mayor-council charters, so that the mayor may be the only popularly elected executive officer. Likewise, such concepts as nonpartisan elections, small councils, and elections at large which have been associated with the council-manager plan are found with increasing frequency in mayor-council charters.

The Council-Manager Plan in Large Cities

One of the interesting facts that stands out to one who has observed the remarkable growth of the council-manager plan has been its failure to receive acceptance in the very large cities of the United States. Since Cleveland, after a brief experience with it, abandoned the plan in 1932, no city with a population in excess of 500,000 has adopted council-manager government. Cincinnati adopted the plan when its population was below that figure and has retained it as it has grown in size. The fact that the largest cities do not have the newer plan cannot be attributed to historical accident; many of these cities, including New Orleans, Philadelphia, and New York, have very recently gone through charter reform and the possibility of adopting the council-manager plan was a matter of debate. For some reasons those who have been able to guide the decisions made in these cities have felt the plan was not adapted to their specific needs.

Evidence is insufficient to permit one to enumerate with confidence the factors which weighed heaviest in swinging the balance against the professional manager in these cities, but certain considerations are rather consistently found in articles dealing with the subject.

1. "The office of mayor—an elected chief executive who is the center of energy and of public leadership and the focus of responsibility for policy and per-formance—had become too important an asset in large cities to be exchanged for the speculative values of legislative supremacy and a city manager as represented in the council-manager plan."[10] This is the way Wallace Sayre explained the failure of the plan to be acceptable to charter reformers in the large cities. The implication is that since councilmen are likely to represent only small segments of the total city population, only a popularly elected mayor can provide the political leadership required to achieve sufficient consensus for effective action. The very nature of the office of city manager precludes any attempt on his part to supply this policy leadership.

The diversity of interests represented in any large city makes the political broker who can put together a policy program sufficiently broad to attract majority support and yet sufficiently limited to be workable an important part of the political process. The complex nature of group-interest politics in the large city may require a leadership personality to achieve any kind of policy decisions that can hope to receive sufficient public acceptance to ensure their implementation. A popularly elected chief executive seems most likely to supply such leadership.

2. In many large cities political parties play a major role in local politics, and political leaders want them to continue to play this role. To them the abandon-ment of mayor-council government constitutes a threat to local party organiza-tion. Even if it can be demonstrated that issues in the political arena bear very little relationship to issues on which parties divide at the national level, party leaders will insist that national parties must depend on local organizations to function effectively. Therefore, leaders of both major parties, and they are often in a position to make the decision, will oppose the adoption of a gov-ernmental structure which they think will add to the difficulty of maintaining strong viable party organizations in the large cities.

3. The problem of securing council action in large cities may be quite different from what it is in the small city. Councilmen from the very diverse wards of the large city are much farther apart in their images of what the council should do than is the case in the more homogeneous small city. A city manager with-out the aid of political pressure may be able by persuasion to achieve council approval for his programs in small cities, but in a large city positive council atcion may require pressure from a strong political figure such as a mayor who has back of him the support of an active party organization and the ability to reach and influence public opinion through his access to the mass media.[11]

Even though proponents of council-manager government present rational arguments to answer those who maintain that it is not a viable system for the very large cities,[12] the fact remains that the people who make the decisions

[10] Wallace Sayre, "The General Manager Idea for Large Cities," *Public Admin-istration Review,* vol. 14, pp. 253–258, autumn, 1954.

[11] For elaboration see Charles R. Adrian, "Recent Concepts in Large City Ad-ministration," in Edward C. Banfield (ed.), *Urban Government,* The Free Press, Glencoe, Ill., 1961, pp. 441–453.

[12] For further discussion see John Bebout, "Management for Large Cities," *Public Administration Review,* vol. 15, pp. 188–195, summer, 1955; and William A. Sommers, "Council Manager Government: A Review," *Western Political Quar-terly,* vol. XI, pp. 144–147, March, 1958.

in these large cities have been unwilling to give it a trial. Table 7.2 gives the forms of government in cities of the United States by size of population groups in 1965.

MAYOR-MANAGER GOVERNMENT

Even though local decision makers have been unwilling to accept the council-manager form of government for large cities, they have more readily accepted the argument that some kind of professional administrator can play a useful role. Measured in terms of total expenditures and personnel employed, city government is in most cities the largest business operation in the city. Businessmen, professionals, and civic leaders recognize that administrative know-how in the form of a professional manager is required at some point in the government to supply unity of direction, coordination, cooperation, and control of city functions if services are to be maintained efficiently and economically. This is the role a city manager is expected to play in the council-manager plan. But since this plan is unacceptable to the charter makers in the large cities, some attempts have been made to provide a strong popularly elected mayor who can furnish the political organizations whose cooperation is essential for popular support and at the same time provide a place for a

TABLE 7.2   Forms of Government in Cities with Population over 5,000 in 1966

Population group	Total no. of cities	Total no. of cities in table	Mayor-council		Commis-sion		Council-manager	
			No.	Per-cent	No.	Per-cent	No.	Per-cent
Over 500,000	27	26	20	76.9	1	3.8	5	19.2
250,000–500,000	27	27	11	40.7	3	11.1	13	48.1
100,000–250,000	96	96	34	35.4	12	12.5	50	52.0
50,000–100,000	232	227	84	37.0	22	9.7	121	53.3
15,000–50,000	476	462	167	36.1	50	10.8	244	52.8
10,000–15,000	1,165	1,105	538	48.7	99	9.0	468	42.4
5,000–10,000	1,171	1,146	746	65.1	58	4.9	344	30.0
All cities over 5,000	3,189	3,089*	1,600	51.8	243	7.9	1,245	40.3

* Not included in this table are Washington, D.C., 40 cities with town meeting government, 26 with representative town meeting government, and 33 other cities for which no information was received.

Source: From International City Managers Association, *The Municipal Year Book*, Chicago, 1966, p. 90.

professional administrator who can furnish the technical competence which few popularly elected mayors possess.

The plan often proposed is essentially the strong-mayor–council form of government to which is added a professional administrative officer who is selected by the mayor and whose direct responsibility is to the mayor.[13] In this respect the plan is a radical departure from the council-manager model in which the professional administrator is selected by the city council and is directly responsible to it. Charter provisions may require that the mayor's appointee be approved by the council, but such approval is also generally required for other major administrative appointments made by the mayor. Since this type of government has not yet become as highly institutionalized as have the others, there is no generally accepted title for the office of the professional administrator; he may be called a general manager, chief administrative officer, or simply administrative assistant to the mayor.

Historically, the idea of a general manager in a mayor-council system began in San Francisco in 1932 when by charter revision the office of chief administrative officer was created.[14] Evidence indicates that the idea was proposed and accepted as a compromise between proponents of the mayor-council and the council-manager plans. In 1938 the city of New York established the office of deputy mayor, which might have become a central management office, and in 1954 the office of city administrator was created.[15] Six other large cities, Boston, Los Angeles, Louisville, Newark, New Orleans, and Philadelphia have created some kind of office to render managerial assistance to their mayors.

No single model for this type of government has yet evolved, since each city has drafted its plan to meet the approval of various groups which were represented in their charter-drafting agencies. The well-established model of council-manager government may be, in part, attributed to the existence of the National Municipal League, a reform-oriented organization that has made the promotion of council-manager government one of its major objectives; no such organizations exist to institutionalize and promote the mayor-manager scheme.

The specific responsibilities assigned to the professional manager in the cities in which this office exists are varied. He is uniformly responsible for administrative planning and what might be called systems-and-methods con-

---

[13] John M. Bollens, *Appointed Executive Local Government: The California Experiment*, The Haynes Foundation, Los Angeles, 1952.

[14] John M. Seliz, "The San Francisco Idea," *National Municipal Review*, vol. 46, pp. 290–295, June, 1957.

[15] Sayre, *op. cit.*, p. 254.

trol, including internal operations and communications. He is not given responsibility for personnel management in any of the large cities.[16] Cities have taken very different approaches to the problem of which major administrative agencies are the primary responsibility of the general manager. In New Orleans, New York, and Philadelphia his chief responsibility is with what are called "line" agencies, i.e., agencies which perform services for the public, while in Los Angeles he is responsible for so-called "management" agencies, those which supply services which the line agencies must have in order to perform their functions effectively.

The one characteristic which more than any other identifies the mayor-manager form from others is that the professional administrator is within the sphere of authority of the mayor rather than the council. Time will be required for this form to evolve into a highly institutionalized pattern, but its continuance in a number of large cities indicates that it is here to stay.

FORM OF GOVERNMENT AND SOCIOECONOMIC CHARACTERISTICS

Earlier in this chapter it was suggested that there probably is a relationship between form of government in cities and the output of their political systems. This speculation was based on some general observations of the kinds of groups which might have greater access to decision makers in the various governmental forms. There is some empirical evidence to indicate a correlation between form of government and the socioeconomic characteristics of cities.

John H. Kessel in 1962 hypothesized that a "frankly political" form of government is likely to be found in cities where there are interests which must be deferred to or whose claims must be arbitrated in the political system, and that when there is no dominant group which is "disposed to cooperate with the policy maker," viable conditions exist for the city manager. In attempting to find evidence to test this hypothesis he examined statistics for the middle-sized (25,000 to 250,000) cities in the United States. Three things seem to stand out in his research.[17]

1. The city-manager form is most consistently found in cities with high growth rates, the mayor-council form is more closely associated with cities of stable population, and the commission form is found "with striking frequency" in cities which lost population during the decade 1950–1960. The implications are that cities with expanding populations are faced with serious management

---

[16] *Ibid.,* p. 255.
[17] This discussion has leaned heavily on John H. Kessel, "Governmental Structure and Political Environment: A Statistical Note about American Cities," *American Political Science Review,* vol. 56, pp. 615–620, September, 1962.

and technical problems for which a professional manager seems to be particularly useful and that in such a mobile situation political groups which could expect to dominate the political scene are not in existence. In stable communities, established political groups are more likely to exist and the political arbitrator in the form of a popularly elected mayor is more in demand than is the professional manager.

2. The higher the percentage of foreign-born in a city, the more likely it is to have a mayor-council government, while city-manager government is most often associated with cities in which the population is mostly native-born. The implication is that foreign-born groups constitute interests that can be best articulated through popular elections and political party organizations.

3. When middle-sized cities are grouped into the following classes: (a) personal service, (b) retail, (c) finance, (d) professional, (e) public administration, (f) wholesale, (g) transportation, (h) diversified, and (i) manufacturing, and their forms of government correlated with economic class, the following observations can be made.

The council-manager form of government decreased in the order in which the classes are listed; i.e., among the personal-service cities was the highest proportion of city-manager systems; among the manufacturing cities, the smallest proportion of such systems. The explanation seems to be that council-manager government is most acceptable to local businessmen and persons whose interests are closely related to their local communities, and that white-collar workers feel the need less than do industrial workers for popular elections to articulate their interests.

Leo F. Schnore and Robert R. Alford also attempted to correlate form of government with certain socioeconomic characteristics, but their study was limited to 300 cities lying within the 25 largest urbanized areas in the United States.[18] In general, they found that council-manager cities tend "to be the natural habitat of the upper middle class," and they tend to be "inhabited by a younger, more mobile, white population that is growing rapidly." Commission-governed suburbs tended to contain persons of lowest socioeconomic status of a higher age bracket and have in their populations more members of minority groups. Mayor-council suburbs fell at points in between these two extremes.

EVALUATION OF GOVERNMENTAL FORMS

The discussion in this chapter focusing on forms of government in American cities should be examined with respect to its relevance to city politics as

[18] Leo F. Schnore and Robert R. Alford, "Forms of Government and Socioeconomic Characteristics of Suburbs," *Administrative Science Quarterly*, vol. 8. pp. 1–17, June, 1963.

defined in the introductory chapter. Analyzed in terms of conflict resolution, form and structure are important because, in themselves, they constitute a subject of conflict. Whether or not sufficient empirical evidence can be mustered to demonstrate the causal correlation between form of government and output of the political system, participants in city politics think that such a relation exists; therefore, any proposal to alter structural form produces opposition and results in group conflict. An analysis of the politics of individual cities might well show that the most heated political battle that appeared over a given time span involved charter revision when the specific point in dispute was mayor-council versus council-manager government.

In the second place there is some evidence to support the contention that form and structure do affect the public decisions made at the city level. Although the differences may be in terms of business-type efficiency in administering regular city services, more significantly, form may affect materially the strength of various groups to influence decisions made by city officials, i.e., some groups may have greater weight in the decision-making process under mayor-council government, while others may fare better with council-manager government.

Analysis of form, therefore, does not lead to an evaluation of which form of government is good or which is bad in an ethical or moral sense, but rather it directs the student to seek evidence to answer the question: Which kinds of groups have access to the centers of decision making in each form?

Some observations can be made which may be useful to anyone who attempts an analysis of a city along these lines:

1. A proposal to make a change in the existing pattern of government in a given city will elicit opposition from those who have in their own minds associated popular election of chief executives with the tenets of American democracy or what they may choose to call the "American way." Their opposition often is emotional rather than rational, and they evoke such symbols as "un-American," "dictatorship," "communist-inspired," and "fascism" in their effort to defeat the proposal.

2. A proposal to make a basic structural change in city government will arouse opposition from a significant segment of the electorate who oppose change for its own sake. Any proposition that must go before the electorate has a built-in opposition of those who dislike deviation from that which they have become familiar with, even before argument on the merits of the change begins.

3. Certain groups present determined resistance to council-manager government on very reasonable grounds. They reason that their ability to influence the system depends on their ability to affect election results. If, for example, organized labor groups are active politically in a city, they may control a large block of votes, be able to raise money for campaign purposes, and carry on an extensive get-out-the-vote campaign. Under such circumstances they will

oppose any change which takes the chief executive out of the political arena as an attempt to remove him from their sphere of influence. This type of analysis may explain the opposition of labor leaders and political party officials to council-manager proposals. Williams and Adrian noted the opposition of labor leaders to council-manager government in their four-city study.[19]

4. Within any city at any given time certain groups feel satisfied with the access they have under existing institutions to the political process; they are therefore, unlikely to swing their support behind any proposal to alter drastically these institutions. In a given case this might apply to a chamber of commerce or a racial minority group. A natural course of action for any group which does not feel seriously disadvantaged by an existing order is to fear proposals for change when they cannot predict with assurance what the new order might bring.

5. City-manager government has become, in the minds of some citizens, associated with reform, honesty and integrity in government, efficiency and economy in administration, political nonpartisanship, and other symbols that elicit favorable responses from good-government and reform-oriented groups. Hence, proposals for council-manager charters are often assured of support from the League of Women Voters, chambers of commerce especially the junior chambers of commerce), nonpartisan leagues, and local members of the National Municipal League. In part, this support is only symbolic, since it represents support on a reform-for-reform's-sake basis, but it also has a pragmatic base. In many cases these groups are not able through existing institutional patterns to control elections or to make a major impact on existing decision-making centers; therefore, they feel that overhauling these institutional arrangements cannot weaken, and might well strengthen, their voice in the output of the system.

6. Often support or opposition to a specific governmental change is based not on an evaluation of the overall change in form or structure but on specific items contained in or associated with the suggested alteration. For example, some group may, in a general way, favor the council-manager form but will oppose a specific proposal which includes the election of some or all aldermen at large. An understanding of this attitude may become more obvious in succeeding chapters which deal specifically with the executive and legislative branches and the municipal courts.

BIBLIOGRAPHY

Books

Adrian, Charles R.: *Governing Urban America*, 2d ed., McGraw-Hill Book Company, New York, 1961.
Banfield, Edward C., and James Q. Wilson: *City Politics*, Vintage Books, Random House, Inc., New York, 1963, chap. 13.

[19] Oliver P. Williams and Charles R. Adrian, *Four Cities: A Study in Comparative Policy Making*, University of Pennsylvania Press, Philadelphia, 1963, p. 145.

Bromage, Arthur W.: *Manager Plan Abandonments*, 5th ed., National Municipal League, New York, 1957.

Chang, T. S.: *History and Analysis of the Commission and City Manager Plans of Municipal Government in the United States*, Ph.D. thesis, University of Iowa, Iowa City, 1918.

East, John Paster: *Council-Manager Government: The Political Thought of Its Founder Richard S. Childs*, University of North Carolina Press, Chapel Hill, 1965.

Kammerer, Gladys M., et al.: *City Managers in Politics: An Analysis of Manager Tenure and Termination*, University of Florida Monographs: Social Science, No. 13, Gainesville, winter, 1962.

————: *The Urban Political Community: Profiles in Town Politics*, Houghton Mifflin Company, Boston, 1963.

Mosher, F. C., et al.: *City Manager Government in Seven Cities*, Public Administration Service, Chicago, 1940.

Stone, H. A., D. K. Price, and K. H. Stone: *City Manager Government in the United States*, Public Administration Service, Chicago, 1940.

————: *City Manager Government in Nine Cities*, Public Administration Service, Chicago, 1940.

Williams, Oliver P., and Charles R. Adrian: *Four Cities; A Study in Comparative Policy Making*, University of Pennsylvania Press, Philadelphia, 1963.

Woodruff, Clinton R.: *City Government by Commission*, Appleton & Company, Inc., New York, 1914.

Articles

Bebout, John: "Management for Large Cities," *Public Administration*, vol. 15, pp. 188–195, summer, 1955.

Fassett, C. M.: "The Weaknesses of Commission Government," *National Municipal League*, vol. 9, pp. 642–647, October, 1920.

Kessel, John H.: "Governmental Structure and Political Environment: A Statistical Note about American Cities," *American Political Science Review*, vol. 56, pp. 615–620, September, 1962.

Mathewson, Kent: "Democracy in Council-Manager Government," *Public Administration Review*, vol. 19, pp. 183–185, summer, 1956.

Sayre, Wallace: "The General Manager Idea for Large Cities," *Public Administration Review*, vol. 14, pp. 253–258, autumn, 1954.

Schnore, Leo F., and Robert R. Alford: "Forms of Government and Socioeconomic Characteristics of Suburbs," *Administrative Science Quarterly*, vol. 8, pp. 1–17, June, 1963.

Selig, John M.: "The San Francisco Idea," *National Municipal Review*, vol. 46, pp. 290–295, June, 1957.

Sherbenou, Edgar L.: "Class, Participation and the Council-Manager Plan," *Public Administration Review*, vol. 21, pp. 131–135, summer, 1961.

Sommers, William A.: "Council Manager Government: A Review," *Western Political Quarterly*, vol. 11, pp. 144–147, March, 1958.

8

THE CITY LEGISLATURE

The idea that every government must have a legislative body to make laws is so well entrenched in the popular image of democracy in this country that we can be sure every city will have included in its governmental structure some body authorized to enact ordinances which will have the effect of law within the boundaries of the city. Although this body will be called a council in most cities, it may be a board of aldermen or a commission in others. The council represents one of the arenas in which conflict issues arise and are debated and in which some kinds of decisions are made. Later discussions will reveal that in most cities policy decisions will also flow from agencies other than the council. Given the favorable attitude toward limited government and dispersal of government power in this country, city legislative bodies will make decisions within certain constraints, either formally spelled out in state laws and city charters or informally imposed by the nature of the political system. Since many decisions of a legislative character emanate from sources other than the council in most American cities, a brief summary of the kind of subjects that generally are within the competence of the council may be useful.

COUNCIL FUNCTIONS

When an observer of American government says the function of a legislature is "to make the laws," he more nearly describes the means through which it discharges its functions than he does the function itself. It is true that many city laws (generally called ordinances) must be formally passed by the council before they can be enforced in courts of law, but the important question is, "Upon what subjects is the council empowered to pass ordinances?" When the areas of decision making which are within the scope of authority of the council are determined, then the passing of ordinances merely becomes the avenue through which this authority is expressed. Without attempting to be all-inclusive, the following classification of functions will serve to direct attention to the kinds of decisions which are assigned to city councils in American cities.

1. City councils adopt ordinances levying taxes, fees, and assessments which produce the city's revenue. Suggestions for new ways to raise revenue or for changes in the established tax pattern may originate elsewhere, but in most cases, favorable action by the council is required before revenue-producing proposals constitute legal demands upon the citizen.

2. City councils by some type of formal action allocate the city's revenue to the various functions which the city performs. Again, detailed and elaborate plans (budgets) for the expenditure of money are supplied to the council by the chief executive or by various administrative agencies, but, in most cases, favorable action of the council is required before tax revenue can be spent.

3. City councils define behavior of persons and organizations which are beyond accepted norms of conduct and provide penalties for violations of these norms. In a sense this constitutes the enactment of criminal legislation, but since the criminal codes of the state apply with cities just as they do elsewhere, the area left to city councils is very limited. City codes usually include such subjects as local traffic regulations, nuisance regulation, peace disturbance, and measures designed to protect public health and sanitation. The latter include ordinances regulating the keeping of animals within the city, rodent and mosquito control, and industrial regulations designed to reduce loss from fire and accidents.

4. City councils influence the physical growth and development of the city through the adoption of master plans, land-use zoning ordinances, and building codes. They also play a role in expansion of the limits of the city through annexation and consolidation proposals. The role of the council in these areas, while a major one, is only a part of the total process by which these kinds of control are exercised.

5. The city council determines the kinds and intensity of public services which will be undertaken. Although certain services such as police and fire protection, street and sewer construction and maintenance, park maintenance, and public health promotion are universally accepted as city functions, there are many types of service which are often performed by private utility companies and any attempt to transfer these services to the city government produces real political conflict.

Although this enumeration of the kinds of subjects about which councils make decisions is not all-inclusive, it points up the fact that they can take action in areas that very significantly affect the life of those who live and work in the city. It also indicates that the areas in which group conflict is likely to be most intense are the areas with which councils are involved.

STRUCTURE OF CITY COUNCILS

Students of politics are not agreed upon the extent to which organizational structure is a significant variable in determining the output of a legislative body. Some insist that the legislative product is in no way affected by the manner in which the lawmaking body is organized, while others are convinced that such organization plays a major role in the political process. There is insufficient empirical evidence to prove which of these opposing views is correct, particularly with respect to city councils. Observation of the behavior of participants in the political process, however, will convince one that those who are politically active *think* structure makes a difference; therefore, structure, itself, becomes a political issue. Since influential people think that their chances of getting legislative decisions that conform to their value judgments depend on maintenance of the existing organizational pattern, any proposal to alter the established structural arrangements provokes bitter political struggles.

Unicameralism

One feature of city legislative bodies that is striking to the student of American politics is the extent to which they have abandoned the two-house structure that is so firmly entrenched at the state and national level. The 1966 *Municipal Year Book* lists only two cities (Everett, Massachusetts, and Waterville, Maine) which still have bicameral legislatures.[1] Perhaps New York City should be added to the list, since the Board of Estimate possesses some legislative power.[2] The unicameral legislature has predominated in American cities from the establishment of the Republic but not to the extent that it does today. In 1900 approximately one-third of all cities in this country with populations of 25,000 or more operated with two-house legislatures.

[1] International City Managers Association, *The Municipal Year Book*, Chicago, 1966, p. 156.
[2] Wallace S. Sayre and Herbert Kaufman, *Governing New York City: Politics in the Metropolis*, The Russell Sage Foundation, New York, 1960, p. 627.

One can only speculate on why the unicameral city council has been so widely accepted when two-house legislatures have persisted at the state level. Certainly, the reform movements which were so effective around the turn of the century were concentrated on reform in city rather than state governments; state reform came later and concentrated attention on administrative reorganization rather than on legislative change. Since these reform movements emphasized responsibility and accountability to the electorate, one may infer that the voter could be expected to keep an eye on his representative better if the council was small and if there was only one house to watch. Another possibility is that the public views cities more as service institutions, not unlike privately owned public utility corporations, than as governmental institutions in which important political issues are debated and compromised; therefore structure which tends to promote quick positive action seems more desirable than structure which maximizes deliberation and debate and which ensures checks upon hasty legislative action.

Size of Councils

Another feature that distinguishes city councils from state legislatures is their small size. In the five cities with populations in excess of one million, the number of councilmen ranges from Detroit's 9 to Chicago's 50; Los Angeles has 15 councilmen, and Philadelphia has 17. Even the smallest states of the union have larger legislative bodies than these very large cities. The number of council members in cities with populations from 250,000 to 500,000 ranges from 4 to 17, with both the mode and mean being 9. For all cities in the United States with populations of 5,000 or more the range is from 3 to 50; the number most commonly found is 5, and the median is 7 in all mayor-council cities and 5 in commission cities and in council-manager cities. The largest council in any commission-governed city has 13 members, and the largest in any council-manager city has 20. In the population group between 25,000 and 250,000, councils in mayor-council–governed cities are somewhat larger than in either commission or council-manager cities; the mode in mayor-council cities is 9, while it is 5 in both the commission and council-manager cities. Table 8.1 shows the size of councils by population classes for the major forms of government.

Again, one can only speculate on the factors which make small councils so acceptable when attempts to reduce the size of state legislatures find such little public approval. The public image of the city as a service institution not unlike business enterprises may cause voters to think of councils as corporate

TABLE 8.1   **Number of Councilmen in Cities of over 5,000 Population**

Population group	Mayor-council			Commission			Council-manager		
	Range	Mode	Median	Range	Mode	Median	Range	Mode	Median
Over 500,000	7–50	9	13						
250,000–500,000	4–41	9	9				5–9	9	8
100,000–250,000	5–40	9	9	3–13	5	5	5–12	7	7
50,000–100,000	4–14	7	9	3–9	5	5	5–18	5	7
25,000–50,000	3–25	7*	8	3–7	5	5	3–20	5	5
10,000–25,000	3–20	6	7	3–9	5	5	3–18	5	5
5,000–10,000	3–19	5	6	2–9	5	4	2–42	5	5
All cities over 5,000	3–50	5	7	2–13	5	5	2–42	5	5

* Both 7 and 9 appear as the mode.

Source: International City Managers Association, *The Municipal Year Book*, Chicago, 1966, p. 94.

boards of directors rather than as forums for the discussion of burning political issues. There is some support for the assumption that sentiment for small councils comes from dissatisfaction with the role played by councilmanic committees in city government, in particular, with the influence of the chairman of these committees in the political process. The assumption is that with a small council, all matters of public business can be discussed and decided in committee of the whole, while with large councils, work must be divided and assigned to a number of standing committees. Debate on each subject of legislation takes place in committees, and action in the full council may be little more than approval of recommendations coming from the committees. Since committee deliberations are often closed to the public, the citizen may find greater access to the small council than to the more elaborate committee system which the large council dictates. Pressure for larger councils is likely to come from organized groups which are so small that they can expect to have a representative only if the number of councilmen is fairly large.

Terms of Office

Of the 2,986 cities reported in *The Municipal Year Book* for 1966, 50.2 percent have four-year terms for their councilmen, 37.7 percent have a two-year term, and 10.2 percent elect councilmen for three years. A few deviate from these patterns, some having one-, five-, or six-year terms and others having a system wherein some councilmen have terms different from those of others. In general, the larger the city the more likely it is to provide four-year terms for councilmen; 47.7 percent of cities with populations between 5,000 and 10,000 have four-year terms, while 76.0 percent of cities over 500,000 use the four-year term. Some variation in council terms is related to form of government. Commission-governed cities have the highest percent (69.0) of cities with four-year terms; council-manager cities are second with 57.1 percent, and mayor-council cities are last with 44.0 percent. See Table 8.2 for terms of office of councilmen in cities classified both by governmental form and population class.

A significant number of American cities provide overlapping terms for councilmen so that the entire membership of the council will never change as the result of a single election. This is most likely to be true in council-manager cities, with 85.9 of these cities having overlapping terms; it is less likely to be true in commission cities and the few with the town-meeting form of government, where the percentages are 37.5 and 46.0 respectively. In mayor-council cities, 55.1 percent use the overlapping principle.

It is interesting to observe the trend toward four-year terms for councilmen over the last few years. In 1934 *The Municipal Year Book* showed that in mayor-council cities the ratio was 2:1 in favor of two-year terms; this contrasts with 57.1 percent of mayor-councils having four-year terms in 1966. In council-manager cities in 1934 the number using two-year and four-year terms was about equal; in 1966 four-year terms were found in 69 percent of the cities.

When one observes the trend toward longer and staggered terms of city councilmen, he must conclude that the forces which are able to produce structural change in city government are those which do not place great stress on frequent popular elections to give direction to those who are charged with responsibility for deciding many of the important issues which arise at the local level.

Representative Base

There is no question but that one of the issues which is most hotly contested in charter-drafting commissions and which takes the longest time to resolve is the basis of representation; i.e., "How shall councilmen be chosen?" At the extreme poles are those who support the election of all councilmen at large and those who argue that all should be chosen from single-member

TABLE 8.2   Terms of Office of Councilmen in Cities of over 5,000 Population

Form of govern-ment or population group	Total no. of cities	No. of cities report-ing	Percent of reporting cities						Over-lap-ping terms (per-cent of total cities)
			1 yr	2 yr	3 yr	4 yr	5 yr	6 yr	
Form of government:									
Mayor-council	1,600	1,516	‡	45.5	10.1	44.0	0	‡	55.1
Commission	243	239	0	15.9	10.0	69.0	3.3	1.7	46.0
Council-manager	1,245	1,164	0	33.0	8.7	57.1	‡	0.9	85.9
Town meeting	40	27	7.4	33.3	51.9	7.4	0	0	37.5
Representative town meeting	26	21	6	33.3	61.9	0	0	0	50.0
All cities over 5,000	3,154*	2,967†	‡	30.8	10.3	50.5	‡	‡	64.0
Population group:									
Over 500,000	27	25	0	24.0	0	76.0	0	0	33.3
250,000–500,000	27	27	0	33.3	3.7	63.0	0	0	37.0
100,000–250,000	96	95	0	31.6	3.2	65.2	0	0	47.4
50,000–100,000	232	225	0	34.7	4.4	59.1	‡	1.3	61.5
25,000–50,000	476	460	‡	34.1	8.5	52.0	‡	1.3	62.1
10,000–25,000	1,165	1,067	0.5	38.2	12.0	47.9	0.5	‡	63.3
5,000–10,000	1,171	1,087	‡	40.3	11.4	47.7	‡	‡	66.8
All cities over 5,000	3,194	2,986†	‡	37.7	10.2	50.2	‡	‡	63.3

* Does not include Washington, D.C., and 39 cities for which the form of government is not known.
† Does not include 96 cities which have two different terms of office.
‡ Less than 0.5 percent.
Source: International City Managers Association, The Municipal Year Book, Chicago, 1966, p. 98.

wards. The first plan permits each voter to vote for as many councilmen as are to be elected; the second permits the voter to vote only for the councilman who is to represent the ward in which he resides. Other schemes for repre-sentation which are discussed in charter commissions may be considered compromises between these two extremes.

If cities having town meetings and representative town-meeting government, of which there are only 47, are disregarded, in 1966 the system of electing all councilmen at large predominated (95 percent) in commission-governed cities. In council-manager cities, 74 percent elected all councilmen at large,

and in cities employing mayor-council government, 44 percent used the at-
large system. Thirty-one percent of mayor-council cities elected all their councilmen from single-member wards, while 25 percent used a combination,
electing some councilmen from wards and others at large. In commission
cities only 5 percent elected commissioners at large, and none employed a
combination plan. Thirteen percent of council-manager cities used single-
member wards as the basis for representation, and 12 percent employed
the combination plan. The type and method of elections for councilmen in
cities classified both as to form of government and population class are shown
in Table 8.3.

Some relationship seems to exist between the size of the city and the basis
of representation used; in general, the larger the city the more likely it is to

**TABLE 8.3   Type and Method of Elections for Councilmen in Cities of over 5,000 Popu-
lation**

| | Type of election | | | Methods of election | | |
| | | | | Percent of reporting cities | | |
Form of govern-ment or population group	No. of cities reporting	Parti-san	Non-parti-san	No. of cities reporting	At large	By wards	Combi-nation of wards and at large
Percent of re-porting cities							
Form of government:							
Mayor-council	1,533	51	49	1,543	44	31	25
Commission	239	39	63	236	95	5	0
Council-manager	1,228	16	84	1,127	74	13	12
Town meeting	26	54	46	25	96	0	4
Representative town meeting	21	24	76	21	86	14	0
Population group:							
Over 500,000	26	31	69	26	42	27	31
250,000–500,000	26	19	81	27	67	7	26
100,000–150,000	95	36	64	94	67	16	18
50,000–100,000	231	32	68	229	55	20	25
25,000–50,000	468	31	69	465	65	18	17
10,000–25,000	1,102	35	65	1,089	64	19	17
5,000–10,000	1,111	40	60	1,122	60	25	15
All cities over 5,000	3,059	36	64	3,052	62	21	17

Source: International City Managers Association, *The Municipal Year Book*, Chicago'
1966, p. 96.

use single-member wards to elect all councilmen. In all cities in the United States with populations of 5,000 or more, 62 percent use the at-large systems, 21 percent employ the single-member ward plan, and 17 percent elect some councilmen at large and some from wards. Of the 26 cities with populations of 500,000 or more, 42 percent elect all councilmen at large, 27 percent elect all of them from wards, and 31 percent employ the combined plan. The group of cities with the highest percentage using at-large elections are those with populations between 100,000 and 500,000. This group, which includes a number of commission-governed cities, has 67 percent using at-large elections for all legislators.

Some cities have attempted to combine the advantages of the two systems. The simplest plan to combine at-large and single-member district systems is to specify in the charter the number of councilmen to be elected by each method, but there is little uniformity in the way the division is made. In some cities only one legislator is elected from the city at large and he, by virtue of his election, becomes the presiding officer of the council. In these cases he will usually have the title of president of the board or council in mayor-council cities and the title of mayor in council-manager cities. In other cities as many as half the councilmen may be elected from the city at large. In Philadelphia, for example, 7 of 17 councilmen are chosen at large, in Houston 3 of 8 councilmen are chosen at large, in Buffalo 6 are elected at large and 9 are chosen from wards. St. Louis elects the chairman of the board of aldermen at large and 28 other aldermen from 28 wards.

Another combination plan that has found favor in some cities is one whereby councilmen are nominated by wards but are chosen by an at-large vote. Under this plan the electors in each ward nominate two candidates for councilmen; these candidates are usually required to have a residence in the ward from which they are nominated. In the general election the voters indicate their preference for one of the candidates from each ward. To reduce the number to be voted on at any single election, terms may be staggered so that councilmen from even-numbered wards will be elected at one time and those from the odd-numbered wards at another time. The rationale that supports this system suggests that it gives each ward a representative easily accessible to residents of a ward and at the same time requires each representative to give attention to problems of the city as a whole since he must stand on his record in an at-large election. The practical problem that arises under the system is that, of the two candidates nominated in a ward, the one with the least support in the ward may be successful in the general election.

The plural-member district system which has been widely used as a basis for representation has not found favor in cities.

EVALUATION OF COUNCIL STRUCTURE

Analysis of council structure must seek to identify the ways in which the ward and at-large systems may operate to give some politically oriented groups an advantage in the decision-making process while working to the disadvantage of other groups that are seeking to influence council action. A fair assumption is that if politically active party, labor, business, or racial groups are convinced that any system gives them an advantage in controlling public decisions they will be found supporting that system without considering whether it is good or bad on moral or ethical grounds. Our purpose, therefore, is to point up the effects that may result from the adoption of one or the other of these systems and leave to the reader the decision as to which results most nearly conform to his values.

A major problem is to find any research efforts that have produced valid generalizations about the effects of representative systems on the decision-making process. In the absence of conclusive evidence supplied by competent researchers directly on this problem, the images which group leaders have of the probable effects of different systems are useful. At least, the behavior of these groups can be predicted if the issue should arise in a city charter election. There is evidence that respected students of municipal politics, as a result of their observations, are convinced that the system of representation does make a difference in politics.[3]

The difficult task is to find out how the various electoral systems affect the distribution of power in a city political system. The observations which follow should not be accepted as statements which have been proved by scientific research, but rather as speculations which follow from observations of municipal politics in action over a long period of time.

1. The electoral system affects the image the councilman has of his role and therefore is a factor in determining his behavior as a representative. The councilman who is elected from a relatively small ward feels the need to cater to the wishes of the voters who are responsible for his election and who can, at any election, replace him. This behavior pattern is reflected in his introduction of and support for measures which are of local rather than city-wide concern. Such bills include provision for the erection of stop signs, specific road and street repairs and improvements, changes in street lighting, spot land-use zoning, neighborhood park improvements, and regulations concerning parking restrictions along city streets. On the other hand, a councilman whose constituency is the entire city feels less pressure to spend time on matters that are primarily of concern to a limited geographic area and, therefore, he feels free to concentrate on issues which are likely to interest great numbers of people in all areas of the city.

[3] Edward C. Banfield and William Q. Wilson, *City Politics*, Vintage Books, Random House, Inc., New York, 1963, p. 87.

A behavior pattern generally known as "aldermanic courtesy" frequently develops in city councils in which all members are elected from single-member wards. This is a scheme whereby the councilman of a single ward expects to be permitted to determine local issues of primary concern to persons living in his ward. The majority will defer to the alderman from the ward most directly involved simply because they expect the same kind of treatment when a local issue involves interests in their ward. When an issue arises over the location of stop signs, parking meters, and changes in existing zoning ordinances the council majority simply support the wishes of the councilman from the ward involved. Each alderman, in return, expects similar treatment when the interests of his ward are involved.

This means that the time of most ward-elected councilmen will be used dealing with issues and problems which concern primarily a local area, while those elected at large are more free to concern themselves with issues of importance to greater numbers of people and broader geographic areas. On the other hand, councilmen elected at large are likely to maintain less direct contact with residents of any single ward since they need to maintain good relations with politically oriented groups whose members are spatially distributed over a wider area. Such groups are more interested in subjects which transcend ward boundaries, such, for example, as traffic flow on major arteries, city-wide physical planning, mass transit, and air pollution. One might predict, therefore, that chambers of commerce, leagues of women voters, and citizen reform groups would favor at-large representation while local party organizations would support ward elections.

2. The system of representation adopted in a city may affect the pattern of recruitment into public service. That is, the kind of persons who are elected to councils or boards of aldermen may be influenced by whether they must appeal to the voters of the whole city or merely to the voters of a single ward. The kind of campaign that is effective in winning an election in a given ward may not be effective in appealing to the voters of the city at large. The local politician who makes politics practically a full-time job is particularly well suited to ward-type politics. Such persons are willing to do all sorts of favors for their local constituents. They can spend time in helping constituents get jobs and city permits, acting as liaison between a citizen and the police department, securing minor street repairs, and listening to all kinds of complaints from constituents who think they have grievances against the city. On the other hand, persons who are willing to make a race that requires an appeal to all the voters of the city are not likely to be ones who think in terms of political favors for constituents; they are apt to pride themselves on being interested in what they refer to as "the general welfare" of all the people. Elections, at large, therefore, have greater appeal to the civic reformer, the businessman or professional man turned politician, and the citizen who for some reason feels that he has a duty to make a contribution to the city by taking a more active part in politics.

3. The system of representation adopted in a city may affect the access that minority groups have to the council and to its members. At-large elections are generally on a winner-take-all basis; i.e., any organized group which can win a majority of the votes of the entire city can put up a slate of as many candidates as there are offices to be filled and secure the election of the entire slate. At-large elections, therefore, tend to maximize the strength of any majority group. This is particularly true in cities with two active parties where one or

the other consistently is in the majority. The minority party is not likely to win a single seat on the council. With such a consistent pattern of defeat, the minority party is likely to remain in name only. With elections from wards, it is unlikely that the majority party can or will want to draw ward boundaries to prevent the minority party from electing some councilmen. The same is true with respect to racial and nationality groups. These groups are usually not evenly distributed over the city and therefore can, in the areas where they are concentrated, be influential in electing a member of the council, but in an at-large election they could be swamped by the majorities piled up in other areas of the city. Even if these minority groups are able to elect one or more of their members to the council, they cannot control decisions made there, but, at least, they have access to someone who can make known their point of view to the council and who can report back to them on what is happening at city hall.

4. The system of representation may affect political party organizations. Banfield and Wilson maintain that, "a small-district system often exists in conjunction with a machine."[4] Their explanation is that the machine is "held together and motivated mainly by the exchange of personal favors for voters;" and that this same principle is used by ward politicians to maintain their hold upon a ward. The political machine is generally built by molding together a majority of ward political leaders who feel that through their relations with the central leadership they can have access to the kinds of favors they need for political currency to maintain their strength in the local district.

In many states the ward constitutes the base for both city and state party organization; the ward committeeman and committeewoman are the most important party officials at the grass roots. If the ward serves no other purpose than as a base for party organization, the significance of the ward committeeman is minimized, but if the ward also serves as an election district, the ward leader may strengthen his position by either winning the council seat himself or securing the election of someone on whom he can count to deliver certain kinds of patronage to maintain ward support.

5. The system of representation may be a factor in determining whose interests will prevail in conflicts that are decided by the legislative body. Leaders of interest organizations whose basis for strength is distributed over the entire area of the city do not want to play the kind of political game necessary to build support in local wards (nor are they particularly good at it); they also usually have at their command the kind of resources necessary to conduct campaigns on a city-wide scale. As Banfield and Wilson point out, "Typically, businessmen, upper-class civic leaders, and reformers oppose small districts."[5] These are the kinds of people who can employ public relations firms, who have social status, and who have ready access to the press, radio, and television to reach mass audiences. Support for the ward system is likely to come from regular political party officials and active party workers, minority group leaders, and politically active labor unions. These people know how to play the game at the local level, and their chances of influencing the election of councilmen are maximized by the ward system. Since councilmen elected under the two systems owe their victory to very different constituencies, they may be ex-

---

[4] *Ibid.*, p. 92.
[5] *Ibid.*, p. 95

pected to reflect in their voting patterns different points of view and thereby determine the kinds of decisions made in councils.

6. The system of representation determines the intensity of conflicts that arise over such issues as malapportionment and gerrymandering of legislative districts. Controversy over the drawing of political district lines has persisted in America from the time that states were organized, but it has reached new heights since the Supreme Court of the United States handed down its decision in the cases of *Baker v. Carr* and *Reynolds v. Sims.* Although these cases dealt specifically with representation in state legislatures, they have now been made applicable to city councils. If city councilmen are all elected from the city at large, no problems of districting arise. The problem becomes more acute as the districts diminish in size. The imbalance in state legislatures that brought conflicts to the Supreme Court involved urban versus rural representation, but there are similar possibilities for malrepresentation in city councils. Gerrymandering, which minimizes representation of a minor political party, or racial groups, or of certain socioeconomic classes, introduces the potential for conflicts over ward boundaries.

Even though boundaries may be drawn which are generally satisfactory at the time, the mobility of population in the city will produce imbalance unless redistricting occurs regularly. Urban renewal projects, public housing programs, large in-migration to certain low-rent areas, and the flight to the suburbs combine to alter the spatial distribution of population and therefore make ward boundaries obsolete soon after they are drawn.

Differences in the total population in wards are likely to work to the disadvantage of Negroes more than any other group. The city is rapidly becoming the home of the Negro, and in general, this group constitutes a preponderance of the unskilled workers, the unemployed, and the lower end of the educational and income scale. Spokesmen for this group feel that only through government action can their problems be solved; therefore there will be increasing demands that the representative system more nearly reflect their interests. But the problem is not solved simply by drawing ward boundaries so that the populations of all wards are relatively equal. The boundaries may be such that they operate to the disadvantage of the total Negro population even though total populations are equal. If the corners of four wards converge near the center of the Negro community, Negroes may find that they are a minority in each of the four districts; or if a single ward is created to encompass as much of a Negro community as possible, the Negroes may be assured only one seat in the council when their numbers would justify two seats if they were divided in two wards. The problem is particularly serious because the legal power to determine the location of boundary lines is usually in the hands of a council or commission which does not at the time adequately represent the minority group which should profit most from redistricting.

The same problem is faced by a minority political party in a city where the machinery by which districts are made is in the hands of the majority party. Self-interest dictates that the majority will, if possible, use its power to draw ward boundaries in a manner that will tend to perpetuate its control of the city council and ensure that the opposing party will continue to be in the minority.

A major problem in representation is simply that there is no generally accepted rationale which can serve as a guide to those who must draw district lines. To say simply that wards shall be compact and contiguous and as nearly equal as possible is of very little use as an objective guide to those who face the districting task. Districts may meet these conditions and still be blatant gerrymanders as far as interest representation is concerned. Adequate answers have never been given to such simple questions as: Should districts include homogeneous groups or should each district include different interest groups roughly in the same proportion as they exist in the total population? In like manner, sufficient evidence about the operation of the political system is not available to predict with any degree of assurance what kind of districting is most advantageous to a particular interest group. If the group has a majority in a single ward, it is assured of a representative in the council; on the other hand, if the group has a sizable minority in two districts, it cannot elect its own representative in either district but, by its balance of power position in each, it may extract promises from the two victorious candidates on issues of first importance to the group. There is also strong evidence to support the contention that a specific group may have its interest better represented in a legislative body by a representative who is not one of the group but who is sensitive to its needs than when the group is represented by one of its own members.

Although the problems associated with drawing district boundaries do not arise if all councilmen are elected at large, the question of equitable representation for minority groups does exist. Certainly, if elections at large continue to be on a winner-take-all basis there will arise demands for reform.

CITY COUNCILMEN

One method to evaluate the significance of any governmental office in the total political process is to determine the kinds of people who are recruited to fill it. The great number of cities in the United States, the wide variation in their sizes, and the differences in the forms of government used make the task of generalizing about typical councilmen very difficult. Certain information about the office, however, may provide clues to the kinds of persons to whom it is attractive.

Formal Qualifications

City charters regularly include statements setting forth the qualifications required of councilmen. These generally include age (at least voting age), United States citizenship, and residence. This latter requirement usually includes both residence for a given period in the city and residence in the ward from which the councilman is elected. Since charters also stipulate that the council itself shall be the sole judge of the qualifications of its members, these formal requirements may not mean, in practice, what they say. The question of legal residence has always been tricky, and it is particularly so in the case of city councilmen. It is not uncommon to find a councilman whose family home is in one part of the city but who represents another area. He supposedly complies with the charter requirement by maintaining a "voting residence" in the ward. This is accomplished by either maintaining an office or business address in the ward, leasing a room or apartment, or listing an address with a relative. In cases of contest the councils have usually upheld the legality of such addresses.

Salaries

The salaries paid to councilmen may furnish some clues to the kinds of persons to whom the office appeals. Table 8.4 gives some summary information on remuneration of councilmen in this country.

From the variations shown in the table, it is obvious that some cities consider that the job of councilman is practically full time for which a regular salary should be paid, while in others the assumption is that a councilman gives his time to the city and should, therefore, receive only a token payment. The tendency for commissioners in commission government to act in the capacity of department heads accounts for the generally higher salaries in these cities. Councilmen, even in the larger cities, receive very small salaries in council-manager cities. This may be explained by the acceptance of the idea that the city manager's office will do most of the work required for councilmen to make intelligent decisions, and the job of councilmen requires a minimum of time. The low salaries may also indicate that the kind of candidates recruited in this governmental form do not need the salary provided by the office; service is to them a civic duty rather than a means of making a living. In practically no case is the salary such as to appeal to professional and businessmen if that is to constitute their chief means of a livelihood. On the other hand, salaries are high enough in some cities to be attractive to many whose regular job income is less than that paid to council-

TABLE 8.4   Salaries of Councilmen in Cities of over 5,000 Population

Population group	No. of of cities reporting	Lowest	Lower quartile	Median	Upper quartile	Highest
Over 500,000:						
Mayor-council	19	$3,000	$5,000	$ 8,000	$10,000	$17,500
250,000–500,000:						
Mayor-council ·	11	1,200	3,000	4,800	7,100	8,500
Council-manager	12	520	1,000	2,400	4,875	8,000
100,000–250,000:						
Mayor-council	28	250	1,080	1,775	2,925	8,500
Commission	9	4,800	6,600	10,000	12,000	13,500
Council-manager	42	120	1,200	1,800	3,000	6,000
50,000–100,000:						
Mayor-council	66	300	1,000	1,338	2,250	10,500
Commission	12	900	3,250	7,100	9,575	11,000
Council-manager	97	120	600	1,200	1,550	6,000
25,000–50,000:						
Mayor-council	120	240	600	900	1,438	6,500
Commission	33	500	2,200	4,500	6,600	9,804
Council-manager	185	10	300	600	1,210	3,600
10,000–25,000:						
Mayor-council	352	12	300	600	900	3,600
Commission	64	60	1,000	1,200	2,325	7,200
Council-manager	343	10	240	400	600	9,000
5,000–10,000:						
Mayor-council	546	12	240	360	600	4,800
Commission	42	100	600	700	1,065	4,500
Council-manager	237	9	125	300	480	3,600

Source: International City Managers Association, *The Municipal Year Book*, Chicago, 1966, p. 96.

men. It may also be true that a councilman's outside income is increased by the fact that he is a councilman. A lawyer may have clients primarily because some people think he is more useful to them because of his office; if a councilman is an insurance broker, he may sell many policies to people who feel they have something to gain from their business relations with him.

The Typical Councilman

The difficulty of describing a typical councilman has already been referred to, but some studies have furnished limited information about these public servants. In a study of six California cities Eugene C. Lee concludes:

> [The] California councilman is a man of 40 to 50 years of age, engaged in some professional, managerial or sales activity and living in the "better" part of town. He belongs to a service club, is probably a Mason, a member of a veteran's group and of the Chamber of Commerce. He is a protestant but not necessarily affiliated with any church. He had no previous official city experiences, although he was active in Community Chest, Red Cross, or related activities. He is a registered Republican but has not taken a very extensive part in partisan politics. He has lived in the city for a considerable length of time.[6]

This description is very similar to the results presented by Huckshorn and Young as a result of their study of councilmen in the city of Los Angeles County.[7] Obviously, differences in sizes of cities and geographic location will make significant differences in the characteristics of typical councilmen. Political affiliation will depend on party strength, but Republicans may often be more successful in city elections than the strength of the party would indicate, particularly if a nonpartisan ballot is used.

The larger the city, the more likely it is that the councilman will be a full-time politician. Meyerson and Banfield found in Chicago: "A few of the aldermen aspired to higher political office, especially (among those who were lawyers) to judgeships, but most of them were in the business of being aldermen as other men are in the business of selling shoes."[8] Religious affiliation is also a matter of local culture, as in Chicago, where two-thirds of the aldermen are Catholics. Charles Adrian contrasts the professional-political type of councilmen found in a large city like Detroit with the nonprofessional politicians who make up the council in a smaller place like Davenport, Iowa.[9]

LEGISLATIVE BEHAVIOR

Information about the qualifications, salaries, and backgrounds of city councilmen is of interest to the extent that it supplies some clues to their behavior as participants in the decision-making process. Other approaches are also available to secure information about legislative behavior; unfortunately most of the research involving these approaches has been applied to the study of

[6] Eugene C. Lee, *The Politics of Non-partisanship*, University of California Press, Berkeley, 1960, p. 50.

[7] R. J. Huckshorn and C. E. Young, "Study of Voting Splits on City Councils in Los Angeles County," *Western Political Quarterly*, vol. 13, pp. 479–497, June, 1960.

[8] Martin Meyerson and Edward C. Banfield, *Politics, Planning and the Public Interest*, The Free Press, Glencoe, Ill., 1955, p. 65.

[9] Charles R. Adrian, *Governing Urban America*, McGraw-Hill Book Company, New York, 1961, pp. 260, 261.

state rather than city legislators. Since some of the work directed toward a better understanding of the behavior patterns of state legislators may be useful to students interested in city politics a summary is included here.

Perhaps the oldest attempt to classify legislative behavior patterns is found in the writings of Edward Burke. He maintained that the representative is selected to be the *agent* of his constituents rather than a *spokesman* for their desires. In other words, he insisted that the legislator should use his own best judgment in making decisions which arise in the legislative process and not merely reflect what his constituents would like. The other extreme is the idea that the legislator is merely a representative sent to do the bidding of those who elected him to office. John Wahlke and others in more modern research efforts refer to the first as the "trustee" role of the legislator and to the second as the "delegate" role. They also identify a third role which they refer to as the "politico," in which the legislator as a skillful politician balances the different roles in terms of how he thinks his action will affect his future political career.[10]

Another approach to the analysis of legislative behavior is to classify such behavior in terms of the perception the legislator has of his role, i.e., in terms of the images legislators have of the role they are expected to play. The Wahlke study referred to above found that state legislators who responded to questions supplied to them could be classified in four categories: Ritualists, Tribunes, Inventors, and Brokers.[11] The *Ritualists* are those who conceive of themselves as the old hands who know the procedural ropes. They are sticklers for knowing and following the rules, and they feel they can be counted on to know how to get things done through the maze of legislative rules and established practices. The *Tribune* perceives of his role as the defender of the people. He seeks to learn what the people want and, knowing that, to translate their desires into legislation. The *Inventor* assumes that his responsibility is to plan and initiate policy. He understands that the government has a responsibility to seek solutions for social problems, and he assumes that he has the obligation to come up with proposed solutions. The *Broker* is the politician type. He views politics as conflict among groups who seek to gain something through governmental action, and considers that his role is to arrange compromises among the competitors and maintain public acceptance of the system. He is, in a sense, an arbitrator of political conflicts that are brought

---

[10] John C. Wahlke, Heinz Eulau, William Buchanan, and LeRoy C. Ferguson, *The Legislative System: Explorations in Legislative Behavior*, John Wiley & Sons, Inc., New York, 1962, pp. 272–280.
[11] *Ibid.*, pp. 247–249.

to the legislative arena for resolution. He is, of course, not unmindful of how his actions will advance or retard his own political career.

James Barber, in his study of state legislators in Connecticut, classified legislators according to their behavior patterns as follows:[12]

1. *The Spectator.* Some legislators looked upon legislative sessions as good shows which they enjoyed but in which they felt little involvement. "Like other members, they have 'competed' for nomination, 'campaigned' for office, and 'won' election, and are now empowered to take an active role in the making of laws. But once in the legislature, they settle back into the role of members of the audience, attending regularly but participating little or not at all. . . . The Spectator, then, stands out as a person of modest achievement, limited skills, and restricted ambitions, political or otherwise."[13]

2. *The Advertiser.* A sizable group of legislators looked upon their job as an opportunity to get their name before the public and to make good contacts that would advance their professional career. Half of this group were lawyers. "The Advertiser, then, takes a hard-headed, calculating stance toward his legislative office. His primary focus of attention is not on the softer rewards of good fellowship but on the use he can make of political office for his own advancement."[14]

3. *The Reluctant.* Another group of legislators appeared to be serving under protest; they did not want to run for office but were persuaded to do so. "The Reluctant Legislative Activity Profile shows a relatively low level of participation in all phases of current political life. . . . [and he] indicates a general lack of interest in political advancement."[15] Barber indicates that "more than most other members, he helps to ensure that the legislative rules of the game will be followed."[16]

4. *The Lawmaker.* Work gets done in legislatures because there exists a minority group of members who take their jobs seriously. Barber says that they "carry the main burdens of business. . . . [and] they appear to devote an unusual amount of attention and energy to the formulation and production of legislation." He concludes: "The politically significant result of the Lawmaker style is the infusion of reason and energy into an all too irrational and sluggish system."[17]

Some significant research designed to discover behavior patterns of city councilmen is being conducted by the City Council Research Project sponsored by the Institute of Political Studies at Stanford University. One study already published distinguishes three types of councilmen with regard to their attitudes toward interest groups.

---

[12] James David Barber, *The Lawmakers: Recruitment and Adaptation to Legislative Life,* Yale University Press, New Haven, Conn., 1965.

[13] *Ibid.,* pp. 23, 24, 25.

[14] *Ibid.,* p. 69.

[15] *Ibid.,* p. 119.

[16] *Ibid.,* p. 159.

[17] *Ibid.,* p. 164.

1. Pluralists are those who esteemed groups, perceived many groups, and attributed their influence to "objective strength or perceived stake."

2. Tolerants are those (a) who maintained a neutral attitude toward groups, perceived many groups, and attributed their influence to "respect," or (b) who esteemed or rejected groups but perceived few groups and attributed their influence to "respect."

3. Antagonists are (a) those who reject groups and attribute their influence to strength or perceived stake, and (b) those who are neutral toward groups, perceive many groups, and attribute their influence to strength and perceived stake.

The pluralists, who are most likely to be receptive to community organizations, constituted only about 25 percent of the sample studied.[18]

COUNCIL ORGANIZATION

Any attempt to describe the organization of city councils is made difficult by the great variation in their size and the degree of complexity of conflict issues which come to them for resolution. Certain features which seem to be significant have been selected for general discussion.

Presiding Officers

The type of officer who presides at council sessions depends to a large extent on the form of government employed and the size of the city. In mayor-council cities with large populations, the presiding officer is likely to be a president of the council or board of aldermen who is elected to the office from the city at large. He may or may not be a regular voting member. If he is a regular member, he may be the only one not elected from a ward or district. The president of the council may be assigned other duties by the charter. For example, in St. Louis, he is, ex officio, a member of the board of estimate and apportionment which considers the city budget before it is presented to the board of aldermen by the mayor. In most cases he will assume the duties of the office of mayor if the mayor is incapacitated or is out of the city.

In smaller mayor-council cities the mayor is often the presiding officer at

---

[18] Betty H. Zisk, Heinz Eulau, and Kenneth Prewitt, "City Councilmen and the Group Struggle: A Typology of Role Orientations," *Journal of Politics*, vol. 27, pp. 618–646, August, 1965.

See also Robert Eyestone and Heinz Eulau, "City Councils and Policy Outcomes: Development Profiles," in James Q. Wilson (ed.), *City Politics and Public Policy*, John Wiley & Sons, Inc., New York, 1968, pp. 37–65.

council meetings, but he has no vote except in cases of a tie; in other instances the council elects one of its own members to serve as the presiding officer.

In commission-governed cities one of the commissioners serves as the presiding officer. The charter often provides that the commissioner of public safety shall automatically be chairman of the commission; in other cities the commission chooses a chairman from among its own members. The title of mayor is often given to the commission chairman in these cities but his responsibilities are usually ceremonial rather than administrative in character.

In cities employing the council-manager form of government the presiding officer is a member of the council. In some cases he is elected specifically to be chairman of the council; in others his selection is by his colleagues on the council. If he is elected as chairman he will be one, and often the only one, of the councilmen elected at large. Although the chairman of the council will officially have the title of mayor, he is not considered an administrative officer.

Meetings

Seldom is the councilman's job considered to be on a full-time basis. Only a few very large cities have specific dates when the council is in regular session. More often, councils meet periodically once or twice a month. In smaller cities where councilmen are professional, business, and working-class people, meetings are held at night so as not to interfere with regular work. Special meetings are fairly common and can usually be called by the chairman or by a certain number of council members.

An agenda for each council meeting is usually prepared before the group convenes. In mayor-council cities the agenda is usually prepared by the city clerk with advice from the council chairman, and the same is true in commission cities. In council-manager cities the city manager prepares the order of business. In any case, provision is made for a time when individual councilmen can introduce matters not included on the agenda.

Rules of Procedure

Many city charters include certain procedural requirements with which the council must comply. These generally relate to the form (ordinance, resolution, or order) of council action, requirements for public notice when action is to be taken, provisions for public hearings, and the number of votes required for positive action. Other matters relating to council procedures are contained in a statement of "Rules and Order of Business" adopted by the council itself. Once such a set of rules is drafted and approved they usually are altered very little from one council to another.

Public participation is provided by holding public hearings. The common practice is to give some kind of public notice that a bill has been introduced and the date at which it will be brought up for debate and final action. On this date citizens who are interested may appear and make known to the council their attitudes. Public notice and public hearing may be absolute requirements in the passage of ordinances setting tax rates, approving budgets, providing for public improvements which are to be financed by special assessments upon property owners, or changes in land-use patterns.

Although final action on legislative matters must take place in a regular council session which complies with all established procedural rules, often this final vote is only a matter of form. The actual decision may have already been made under some kind of informal relationships. In many cities, councils have established the custom of having an informal meeting prior to the time set in public notices for the formal session. At these informal caucuses members often decide what they will do at the formal sessions. Compromises and deals can be arranged within these caucuses which might be much more difficult to accomplish in open sessions; it is often in these caucus sessions that conflicts are aired and real debate takes place. Only after a fairly high degree of consensus is achieved will an issue be brought before an open council session for passage. Williams and Adrian, in their four cities study, make the following comment about councils they observed.

> Unlike representative assemblies at higher levels of government the city legislature does not provide the public forum to bare the character of disputes among groups. . . . There were occasional individuals who enjoyed conflict in the public limelight, but these men were rare. Consequently, most councilmen were quite willing for the drama of city policy formation to be played off-stage where they and their colleagues were scarcely identified as participants.[19]

The so-called executive session of the city council is not uncommon in American cities. These sessions are more official than the caucus session discussed above. They are essentially sessions from which the public and press are barred, and the assumption is that matters are to be discussed that

---

[19] Oliver P. Williams and Charles R. Adrian, *Four Cities; A Study in Comparative Policy Making*, University of Pennsylvania Press, Philadelphia, 1963, pp. 294, 295.

should not be debated publicly. Executive sessions are common when personnel matters come before the council. Since charges made against a public official, if made publicly, might be injurious to him whether or not they can be substantiated, councils prefer to discuss these charges secretly until they are convinced that the evidence is sufficient to justify punitive action. The executive session is also used when the subject for discussion may, if publicized, affect property values. Probable public improvements, changes in land use, and park improvements fall in this category. Once the council has agreed on the nature of the action it will take, the decision may be legitimized in an open session.

POWERS OF CITY LEGISLATURES

Cities, as creatures of the state, can exercise only those powers which are specifically given to them by state constitutions, state statutes, or city charters drafted in conformity with constitution and statute. Strictly speaking, the powers which are conferred upon the city belong to the council or board of aldermen unless they are specifically delegated to another agency. It is not uncommon, however, to find that many powers which might well be classified as legislative in character have been specifically delegated by the state to some other agency of city government. In many cities the library board and the park board may be legally authorized to levy taxes for their specific purposes and to decide how revenue derived from these levies will be budgeted. Boards of health promulgate regulations relating to waste disposal and restaurant sanitation, traffic commissioners determine speed limits, location of control signals, and direction of traffic flow on streets, and park boards promulgate rules defining acceptable conduct in public parks. In many other types of legislation the council may do little more than give final approval to legislative measures which have been prepared and recommended for passage by city boards, commissions, or authorities.

The most extensive list of powers assigned to city councils is usually to be found in city charters. These lists include all the objects on which the council can legislate. The *Model City Charter* promulgated by the National Municipal League seeks to convey legislative power upon the council by the general statement: "All powers of the city and the determination of all matters of policy shall be vested in the council."[20] Because of specific provisions of law in some states, consultants to charter-writing commissions advise the more

[20] National Municipal League, *The Model City Charter*, New York, 1941, p. 5.

cumbersome method of including in long lists the specific areas of policy in which the council may enter in order to ensure compliance with state statutes.

Nonlegislative Functions

Although most of the efforts of city councils will be devoted to legislative matters, numerous other types of action are presented to them for consideration. In many cases these matters may provoke more serious conflict than do matters of a legislative character.

1. The council may be required to approve appointments of administrators, particularly appointments to boards and commissions.

2. The council may have power to remove some officials from office. In the case of city managers, this power to remove at any time is considered a part of the system. In many mayor-council cities the mayor and other administrative officials are subject to removal by the council for cause by the process of impeachment.

3. The council may be authorized to determine the qualification of its own members.

4. The council may conduct investigations. This investigative power is generally assumed to be associated with the power to make laws.

5. Councils may adopt resolutions expressing the sentiments of the council on matters over which it has no authority to take more positive action. Often such resolutions are intended to seek some kind of action from federal, state, or county officials on matters affecting the city.

6. Councils have certain powers related to charter making. The council may submit to the voters the question as to whether or not a commission should be organized to draft a new charter. It may formally propose amendments to an existing charter, or create a commission to recommend to it proposals for charter change.

BIBLIOGRAPHY

Books

Adrian, Charles R.: *Governing Urban America*, 2d ed., McGraw-Hill Book Company, New York, 1964, chap. 10.

Banfield, Edward C., and James Q. Wilson: *City Politics*, Vintage Books, Random House, Inc., New York, 1963, chap. 3.

Barber, James David: *The Lawmakers: Recruitment and Adaptation to Legislative Behavior*, Yale University Press, New Haven, 1965.

Lee, Eugene C.: *The Politics of Non-Partisanship*, University of California Press, Berkeley, 1960.

Meyerson, Martin, and Edward C. Banfield: *Politics, Planning and the Public Interest*, The Free Press, Glencoe, Ill., 1955, chap. 3.

Sayre, Wallace S., and Herbert Kaufman: *Governing New York City: Politics in the Metropolis,* The Russell Sage Foundation, New York, 1960, chap. 16.

Wahlke, John C., Heinz Eulau, William Buchanan, and LeRoy Ferguson: *The Legislative System: Explorations in Legislative Behavior,* John Wiley Sons, Inc., New York, 1962.

Articles

Bromage, Arthur W.: "Ten Traits of City Councilmen," *Public Management,* vol. 33, pp. 74–77, April, 1951.

Ebel, Alice L.: "Investigatory Powers of City Councils," *Marquette Law Review,* vol. 38, pp. 223–236, spring, 1955.

Eystone, Robert, and Heinz Eulau, "City Councils and Policy Outcomes: Development Profiles," in James Q. Wilson (ed.), *City Politics and Public Policy,* John Wiley & Sons, Inc., New York, 1962, pp. 37–65.

Huckshorn, R. J., and C. E. Young: "A Study of Voting Splits on City Councils in Los Angeles County," *Western Political Quarterly,* vol. 13, pp. 479–497, June, 1960.

McGeary, M. Nelson: "The Councilman Learns His Job," *National Municipal Review,* vol. 43, pp. 284–287, June, 1954.

Zisk, Betty H., Heinz Eulau, and Kenneth Prewitt: "City Councilmen and the Group Struggle: A Typology of Role Orientation," *Journal of Politics,* vol. 27, pp. 618–646, August, 1965.

9

THE CITY CHIEF EXECUTIVE

If a fictional man from Mars should land in the backyard of a typical city resident and say, "Take me to your leader," the mayor of the city would soon have a visitor. The mayor of American cities has become so strongly identified with local leadership in the public mind that citizens look to his office for solutions to the city's problems and place the blame there if they are unhappy with the results. In all forms of human organization some person or office is singled out, in the minds of the public, to project a single image of the total organization. In governmental organizations this role is associated with the chief executive: the President, the governor, or the mayor. Since this officer, as perceived by the public, represents the government, any accolades or criticisms which the citizen wishes to bestow upon government in general are apt to be aimed directly and specifically at the chief executive. Whether or not the mayor has the formal legal powers or the organizational support required to make a major impact on policy making, he will be expected to have such competence, and behavior toward him will be governed accordingly.

It is not the purpose of this chapter to discuss and evaluate various theories of leadership, to enumerate the personal characteristics of leaders, or to classify the situational factors which produce different kinds of leaders, but some observations about leadership may be useful for an understanding of the role of the chief executive in American cities. One element of leadership found consistently in the literature is that the leader understands and gives effect to forces found among those he leads. Tolstoi's expression was, "The leader exists only to give form and expression to the energy of his followers."[1] Woodrow Wilson supported this notion of leadership when he described political leadership as "the capacity to give sight to the blind forces of public thought."[2] Thomas Gordon concluded that the leader must perceive what it is that the group wants, he must contribute something that will move them closer to that goal, and the contribution must be acceptable to the group.[3]

The concept of leadership contained in these statements seems most nearly to describe the position of the mayor. He is not likely to be possessed of the charismatic quality which by force of his attractive personality wins followers with religious fervor. He much more likely will be accepted by the voters because he has convinced them that he knows what they want and he has the ability to propose and secure approval of ways and means to accomplish these desires. This is not to imply that all mayors have such a clear perspective of the needs of their constituents or of the means for their fulfillment, but those who, in their tenure of office, receive widespread approval do possess this quality of leadership in some degree.

Each mayor, even though he may see clearly the problems he must face and has developed what he conceives to be workable solutions, is faced with the practical task of effecting these solutions. Organizational, legal, and political considerations combine to set limits to the amount of change any single mayor can achieve. The mayors who score a record of achievement are often those who can secure positive action in the face of formal and political obstacles that are present in most city political systems.

DEVELOPMENT OF THE OFFICE OF MAYOR

The following discussion of the office of mayor is limited to the office as it has developed in cities using the mayor-council plan of government; the office of mayor in other governmental forms is quite different. The term "mayor" used to refer to the city executive was brought to this country from England and was in use before the revolution. Mayors in colonial cities re-

---

[1] Quoted from Stephen K. Bailey, "Leadership in Local Government," *Yale Law Review*, vol. 46, pp. 563–566, 569–571, summer, 1965.

[2] *Ibid.*

[3] Thomas Gordon, *Group Centered Leadership*, Houghton Mifflin Company, Boston, 1955, p. 51.

ceived their appointments from the colonial governors. After the American federal system was established, city charters modeled governmental structure along the lines of the federal and state governments. Early mayors, however, were chosen by city councils, their terms of office were for only one year, and their powers were narrowly circumscribed. After 1820 mayors were usually popularly elected but the office had little prestige and most governmental power remained in the council. Administrative functions which are now regularly associated with the office of mayor were performed by councilmen, usually through committee chairmen.

In the years following 1850 cities experienced rapid growth both in their population and in the complexity of administrative tasks which they faced. For a number of years cities attempted to cope with their new administrative load by creating boards and commissions, each with a specific function to perform, rather than by strengthening the office of mayor. After 1880 the office of mayor as a chief administrative office began to take shape. The term of office was extended, the mayor was given greater authority to appoint and remove other administrative officers, and his position vis-à-vis the council was strengthened. The reform movements following 1900 produced a significant swing toward the strong executive at all levels of government, and the office of mayor was strengthened in both power and prestige. In most modern mayor-council cities, the office of mayor possesses the legal powers and the tools of executive leadership that give it the same status locally that the office of the governor has on a statewide basis.[4]

Since the kind of persons who are recruited for the position of mayor and the ability of mayors to play a dominant role in decision making depends, in part, on the provision of city charters that establish the formal characteristics of the office, these will be discussed before any attempt will be made to consider the functions of the office.

STRUCTURE OF THE OFFICE

Direct popular election is the prevailing pattern found in mayor-council cities for selection of the mayors; of cities over 5,000, 96.6 percent of all mayors are selected in this manner, 3.9 percent are selected by the council, and in 0.5 percent the councilman receiving the highest vote in the election is auto-

[4] For a more extensive discussion of the historical development of the office of mayor, see John A. Fairlie, *Municipal Administration*, The Macmillan Company, New York, 1901, chaps. 5, 19; and William B. Munro, *The Government of American Cities*, 3d ed., The Macmillan Company, New York, 1920, chap. 1.

matically declared to be the mayor. The few mayor-council cities which do not elect their mayors directly by popular vote are in the 5,000 to 10,000 population range. Most popularly elected mayors have no regular vote in the council but can vote to break a tie; only 13.5 percent are permitted to vote on all issues, while 64.7 percent can vote in case of a tie.[5]

Term of Office

Of the 1,490 mayor-council cities with populations of 5,000 or more for which data are available, 53.6 percent provide a four-year term for mayor and 42.4 percent use a two-year term, with the remainder having either one- or three-year terms. In general the larger cities provide four-year terms. Of the 20 cities with populations of 500,000 or more which are operating under the mayor-council plan, only Cleveland and Houston have two-year terms; all others provide terms of four years. Only 11 of the 27 cities with populations between 250,000 and 500,000 have mayor-council government, and all but two of these give their mayors four-year terms.[6]

The salary provided for city mayors is closely related to the size of the city. Table 9.1 shows the highest, lowest, and median salaries of mayors in cities of various population ranges. The very low salaries attached to the office in smaller cities indicates that the office is considered to be a part-time one and the incumbent is expected to continue in his profession, trade, or business while holding the office.

Legal Qualifications

The practice of including specific qualifications for officeholders in constitutions and charters is well established in this country. In some instances general state statutes will require that all mayors have a certain period of residence in the state to be eligible to serve. Certainly, most city charters spell out some formal requirements. In general these would include age, residence, and citizenship. The minimum will be the same requirements as are demanded for qualified voters, but many charters require an age greater than 21 years and a specific period of United States citizenship. Such legal qualifications are much less significant than are political considerations in determining the kind of person who is able to put together enough support to be nominated in a

[5] International City Managers Association, *The Municipal Year Book*, Chicago, 1966, p. 91.
[6] *Ibid.*, p. 92.

TABLE 9.1   Salaries of Mayors in Mayor-Council Cities

Population	Highest	Median	Lowest
500,000 and over	$50,000	$25,000	$14,000
250,000–500,000	30,000	20,000	9,600
100,000–250,000	20,000	15,250	7,200
50,000–100,000	20,000	12,000	1,500
25,000–50,000	20,000	7,500	100
10,000–25,000	15,000	3,000	20

Source: International City Managers Association, *The Municipal Year Book,* Chicago, 1966, p. 92.

primary and persuade a majority of voters to choose him in a city-wide vote. Factors such as religion, nationality, race, and personality may be far more important than age, residence, or length of citizenship.

Removal

Most mayors are removed from office simply by the expiration of their term and failure to be reelected or by voluntary retirement. In many cities, however, the mayor can be removed from office before his regular term expires. State statutes may provide that any locally elected official will be removed from office upon his conviction of a felony or of a crime "involving moral turpitude." In some states the governor can remove a mayor from office for cause, as outlined in the statutes. The city council may be empowered by charter to bring charges against a mayor, and through a process similar to impeachment it may remove him from office. In such cases a greater than a simple majority vote is usually required.

By a process known as "recall," mayors may be removed by the electorate without any kind of formal accusation or trial. If a petition to remove a mayor is signed by a sufficient number of qualified voters (usually from 10 to 25 percent), a special election is held at which the voters decide to remove or retain the mayor in office. To prevent the use of the recall to harass the mayor, provisions are usually made so that only one recall election is possible during a single term of office.

Very little information is available from which one can judge the impact of legal means of removal upon the behavior of mayors. The resignation of James Walker from his position as mayor of New York City in 1932 in the face of a hearing before the state governor is often cited as evidence of the effectiveness of this method of removal. Even if data were available to show

how many mayors were removed from office before their terms expired, generalizations about removal procedures would be difficult. The argument can be made that the effectiveness of such devices is measured not in terms of how many mayors were removed but in terms of the number not removed; i.e., the prospect of removal may be "a gun behind the door" that conditions the behavior of mayors so that sentiment for removal does not develop.

Succession

Vacancies in the office of mayor may occur for a number of reasons, including death, disability, or removal from office. More often, however, the office may become vacant due to resignation. A mayor may elect to run for governor or United States senator or he may accept an appointment from the President. In the larger cities which have a president of the council or board of aldermen, this officer is generally first in line of succession. In other cities a popularly elected administrator may succeed to the office of mayor or the council may be empowered to elect a successor. Some charters provide that if a major part of the unexpired term is remaining, a special election will be called by the council to fill the vacancy. Whenever the charter provides for the holder of a specific office to be first in line of succession, this official assumes the duties of the mayor temporarily when the mayor is out of the city.

FUNCTIONS OF THE MAYOR

Because of the great number of cities involved and the variations in their size it is very difficult to generalize about the function of the mayor even when the cities are operating under the mayor-council system. One of the best discussions of the function of the office of mayor is found in the description by Sayre and Kaufman of this office in New York City.[7] Obviously, this office in the nation's largest city is a special case; yet much of what they say is applicable generally to other cities. At least, their classification of the functions of the office is useful in examining any city. They use four categories to group the functions of the office of mayor and refer to the holder of the office as chief of state for the city, chief executive, chief legislator, and chief of party. Each of these will be considered separately.

[7] Wallace S. Sayre and Herbert Kaufman, *Governing New York City: Politics in the Metropolis*, Russell Sage Foundation, New York, 1960, pp. 658–662.

Chief of State for the City

Early in the development of the office in this country the mayor was looked upon as a ceremonial head of the city long before he became a chief administrative officer. To most city residents and to visitors to the city the mayor personifies the city, and he is expected to represent the city at all major ceremonial occasions. Because of the public image of the office as the personification of the city, all kinds of private and public organizations seek to use the prestige of the office to promote their causes. The following quotation from Sayre and Kaufman is expressive of this ceremonial function.

> He must issue formal proclamations launching community drives or awarding the city's recognition to deserving groups or persons; he must welcome distinguished visitors; he must appear as principal speaker or guest of honor at scores of meetings, breakfasts, luncheons, and dinners each month; he must see an unending stream of citizens great and small, listen to their petitions or demands and respond to many other intercessions that come to him by letter or telephone. In short he must make himself visible, accessible, communicative, and responsive to the city and its people. This is one of the most important ways the mayor establishes the popular image of himself and his office.[8]

These ceremonial functions of the mayor of New York City differ from those of mayors of other cities only in the intensity of demands made upon him, not in the kind of demands.

Chief Executive

Most city charters which prescribe the mayor-council form of government specifically charge the mayor with responsibility for the faithful execution of the ordinances even though in many instances other officers or agencies are created to administer specific functions of the city. For example, city parks, land-use planning, and city libraries may be operated under boards or commissions over which the mayor exercises very little control. In fact, the significant differences between weak-mayor-council government and strong-mayor-council government is in the degree to which administrative activities are concentrated under the mayor or are dispersed among a number of semi-independent boards and commissions or popularly elected department heads. Even though structurally the mayor is not responsible for, nor in a position to influence, many administrative functions of the city, he will nevertheless, be

[8] *Ibid.*, p. 658.

blamed for their failures by the citizens who are not aware of existing charter limitations.

Many cities which have written new mayor-council charters or have revised old ones in the last thirty years now give formal authority to the mayor which enables him to exert strong influence over most city administrators and the activities of the departments which they head.

Attempts to enumerate the functions of chief executives have never been very satisfactory, but activities of city mayors can be identified with sufficient accuracy to be useful to the student.

1. The mayor in his relations with those who carry on the day-to-day work of the city can set the tone or determine the style of administrative personnel. He may emphasize efficiency and courtesy on the part of workers who have contacts with the public and may by word and behavior stress "equal treatment" for all citizens by all city employees.

2. The mayor may act as spokesman for administrative employees of the city by pleading their cause for more adequate salaries and working conditions in public discussions and before city councils or their committees.

3. The mayor may make a strong impact on the enforcement of ordinances by executive decrees, orders, and directives which are necessary to clarify language in ordinances or to determine conditions under which ordinances become effective.

4. He may achieve greater coordination of effort of various administrative agencies by meeting with responsible administrators and working out plans which clarify the areas in which each agency is to function and which establish specific means for settling any jurisdictional problems that arise in practice.

5. He may stimulate long-range planning by departments through cabinet meetings where innovations and new ideas are encouraged. In fact, he may, by virtue of his position, require such plans from his subordinates which then become the basis for discussion in cabinet sessions.

6. He may select certain problems which face the city for special treatment and through his contacts with administrators secure a concentrated effort toward their solution even though other problems may have to be shelved for the time.

Most mayors in American cities now have available to them in some degree the tools they need to be effective in setting administrative style in their cities. Some of these are worth special notice.

1. The power to appoint and remove from office chief administrative officials is now fairly well established. Although council approval may be required for top-level appointments, this approval is often a matter of form only. Some cities still require the popular election of one or more top-level administrators (e.g., comptroller), but in many cases the victorious candidate has won his office with the support of the mayor and he may be as willing to cooperate as if he were appointed. In some large cities the mayor's appointive power is limited by a merit system of personnel administration which includes top-level

administrators, but in general, department heads are exempt from tenure provisions of the civil service code.

2. The mayor is generally required to prepare a budget for submission to the council, and after final legislative action on the budget, he controls the expenditure of funds in conformance with legislative intent. The fact that administrative officers must plead their case with the mayor in order to get their monetary needs included in the budget gives to the mayor a strong hand in assuring their cooperation in his overall program. Likewise, the fact that money authorized by council action is not available to a spending agency until released by the mayor or his budget officer strengthens the mayor's hand in dealing with his administrators.

3. The mayor's access to the press, radio, and local TV gives him a strong position to carry his case to the public in the event that an administrative officer should try to operate outside the policy lines presented by him or worked out in staff and cabinet conferences. It would be an unusual administrator who would feel that he could win public opinion to his side in an open contest with the mayor.

4. The mayor's position as a political leader increases his prestige in person-to-person relations with administrators. Most top administrators, in large cities at least, are politicians in that they have been active in election campaigns and they may have future political ambitions. Working with the mayor may be one of the ways they can strengthen their position and win organization support for these ambitions.

Although the mayor has available to him both formal and informal means to exercise great influence in decisions made by all administrative agencies, the extent to which he uses his position depends on his own personality and political style. Meyerson and Banfield point out the significance for the public housing program in Chicago of the difference between the method of operation of Mayor Kelley and that of Mayor Kennelly.

During Mayor Kelley's regime the Authority could be independent because Kelley paid its political bills. . . . After his retirement the Authority had only a shell of its independence. . . . It was not until late in 1947 or early in 1948 that the heads of the Authority realized that Mayor Kennelly was not going to be a mayor in the same sense that Mayor Kelley had been or, indeed, in any significant sense at all. Until 1948 it was reasonable for them to suppose that the Mayor was the person with whom a general understanding would have to be reached. But when at last it became evident that the city government was to be run by the "Big Boys" of the Council it would not have been easy for the heads of the Authority, even if they had tried, to reach an understanding with them.[9]

[9] Reprinted with permission of The Macmillan Company from *Politics, Planning and the Public Interest*, by Martin Meyerson and Edward C. Banfield, copyright 1955 by The Free Press, a division of The Macmillan Company, New York, p. 258.

The nature of the office of mayor gives to its occupant a position of power and influence not possessed by any other official of the city. Robert Salisbury noted this in his essay dealing with what he calls "the new congruence of power" in urban politics.

> Of what is mayoral influence composed? Much of it is contained in the office itself. Of all the roles in the community none is so well situated with respect to the flow of information concerning the city's problems. This alone gives the occupant of the office a great advantage over other influentials. He knows more about more things than anyone else.[10]

Insofar as "knowledge is power," no other administrator can compete with the mayor. Each top administrator may know more about the internal operations of his own department than does the mayor, but he knows much less about other administrative operations, about council action, or about party and interest-group pressures. Salisbury also suggests that some of the influence that attaches to the office of mayor results from the fact that he can co-opt almost any business or civic leader in the city to serve on ad hoc citizen committees to work on major issues which arise.

Chief Legislator

The role of the chief executive in the legislative process is becoming more significant at all levels of government; this is particularly true of the mayor in city politics. The influence of the mayor in legislative action arises, in part, from the fact that he is the most visible official in the city. Scott Greer, in a study following the defeat of a city-county coordination proposal in the St. Louis area, found that more people knew where Mayor Tucker stood on the proposition than any other person involved. Although only one-third of the samples studied knew where the *Post-Dispatch* stood on the issue, 55 percent in the county and 33 percent in the city knew where Mayor Tucker stood.[11] Not only do people know who the mayor is and what his position is on important conflict issues, but they expect him to do something about their problems. Very few citizens who become involved in political issues and campaigns know or care about theories of separation of legislative and executive powers. If a housewife is thoroughly disgusted with the city's garbage and

[10] Robert H. Salisbury, "Urban Politics: The New Convergence of Power," *Journal of Politics*, vol. 26, pp. 788, 789, November, 1964.
[11] Scott Greer, *Metropolitics: A Study of Political Culture*, John Wiley & Sons, Inc., New York, 1963, pp. 105–109.

refuse collection, she will direct her criticism at the mayor without seeking to find out whether the council has failed to pass ordinances designed to improve the service. If new ordinances are required, she will expect the mayor to see that they are passed. Mayors are aware of this public image of their job, and, in order to maintain their popularity with the electorate, they try to fulfill their expectations. Therefore, a mayor may give as much time to his legislative program as he does to his administrative duties.

Although much of the mayor's influence will be exerted informally through personal contacts or through appeals for public support in the press and on the airwaves, a number of avenues for influencing the final legislative product are made available to him by the structural form of government.

1. He may participate personally in sessions of the council or board of aldermen. In many small cities the mayor is the presiding officer of the council and, as such, he can be effective in controlling the agenda, the nature of debate, and the kind of action that may be in order at council sessions. Some city charters specifically authorize the mayor to introduce proposed ordinances, but even if no such formal power is provided, he can always find a councilman who is willing to introduce bills for him. Most mayors in large cities prepare regular messages which they deliver to the council. These messages are designed to give the mayor an opportunity to prepare a legislative program and lay it before the legislature. Such messages are given widespread publicity as the mayor's program, and his personal prestige, as well as that of his office, forces the council to give them careful attention. Special messages which deal in greater detail with specific subjects may be presented to the council at any time by the mayor. In most mayor-council–governed cities the mayor may vote on legislative matters only in case of a tie. Of the popularly elected mayors in cities with a population of 5,000 or more which operate under the mayor-council form, 13.5 percent can vote on all issues and 64.7 percent vote only in case of a tie.[12] Obviously, the percentage of mayors with regular voting rights in commission and council-manager cities is much higher. The larger the city, the less likely it is that the mayor will regularly attend council meetings and the more likely that he will have to use informal approaches to exercise influence over the legislative process.

2. *The Veto*   The power to sign into law or veto acts of legislative bodies has been regularly associated with the chief executive at all levels of government in this country. Although this power is very infrequently given to mayors in commission or council-manager cities, it is quite commonly delegated by charter to mayors in mayor-council cities. Of 1,489 mayor-council cities reporting in 1966, in only 32.6 percent did the mayor not have any veto; in 33.6 percent the mayor could veto all measures passed by the council, and in 33.8 percent the veto applied only to selected items.[13] In most cities vetoes may be overridden by the council, but more than a simple majority vote is usually required. The mayor is often given added strength to control expenditures through the item

[12] International City Managers Association, *op. cit.*, p. 91.
[13] *Ibid.*, p. 92.

veto, which permits him to disapprove of single items of expenditure in appropriation or budget ordinances while approving other items in the same ordinances. He may also be permitted to reduce the amount provided in an ordinance and then approve it for the reduced amount; he cannot, however, increase items of expenditure.

The importance of the mayor's veto power cannot be measured in terms of the number of times it is used. A public threat to use the veto by the mayor may have sufficient effect on councilmen to make an actual veto unnecessary. An interesting phenomenon in American politics is the tendency for the articulate public to support the executive when an open conflict between the legislature and the executive develops.

Chief of Party

Seymour Freegood, in describing new strength in city hall, catches in a highly literate fashion the concept of the mayor as a political leader.

> The big problem at city hall is no longer honesty, or even simple efficiency. The fight for these virtues is a continuous one, of course, and Lucifer is always lurking in the Hall but most big-city governments have become reasonably honest and efficient. Today, the big problem is not good housekeeping: it is whether the mayor can provide the aggressive leadership and the positive programs without which no big city has a prayer. What is to get priority? (and for whom?) There is only so much money, and if hard policy decision are not made, the city's energies will be diffused in programs "broad" but not bold. . . .
>
> Above all the mayor is a politician. True, he may have risen to office on the back of a reform movement. But he is not, as has happened too often in the past, a "non-political" civic leader who rallies the do-gooders, drives the rascals out of City Hall, serves an undistinguished term or two, and then withdraws—or gets driven out—leaving the city to another cycle of corruption. Instead, he fits the qualifications of the mayors whom Lincoln Steffens called on the public to elect: "Politicians working for the reform of the city with the methods of politics."[14]

In order for a mayor to perform a leadership role and actively participate in the legislative and administrative decision-making process he must have an organizational base of support. In small cities this may come from a more-or-less permanent citizens' committee or a federation of semipolitical good-government organizations, but in large cities it is more likely to come from the local organization of one or the other of the two national political parties. In these large cities the candidate for mayor must establish a degree of leadership in a party before he can be elected. Once he wins the office he can

[14] The Editors of *Fortune, The Exploding Metropolis,* Anchor Books, Doubleday & Company, Inc., Garden City, N.Y., 1958, pp. 63, 64, 68.

use the patronage of the office to consolidate and perpetuate his position of power. The nominating process is the avenue through which the mayor has established his party position; effective dispensing of rewards available to the holder of the office is the tool he uses to strengthen his leadership position. The existence of nonpartisan ballots in most smaller cities and in some of the larger ones may complicate the process through which party leadership is established and maintained, but it does not constitute an impossible barrier. Even though party labels cannot appear on official ballots or the faces of voting machines, party organizations through advertisements, sample ballots, door-to-door visits, and in campaign oratory give the voter ample opportunity to know who the party-sponsored candidates are. The nature of the legal party organization in many states complicates the process of building party support within small and middle-sized cities. Except in large cities the geographic base of party organization is usually the township and the county, and in many instances a single city may be located in two or more townships. This makes it practically impossible for a party committeeman or committeewoman at the county level to represent a single city. In fact, under the party organization prescribed by law in some states, it is very unlikely that any formal city party organization can exist except in very large cities where the ward replaces the township as the base for county organization.

In some American cities attempts have been made to give the mayor party support by organizing what might be called a local party. Its membership might well be drawn from members of both state parties, and it might perform locally most of the functions that regular parties perform at the state and national level. In many instances such organizations were put together to accomplish some major structural change, such as home rule for the city or a city-wide merit system, and then it was decided to continue their existence to ensure continuity for the reform that had been achieved.

THE MAYOR AND OTHER GOVERNMENTS

In the discussion of the legal position of the city in relation to the state, the point was emphasized that in many cases positive action by the city on matters of local policy depended on the ability of city leaders to persuade the state legislature to pass some kind of enabling statutes. The burden of presenting the city's case before the public in general, and state legislators in particular, usually falls upon the mayor. He is the one person who may be presumed to speak for the city. In some cases the appeal to the state legislature is for action on a specific function which the city would like to perform but cannot under existing laws; again, it might be a request for legislative permission to levy a new kind of tax not at the time authorized by state law. Some city mayors have preferred to prepare a package deal which includes a number of subjects on which they seek action at the state level. Such a package may range from a request enabling the city to engage in a function which will be wholly supported out of city taxes to a request that the state take over and finance an activity which at the time is financed locally. An example of the first is a request to permit a city to construct off-street parking facilities and pay the costs out of parking-meter receipts; an example of the second is a plea by the city that the state take over and operate a mental hospital that has been the responsibility of the city. Regardless of the nature of the action requested from the state, the mayor will be expected to carry the brunt of the burden of securing favorable action. Many large cities maintain regular lobbyists at state capitals during legislative sessions to assist the mayor in his relations with legislators. A major factor in determining the mayor's effectiveness at the state capital will be the strength of his party leadership. If a state governor or state legislature needs his support to win the city vote, his voice will carry great weight at the state capital.

Recent years have seen great changes in the interest of the federal Congress in matters of concern to urban areas. Extensive federally aided programs of slum clearance, urban renewal, public housing, and vocational training have brought city officials closer to the federal government than was formerly the case. The complexity of these programs requires extensive negotiations between federal and city officials. The mayor as the spokesman for the city spends more and more of his time in appeals to Washington for federal aid for local programs and in negotiation with federal officials who approve these programs at the various stages of completion.

Most large cities in this country are parts of complex metropolitan areas in which the city government is only one of many numerous governments operating within the area. Complications arising out of the tangle of local governments require the mayor to negotiate with other mayors, county officials, and agents of super special-purpose district governments. The problems inherent in these areas were discussed at greater length in an earlier chapter.

EVALUATION OF POSITION OF MAYOR

Certainly no public office in a mayor-council city is as important politically as the mayor. The holder of this office personifies the city, not only to residents of the city but also to decision makers at the state and national level. The mayor is expected to be accessible to leaders of all interest groups which seek to influence the decisions that are made by the city government. Form and structure of city government in some instances reinforce the authority of the mayor by broad prescriptions of power, while in others they tend to set limits to his power to exert influence by decentralizing and scattering formal powers among semi-independent boards and commissions. In most cities, however, the role of the mayor in the resolution of conflict among divergent political forces is determined by the personality, values, and political competence of the men who are recruited for the office. If one could view the political history of a large city as a curve with peaks representing periods of progress in terms of physical development and social sensitivity separated by troughs of complacency when government was little more than a spectator to the events taking place in the city, he would find that the peaks corresponded closely to periods when the city had a mayor who was willing and able to maximize both the formal and the political strength available to the office to influence decisions in all governmental agencies, while on the other hand the periods of inactivity would correspond with terms of service of mayors who were either unwilling or unable to take advantage of the great resources available to the office. The description by Sayre and Kaufman is meant to apply specifically to the office of mayor of New York City, but it is useful in studying the same office in other large cities.

> The greater powers of the office are available only to those Mayors who understand its full political dimensions. They must possess, as did La Guardia, a high sophistication about the nature and uses of political power, and a strong appetite for exercising such power themselves. . . .
>
> For lesser men the Office of Mayor is an office of weakness. Average men as President are more fortunate; the office reinforces the man. But the mayoralty is the highest vulnerable symbol of all defects in the city and its government. It is within close reach of its critics. And against these demands, an ordinary mayor can bring only limited resources to bear.[15]

THE CITY MANAGER

Although the city charter in a council-manager form of government defines the formal powers of the manager in terms very much like those which confer power upon the mayor in a mayor-council charter, the offices, operationally, are quite different and the occupants of the two offices present sharp contrasts. The city manager comes as near to the establishment of a discrete

[15] Sayre and Kaufman, op. cit., pp. 698–699.

profession in public administration as one can find in American government. The office of superintendent of public schools comes the nearest in matching its professional character. It is true that all levels of government employ professional men such as lawyers, doctors, accountants, engineers, and nurses, but these persons are trained in regular professional schools from which most graduates do not go into government service. In fact, many of these professionals enter public service without any intent to carve out their career in government service. For the most part these professionals maintain their membership in professional societies whose members are predominantly employed outside government, and their reference groups are not confined to those in public service. The city manager, as a professional, is quite different. If he has, as a young man, decided to train himself for this kind of work, he has entered one of a limited number of colleges or universities that profess to train prospective city managers. Most of such trainees are aware that about the only professional avenue open to them is city management, and once they are placed in a job, they become members of a professional organization (The International City Managers' Association) whose full membership is open only to their counterparts. Upward mobility and promotion are available only by moving from one city to another which because of size, salary, or location is more attractive. It is true that the training obtained as an administrator may make a person attractive to public utility corporations and other governmental agencies, and there is some mobility from city management to other kinds of employment, but such a change in employment carries with it a change in professional standing. The nature of this well-established profession in American politics deserves more empirical research from social scientists interested in decision making at the local level than it has received.

Formal Powers of the City Manager

For a general statement of the formal powers of city managers the reader is referred to the *Model City Charter*, which has served as a guide for many city charter-writing commissions in this country.

Two features of the formally stated powers of the city manager stand out as of special significance.

1. "He shall be responsible to the council for the administration of city affairs placed in his charge by or under this charter." This type of statement is designed to make clear that the council holds the manager responsible for the administrative acts of all other city employees; the council therefore will not be expected to deal with the chief of police if dissatisfaction arises in the police department or with the fire chief if the efficiency of fire protection is ques-

tioned. The council will hold the manager responsible for any shortcomings within any of his departments. The nature of this responsibility is further spelled out in the *Model City Charter* (and in many others patterned after it). "Except for purpose of inquiry . . . the council or its members shall deal with city officers and employees who are subject to the direction and supervision of the manager solely through the manager and neither the council nor any of its members thereof shall give orders to any such officer or employee, either publicly or privately."[16]

2. "He shall appoint, and when he deems it necessary for the good of the service suspend or remove all city employees and appointed administrative officers provided for by or under this charter, except as otherwise provided by law, this charter or personnel rules adopted pursuant to this charter."[17] The exceptions generally relate to the method of removal of tenure members of the civil service, judicial officers, or members of independent boards and commissions. The power to appoint and remove is usually without limitation so that no approval of the council is required for appointments and no appeal is available in case of removal except for tenure personnel under the merit system. Again the *Model City Charter* sets a pattern to ensure that the council will not interfere with the manager in his performance of this function. "Neither the council nor any of its members shall direct or request the appointment of any person to, or his removal from office by the city manager or by any of his subordinates, or in any manner take part in the appointment or removal of officers and employees in the administrative service of the city."[18] Usually the penalty for violation of the provisions designed to prevent council interference with powers assigned to the manager is removal from office.

Appointment and Tenure

The International City Manager's Association reported that as of the end of 1965, 1,698 city managers were members of the Association; this represented an increase of 2.6 percent over the previous year. A total of 354 manager appointments were made during 1965. Of these, 33 percent were already city managers and accepted appointments to new positions, and 12 percent were former managers who returned to the profession. Probably more significant in terms of professional development is the fact that of the appointments made in 1965, 15 percent were assistant city managers, administrative assistants, or interns prior to their appointment. Eighty-one percent of the persons receiving appointments in 1965 had some previous experience in public administration; only 7 percent came from nongovernmental positions—generally from business and industry.[19]

[16] National Municipal League, *Model City Charter*, 6th ed., New York, 1964, p. 7.
[17] *Ibid.*, p. 23.
[18] *Ibid.*
[19] International City Managers Association, *op. cit.*, p. 521.

Data are available for 195 of the managers who were appointed in 1965; 20 percent had a master's degree in public administration, 40 percent held a bachelor's degree only, and 14 percent had only a high school education or less. Of those with bachelor's degrees, 47 percent had majored in political science, government and law, or public administration. Further evidence of the professionalization of the service is the fact that of all managers appointed in 1965, 66 percent were brought in from outside the city, and 33 percent were under forty years of age.[20]

Some evidence as to the tenure of managers is found in a study of 235 persons who were managers in 1965 but were not serving at the end of the year; 24 died or retired, leaving 211 who, it is assumed, resigned or were removed from office and did not either receive or accept another manager appointment. Of the 24 who died or retired in 1965, the average tenure in office was 12.4 years for all cities served and 8.3 years per city; 17 had served only one city. The average tenure of the 211 who either resigned or were removed from office was 5.7 years for all cities served.[21]

Salaries

Attention has previously been called to the similarity in the professional character of the office of city manager and that of superintendent of schools; therefore a comparison of salaries for these positions is interesting. Table 9.2 shows these comparisons.

TABLE 9.2   Comparative Salaries of City Managers and School Superintendents

Population	City manager			Superintendent of schools		
	High	Medium	Low	High	Medium	Low
250,000–500,000	$35,000	$27,500	$22,500	$32,000	$29,000	$23,500
100,000–250,000	31,500	21,000	16,500	30,000	21,088	7,500
50,000–100,000	30,624	18,000	7,525	28,000	20,000	7,500
25,000–50,000	24,000	15,365	9,300	25,500	17,000	8,500
10,000–25,000	24,000	12,300	6,600	35,000	15,000	4,680

Source: From International City Managers Association, *The Municipal Year Book*, Chicago 1966, pp. 664, 666.

[20] *Ibid.*, p. 522.
[21] *Ibid.*

The Typical City Manager

Walter L. Webb and David S. Arnold, using data in *The City Manager Directory, 1964*, give this summary of their analysis:

> The average city manager is a college graduate holding a bachelor's degree with major course work in one of the social sciences, usually political science. He is in his early 40's and is earning $11,343 per year. He is likely to be serving his first city and was a nonresident at the time of his appointment.[22]

It is interesting to note that in this study 56 percent of the managers were serving cities outside metropolitan areas and that 53 percent of them were in cities with populations under 10,000. Twenty-three percent of the managers had master's or other graduate and professional degrees.

Formal Qualifications

City charters usually contain broad statements outlining the qualifications of the city manager and leave fairly broad discretion to the council in applying the statements in the actual selection process. The statement contained in the *Model City Charter* is fairly typical.

> The council shall appoint a city manager for an indefinite term and fix his compensation. The manager shall be appointed solely on the basis of his executive and administrative qualifications. He need not be a resident of the city or state at the time of his appointment but may reside outside the city while in office only with approval of the council.[23]

In line with the comparison of the city manager and the superintendent of schools it is interesting to note that although certification of competence by some state agency is regularly required for school superintendents, such certification has not become an accepted practice for city managers. Some states do have requirements that all public officers be citizens of the United States and such general requirements would probably apply to city managers.

[22] David S. Arnold, "A Profile of City Managers," *Public Management*, vol. 46, pp. 56–60, March, 1964.
[23] National Municipal League, *op. cit.*, p. 22.

Term of Office and Removal

Although a few cities have contracted with city managers for a specific term, the majority of cities employ city managers for an indefinite term subject to removal by the council at any time. This, again, is different from the practice that has become well established in the employment of school administrators. Superintendents are generally employed by school boards under terms of a written contract and for a definite time period—in many cases as long as three years.

The theory of city manager government holds that the manager is subject to removal by the council at any time. In practice, however, removal may not be as easy as it might appear. Many city charters follow the pattern set by the *Model City Charter,* which, although it clearly states that the manager can be removed by a simple majority vote of the council, affords him an opportunity for a public hearing on the charges the council has made against him. In fact, under the procedures prescribed, the council is required to adopt a resolution, at least thirty days before removal is to become effective, stating the reasons for his removal. The manager may then demand a public hearing on the charges, after which the council must pass a final resolution of removal. It is unlikely that any city manager has not made enough friends in a city to ensure some public opposition to his removal; therefore the question of removal often enters the arena of political conflict. There are many councilmanic elections in which the chief issue is the retention or removal of the existing city manager. Since the market for city managers is good, a city manager may seek a new job as soon as he sees he is losing support of councilmen; he then resigns when he has found a new job, making removal procedures unnecessary.

The Nature of City Management

The rationale undergirding council-manager government is that administrative functions have an identity that separates them from policy-making functions and that these functions can be collected into a single package and assigned by charter to a city manager who possesses certain professional qualifications that equip him to discharge his responsibilities in an impersonal way, "without fear or favor." The presumption is that the selection of a manager as chief administrator for a city will be based on professional training and experience and that personal and political factors will not be permitted to enter in the selection process. It is true that a selection committee may consider the personality of a candidate to determine if he fits the image the community might expect, but consideration of this factor is not intended to give to any one group in the city an advantage over others in the political process.

The terms of reference used by manager candidates and by those responsible for their selection is that, once employed, the manager will expect the city council to establish policy in rather definite terms, and the manager will confine his efforts toward the efficient implementation of such policy. The assumption is that conflict issues will arise and be resolved in the council and the manager will not become enmeshed in such conflict issues; he will be neutral until a clear decision has been reached by the council. The manager stands as ready to administer one kind of decision as another, depending upon which happens to survive after council debate. The manager seeks to project his role in city government as a nonpolitical one, and he is apt to measure his own performance in terms of management coordination, efficency, and economy in administration rather than in terms of the kinds of policies adopted in the city for handling such problems as civil rights, elimination of slums, and constructive measures to eliminate poverty.

The discussion above states the extreme position of relations between manager and council, and council-manager government got its start from this theoretical base. In the years of experience with this form of government, adjustments have been made in the theory and in the practice relative to the acceptable role for a city manager to play in the political process. The volume, *The Technique of Municipal Administration,* published for the Institute for Training in Municipal Administration by the International City Managers' Association, gives one the impression that city managers themselves are recognizing that they cannot avoid a leadership role if the system is to remain a viable form of government in modern cities. For example, the prospective city manager is told:

> Both the council and the city manager deal with municipal policy. This is not to say that the council deals only with policy making and the city manager only with administration of policy—a distinction which is unrealistic. No one can divide the subject matter of municipal government into two categories, policy and administration, in order to assign them as exclusive provinces to the council and city manager respectively.
> In solving the more important problems of municipal government, the city manager and the council must work together on the same subject matter. . . .[24]

[24] International City Managers Association, *The Technique of Municipal Administration,* 4th ed., Chicago, 1958, p. 18.

Again, in the discussion of how the city manager should represent the city government to the public, the instructions do not limit the manager to purely administrative actions.

> The city manager need not hesitate to discuss matters on which the council has made a decision with which he agrees. If, for example, the council has voted a bond issue which requires approval in a public referendum, the city manager may publicly advocate the passage of the issue. . . .
> The city manager is free to act as a community leader in the great majority of municipal policies which do not involve political controversies. . . . Many city managers have rendered their most valuable service to their communities by inducing their councils and electorates to approve of the services which had formerly been entirely unknown to them.[25]

These quotations demonstrate that the philosophy of exponents of the profession recognize that the role of the city manager cannot be a passive one in certain areas of policy making. However, it must be emphasized that this same source goes on to considerable length to make clear that the manager is always subordinate to the council. A single quotation selected from many which are available will illustrate this position.

> The city manager should make clear his subordination to the council and should not compete with its members for attention. He should urge the mayor and councilmen to assume publicly the responsibility for controversial decisions and when he himself speaks, he should make it clear to the audience the ultimate decision is to be made by the council—not by himself.[26]

Adrian, in reporting on a study of leadership in three middle-sized council-manager cities, comments on the role played by the city manager.

> Tentative conclusions reached in this preliminary report indicate that the manager and his administration are the principal sources of policy innovation and leadership in council-manager cities, even though the manager seeks to avoid a public posture of policy leadership; that the manager has resources and techniques that enable him to withstand even strong attempts by some councilmen to take policy leadership away from him; that nonofficial groups provide a greater amount of leadership in council-manager cities than is allowed for in the theory of the plan; and that this leadership is a result of councilmanic leadership falling short of the idealized role assigned to it by the theory.[27]

[25] *Ibid.,* p. 19.
[26] *Ibid.,* p. 31.
[27] Charles R. Adrian, "Leadership and Decision-making in Manager Cities: A Study of Three Communities," *Public Administration Review,* vol. 18, p. 208, summer, 1958.

The limited number of references quoted here indicates that the development of the institution of city manager has brought the office into an important place in policy making in cities. Although, as is claimed by some practicing managers, "The manager is not a political leader nor a partisan messenger boy for groups within the council or the community. The city manager, in other words, is not tied to the strings of a political mentor, be it mayor, council, or special interest group,"[28] he cannot avoid in practice the conflicting issues that arise in every city and come to governmental agencies for debate and resolution. The manager may maintain a public image of policy neutrality, but in the council he cannot avoid the policy questions that individual councilmen put to him.

The emergence of the manager as leader may simply be due to his realization of the necessity to fill a leadership gap which the system fails to supply. If the theory of the plan implies that the chairman of the council, who usually has the title of mayor, can provide policy leadership, it fails to take into account the fact that this office does not possess the prerequisites of effective leadership. With no appointive power and no other kind of patronage, the office is in no way comparable to that of the mayor in the mayor-council system. Furthermore, it is the manager, rather than the mayor, who has access to the technical know-how now recognized as an essential element in establishing a position of policy leadership. Salisbury makes the point: "Technical criteria play a far greater role than before in determining choices, and the specification of alternatives is likewise largely a function of the technician who, often alone, knows what is possible."[29] Banfield and Wilson maintain that the city manager often acquires power because of his "virtual monopoly of technical and other detailed information."[30] There is also a tendency for the citizen to defer to the so-called "expert" when difficult decisions have to be made, and it is not uncommon for a councilman to justify his vote on a conflict issue to his constituents by saying that he simply felt compelled to support the recommendations of the expert in the field, who turns out to be the city manager.

Even if we accepted the unrealistic position that the city manager was not a major force in the policy-making process which centers in the city council, we would still have ample reason to consider him as a political force in the terms of reference in which politics has been used throughout this text. If

---

[28] William A. Sommers, "Council Manager Government: A Review," *Western Political Quarterly*, vol. 11, p. 146, March, 1958.

[29] Salisbury, *op. cit.*, p. 786.

[30] Edward C. Banfield and James Q. Wilson, *City Politics*, Vintage Books, Random House, Inc., New York, 1963, p. 175.

only his activities within the administrative system are considered, he must make important decisions which determine the allocation of scarce resources. As the responsible budget officer, he must weigh the needs of the police department against those of the fire department. He must decide if the demands for higher wages coming from street department employees can be met without producing impossible demands from workers in other departments. Interest-group demands for more recreational facilities compete for scarce funds with demands from business organizations for improved parking facilities or better street lighting. In all these conflicts the manager must act as conflict resolver and negotiator, and in this capacity he needs political ingenuity as much as technical competence.

In all cities with major service departments, interdepartmental conflicts arise over jurisdiction and priority of needs. In the final analysis the city manager is forced to intervene and mediate these disputes. Often patient application of the skills of the politician are more effective in the resolution of such conflicts than is the application of any formal set of administrative principles.[31]

City-manager Style

In the discussion of mayors it was noted that the styles by which different mayors sought to exert influence to make their programs effective were very different. The same is true of city managers. Managers with different backgrounds, personalities, and values achieve success with quite different approaches to their jobs. Karl A. Bosworth has described three styles of managers, which to some extent represent a historical development of the office.[32]

The first he calls the *Administrative Manager,* who views his job as primarily administrative, i.e., carrying out the custom of the council. This style places such heavy emphasis on administrative management that it leaves little or no room for initiating or influencing policy.

The second is the *Policy Researcher and Manager,* who understands that policy issues impinge upon administrative decision and therefore does not hesitate to advise the council on the probable administrative consequences of their proposed decisions. This style of manager studies the problems that are likely to come before the council and brings to the discussion not only his

---

[31] For a study of city manager tenure in Florida see Gladys Kammerer et al., *City Managers in Politics: An Analysis of Manager Tenure and Termination,* University of Florida Press, Gainesville, 1962.

[32] Karl A. Bosworth, "The Manager Is a Politician," *Public Administration Review,* vol. 18, pp. 216–222, summer, 1958.

own expertise but the results of his specific research as well. In no case is he merely a passive observer of council debate simply waiting for them to take action so that he can then put their decisions into effect.

The third style is the *Community Leader and Manager,* who assumes a role of active policy leadership. Such managers seek out the persons whose help is required to ensure popular support for his policies, and he uses these persons to achieve his program. He represents the city, and often speaks for it, at meetings with state and other city officials and works with various community groups to assist them in their programs when they are not in conflict with his own policies. The fact that the city manager is the one person who has the information most often requested by policy-oriented groups gives him a strategic position in dealing with them.

EVALUATION OF THE POSITION OF MANAGER

The growth of the council-manager plan of city government has furnished a firm base for the development of a profession of city management. The large majority of cities which adopt the plan accept the notion that the manager should be a professional, and they search for such a person to be chief administrator of their city. Schools of public administration have accepted some responsibility for training city managers, and the attitudes of managers toward their work have been influenced by the values of those who staff these schools. In some instances young managers have been so sure that the "principles of public administration" which they learned in their training programs should be followed to the letter that they encounter difficulty in adjusting to real political systems where demands are made upon public officials by groups who are far more interested in specific decisions about city problems than they are in demonstrating the viability of any administrative principle.

Most successful city managers soon learn that their job places them in the center of a political system which, if it functions effectively, will be called upon to debate and resolve conflicts among groups with different values and demands. And the best that can be expected of a professional administrator is that he assist the council to understand the sources of conflict and propose alternate ways to compromise the opposing forces without completely alienating any of those who have potential strength to overturn the system. This means that the manager must enter politics, not as a partisan seeking political office for himself or for anyone else, but as a student of the political process who recognizes that the city system must allow for political conflict and that when it occurs, continuity may demand that there be sufficient flexibility in the system to permit compromise decisions. Any manager who attempts to stand on the premise that problems which he faces can be approached on the basis of what is *good* government and what is *bad* government will find that his concept of what is good or bad will not be in accord with the concepts of others and that such a position leaves little room for adjustment. No one wants to admit that he is willing to compromise with evil. However, if conflicts are viewed as resulting from differences in values among equally good people all of whom are seeking to use government to achieve some goal, compromise in substance without giving up principle is always possible.

The literature which is prepared primarily for a city-manager audience indicates that the political position in which managers must operate is recognized by them and that an understanding of decision making in a political environment may be as important to a prospective manager as is technical training in the principles of administration.

BIBLIOGRAPHY

Books

Adrian, Charles R.: *Governing Urban America*, 2d ed., McGraw-Hill Book Company, New York, 1961, chap. 9.

Bollens, John C.: *Appointed Executive Local Government*, The Haynes Foundation, Los Angeles, 1952.

Fairlie, John A.: *Municipal Administration*, The Macmillan Company, New York, 1901.

Gordon, Thomas: *Group Centered Leadership*, Houghton Mifflin Company, Boston, 1955.

Kammerer, Gladys, Charles D. Farris, John M. DeGrove, and Alfred B. Clubok: *The Urban Political Community: Profiles in Town Politics*, Houghton Mifflin Company, Boston, 1963.

————: *City Manager Politics: An Analysis of Manager Tenure and Termination*, University of Florida Press, Gainesville, 1962.

Ridley, Clarence E.: *The Role of the City Manager in Policy Formulation*, International City Managers Association, Chicago, 1958.

Sayre, Wallace S., and Herbert Kaufman: *Governing New York City: Politics in the Metropolis*, Russell Sage Foundation, New York, 1960, chap. 18.

Sweeney, Stephen B., and Thomas J. Davy (eds.): *Education for Careers in Government Service*, University of Pennsylvania Press, Philadelphia, 1958.

Articles

Adrian, Charles R.: "Leadership and Decision-making in Manager Cities: A Study of Three Communities," *Public Administration Review*, vol. 18, pp. 208–213, summer, 1958.

Arnold, David S.: "A Profile of City Managers," *Public Management*, vol. 46, pp. 56–60, March, 1964.

Bailey, Stephen K.: "Leadership in Local Government," *Yale Law Review*, vol. 46, pp. 563–566, 569–571, summer, 1965.

Bosworth, Karl A.: "The Manager Is a Politician," *Public Administration Review*, vol. 18, pp. 216–222, summer, 1958.

Carrell, Jeptha: "The Role of the City Manager: A Survey Report," *Public Management*, vol. 44, pp. 74–78, April, 1962.

———: "The City Manager and His Council: Sources of Conflict," *Public Administration Review*, vol. 22, pp. 203–208, December, 1962.

Freegood, Seymour: "New Strength at City Hall," in Editors of *Fortune, The Exploding Metropolis*, Anchor Books, Doubleday & Company, Inc., New York, 1958, pp. 62–91.

Harrell, C. A., and D. G. Weiford: "The City Manager and the Policy Process," *Public Administration Review*, vol. 19, pp. 101–107, spring, 1959.

Lockard, Duane: "The City Manager, Administrative Theory and Political Power," *Political Science Quarterly*, vol. 77, pp. 224–236, June, 1962.

Pealy, Dorothy S.: "The Need for Elected Leadership," *Public Administration Review*, vol. 18, pp. 214–216, summer, 1958.

Salisbury, Robert R.: "Urban Politics: The New Convergence of Power," *Journal of Politics*, vol. 26, pp. 775–797, November, 1964.

Sommers, William A.: "Council Manager Government: A Review," *Western Political Quarterly*, vol. 11, pp. 137–148, March, 1958.

10

THE JUDICIAL FUNCTION IN CITIES

The concept of separation of powers, which holds that total powers of government are separated into legislative, executive, and judicial branches, is so firmly implanted in American political theory that one is surprised to find that the Model City Charter prepared by competent observers of municipal government makes no mention of municipal courts in its 76 pages. This cannot be explained as merely an oversight, since the drafters of the document were thoroughly familiar with the operation of city government. The omission of any provision for city courts simply points up the fact that the judicial function is generally considered to belong to state government rather than to cities. Sayre and Kaufman, in their excellent study of New York City politics, introduce the discussion of courts with the statement, "In a strict sense, there is no such thing as a wholly local court in the state of New York."[1]

There are, of course, courts functioning within cities in this country, but the great majority of them are part of the state court system, and their organization, jurisdiction, and methods of procedure are determined by state law rather than by city charter or ordinance. There is, however, a distinction in type of jurisdiction which needs consideration. Since cities are merely parts

[1] Wallace S. Sayre and Herbert Kaufman, *Governing New York City*, Russell Sage Foundation, New York, 1960, p. 522.

of the state, all state civil and criminal law applies within the boundaries of the city, just as it does elsewhere in the state. Therefore, court cases which involve civil or criminal matters are concerned with state law even though they arise within city boundaries, and such cases proceed through the regular state courts. But cities, by their status as municipal corporations, have been given, either by state constitution or state statutes, power to make laws applicable only within their boundaries. The question, then, arises as to what kind of court will be called upon to hear and decide cases where city ordinances rather than state laws are involved. Certainly the state legislature, unless limited by the state constitution, has ample power to assign such jurisdiction to state courts whose territorial jurisdiction includes the city whose ordinances are involved. But, if it chooses to do so, the state, either by constitution or statute, can authorize cities to create purely municipal courts to deal with cases arising under its own ordinances, and if such courts are created, the state could expand their jurisdiction beyond the limits of disputes over city ordinances. As a matter of fact, many cities do have municipal courts provided for in their home rule charters, and in some cases in statutory charters, which confine their work to cases arising out of city charters and ordinances.

The discussion in this chapter will use this distinction in describing the judicial function in cities, but in some states a single system of state courts may be responsible for handling cases arising under both state law and city ordinances.

PURELY MUNICIPAL COURTS

The following provision from a home rule charter will illustrate what is referred to here as a purely municipal court.

> There shall be a municipal court which shall have jurisdiction to hear and determine all cases arising under this charter or the ordinances of the city, and to assess punishment as therein provided. . . . The municipal court may punish contempt of court by fine not to exceed fifty dollars or by imprisonment not exceeding ten days, or both. It may enforce its orders and judgments as a court of record may, and render final judgment on any forfeited bond or recognizance returnable to such court, subject to appeal as in other cases.[2]

The police department is required to serve as marshal for the municipal court and is charged with the duty of enforcing its orders, judgments, and decrees, and the city attorney's office assigns a lawyer to represent the city

---

[2] Charter of City of Clayton, Missouri, p. 15.

in the prosecution of all cases in which violations of the charters or ordinances are involved. The number of such municipal courts or the number of judges required if the court is unified depends on the size of the city. In large cities these courts may operate on both day and night shifts and a substantial number of judges may be required while in small cities one judge is sufficient and he may hold court only once or twice a week.

Where such a purely municipal court is provided by a statutory charter for small cities outside metropolitan areas, the mayor is often designated as judge of the court and he holds court as the need arises. The term "mayor's court" is often applied to such municipal courts.

NATURE OF CASES

Observation of the work load of purely municipal courts reveals that they follow fairly regular patterns. The vast majority of cases involve persons brought in by police summonses for violation of the city ordinances relating to parking, speed limits, and imprudent operation of motor vehicles. Other cases involve violations of health and sanitary codes, including failure to keep premises clean and free of rats, keeping of farm animals within the city limits, or operating food-dispensing establishments without adequate sanitary precautions. More serious cases arise over enforcement of the city's land-use zoning ordinances, various kinds of building codes, and rooming and boardinghouse regulations.

Appeals from the municipal courts are available in all types of cases, but in practice such appeals are usually made only in cases involving zoning and building-code enforcement. In most such cases the issue is not whether a violation of the ordinance has occurred, but rather whether the ordinance itself violates state statutes or the state and federal constitutions.

Cases in municipal court are generally heard by a judge without a jury, although the accused can require a jury if he desires it. Often the defendant is not represented by a lawyer and few witnesses are called. The testimony consists largely of statements of the police officer or officers who issued the summons, the health officer who made the inspection that discovered a violation, or the building commissioner who made the complaint against the defendant. In a great majority of instances in which citizens are issued tickets for less serious traffic violations, court appearance is not required if the offender goes to police headquarters and, in effect, pleads guilty and pays a standardized minimum fine.

These purely municipal courts may have a greater significance in the total political process than the nature of the cases they decide might indicate. Many citizens who are required to appear before them have no other direct contacts with city government or with any higher levels of the judiciary. Hence, attitudes toward government in general, and the court system in particular, may be formed by experiences in municipal court. To this extent citizen reaction at election time and particularly attitude toward referendum proposals on tax levies and on bond issues may be influenced by personal reactions to the city's court system. Those who appear before these courts are often from underprivileged classes and from minority groups who are less able to employ adequate defense help and are less able to appeal from what they consider unjust treatment.

In many cities the judge is without legal training and often with even less understanding of the social and psychological factors that have produced the behavior that brought the defendant into court. Procedures are, in many instances, not designed to increase respect for the judicial process, and although the defendant has a legal right to appeal a verdict in municipal court, the time consumed and the cost make an appeal unlikely. Many more recent home rule charters, particularly in metropolitan suburbs, are specifying that the judge be a licensed lawyer and that due process be followed in all cases coming before him.

THE JUDICIAL PROCESS WITHIN CITIES

In order to understand how the judicial process fits into the total political process within municipalities, the discussion must not be restricted to purely municipal courts. Within all cities there are numerous courts hearing many kinds of cases, and although technically they must be classified as state courts, their territorial jurisdiction is within the corporate limits of a city. Decisions made by governmental agencies to resolve conflicts affecting individuals and groups are political decisions. This applies to decisions flowing from the courts the same as it does to those made in city councils or in administrative departments. If there is a difference, it is in the nature of the conflict and the environment in which the issues are considered and a decision made. Another quotation from the Sayre and Kaufman study illustrates this point:

Like all governmental officials and employees engaged in the quest for the stakes of political contest, judges and their staffs are both claimants and distributors. The special character of the judicial process sets them apart from those whose primary functions are the formulation and management of government programs, so they are conventionally treated separately. Nevertheless, they are participants in the political contest, involved as fully as all the others who take part in it. Many individuals and groups expend a great deal of energy trying to influence court personnel (from judges down); judges and other court personnel, in turn, exert all the influence they can bring to bear upon some other contestants when certain questions are to be decided. Judges and their staffs are not without their modes of exercising influence, nor are they invulnerable to the pressures of others.[3]

THE NATURE OF THE JUDICIAL FUNCTION

In order to understand the nature of the role played by courts in the total political process, it is necessary to examine the nature of their function. Ordinarily, courts are not initiators of policy, although judges may either in a written opinion or in a public discourse imply that if someone should bring a certain kind of case to the court, precedents might be discarded and a new line of argument applied in reaching a decision. Courts normally are passive, waiting to enter the decision-making process until some person or group brings a specific issue to them for a decision. In general, issues are presented to courts in the form of specific cases, with actual contestants ready to argue their cases, but in some instances courts are authorized to render advisory opinions when called upon to do so by competent sources—usually legislative or administrative officers.

The case presents certain conflict issues which the court is requested to decide; these may include one or more of the following kinds of contest.

1. Conflict over sets of facts. The introductory question as to whether the court has jurisdiction over the case may depend on factual issues. In what location did the action complained of take place, what is the legal residence of the parties, and what specific behavior actually took place? The fact that a number of persons who are present to see a certain live drama take place can come away with quite different images and give conflicting accounts of what really happened gives rise to many court cases in which the chief point at issue is conflict over facts.

2. What law is to be applied to an established set of facts? The plural nature of the American legal system accentuates the possibility of this type of contest. In a given case, any of the following might rationally be held to apply: a city ordinance, a state statute, a state constitution, a federal statute, or the United States Constitution. Equally competent lawyers might well have honest disagreements over the specific law which should serve as the basis for the settlement of a specific legal contest. One need only look at the number of very important cases that have been decided by applying the "equal protection of law" clause

[3] Sayre and Kaufman, op. cit., p. 522.

of the Fourteenth Amendment to understand how disagreements over what law is to be applied reach the courts.

3. What interpretation of the law is the correct one to be applied in a specific case? It may well be that opposing lawyers can reach substantial agreement on facts that were first at issue and that they can agree upon the exact section of a statute or a constitution that should decide the issue, but they may honestly differ as to the meaning to be attached to words, phrases, and sentences contained in the section involved. Some of the most important court cases that have become landmarks in the development of American law have involved the interpretation of such phrases as "freedom of speech," "trial by jury," "due process of law," "testify against himself," and "equal protection of the law." Anyone who reads state statutes and city ordinances is struck by the fact that so many sections are subject to different interpretations by equally competent persons.

4. What decision in the specific case will produce substantial justice in the light of established facts and law which must be applied? In many instances the range of decisions which are possible even after factual and legal conflicts have been settled is quite large. Punishment for a certain crime may range from a short term in prison to imprisonment for life, and money damages to be awarded to a plaintiff in a civil lawsuit may range from one dollar to many thousands of dollars.

5. How shall the final decision of the court be made effective? In general, it is assumed that administrative officials will proceed to carry out court decisions, and the court is no longer involved once its opinion is announced. This is true in many cases; a convicted criminal is taken off to prison by a sheriff or marshal, a defendant in a civil lawsuit pays his judgment to the plaintiff and the case is closed. But in many instances enforcement is not so simple. If a defendant fails to pay a claim assessed by the court, another court order may be required authorizing some officer to seize and sell property to satisfy the judgment, or a case involving corporate bankruptcy may require the court to exercise continuous supervision over a referee who is authorized to dispose of and allocate assets. A more dramatic example is found in court cases involving reapportionment of legislative seats. Courts, after holding existing districts unlawful, have had to redraw districts themselves in some cases and maintain jurisdiction in others where redistricting is in process. The same problem faced the courts when they ordered that schools be integrated. The point is that the judicial function does not always end with the announcement of a decision.

The obvious conclusion to be drawn from a discussion of the nature of the judicial function is that it involves far more than a mechanical process in which the court lays out the facts alongside the law and automatically the right decision emerges.[4] Most contests in which the decision emerges so simply never reach the courts, since lawyers arrange settlements out of court. The contests which must be tried out in the court system are sufficiently

[4] For a discussion of the politics of decision making in courts, see Kenneth N. Vines, "Courts as Political and Governmental Agencies," in Herbert Jacob and Kenneth N. Vines (eds.), *Politics in the American States*, Little, Brown and Company, Boston, 1965, pp. 267–283.

complex that decisions depend to a large extent on the values, attitudes, experiences, and philosophy of the judges who make the decisions. And in most cases, equally competent judges—as measured in terms of legal knowledge—may reach different opinions on the final decision that should be promulgated.

This is the characteristic of the judicial function that puts it within the scope of politics. Decisions which flow from the process are intended to resolve conflicts, and they very often determine how the scarce values of society are to be allocated.

STRUCTURE OF COURTS

The nature of purely municipal courts has already been referred to; they are created to serve the judicial function as it relates to local ordinances and local administrative rules and regulations. This constitutes only a minor part of the total judicial function performed in a modern city. Federal court structure will not be included in this discussion, since its territorial jurisdiction is not usually related to municipal boundaries. The structure of state courts varies from one state to another, but a simplified generalized pattern will be useful; examination of the courts of any single state will be easier if the generalized form is used as a model. Most states have the following kinds of courts: (1) minor courts, (2) regular trial courts, (3) intermediate courts of appeals, (4) courts of last resort, and (5) specialized courts.

Minor Courts

Minor courts have jurisdiction to hear and decide a wide variety of cases as far as subject matter is concerned, but they are limited both in terms of the seriousness of the case and in terms of area. The most common title applied to such courts is *justice of the peace courts*,[5] although they are referred to as *magistrate courts*[6] in some states. Often the justice of the peace who presides over these minor courts is a layman without legal training; in those states which have replaced the justice of the peace with a magistrate, the magistrate is required to be licensed to practice law. The area base for

[5] For a general discussion of justice of the peace courts, see Clyde F. Snider, *Local Government in Rural America*, Appleton-Century-Crofts, Inc., New York, 1957, pp. 305–315.

[6] For a discussion of magistrate courts, see H. H. Curran, *Magistrate Courts*, Charles Scribner's Sons, New York, 1942.

these minor courts is usually the political township or the county, and these courts usually hold their sessions in the city or cities located within their territorial jurisdiction. The number of justices of the peace or magistrates is dependent on the case load, which, in turn, is dependent on the degree of urbanization of the area.

Cases of both a civil and criminal character are heard in the minor courts, but legal limits are imposed upon the jurisdiction in terms of the importance of the case. With respect to criminal cases, minor courts are usually limited to those in which the defendant is accused of a misdemeanor, not a felony. Roughly, this means that maximum punishment, if the accused is judged guilty, is a monetary fine or sentence to a local jail or workhouse. In no case would the punishment include sentence to a state penal institution. Civil cases, which usually are suits for money damages, can be heard in the minor courts only if the amount of damages does not exceed a certain amount. This amount is generally determined by state statutes and varies from state to state: $1,000 may be considered typical.

These minor courts may also perform a function related to the trial of serious criminal cases, but they do not hold trials or decide guilt or innocence in these felony cases. Persons accused by the prosecutor of a felony must either be indicted (formally accused of a felony) by a grand jury or they must be given a preliminary hearing before they can be brought to trial in a regular trial court. The minor courts discussed here are often empowered to conduct such preliminary hearings and, if there is sufficient evidence, authorize holding the accused for trial.

Minor courts normally do not make complete records of their sessions and do not have final jurisdiction; i.e., persons who feel they did not receive substantial justice in a minor court may appeal to have the case heard in a regular trial court. In such appeals the case would be tried *de novo* (as though it had not been heard before).

Criticism of the justice of the peace courts has been widespread, often on the grounds that citizens who are involved in court cases will probably have their first experience with American justice in these courts and the result is not likely to leave a favorable impression. The criticism usually concentrates on the lack of legal competence and lack of judicial demeanor of the justice, and upon the fact that their compensation often comes from fees collected from those who are adjudged guilty in cases before them. Reforms to meet these arguments have been achieved in some states where minor court judges are required to be lawyers and are compensated by regular salaries rather than by fees.

Regular Trial Courts

All states have courts in which the trials of most major criminal and civil cases are held in the first instance.[7] As indicated above, the trial of minor cases is held in these courts when appealed from a minor court. There are usually no limits to the jurisdiction of these courts insofar as seriousness of the crime is concerned or the amount of damages that may be sought in a civil case. The limits of jurisdiction of trial courts are territorial rather than substantive. States are usually divided into judicial districts (often called circuits), and a trial court is created by law for each district. The number of judges in each district is determined by the size of the anticipated case load. Large cities, which usually constitute a single district, may require as many as 50 judges; in other areas a single judge will serve the needs of four or five counties which constitute a single district. Regardless of the number of judges serving a single district, only one judge presides at a single trial.

In large cities with a number of trial judges, one judge presides over what is often called the assignment division, and he is responsible for assigning cases which are placed on the docket to the division where they will be tried. Some sort of division of labor is required; this is often based upon subject matter. Some judges will be assigned to the criminal division, and others to the civil division. Further specialization may provide for a juvenile division, domestic relations (divorce) division, and an equity division. In some cities judges are selected for specific divisions and serve their full terms in the same division, while in others some sort of rotation plan is followed.

The regular trial courts are the scenes of what most persons think of as a trial. Juries are selected, witnesses are placed on the stand and questioned, and lawyers perform their dramatic roles. When cases are appealed from these courts to a higher level, few of these features are repeated.

Intermediate Courts of Appeals

A part of the popular image of American justice is that a person who is dissatisfied with the outcome of his trial can appeal to a court with higher authority. In some states because of the number of appeals taken from regular trial courts, only a supreme court is necessary to provide reasonably quick hearing of appeals, but most states try to reduce the load on the state's highest court by providing a set of intermediate courts of appeals. These courts are usually assigned territorial jurisdiction by dividing the state into

[7] For a discussion of trial courts, see Council of State Governments, *Trial Courts of General Jurisdiction in the Forty-eight States*, Chicago, 1951.

appellate court districts; each appellate court hears cases arising out of the trial courts of its district. As is true of most appellate courts, these are multi-judge courts. For example, three judges may be provided for a single district, and they sit together to judge appeals; if the load is greater than they can handle, three additional judges are provided and they sit as a single court to hear other appeals.

The variety of court procedure from state to state makes it difficult to discuss generally the limits of jurisdiction of these appeals courts. In Missouri, for example, the courts of appeals have no authority to hear appeals from criminal trials, which go directly to the supreme court, and they hear appeals in civil cases only when the damages involved do not exceed a figure stipulated in the statutes; nor do they handle cases where the issue in conflict is the constitutionality of a state statute. The student will often find it difficult to be certain of the jurisdiction of these courts in a single state, since experienced lawyers find ample room for disagreement as to the particular court that is competent to handle a specific case.

Appellate courts do not decide cases in the same sense as do trial courts; their chief function is to judge whether or not the trial courts have made any errors in law or judgment in the original trial. The lawyers who prepare an appeal specify as a basis for appeal the instances in the trial record where they contend the trial court erred. They may plead that incorrect interpretations of law were made or that procedures did not conform to "due process." The appellate courts rely on the record which has been certified to them and the briefs and arguments of opposing counsel for the information they need to reach a decision. If the judges feel a substantive error has been made, they order that the case be returned to the trial court in which it originated so that it can be retried, this time under instructions outlined in the appellate court's decision.

The Supreme Court

All states have a court which represents, as far as the state is concerned, a court of last resort, and in most states it is called the supreme court. Appeals from this highest court of a state lie only to the United States Supreme Court. The number of judges in these courts varies among the states, but seven is a common number. In some cases appeal has come to this court directly from trial courts, while in others cases have been appealed from the intermediate appeals courts. The main function of this court is to make judgments on issues of law and procedure on the basis of a record made in other courts. It is true that state constitutions confer some original jurisdiction upon a supreme court, but very little of the court's time is spent in this type of work. In many instances the decisions of this court either uphold the record and decision of another court or, if they find substantial error in the record, send the case back with instructions for rehearing.

Specialized Courts

In most states some kind of courts are provided to deal with very specialized types of legal problems.[8] Perhaps one of the most common of these is the probate court. These courts are limited to the handling of legal problems resulting from the administration of the estates of deceased persons. Such problems may result from the probation and execution of the terms of a will or from the administration of the estate of a deceased person who died without leaving a will. Probate courts are usually located in each of the counties of a state.

Juvenile courts as organized in some states may be considered to be special courts since they deal only with juvenile offenders and their informal procedures in dealing with individual cases is quite different from the stylized procedures of regular trial courts. States have in a few instances created what are called small-claims courts, whose purpose it is to permit a citizen to recover small claims in instances where use of regular civil courts would cost more than the damages claimed.

EVALUATION OF THE JUDICIAL PROCESS

The assumption made here is that the judicial process is simply a part of the total political process. Decisions which flow from the courts in some cases, just as do decisions made in legislative bodies, determine, for operating purposes, what policy will be enforced through the sanctions of government and how values shall be allocated. Few would deny that decisions flowing from the judicial rather than from the legislative process produced reapportionment of legislative seats, required racial integration of public schools, and opened public facilities to all without regard to race. In fact, one may predict that if these issues had been decided in the legislative arena alone, the resulting decisions might have been quite different from the judicial mandates.

The courts may be looked upon simply as other political arenas to which conflicts may be taken for resolution, and, at some times and with some kinds of issues, a contestant may find a much more sympathetic audience in the

---

[8] See Clyde F. Snider, *op. cit.*, pp. 303–305.

courts than in the legislature or at the executive mansion.[9] Many of the conflicts with respect to the legal competence of a municipal corporation to take action find their way into the judicial arena for settlement; therefore, students of city politics must recognize that the city's role as policy maker is dependent to a large extent on the attitude of the courts to the general idea of city independence and on their attitudes toward policy innovations with which a city wishes to experiment.

Since the judgments of courts have such profound consequences for policy action, it would be difficult to imagine that parties who feel their interests are directly affected by court decisions would not contrive legal means of trying to influence these decisions. Although historically, evidence of outright bribery of judicial officials has occurred, there is little evidence that such crude attempts to influence the judgments of courts is practiced on any large scale today or that it would be successful if it were attempted. Forces which in a legitimate fashion seek to influence the judicial phase of the total political process are much more likely to concentrate their efforts on influencing the process by which judges are selected and on controlling the environment in which courts are forced to operate. Here again the insightful comments of Sayre and Kaufman are pertinent.

> Judicial decisions, like the decisions of other governmental institutions, are vehicles of public policy. Inevitably, therefore, judges are targets of influence exerted by other contestants in the struggle for the stakes of politics. . . .
> The methods of influencing policy decisions made by judges are somewhat different from those applied to other organs of government. Tenure, tradition, procedure, and myth render them less susceptible than other officials to many of the standard techniques of political pressure. . . . Policy decisions of judges are thus made in a field of forces in which the contestants are of limited effectiveness at best, and from which many are excluded for all practical purposes.[10]

SELECTION AND TENURE OF JUDGES

If the nature of the American judicial system tends to place judges in positions that make them less susceptible to the regular political influences that affect other policy officials, the system by which judges are recruited to their positions and the forces which can end their tenure take on increased importance.

[9] See Glendon Shubert, *The Political Role of the Courts: Judicial Policy-Making*, Scott, Foresman and Company, Chicago, 1965.
[10] Sayre and Kaufman, *op. cit.*, p. 553.

Except for judges of minor courts, one may assume that the minimum qualification of judges will be those that are required by the state for the practice of law. This, alone, circumscribes the area from which judges can be recruited and dictates that all judges will have been subjected to the socialization process inherent in a three-year study in law school. It further limits the field of selection socially and economically to those young men and women who were able to get into a law school and who were able to finance their stay there. This is not to say that the available pool is better or worse than the total population, but it is different. To the extent that the pool is different, one may assume that the attitudes, values, and biases of judges will be different from those of the general population.

The procedure by which those who are to sit as judges in our courts are selected from the available pool depends on the constitutions and statutes of the 50 states, but some categories are discernible. At one extreme are those judges who receive their appointment from the chief executive, usually with some kind of legislative approval, and who hold their office during good behavior which means, generally, until retirement or death. At the other extreme are those judges who are popularly elected in regular political party elections and who must stand for reelection as their terms expire. Again, no attempt is made to say that one system produces better or worse judges than the other, but there is a good possibility that the two systems produce judges who are different from each other. Popular election tends to be a self-selection process; a candidate for a judgeship announces his candidacy because he wants to be a judge. Under an appointive process a lawyer may be asked to take a judgeship and he may accept when he never would have, on his own initiative, run for the post in a party primary. In a loose sense, in the one case the man seeks the office while in the other the office seeks the man. Without empirical evidence to prove the point, one may conjecture that the popularly elected judge will be more sensitive to what he perceives to be the public attitude when he is required to make policy decisions in his judicial capacity. On the other hand the appointive judge may feel inclined to let his own values, attitudes, and prejudices weigh more heavily when policy issues confront him.[11]

In some popular elections judges run for elections on ballots without party identification and at times when other popularly elected officers are not contesting for office. This pattern is supported by those who cling to the Jack-

[11] For further discussion see Stuart Nagel, "Political Affiliation and Judges' Decisions," *American Political Science Review*, vol. 55, pp. 643–651, September, 1961.

sonian philosophy of popular election of officials but fear the influence that parties might have upon judges. Party officers are likely to be more interested in the patronage available through judges than they are in influencing their policy decisions.[12] The amount and kind of judicial patronage varies from state to state, but it is probably more than is generally known. A few examples will serve to point up the significance of this kind of patronage. In the first place, a certain amount of job patronage is available through judges; clerks, reporters, and commissioners will serve as illustrations.[13] In cases involving public condemnation of land for public use, the court is required to appoint appraisers, and the fees approved for this work make these appointments very desirable. In metropolitan areas where a large amount of road construction and public building construction is always in progress, this kind of patronage is very significant. In bankruptcy cases courts are required to appoint referees to take over the assets of a corporation and supervise the allocation of assets to satisfy creditors. Often the fees for this service make these jobs attractive. The administration of estates also requires appointment of lawyers to compute estate taxes or for other legal service; these jobs may also be allocated on a patronage basis.

Lawyers have evidenced greater interest in the process of the selection of judges than have laymen.[14] Since lawyers have the closest contact with the courts and are most directly affected by their decisions as well as by the manner in which they conduct proceedings that come before them, it is not difficult to understand their interest. Insofar as lawyers view the judicial process as one requiring knowledge and understanding of established lines of precedents and intellectual capacity to see the relevance of these precedents to the issues at hand, they hope to practice before judges who have both understanding and intelligence. Legal associations have generally favored schemes other than popular election for the selection of judges.

The Missouri Nonpartisan Plan

A constitutional amendment adopted in Missouri in 1940 put into operation a procedure for selecting judges that has now, with some modifications, been

[12] Sayre and Kaufman, *op. cit.*, p. 554.
[13] *Ibid.*, p. 530.
[14] For an excellent discussion of the part played by lawyers in the process of selecting judges under the Missouri Nonpartisan Court Plan, see Richard A. Watson, Ronald G. Downing, and Frederick C. Spiegel, "Bar Politics, Judicial Selection and the Representation of Social Interests," *American Political Science Review*, vol. 61, pp. 54–71, March, 1967.

adopted in a number of other states. The plan provides that when a vacancy occurs on the supreme court or on any of the three courts of appeals, an appellate judicial commission shall select the names of three properly qualified persons as candidates for the vacant position. These three names are transmitted to the governor, who appoints one of them to the post. After the newly appointed judge has served for a period of twelve months, the secretary of state is required to prepare a ballot to be given to all voters at the next regular election so that they can either approve or reject the newly appointed judge. If the judge wishes to serve another term, he must so notify the secretary of state, who prepares a ballot like the one previously used to give the voters a chance to pass judgment on him. No political party descriptions can appear on the ballot, and if paper ballots are used in regular elections, the judicial ballot must be separate from the regular ballot on which names of candidates for other offices appear.

The significant features of the plan are the screening of candidates for a judicial appointment by a commission, selection by the governor from a list of three, and a mandatory election procedure at which voters can approve or disapprove a judge without his having to conduct a campaign in competition with other candidates, and the nonpartisan character of the ballot. There is by no means unqualified support for the plan in Missouri. The fact that the state legislature has failed to follow the constitutional mandate to pass enabling legislation whereby regular trial court districts throughout the state can choose the plan is fairly clear evidence of opposition on the part of legislative leaders. Even those who are strongly in favor of the basic principles embodied in the plan are aware of problems that have arisen in its operation.

EVALUATION OF SELECTION METHODS

The various methods which might be used to select judges to preside in local and state courts are of importance only to the extent that they are factors in determining the kinds of lawyers who occupy these positions and in giving them freedom to let their own attitudes and values shape their judgments. Very little political conflict can be generated with respect to judicial behavior in cases which involve the application of laws of such long standing and popular acceptance that the primary qualification required of the judge is legal knowledge of precedents. But since the function of judges in many cases is to establish the kind of policy which will become the operational guide for administration of law, groups affected by these policies are concerned with the attitudes and values of judges who are empowered to make these decisions. To the extent that judges are removed from large-interest-group influences, their decisions on policy issues may be less sympathetic to these groups. If processes other than popular election tend to recruit into judicial positions the more successful lawyers with upper- and middle-class values, and observation tends to support this notion, one may expect labor unions and lower-class voters to argue for direct elections in judicial selection. The use of court injunctions in disputes between labor and management is a typical example of the type of judicial action in which decisions have significant policy implications and in which large interest groups are affected by the behavior of judges.

The significant point is that group attitudes toward the process by which judges are recruited will be determined not by abstract ideas about which is good or bad but by images of the kinds of judges, in terms of attitudes, values, and biases, that are likely to be selected under the various schemes.

NONJUDICIAL FUNCTIONS OF JUDGES

Many reforms in governmental structure and procedures have, rightly or wrongly, been based on the premise that certain kinds of public actions should be taken out of politics. Included in these so-called nonpolitical actions at the local level are efforts to make changes in the basic law or in existing governmental structure. Since judges are often considered to be farthest removed from partisan politics, they are assigned functions unrelated to their judicial responsibilities. In some cases judges select the members of boards of freeholders or commissions which are created to write charters or produce plans for overhauling existing local government structure. The Missouri constitution, for example, provides that the boards of freeholders required to draft a charter for the government of home rule counties shall be selected by the judges of the county. A similar provision empowers the judges of the City of St. Louis and St. Louis County to select the members of a board of freeholders to study and recommend plans for greater integration of the county and city governments.

OTHER OFFICES ASSOCIATED WITH COURTS

A number of official functions found in most large cities and in county governments outside the large cities, although not a part of the judicial structure, are closely related to the judicial process. Strictly speaking, these functions may be classified as state functions performed locally by local officers. In that respect they are similar to judges in state courts whose jurisdiction is confined to local areas.

The Prosecutor

To the extent that courts act as an official arbiter in legal disputes among citizens or private corporations in civil cases, the office of prosecutor plays no role, but in criminal cases in which the government as protector of the public initiates court procedure to punish a person accused of violating criminal law, the prosecutor represents the government.[15] Although the prosecutor's office may have criminal investigators on its own staff, most cases in which it becomes involved result from action by police officers who present evidence they have collected for prosecution. The prosecutor decides on the basis of evidence made available to him by the police whether prosecution is justified. If, in his judgment, prosecution is in order, he prepares the formal accusation and organizes the evidence for presentation in a court trial. He may elect to present the evidence to a grand jury and ask for a true bill of indictment as the legal instrument by which a trial is justified, or in many states he may simply file an information in which the person is officially charged with a crime and present sufficient evidence to a magistrate in a preliminary hearing and ask that the accused be held for trial.

In cases before what have previously been called purely municipal courts, the city attorney or one of his assistants acts as the prosecutor and the procedure is much less involved. In the trial of cases before regular trial courts, the prosecuting officer is usually considered a county or state officer. He is variously known as prosecuting attorney, state's attorney, circuit attorney, or county prosecutor. Although city attorneys are very often appointed by the mayor or city manager, state prosecutors are usually elected popularly on a county-wide basis. The office is generally not a high-salaried one, and it often appeals to young lawyers who are anxious to get the experience the office affords and the publicity that always comes to its holder.

The Coroner

Although the traditional office of coroner is being replaced by an office of the medical examiner in some areas, it still exists in most states.[16] The

---

[15] See Clyde F. Snider, *op. cit.*, pp. 337–341.
[16] *Ibid.*, pp. 328–336.

coroner is charged by law with the responsibility to investigate deaths which have resulted from unusual circumstances, from violence, or from unknown causes, determine cause of death and report to the prosecutor if he has reason to believe a crime has been committed. The coroner may have no legal or medical training; therefore he must rely heavily on police for investigative work and on medical examiners whom they employ to establish cause of death. The coroner's inquest may employ a jury selected by the coroner which hears witnesses called by him to testify. Such an inquiry cannot establish guilt or innocence or assess punishment, but it may submit reports that are made public and thereby influence public opinion toward a person officially accused of crime.

Coroners are usually popularly elected on a county-wide basis, and in metropolitan counties they may have considerable patronage to dispense.

The Marshal or Bailiff

Trial courts, in the performance of their function, must have officers who can serve various kinds of court orders upon the persons named in the orders and who are on duty at court sessions to maintain order and serve to guard juries from outside contacts. In some cities the regular police department may serve these functions by assigning regular police officers to serve the various divisions of the court; in rural areas the sheriff and his deputies perform these functions, while in others the court may appoint its own bailiffs. In purely city courts a marshal is often popularly elected to act as a peace officer for the municipal court, and in justice of the peace courts, a popularly elected constable acts in this capacity.

The Grand Jury

The Fifth Amendment to the United States Constitution stipulates that "no person shall be held for a capital or infamous crime except upon presentment of an indictment by a grand jury." Since the guarantees of this amendment were held by the Supreme Court to apply to the federal courts only, many states by their constitutions permit the prosecutor to substitute an information under his own signature and a preliminary hearing for the grand jury indictment. The grand jury, however, did not cease to exist in state court procedure, and with the possibility that the United States Supreme Court may include grand jury indictment as a part of "due process of law" required of states by the Fourteenth Amendment, its use will probably increase.

The grand jury is used in many instances to justify the trial of an accused person. The prosecutor submits the evidence that he has against the person accused and asks the jury, on the basis of the evidence, to vote a true bill of indictment. The evidence is presented in a secret session, and all jurors are sworn not to divulge information discussed in grand jury session. Should the jury feel that the evidence presented by the prosecutor was wholly inadequate to justify a trial, it can return, "no true bill."

Grand juries are also used as investigative agencies. Regular trial courts may convene grand juries to investigate the conduct of public officers, the efficiency of government departments, or activities of private persons or corporations where law violations are suspected. Grand juries may be assigned special personnel to assist in their investigations, and they may compel the attendance of witnesses. Since their hearings are held in secret, reputations are not impaired by publicity unless a public report or an indictment is issued. Since judges often use selective lists from which an investigative grand jury is drawn, the term "blue ribbon" juries has often been used to refer to those that have investigated very important issues.

The Petit Jury

English and American jurisprudence has for many years held to the principle that every person brought to trial shall have the right to a trial by jury. The jury implied in this right is known as a petit jury. The purpose of such juries is to sit in open court to hear evidence presented and render a verdict based on the facts and the law as it is explained to them in the judge's instructions. Members of petit juries are laymen generally selected from jury lists by some random method of choice. Jury lists may be compiled by use of voter registration lists, from the election poll books, or by house-to-house canvass. Eligibility for jury service varies widely from state to state, but eligibility to vote is usually a minimum requirement. Lawyers as a profession are usually not eligible for jury service, and persons convicted of a felony may be made ineligible. Many groups, although eligible for jury service, are not required to serve if they elect not to. In some states women are in this group, as are teachers, doctors, railroad workers, and many others. If a student will take the time to read the statutes of his own state that relate to jury exemptions, he may well wonder where enough jurors can be found to supply the demand. Since American culture often equates jury service with the duties of citizenship, many persons accept jury service even though legally they could receive exemption. The administrative work connected with jury selection is usually assigned to a jury commissioner who is under broad general supervision of the court.

SUMMARY

Constitutions and statutory law have been highly developed in the United States; just as the making of constitutions and statutes has involved group conflict, their application and interpretation produces conflicts which are often brought to courts for settlement. Since the language of laws has developed through compromises in order to arrive at consensus, they contain the seeds of continuous conflict. Therefore, the courts in applying and interpreting laws are confronted with conflicts not unlike those which were waged in constitutional conventions and legislative halls. Since judges may be recruited from different segments of society than are legislators, they bring to the decision-making process different attitudes, biases, and scales of values; therefore groups which were unable to win what they contested for in the lawmaking process may secure more favorable results from the courts as they give operational meaning to law. The courts, therefore, must be considered a part of the total political process, and the arguments of opposing lawyers in a specific case are, in a sense, the continuation of the debates that filled the legislative chambers before the law was passed.

Since courts are not neutral in the political process, the systems by which judges are selected become matters of concern to groups who are affected by decisions made in the judicial branch. Therefore, the conflicts that develop over popular election of judges versus other methods of selection must be considered as a political struggle to control the decision-making process, rather than as a difference in moral or ethical principles between those who want good judges and those who want judges who are corruptible.

The nature of the law, itself, is never neutral in a political system. Existing substance and procedure are more favorable to some than to others; therefore group action to revamp the content of law and of court procedures is an avenue open to those who feel that the system is producing decisions not in conformity with their interests. And although opponents of change may argue that existing machinery has a degree of sanctity that should not be challenged, they are often merely anxious to preserve it because it operates to produce decisions which conform to their image of their interests.

BIBLIOGRAPHY

Books

Adrian, Charles R.: *State and Local Governments*, 2d ed., McGraw-Hill Book Company, New York, 1967, chap. 15.

Aumann, Francis R.: *The Instrumentalities of Justice*, Ohio State University Press, Columbus, 1956.

Council of State Governments: *Trial Courts of General Jurisdiction in the Forty-Eight States*, Chicago, 1951.

Curran, H. H.: *Magistrate Courts*, Charles Scribner's Sons, New York, 1942.

Frank, Jerome: *Courts on Trial*, Princeton University Press, Princeton, N.J., 1949.

Peltason, Jack W.: *The Missouri Plan for Selection of Judges*, University of Missouri Press, Columbia, 1945.

Rosenblum, Victor G.: *Law as a Political Instrument*, Random House, Inc., New York, 1955.

Sayre, Wallace S., and Herbert Kaufman: *Governing New York City*, Russell Sage Foundation, New York, 1960, chap. 14.

Schubert, Glendon: *The Political Role of the Courts*, Scott, Foresman and Company, Chicago, 1965.

Snider, Clyde F.: *Local Governments in Rural America*, Appleton-Century-Crofts, Inc., New York, 1957, chaps. 12, 13.

Vanderbilt, Arthur T.: *Judges and Juries: Their Functions, Qualifications and Selection*, Boston University Press, Boston, 1956.

Vines, Kenneth N.: "Courts and Political and Governmental Agencies," chap. 7 in Herbert Jacob and Kenneth N. Vines (eds.), *Politics in the American States: A Comparative Analysis*, Little, Brown and Company, Boston, 1965.

Articles

Bok, Curtis: "The Jury System in America," *Annals of the American Academy of Political and Social Science*, vol. 187, pp. 92–96, May, 1953.

Keefe, William J.: "Judges and Politics," *University of Pittsburgh Law Review*, vol. 20, pp. 621–631, March, 1959.

McMurry, Carl D., and Malcolm B. Parsons: "Public Attitudes toward the Representational Role of Legislators and Judges," *Midwest Journal of Political Science*, vol. 9, pp. 167–185, May, 1965.

Nagel, Stuart: "Political Affiliation and Judges' Decisions," *American Political Science Review*, vol. 55, pp. 843–851, September, 1961.

————: "Ethnic Affiliation and Judicial Propensities," *Journal of Politics*, vol. 24, pp. 92–110, May, 1962.

Ploscowe, Morris: "The Inferior Courts in Action," *Annals of the American Academy of Political and Social Science*, vol. 287, pp. 8–12, May, 1953.

Watson, Richard A., Ronald G. Downing, and Fredrick C. Spiegel: "Bar Politics, Judicial Selection and the Representation of Social Interests," *American Political Science Review*, vol. 61, pp. 54–71, March, 1967.

11

ADMINISTRATIVE ORGANIZATION

Anyone who even casually observes city government in operation knows that when the city council passes an ordinance to pave a defined portion of a street, that action of itself does not make the street any different than it was before. Passage of an ordinance limiting the speed of motor vehicles will, by itself, not regulate speed of all city drivers, and ordinances which define the type of building construction to be permitted in the city do not, by simply being on the books, ensure compliance by builders who are engaged in the construction industry. A part of the total political process was consummated when, probably after a number of compromises were achieved, the council finally passed an ordinance, but the total process is not complete until some means is available to grade and pave the street, patrol the streets and apprehend violators of the legal limits, and make on-site inspections of construction projects. Although these two kinds of activities are in practice performed by different sets of officers and employees, they are both parts of a total process by which city governments accomplish the purposes for which they exist.

Groups and their leaders who make it a part of their business to influence this total process are just as much interested in the manner in which city officials pave streets, enforce speed laws, or supervise construction as they are in the nature of the ordinances which authorized these activities. For purposes of study, the part of the process which authorized the activities is called legislation, and the part of the process which involves enforcement of the contents of the ordinances is referred to as administration. Under the commission form of government, both parts of the process are controlled by the same set of city officers, but other institutional arrangements assign the administrative stage to a different set of officers from those who control the legislative stage. This discussion will be concerned with the administrative part of the political process, although there are numerous interrelations among legislators and administrators by which the behavior of each is affected by its contacts with the other.

Since administration is a part of the total political process, it will be involved with conflicts, and one of its major functions will be to resolve these conflicts by making decisions which will permit routine activities to proceed. For example, an ordinance of the council may authorize the paving of a defined section of a street and provide the method by which the cost will be assessed, but it may not specify the nature of the paving material, the specifications with which construction must comply, or whether the job is to be done by the city's own crews or let out to private contractors. Each of these decisions provides the basis for conflict. The Portland Cement Association may seek to have a cement concrete pavement, while the asphalt suppliers may be expected to expound the advantages of their product. Contractors acting through their association will insist that the job be let out to a private contractor, and they may have the support of labor organizations who have contracts with the construction companies. On the other hand the head of the department of public works and his employees will have supporters in the city who will insist that the work be left to city crews.

The point to remember is that the difference between the legislative function and the administrative function is not that one makes decisions and the other merely carries out decisions. Both make decisions, and each is more or less influenced by the other in the process. In a formal way the city charter and city ordinances define the nature of the decisions that will be within the province of the council and the nature of decisions that are left to administrators, but these provisions are never sufficiently precise to avoid conflicts of jurisdiction.

INSTITUTIONALIZATION OF ADMINISTRATION

As city legislatures, under pressure produced by rapid urbanization, have authorized the expansion of existing functions and accepted municipal responsibility for new ones, the task of administration has increased enormously. Measured in terms of number of employees, the amount of money spent, and the complexity of the job, the administrative branch of city government has outstripped other branches in growth. Administrative work in cities has become highly organized, and certain institutional patterns have become so acceptable that they are to be found in most American cities. These institutional patterns, staffed by a variety of professional, skilled, and unskilled workers with specially assigned tasks all designed to achieve a common purpose, constitute social organizations.[1] The extent to which the organization achieves its purpose depends, in part, on the extent to which individuals within it give up their individual preferences in favor of organization goals; i.e., the performance of an organization is affected by the individual behavior of those who are employed in it, but in turn, the organization conditions the behavior of those who are responsible for its performance.

Bureaucracy

The term most often used to refer to an organization which administers governmental policy is "bureaucracy." Although in public use the term may have unfavorable connotations, in administrative literature it carries no value orientations. Max Weber considered the bureaucracy one of the three major power forces operating in society, and he set out what he considered to be the characteristics of the ideal type or model bureaucracy. Although Weber's concepts have been criticized by modern students of complex organizations, they serve a useful purpose for those who are just beginning to become acquainted with bureaucratic behavior. The following are the chief characteristics of bureaucracy.[2]

1. *Specialization or division of labor.* "The regular activities required for the purposes of the organization are distributed in a fixed way as official duties."
2. *Hierarchy of structure.* "The organization of offices follows the principle of hierarchy; that is, each lower office is under the control and supervision of a higher one."
3. *Fixed set of rules.* The expected ways of behaving of each person in the bureaucracy are governed "by a consistent system of abstract rules . . . [and] consist of the application of these rules to particular cases."
4. *Impersonality of relations.* "The ideal official conducts his office . . . [in]

---

[1] See John M. Pfiffner and Frank P. Sherwood, *Administrative Organization,* Prentice-Hall, Inc., Englewood Cliffs, N.J., 1960, p. 30.
[2] Summarized from Peter Blau, *Bureaucracy in Modern Society,* Random House, Inc., New York, 1965, pp. 28–30.

a spirit of formalistic impersonality, '*sine ira et studio*', without hatred or passion, and hence without affection or enthusiasm."

5. *Career employment.* The assumption is that employees are brought into the organization on the basis of competence; their tenure is protected against dismissal without cause; they are promoted according to established standards; and therefore, they make their career in the organization.

Weber maintains that organizations which meet the standards of bureaucracies are capable of attaining the highest degree of efficiency. Examination of the highly developed and formalized civil service systems found in many of our large cities will demonstrate striking similarities to the model of bureaucracy described by Weber. Many observers are now convinced that such highly structured bureaucracies have their disadvantages as well as advantages; they tend to force conformity and maintenance of established routine, thereby stifling creativeness and experimentation. Observers are also giving greater attention to the effects of bureaucracies upon those who work in the kind of environment which they foster.

Peter Blau, a student of human organizations, has made some very pertinent observations about bureaucracies and efficiency.

> If an association among men is established for the explicit purpose of producing jointly certain end-products, whether it is manufacturing cars or winning wars, considerations of efficiency are of primary importance; hence bureaucratization will further the achievement of the objective. However, if an association is established for the purpose of finding intrinsic satisfaction in common activities, say in religious worship, considerations of efficiency are less relevant. . . . If an association is established for the purpose of deciding upon common goals and courses of action, which is the function of democratic government (but not that of government agencies), the free expression of opinion must be safeguarded against other considerations, including those of efficiency. Since bureaucratization prevents the attainment of this objective, it must be avoided at all costs.[3]

DEVELOPMENT OF ADMINISTRATIVE INSTITUTIONS

In order to understand the existing organizational pattern of administration in American cities it is necessary to have some knowledge of how it came to be; i.e., the rationale or philosophy that has shaped its development. The Jacksonian philosophy of equalitarianism tended to produce a nonintegrated administration with few of the elements of Weber's model. With popular elec-

---

[3] Peter Blau, *Bureaucracy in Modern Society*, Random House, Inc., New York, 1965, p. 23. Copyright by Random House, Inc., 1965.

tion of chief administrators and the selection of other personnel on the basis of party patronage, rather than qualifications relevant to the nature of the work to be performed, central direction, interdepartmental coordination, and a career service did not find a favorable environment.[4] Although the position of the mayor as a chief executive was strengthened during the latter part of the nineteenth century, the highly centralized organizations now common in cities were not developed until the twentieth century.

Accounting in part for the change in administrative institutions was the general acceptance of the philosophy of Woodrow Wilson and Frank J. Goodnow. These men gave acceptability to the doctrine that administration and politics (policy making) can be separated, and that those who administer can be isolated and treated institutionally in one way while those who are in politics can be treated in another. Wilson, in his attempt to justify the creation of a nonpolitical civil service, emphasized this philosophy.

> Most important to be observed is the truth already so much and so fortunately insisted upon by our civil service reformers; namely, that administration lies outside the proper sphere of *politics*. Administrative questions are not political questions. Although politics sets the tasks for administration, it should not be suffered to manipulate its offices. . . . It [administration] is a part of political life only as the methods of the counting house are a part of the life of society; only as machinery is part of the manufactured product.[5]

A number of academicians writing after 1920 who did so much to shape the subdiscipline of public administration also had a profound influence on practitioners who as reformers altered administrative structure. W. F. Willoughby, Leonard D. White, John M. Pfiffner, Luther Gulick, and others, although not accepting completely the dichotomy of politics and administration, did proclaim the need for a professionalized administrative structure so that highly qualified civil servants could be recruited into a system which would offer them an attractive career free from interference from politicians. But these leaders of their day were interested in more than just a nonpolitical administration; they were also interested in developing organizational structure and principles of administration that would maximize efficiency and economy in government.[6]

[4] See O. Glen Stahl, *Public Personnel Administration*, 5th ed., Harper & Row, Publishers, Incorporated, New York, 1962, pp. 29–35.
[5] Woodrow Wilson, "The Study of Public Administration," reprinted with permission from the *Political Science Quarterly*, vol. 56, p. 494, December, 1914.
[6] See Leonard D. White, *Introduction to the Study of Public Administration*, 4th ed., pp. 4–12, The Macmillan Company, New York, 1948.

Search for Principles of Organization

As a result of study and observation and without the kinds of empirical tests now demanded by social science researchers, these students of public administration devised a series of statements about administration that were regularly referred to as principles of administration. Although more recent students have effectively questioned these principles as operational guides, they were so generally accepted at the time that one can understand modern municipal administrative structure only if he is familiar with them. These statements are found in different forms in different places, but the following summary will serve to illustrate their substance.[7]

1. *Centralization of administration.*   All administrative activities of any governmental unit should be made the responsibility of a chief executive who would direct, control, and coordinate all other administrative officers. This philosophy accounts for the support of the strong mayor or the city manager in city government.

2. *Delegation of authority and hierarchical organization.*   The chief executive, by necessity, would have to delegate to others the authority over certain activities, and these subadministrators would, in turn, have to delegate to others under them some areas of authority. This would produce a structure in which each employees would have a clear line of responsibility to a higher official, and at the top all lines would converge in the office of the chief executive. A number of formal models were devised, all of which conform to this principle.

3. *Limited span of control.*   Since administrators are human beings, they have physical and mental limitations as well as limitations of time; therefore in creating an organizational structure, no one person should be required to supervise directly and have report directly to him more than a limited number of subordinates. Adherence to this principle meant that as the size of the administrative branch increased, the number of echelons required in the structure from top to bottom increased. Although the number of subordinates that constituted a satisfactory span of control was never clearly determined, six seemed to be a nice figure.

4. *Unifunctional departmentalization.*   Although there was some argument that administrative departments could be organized on the basis of the nature of specialization required for the tasks to be performed, or the character of the process involved, proper structure should be based on the type of function to be administered. Acceptance of this basis for organization, operationally, presented some problems, since the number of functions which could be identified and therefore should be made into separate departments was greater than the number that a chief executive could be expected to supervise directly. To solve this dilemma, another principle was devised.

5. *Staff aides.*   A chief executive should have sufficient staff officers to make it possible for him to perform his duties more effectively. These staff officers

[7] *Ibid.*, pp. 40–43; see also John M. Pfiffner and Robert Presthus, *Public Administration*, 5th ed., The Ronald Press Company, New York, 1967, chaps. 7, 8.

would have no supervisory powers of their own but would provide many services to assist the chief executive in the performance of his duties.

6. *Executive control of budget and personnel.*   The chief executive should be responsible for the preparation of and implementation of the budget and of personnel administration, since these are the most effective tools through which he can ensure control of the entire administration.

7. *Single-headed departments.*   Since boards and commissions tend to difuse authority and weaken the line of responsibility to the chief, they should never be used to head departments. If, for other reasons, boards and commissions should be deemed advisable, they should be advisory in character and should not have authority to make binding decisions.

There is no intention here to evaluate these statements of administrative principles; whether or not they are valid or desirable is not the question. The point is that their validity was accepted by professionals who conducted reorganization surveys and by nonprofessionals who acted on the recommendations of these surveys and therefore played a role in shaping the present administrative structure found in our cities.

Resistance to Integration

The reform forces which were supporting the professionals in their efforts to integrate all administrative officers under a single chief executive were not without opposition, and examination of the administrative branch of any city today will reveal that, although evidences of successful integration are apparent, there is also much left to reveal the strength of the opposition. Park boards, library commissions, popularly elected comptrollers and treasurers, planning commissions, and other agencies continue to function with a fairly high degree of freedom from direct control of a strong mayor or city manager. The kind of opposition faced by proponents of complete administrative integration in the 1920–1940 period still exists to produce intense political conflict when structural changes are proposed.

1. Existing department heads and members of boards and commissions tend to resist change which will restrict their freedom of action. They view any attempt to strengthen their line of responsibility to the chief executive as an invasion of their independence. The fact that these persons occupy high positions indicates they have some friends and public support; therefore, they constitute a core of what has proved to be substantial opposition to change in their status.

2. Democratic philosophy has been used effectively as a popular argument against integration. Fear of one-man rule remains a potent force determining political behavior in this country, and opponents of the strong executive have been able to play upon this fear to arouse opposition to charter proposals that placed all administrators under control of a mayor or manager.

3. Certain kinds of city functions have required fairly strong clientele groups to secure their establishment as city functions, and, in general, these clientele groups, who continue to support the function in some organized way, fight for a high degree of autonomy.[8] Public zoos, libraries, art museums, parks, and airports are examples of services which, although supported by taxation, need additional aid from citizen organizations if they are to prosper. Administrators of these functions are often instrumental in organizing these citizen support groups, and they can count on public support if their independence is threatened.

4. Similar to the point raised above is the myth that certain kinds of public functions should be kept out of politics. Placing any function under the direction and control of the mayor or manager will be viewed as giving control to the politicians, who supposedly will use the functions for political patronage. The outstanding example is the administration of public schools. This public attitude accounts for many of the nonpartisan or bipartisan boards that still exist to administer certain city functions.

5. Friends of some special services are not willing to have their available funds determined in the regular budgetary process, in which their agencies must compete for scarce resources with other functions which seem to have greater popular support. Many city services are, at least in part, supported by taxes earmarked for their use, or they are guaranteed by charter a certain level of support. Opponents of integration view it as an attempt to deprive these functions of their independence as far as funds for support are concerned.

The present administrative structure in any American city is the result of these opposing pressures, and, as is true of other conflicts in the political arena, compromise solutions have been achieved.

CLASSIFICATION OF ADMINISTRATIVE FUNCTIONS

Another feature of the 1920–1940 movement for professionalizing the public service must be discussed before one can understand the present organizational structure in city government. This is the tendency to classify administrative functions according to their nature. Luther Gulick, Leonard White, and others were very convincing in arguing that such a classification was useful, operationally, as a guide to those who were trying to reorganize administrative structure to produce maximum service with a minimum expenditure of manpower, materials, and resources. Although there were differences in terminology used, the concepts were pretty much the same in most of the professional literature. The terminology used by Professor White will be followed here.[9]

[8] See Pfiffner and Presthus, *op. cit.*, pp. 148–150.
[9] White, *op. cit.*, pp. 31–35; see also Luther Gulick and L. Urwick (eds.), *Papers on the Science of Administration*, Institute of Public Administration, New York, 1937.

Line Functions

Line functions are defined as those functions which the organization was created to perform. The national government, for example, was created to provide national defense, regulate interstate commerce, and establish a uniform currency; these and others like them, then, are its line functions. The state was created to provide public education, adopt and enforce criminal and civil codes, and build and maintain highways; such functions are, therefore, its line functions. Applying the definition to cities, their line functions will include fire protection, police protection, street construction and maintenance, providing parks and playgrounds, public health protection, and certain welfare services. The number of line services which any city performs depends on the legal system within which it operates and the willingness of the citizens to support such services financially.

Auxiliary Functions

Auxiliary administrative functions are defined as those functions which must be performed in order to accomplish line functions. They are not services for which the government unit was created. For example, no one would argue that a city was created so that it could collect taxes, yet all agree that a city cannot supply fire and police protection if it does not collect taxes. Likewise, cities are not created so they can hire employees and do all the other things related to administering a personnel system, but personnel administration is necessary so that streets can be built and parks can be maintained. In other words, auxiliary functions are performed as services to line administrative agencies, rather than as services directly to the public. The most common auxiliary functions include budgeting and accounting, tax collection, personnel administration, legal counseling, research and reporting, and purchasing of supplies. It would be possible to set up organizational structure in such a way that each line department would be self-sufficient in that it would have its own personnel officer to recruit, examine, and hire its own employees, have its own legal advisor, collect its own taxes, and have its own accounting division. But, on the other hand, it is possible to establish a central personnel department to service all line departments, to have a single legal office to supply legal services to all line departments, and to concentrate all tax collection and accounting in a single financial office.

Staff Functions

The staff function is advisory in character. The assumption is that any major administrator in government will have a span of control beyond his limited capacity; he will have more reports available than he has time to read; he will need information he is unable to gather himself; he will need technical advice on matters about which he has no technical expertise. To fill this need the chief executive must have aides who summarize reports, supply factual information by research, make inspections, secure technical advice, and in general, do for the executive those things which he needs to have done so that he can fulfill the obligations of his office. The people who perform these services are staff officers, and they may carry such titles as administrative assistant, executive secretary, or assistant to the mayor or manager. Regardless of their title, the theory is that these officers do not direct, control, or supervise the people who operate other departments. Although they may act as liaison between the chief and a department, they are not authorized to make decisions affecting the departments. In practice the nature of staff jobs will depend on the personal style of the chief executive and the extent to which he respects the ability and judgment of his staff employees.

TYPICAL ADMINISTRATIVE STRUCTURE

The chart in Figure 11.1 is not designed to represent the existing pattern of organization in any city. It is, rather, intended to show graphically a typical nonintegrated structure and how the theoretical considerations discussed above may have had an impact in determining the structure prevalent in many American cities today.

Figure 11.1   Typical nonintegrated administrative structure.

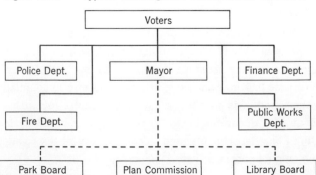

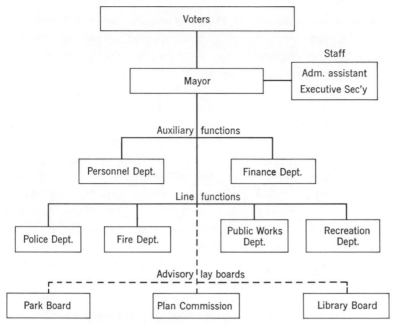

Figure 11.2   Typical integrated administrative structure with separation of line, staff, and auxiliary functions.

The organization chart shown in Figure 11.2 represents a fairly highly integrated system with all departments operating directly under the control of the chief executive; the only exceptions are the lay boards. It also represents a structure which identifies the three kinds of functions previously discussed. In a very large city any one of the departments is large enough that if its internal structure were charted, it would fit into the general form shown for the entire city. The chief would be the departmental director, subdivisions would be called divisions rather than departments, and the boards would become interdepartmental committees.

CONFLICT ISSUES IN ADMINISTRATIVE REORGANIZATION

After the Hoover Commission was created in 1947 to study organizational structure at the national level and to make recommendations for change, many states followed with Little Hoover Commissions to propose specific changes in state administrative organization. Similar studies have been undertaken in many large cities. To a great extent, these administrative reform efforts are a result of the demand for economy and efficiency that was a part of the new science of public administration referred to earlier, but they were also supported by many who felt that the existing structure was not adequate to cope with the increasingly large and complex problems that modern city governments are required to handle. Little difficulty was encountered in getting legislatures to recognize the need for a general reorganization of administration; the real conflicts developed when the recommendations for change were put in definite form for legislative action. Overwhelming evidence of overlapping jurisdiction, duplication of authority, and indefinite lines of administrative responsibility could be readily assembled in most any large city. When these characteristics were discussed as general issues, consensus that changes were needed followed with little difficulty. Only after legislators, some administrators, interest-group leaders, and party officials had the specific proposals before them could they see what they construed to be threats to their power positions; conflict was then inevitable.

There are numerous power centers within the administrative structure of any large city; i.e., there are many places where decisions can be made that affect interests that are able to call upon group support in their defense. Any change which alters the authority of these centers constitutes a potential conflict issue. If, for example, a citizen's group has been formed in a city to sponsor a program for the creation, over a period of time, of a park system, and it has been successful in securing a park board, a director of parks and recreation, and a park-improvement tax, and through cooperation of the board, the director, and the citizen group progress is evident to all, there will be a strong built-in opposition to any administrative reorganization plan that calls for the park department to be moved from its rather autonomous position and made directly responsible to the mayor or city manager. This is only a simple example to illustrate the point that interest-group leaders will react to proposals to alter administrative structure in much the same way that they react to any political issue. They will oppose any suggestion which they conceive to be a threat to their present power position, and support those changes which they think will strengthen their position in the decision-making process. Formal arguments about good administrative organization will not prevail when the good organization proposed is perceived to alter the locus of power to the disadvantage of interested citizen groups.

Degree of Integration

The idea of an integrated administrative organization in which formal lines of authority run clearly from the lowest office through section heads, division heads, and department heads and finally converge in the office of the chief executive draws sympathetic responses when discussed in general and abstract terms; responses change, however, when the integration proposal affects certain sensitive areas of administration. The principle of the fable about "whose ox is gored" often determines who will favor and who will oppose administrative integration. A few examples will illustrate the nature of conflicts that regularly arise. Some administration specialists, in order to keep the executive's span of control within what they consider reasonable limits, propose the combination of the police department and the fire department into a single department of public safety. This may make sense in the abstract, but such a proposal invariably produces heated political conflict. It is not likely that the police, the firemen, or their top administrators will react favorably. Either the policemen will fear a department head who is more interested in fire protection than in police work, or vice versa. The skills of the two professions are quite different, and all sorts of evil consequences are conjured up that might result from the change. Citizens who have any contacts with these two professional groups will take their cues from the attitudes of policemen and firemen, both of whom will probably oppose the change.

Likewise, suggestions have been made to combine the department of health with the welfare department, to make a single department of health and welfare. This also makes a lot of sense in terms of limiting span of control, combining clerical and secretarial services, and the two functions appear not to be unlike in nature. But the philosophy of professional social workers is so different from that of medical men who staff health departments that neither group can conceive of working harmoniously with the other. Since each group has a fairly strong professional association to support them, such a change is sure to provoke intense political conflict.

The demand of supporters of such functions as education, libraries, and parks for a high degree of autonomy so that they can keep their activities "out of politics" has already been referred to. Any attempt to integrate such services under a strong chief executive is sure to draw the fire of their clientele groups.

Single- or Multiple-headed departments

The question of using boards or commissions rather than single directors to head departments is always good for extended debate. The formal arguments are fairly well known. The single administrator concentrates responsibility, assures positive action without undue delay, gives the chief executive more direct control, and tends to assure unity of administrative policy. On the other hand, a board or commission provides for presentation of more than one point of view, ensures debate and deliberation on policies, permits greater citizen participation, and provides better means to win citizen support for department programs. No doubt these arguments have some validity, but although used in the formal debates on the issue, they are probably not the factors which determine how the issue will be resolved. Any administrative department has available to it what may be called patronage; i.e., it is in a position to adopt policies and procedures which are advantageous to some and disadvantageous to others. Groups close to the central administration or "the establishment" are quite content to have a single-headed administrative department, since such a structure will strengthen the chief executive. This means that those who have most access to the mayor will also have access to the department heads. On the other hand, groups who are generally perceived to be nonpolitical and who find their access to the mayor limited or, at least, their influence slight, will feel that a board or commission will be more approachable. Minority groups that regularly lose in their effort to elect a mayor are usually assured some representation on an administrative board or commission; hence their support for a plan which abolishes boards and commissions is difficult to get.

This issue is also debated in terms of the nature of the functions which are to be assigned to a department. In certain long-established departments, broad policies have been established over time, and internal administration may be perceived to be more important than substantive issues that might arise. Other departments administer functions where substantive policies and basic procedures are still being worked out by debate and compromise. The same interest groups may support a single director for the first department but insist on a citizen board to head the second because of the policy implications of the work involved.

Even in highly integrated systems with administrative leadership centered in a city manager, attempts are made to get more citizens involved in the political process. This is accomplished by the creation of citizen boards and commissions and inviting persons identified as community influentials to serve on them. Formally, however, the function of these boards and commissions is to advise and consult with responsible city officials rather than to make final decisions. The very fact, however, that community leaders serve on such boards gives them a voice in decision making that city officers cannot fail to heed. Certainly the types of persons who are willing to give their time for this kind of service will be determined by the extent to which their advice is influential in determining final administrative policy.

Centralization of Auxiliary Functions

Such functions as purchasing of materials, recruitment of employees, and legal counseling are recognized as functions which must be performed in any large organization, but since there is more than one way by which they can be performed, they constitute sources of conflict. This type of conflict may divide professional administrators more than it does interest-group or political leaders. Those who argue that formal structure should always seek to concentrate authority in a single person maintain that each major administrator (department head) must be given authority to hire his own employees, make his own purchases, and seek his own legal advisor. They take the position that to give these kinds of responsibilities to someone outside the control of the department head divides responsibility and makes it more difficult to fix blame for inefficient operation. On the other hand, there are those who prefer to see these auxiliary functions concentrated in single administrative units so that all departments can be served from the same unit. Arguments for centralization are fairly convincing. Centralization of personnel administration in a single agency tends to eliminate political influence in hiring, ensures greater uniformity in personnel policies throughout the city service, and permits the employment of persons specially trained for personnel work. Central purchasing allows quantity purchasing and competitive bidding by suppliers, and permits quality controls of materials delivered. Furthermore, the auxiliary services may be used by the chief executive as tools by which he exercises control over line departments. Although the trend has been to centralize these functions, the debate continues, and any attempt to centralize in a city where decentralization has been the rule will arouse vigorous opposition.

Professionalization of Top Administrators

Some conflict arises in administrative reorganization over the extent to which major departments should be headed by professionals. There are those who insist that each top administrator should be a professional even if he has to be imported from another city, while others maintain that top administrators should be leaders who command respect in the community, but that they need not have special training in the kind of work in which their department is engaged. That is, the head of the department of public works need not be an engineer, even though his department builds streets, bridges, and all kinds of physical facilities. His own time may be taken up by public relations, contacting legislators and the chief executive, and keeping the support of civic and political leaders, rather than in dealing with matters requiring technical knowledge. Although the nonprofessional head may suffer from lower prestige in the eyes of the professionals in his department, he may make up for this deficiency by his ability to win support for the department's activities from the general public and the city council.

This conflict with respect to professionalism also takes another form. There has been developing in this country since about 1930 a select group that may be called professional administrators. Members of this group are often referred to as administrative generalists, and their claim to special competence is in the possession of what are called administrative skills.[10] A few American universities have special programs to train these administrative generalists for the public service. The issue in conflict, then, is not whether top administrators should be professionals or nonprofessionals, but whether they should be administrative generalists or professional specialists. The kind of questions posed are: Should the head of a department of health be a professional administrator or a doctor? Should the finance department be headed by a person trained in general administrative skills, or by a banker or professional accountant? This kind of conflict will probably never be fully resolved. If doctors, engineers, and accountants could be given administrative training along with their specialized training, the ideal type of department head might be available, but since this is not the present pattern of training in our professional schools, the administrative generalist can make a good case for himself. Even if the professional specialists win the struggle for top-line department jobs, the generalists will find their services in demand as staff officers and in centralized auxiliary departments.

Civil Service Conflicts

Problems related to recruitment, pay, working conditions, and tenure of office have produced significant conflicts in the civil service of cities since the turn of the century. Since 1960 new and more intense conflicts have developed between organized public service employees and the political decision makers of the city.

10 See John M. Pfiffner and Robert Presthus, *Public Administration*, 5th ed., The Ronald Press Company, New York, 1967, pp. 281–283; and Stephen B. Sweeney, *op. cit.*, chap. 6.

The traditional conflict between party leaders who wanted to use city jobs as political patronage and civic reformers who insisted that employees should be selected on the basis of competitive examinations and should hold their jobs as long as their work was satisfactory has been reduced in intensity. Most large cities have established formal merit systems with elaborate rules designed to remove the selection process from party control. Institutionalization of the merit system has satisfied the reformers, and party leaders have learned to work within the system, although they would still prefer more job patronage. Loopholes in many formal rules, laxity of enforcement, and exemptions of certain groups of employees have left party leaders with some influence over the selection process.

The success of efforts to professionalize the public service and to give reasonable assurances of permanence in employment, however, have produced new kinds of conflicts within the civil service. Common interests of groups of public employees have led to organizations of employees that are very similar to labor unions. In some cases the public employees are affiliated with national unions; in others they are independent but operate very much like unions. Teachers, firemen, policemen, welfare workers, and garbage collectors have in one city or another since 1960 backed up their demands by the strikes, slowdowns, or threats of the use of these weapons that are so well known in labor relations when collective bargaining breaks down.

The public inconvenience resulting from activities of public service employees who were dissatisfied with their pay or working conditions has forced policy makers to review their methods of dealing with employee demands. For years the question of recognition of organizations for collective bargaining and the use of the strike have been discussed almost wholly in legalistic terms, with arguments turning on whether recognition of a group was legal and whether public employees could legally strike. The strength of modern organizations and their willingness to use slowdowns and strikes in New York, Detroit, St. Louis, Memphis, and elsewhere have forced political decision makers to face up to the fact that professional city employees are in a position to back up demands with action which practically shuts down essential services. Some means must be devised to resolve these kinds of conflict if cities are to maintain essential services on a continuous basis and at a high level. Discussion of the issues in terms of legalisms has not produced solutions, and there is no reason to assume it will in the future.[11]

[11] For a good discussion of these issues see the five articles in a symposium edited by Felix Nigro, "Collective Negotiations in the Public Service," *Public Administration Review*, vol. 28, March–April, 1968.

CHANGES IN EMPHASIS IN PUBLIC ADMINISTRATION

The discussion in this chapter thus far has tried to identify the factors and forces which have operated to mold existing administrative structures in our cities and to explain the philosophy and rationale behind the movements for reform that made their imprint upon structure in the 1930–1960 period. The reforms instituted along with the scientific-management movement were aimed at achieving greater economy and efficiency by applying certain criteria which were enunciated as principles of administration. Although the movement attracted strong good-government support, it also faced opposition from party leaders and many interest groups. Therefore, changes never went far enough to satisfy the reformers, but often they went too far to please the opposition, so that seeds of future conflict always remained. Sayre and Kaufman make this point in discussing the administrative reform movements in New York City.

> The net consequence of these opposed views has actually been a compromise among the participants most directly involved in the change; the values of efficiency, economy, and rationality are endorsed by all, while the gains and losses in power by the participants are held within the limits established by the vigorous bargaining among them. The gaps between the proposals and the changes actually made provide much of the grist for the next administrative survey and its new package of recommendations. Administrative reorganization and management improvement efforts have tended to become a continuous activity within the city's governmental and political system, as the four surveys of the 1950's and the recent institutionalization of the function in the work of the City Administrator's Office, all eloquently testify.[12]

There is reason to predict, however, that future surveys may be pursued with different emphasis and conducted by so-called experts who take to their task different schemes of analysis and, in some cases, different sets of values that determine the goals they seek to attain. This prediction is based on the assumption that the new crop of public administration specialists, particularly if they are drawn from the ranks of academicians, will have read more from Herbert A. Simon, Peter Blau, Victor Thompson, Wallace Sayre, Robert Presthus, and others like them than they will have from Luther Gulick, Leonard White, W. F. Willoughby, and Lyndall Urwick.

The changes which stand out in the contributions of more recent students which distinguish them from earlier works on public administration are the commitments to the scientific method and the emphasis upon organizations

[12] Wallace Sayre and Herbert Kaufman, *Governing New York City*, Russell Sage Foundation, New York, 1960, p. 734.

as forms of human associations and the factors and forces that are determinants of behavior in such organizations. Concern for scientific method implies that studies of existing administrative agencies proceed by first determining the aims and goals which organizations are expected to accomplish, identifying the alternative choice available for accomplishing the goals, then selecting the alternative that maximizes goal achievement. Such a procedure contemplates the clear separation of facts and values;[13] i.e., administrative organization research can be conducted in a value-free manner. The aims and goals may be reduced to such clear statements that the researcher need concern himself only with the search for alternatives; the correct alternative will then become obvious in the light of the goals defined. Rather than differentiate between what is policy and what is administration to allocate responsibilities, the newer approach differentiates between value decisions which establish aims and goals and factual decisions which state alternatives and predict consequences to be expected from the choice of each possible alternative.[14]

Commitment to the scientific approach also rejects what have been described earlier as principles of administrative organization which constituted the norms for reorganization task forces that submitted recommendations for reform at all levels of government in the 1930–1955 period. In fact, the values of efficiency and economy as the ultimate goals of reorganization are challenged. Simon refers to these principles as proverbs and suggests that they are often contradictory and have never been submitted to empirical testing.[15]

Organizational Behavior

More and more studies in public administration have concentrated attention on the organization (the bureaucracy) as a form of political power itself, upon the effect the bureaucracy has upon those who work in it, the responses of those in it to the pressures it exerts, and upon the impact of modern bureaucracies upon traditional democratic theory. Blau suggests very cogent reasons for concentrating attention on bureaucracies:

> The prevalence of bureaucracies in our society furnishes a practical reason for studying them; the fact that they endanger democratic insti-

[13] See Herbert Simon, *Administrative Behavior*, The Macmillan Company, New York, 1947, pp. 4, 5.
[14] *Ibid.*, pp. 5 and 6 and chap. 3.
[15] *Ibid.*, chaps. 2, 9.

tutions supplies an ideological reason; and the contribution their study can make to sociological knowledge provides a scientific reason for undertaking the task.[16]

Greater concentration on the nature of organizational behavior rather than on the nature of organizational structure forces attention on phases of the administrative process which were generally neglected in former organization studies.

Informal Structure

Reorganization studies have usually taken as their first task the preparation of a master organization chart which graphically depicted the major units of the total organization in such a manner as to show how lines of authority and responsibility run; or, in other words, who takes orders from whom. The charts were constructed from reference to city charters, state laws, city ordinances, and executive orders. In short, they represented the formal or legalistic relationships among the officers who made up the bureaucracy. There is no question but that the formal relationships as displayed on the chart constituted a force conditioning behavior, but recent research demonstrates that individual behavior is also affected by interorganizational relationships that do not appear on the chart, as well as by relationships external to the organization.[17] These uncharted relationships that develop and often become institutionalized in the system are referred to as the informal organization. Knowledge of these patterns of informal relations in which one member defers to another who formally has no control over him may be as important in understanding why an organizational unit has high output as is knowledge of formal structure. An entirely different research technique is required to chart these informal lines of power and authority than is needed to show formal relations graphically. Research may show that a given employee takes the cues that determine his behavior in a bureaucracy from his professional colleagues who are employed by other agencies or from someone in his own agency with whom he meets regularly on a social level rather than from his immediate supervisory officer as shown on the formal chart. No amount of formal structure juggling is apt to alter these informal relations.

[16] Peter Blau, *Bureaucracy in Modern Society*, Random House, Inc., New York, 1965, p. 25. Copyright by Random House, Inc., 1965.
[17] For discussion of informal organizational structure, see Chester I. Barnard, *The Functions of the Executive*, Harvard University Press, Cambridge, Mass., 1938.

Communications in Organizations

The larger an organization becomes the more difficult it is to maintain a system of communication that keeps all its members aware of organization goals and the part each individual plays in achieving these goals. Inefficiency in governmental bureaucracies may result from inadequate internal communications as often as it does from deficiencies in formal structures. Eugene Walton, in a study of organizational communication systems, contends "that the most significant factor accounting for the total behavior of the organization in its communication system, and that the dynamics of the organization can be best understood by understanding its system of communication."[18] One might be able to construct an organizational chart showing lines of influence within an organization if he could know how messages flow within the system, and it is very unlikely that these authority lines would be the same as those shown on the formal organization chart displayed in conspicuous places in supervisory offices.

Messages, supposedly, start with some top administrator and travel along authority lines to the next-lower administrator and on down to the operational employees who are supposed to carry out the intent of the message. But in the process of travel, alterations in oral communications or differences in interpretation of the meaning of written messages may result in behavior patterns quite different from what was originally intended. Norbert Weiner made the term "cybernetics" popular in the literature of organization theory. He emphasized the importance of communications in organizations and called attention to their two-way character. He insisted that a communication system must provide a *feedback* mechanism which keeps the originator of messages informed about the effects achieved by the messages.[19] If a message which is intended to produce certain kinds of behavior produces results different from what was expected, feedback systems show how actual behavior is different from expected behavior so that the original sender can make necessary adjustments to achieve his goals.

Insofar as behavior of workers in a bureaucracy is affected by the image they have of their role in achieving the goals of the bureaucracy, communications are a critical variable in organizational behavior. Certainly in large organizations the communication system is about the only way the organiza-

[18] Eugene Walton, "A Study of Communication Systems," *Personnel Administration,* vol. 26, p. 46, May–June, 1963.
[19] Norbert Weiner, *The Human Use of Human Beings,* Houghton Mifflin Company, Boston, 1954, pp. 23–33, 58–59, 151–153, 156–158.

tion members can be made aware of what the organization is trying to accomplish and how their job contributes to these objectives. More recent studies designed to increase organizational output are giving greater attention to internal communications.

Individual Reaction to Organization

Considerable attention in recent studies of organizational behavior has been directed to the responses of those who work in the organization to pressures that the organization places upon them. The assumption is that organization goals can be achieved most efficiently if worker reaction to organizational expectations is favorable, and conversely unfavorable response to organizational demands reduces output in relation to expenditures of manpower and materials. Robert Presthus, among others, has given some attention to this phase of organizational behavior. He has tried to classify response patterns that have significance in determining organizational effectiveness. He identifies three classes of employee, the *upward-mobiles*, the *indifferents*, and the *ambivalents*. The upward-mobiles, as identified by Presthus, are:

> . . . typically distinguished by high morale; their level of job satisfaction is high. Indeed, the process and criteria by which they are selected insures that they will have an unfailing optimism. The reasons for this are clear. They identify strongly with the organization and derive strength from their involvement. Their dividends also include disproportionate shares of the organization's rewards in power, income, and ego reinforcement.[20]

This class of employee becomes the "organization man" who accepts without question the prescribed goals of the organization, and who has little sympathy with dissent, since it tends to call these goals into question. Under existing patterns of deference in large organizations, the upward-mobiles may well be the ones first chosen for promotion to formal positions of power.

The indifferents, unlike the upward-mobiles, refuse to compete for the rewards that conformity to organizational goals promises. They have reached an accommodation with the organization by contributing what they must in order to stay on the payroll, but they depend for their personal satisfactions upon contacts outside the organization. They do not seek, and may reject, promotions when offered if new responsibilities would interfere with their

---

[20] Robert Presthus, *The Organizational Society*, Alfred A. Knopf, Inc., New York, 1962, p. 167.

freedom to pursue outside activities in which they find their greatest satis-faction.[21] The large number of persons in any bureaucracy who have adjusted to the organization in this way sets strict limits on the pool from which pro-motions to higher posts can be recruited.

The ambivalent, as described by Presthus, is, "creative and anxious, his values conflict with bureaucratic claims for loyalty and adaptability. While the upward-mobile finds the organization congenial, and the indifferent refuses to become engaged, the ambivalent can neither reject its promise of success and power nor can he play the roles required to compete for them."[22] The am-bivalents are often specialists whose value systems demand that rewards be meted out according to knowledge and skill, and they tend to rebel when they see rewards in the bureaucracy allocated on some other basis. Although the response of the ambivalents is dysfunctional to the system, they often provide the force for reexamination and change. The implication may be that the existing system which generates this kind of response from persons socialized in a certain way needs to reexamine its reward system so as to evoke a more sympathetic response.

THE ROLE OF SKILL AND EXPERTISE

The discussion thus far has attempted to center attention on the role of ad-ministrative personnel in the total decision-making process, since they must, themselves, make choices among alternatives as well as act in an advisory capacity to policy-making executives, but a further word is necessary to call attention to the role of administrative personnel in helping to fashion the responses of councilmen and voters at large to conflict issues. As the tasks involved in the administration of the functions of large cities become more complex and dependent more and more upon scientific and engineering find-ings, the average councilmen and voters, both of whom are laymen, are inclined to lean upon technical and professional opinion to help them reach decisions. Within the political system the administrators have a practical monopoly on the information and expertise required to understand the nature of the issues to be decided. This posture places them in a position to secure deference from councilmen and voters when critical decisions must be made. The administrator's position is often strengthened further by the mass media, since the inclination of editorial writers is to support the opinion of the expert and the specialist on issues which they as laymen do not feel competent to judge.

[21] *Ibid.*, p. 205.
[22] *Ibid.*, p. 257.

EVALUATION AND SUMMARY

In this chapter an attempt has been made to impress upon the student the importance of the administrative organization of city government in the total decision-making process. Most city employees are in administrative work, and practically all city expenditures are made by administrative workers. Present patterns of administrative organization have been determined to a great extent by the reform movement that began about 1920, and this movement was guided by administrative theory developed and expounded by an able group who helped make public administration a profession. Principles of administration developed by these theorists and practitioners became the guides for those who were called on to revise and reorganize the administrative structure of governments at all levels.

Beginning about 1950 reevaluation of administrative theory that had become so widely accepted has changed the direction of research in public administration. The thrust of the newer approach has been to give greater emphasis to administrative behavior and less to formal organizational structure as the major determinant of administrative performance. With this change in emphasis came more attention to communication in organizations and the responses of workers to their bureaucratic environment. Although all agree that structure is one variable which influences organizational output, most observers are ready to agree that it is not the only variable and may not be the most important one.

The central theme to be kept in mind is that the administrative organization is but a part of the overall governmental machinery in which political decisions are made, and that some groups in the population may find they have easier access to, and therefore, greater influence on, administrative agencies than they have on the city council. Group leaders soon learn what part of the total governmental organization is most responsive to their demands, and they tend to concentrate their efforts where they think they will do the most good.

BIBLIOGRAPHY

Books

Adrian, Charles R.: *Governing Urban America*, 2d ed., The McGraw-Hill Book Company, New York, 1961, chap. 13.
Argyris, Chris: *Understanding Organizational Behavior*, The Dorsey Press, Homewood, Ill., 1960.
Barnard, Chester I.: *The Functions of the Executive*, Harvard University Press, Cambridge, Mass., 1954.

Blau, Peter: *Bureaucracy in Modern Society*, Random House, Inc., New York, 1965.

————: *The Dynamics of Bureaucracy: A Study of Social Pressures*, University of Chicago Press, Chicago, 1955.

Gulick, Luther, and L. Urwick (eds.): *Papers on the Science of Administration*, Institute of Public Administration, New York, 1937.

Joiner, Charles A.: *Organizational Analysis: Political, Sociological and Administrative Process of Local Government*, The Michigan State University Press, East Lansing, 1964.

Pfiffner, John M., and Robert Presthus: *Public Administration*, 5th ed., The Ronald Press Company, New York, 1967, chaps. 9 to 13.

————: and Frank P. Sherwood: *Administrative Organization*, Prentice-Hall, Inc., Englewood Cliffs, N.J., 1960.

Presthus, Robert: *The Organizational Society*, Alfred A. Knopf, Inc., New York, 1962.

Sayre, Wallace, and Herbert Kaufman: *Governing New York City*, Russell Sage Foundation, New York, 1960, chaps. 8 to 11.

Simon, Herbert: *Administrative Behavior*, The Macmillan Company, New York 1947.

Thompson, Victor: *Modern Organization*, Alfred A. Knopf, Inc., New York, 1961.

Waldo, Dwight: *The Administrative State: A Study of the Political Theory of American Public Administration*, The Ronald Press Company, New York, 1948.

Weiner, Norbert: *The Human Use of Human Beings*, Houghton Mifflin Company, Boston, 1954.

White, Leonard D.: *Introduction to the Study of Public Administration*, 4th ed., The Macmillan Company, New York, 1948, chaps. 3, 4, 14, 15.

Articles

Freeman, J. Leiper: "The Bureaucracy in Pressure Politics," *Annals of the American Academy of Political and Social Science*, vol. 119, pp. 10–29, September, 1958.

Joiner, Charles A.: "Organizational Theory and Public Administration: Bits and Pieces," *Public Administration Review*, vol. 21, pp. 99–104, spring, 1961.

Kaufman, Herbert: "Emerging Conflicts in the Doctrine of Public Administration," *American Political Science Review*, vol. 50, pp. 1057–1073, December, 1916.

Long, Norton: "Public Policy and Administration: The Goals of Rationality and Responsibility," *Public Administration Review*, vol. 14, pp. 22–31, winter, 1954.

Nigro, Felix (Ed.): Symposium, *Public Administration Review*, vol. 28, (March–April, 1968): Rollin B. Posey, "The New Militancy of Public Employees;" Chester A. Newlan, "Collective Bargaining Concepts: Applications in Governments;" Gordon T. Nesvig, "The New Dimensions of the Strike Question;" Paul Camp and Richard Lomax; "Bilateralism and the Merit Principle;" Felix Nigro, "The Implications for Public Administration."

Walton, Eugene: "A Study of Communication Systems," *Personnel Administration*, vol. 26, pp. 46–49, May–June, 1963.

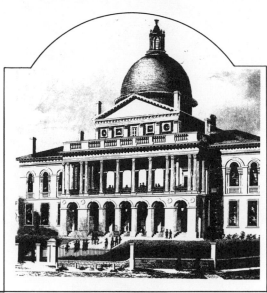

PART 4

**CITIZEN PARTICIPATION IN THE URBAN
POLITICAL PROCESS**

12

ELECTION PROCESSES

A part of the political process in all American cities is the election, in which qualified persons express their preferences for candidates for office as well as for propositions involving tax rates, bond proposals, and charter amendments. Elections become institutionalized within a political system, and the rules, regulations, and mechanical processes change little from year to year. Each political group which seeks to control decisions made in the city government views the election as one place where it can exert influence on the system. In general, politically oriented groups accept existing electoral rules and devices and plan their strategies around these institutionalized procedures. If an existing system appears to work to the serious disadvantage of any organized group and they are unable to overcome this disadvantage by any strategy they can devise, the group will probably make a frontal attack on the election machinery and seek electoral reforms.

Any electoral system will, in practice, work to the advantage of some groups and the disadvantage of others; and although changes may alter the relative advantages or disadvantages of competing groups, it is unlikely that any system can be devised that is entirely neutral in election contests. Banfield and Wilson have stressed the importance of electoral systems.

Around such [electoral] systems there develops a set of strategies for the gaining of power. The strategies take account both of the "rules of the game" and each other's strategies, and there arises by mutual adjustment an equilibrium that becomes in time so familiar and taken for granted that the electoral system appears to be a purely technical, and therefore trivial feature of the city's politics. But this is an illusion, for the electoral system profoundly affects the character of politics. It should not be surprising then that efforts to change fundamentally the distribution of power within a city are often directed toward changing the electoral system. And it should, likewise, not be surprising that the changes proposed are discussed by proponents and opponents as if they could be judged on purely technical grounds.[1]

PARTICIPATION IN THE ELECTORAL PROCESS

Democratic theory has placed great emphasis on the right to vote, and, in general, the percentage of a total population that is permitted to vote is considered to be one measure of democracy. The voting booth is supposed to be the one place where the voice of all persons carries the same weight, regardless of wealth, social status, or political position. The extent to which this equality is translated into practice will depend on the rules and procedures under which elections are administered. Free expression at the ballot box will depend, in part, on the extent to which the voter feels assured that his vote will be counted as he casts it and that no one will be able to find out how he voted.

VOTER QUALIFICATIONS

Traditionally, the American legal system has recognized two kinds of rights, political and civil. Civil rights have been assumed to include freedom of speech and religion, right of trial by jury, and those other rights incorporated in constitutional bills of rights. Supposedly, these rights attach to the individual regardless of age, place of residence, or citizenship, and no agency of government can place restriction on them. Political rights, on the other hand, must be conferred on individuals by government and can be withheld from certain classes provided the classification scheme is reasonable. The right to vote and to hold office are the two most easily recognized political rights, i.e., rights which the individual does not achieve merely through citizenship.[2]

[1] Reprinted by permission of the publishers from Edward C. Banfield and James Q. Wilson, *City Politics*, copyright 1963, the President and Fellows of Harvard College and the Massachusetts Institute of Technology, p. 87.

[2] For a discussion of the separation of citizenship and suffrage see *Minor v. Happersett*, 21 Wallace 162 (1875).

Recent court decisions interpreting the "equal protection" clause of the Fourteenth Amendment indicate that the right to vote may be considered more like a civil right than has been previously supposed.[3]

In the American federal system legal authority to determine qualifications for voting was left to the states. The provisions in the body of the constitution stipulated only that persons who were eligible to vote for a member of the most numerous branch of the state legislature could also vote for a member of the United States House of Representatives. A similar provision was included in the Sixteenth Amendment, which provided for the popular election of United States senators. The suffrage was extended to women on the same basis as men by the Nineteenth Amendment. Although states still determine the basic qualifications for voters, constitutional amendments have placed limits on this power in order to prevent them from denying the suffrage to certain groups in the population.

Legally states could have delegated to cities power to establish their own qualifications for voting in city elections, but they have not done so. In certain kinds of local elections, such as approval of bond issues and increases in property tax rates, ownership of property was set up as a qualification for voting, but only a few states retain this requirement.[4]

State Suffrage Laws

Since suffrage qualifications in cities are contained in state constitutions and statutes, a summary of state laws on the subject is in order. Three qualifications for voting (age, citizenship, and residence) are found in all 50 states. Georgia and Kentucky set the minimum age at eighteen years, it is nineteen in Alaska and twenty in Hawaii; all other states have made twenty-one the minimum voting age. Although there has been some agitation for making the minimum voting age the same as the compulsory military service age, proposals to achieve this end have been defeated in a number of states.

All states now require voters to be United States citizens. Many states at one time permitted aliens to vote as soon as they had taken out their first citizenship papers and declared their intentions to become a citizen. Many of these aliens were concentrated in the large cities, and they became an important factor in the strength of local political bosses.

Although all states have a residence requirement for voters, there is considerable variation in its application. A few Southern states require two years'

[3] See *Ex parte Yarborough*, 110 U.S. 651 (1844); *U.S. v. Classic*, 313 U.S. 299 (1941); *Smith v. Allwright*, 321 U.S. 649 (1944).
[4] Council of State Governments, *Book of the States*, Chicago, 1966–1967, p. 22.

residence in the state, a dozen states have only a six-month residence require-ment, others have set the requirement at one year. The residence qualification has received increased attention as the mobility of the United States popula-tion has increased. Ordinarily residence for voting purposes is neither gained nor lost by reason of one's geographic assignment when in the armed forces.

Most states deny the right to vote to certain classes of persons even though they may meet the established minimum qualifications of age, citizenship, and residence. These restrictions apply to insane persons and to those who have committed serious crimes. Certainly, those who are incarcerated in penal institutions and those committed to mental institutions are denied the right to vote, and in some states a felon may be disfranchised even though he has served out his prison term, unless his political rights have been restored by the governor.

The depression of the 1930s and federal legislation to provide assistance to the poor have brought interesting responses that relate to voting. Deter-mined attempts were made to deny voting rights to anyone on the relief rolls during the depression years, and similar attempts have been made to remove from the registration rolls those who were receiving old age and public wel-fare payments. The ability of the federal government to attach conditions to its grants to the states for these purposes has probably been the strongest force operating to prevent such limitations on suffrage.

Negro Voting Rights   The problem of equal voting rights for Negroes constitutes an excellent case study of attempts, within the concepts of Amer-ican democracy, to deny the suffrage on a class basis. This was possible in the United States only because under the federal system the states rather than the federal government possessed power to determine qualifications for voting. The Fifteenth Amendment furnishes ample evidence of the federal government's willingness to extend suffrage to Negroes. The amendment had to secure a two-thirds favorable vote in both houses of Congress before it could be submitted to the states for ratification. In most states Negroes were permitted to vote without difficulty, but Southern states devised means whereby they could deny them voting rights without violating the letter of the amendment.[5]

Long residence requirements, both within the state and in the county or election district, were established to disenfranchise the most mobile of the

[5] For a discussion of attempts to disenfranchise Negroes, see C. Herman Pritchett, *American Constitutional Issues*, McGraw-Hill Book Company, New York, 1962, pp. 57–76; and G. Theodore Mitau, *State and Local Government: Politics and Processes*, Charles Scribner's Sons, New York, 1966, pp. 228–240.

population. Although this restriction was general in its applicability, it hit hardest at Negroes and poor whites. Attempts to limit suffrage through "grandfather clauses" were nullified by the United States Supreme Court.[6] These laws incorporated some kind of test for voting such as payment of poll taxes or ability to read and understand the Constitution but exempted from the requirement persons who were eligible to vote in 1867 and their descendants. The poll tax and the literacy test without the grandfather clause continued to be used in a number of Southern states.

The poll tax (or head tax) is a fixed tax per person; it was often used to maintain local roads in many states and was not related in any way to the right to vote, but Southern states seized upon it as a legal way to disenfranchise the Negro. Although the poll tax was small, usually around $2, it was often cumulative, so that a person who tried to vote at a particular election would have to pay back taxes for a fixed period of years. There seems little doubt that this tax and the method by which it was administered kept many Negroes as well as poor whites away from the polls. Only four states, as of 1965, used the poll tax as a qualification for voting.[7] The Twenty-fourth Amendment to the United States Constitution has now made the poll tax illegal as far as elections for federal officers are concerned, and the Supreme Court, in *Harper v. Virginia Board of Education,*[8] has ruled it out in state and local elections.

Some kind of literacy test has also operated to keep minority groups from freely entering the election process. In many Southern states prospective voters could be required to take a test to demonstrate ability to read and *understand* the Constitution. Since the tests were administered by election officials, intentional discrimination was possible. The 1965 Voting Rights Act addressed itself specifically to the literacy test as it was used in the Southern states. The act automatically suspended the test in any state or county in which less than 50 percent of the voting-age population were registered to vote or actually voted in the 1964 presidential election.

The New York literacy test, although administered objectively, actually disenfranchized large numbers of Puerto Ricans because it was given only in the English language. The 1965 act also provided that no literacy test could be required for any prospective voters who had successfully completed six grades in any school operating under the United States flag even though instruction

---

[6] *Guinn v. United States,* 238 U.S. 347 (1915).
[7] Council of State Governments, *op. cit.,* p. 22, Alabama, Mississippi, Texas, Virginia.
[8] 383 U.S. 663 (1966).

was not in the English language. In 1966 the Supreme Court ruled that the New York test must be made available in Spanish as well as English.

The Lily-white Primary   In 1921 the United States Supreme Court handed down a decision which, in itself, was unrelated to Negro suffrage but was seized upon by Southern states as a legal means for making the Negro vote ineffective. In the *Newberry* decision[9] the Court was asked to determine if the federal law which limited the amount of money a candidate for the United States Senate could spend in an *election* applied to the direct primary as well as the general election. Although, because of the manner in which the judges divided, the full import of the decision was not clear, many lawyers interpreted it to mean that a direct primary was not a part of the election as far as federal restrictions were concerned. If this were true, states would be free to place any restrictions upon voting in the primary without violating the Fifteenth Amendment. Since the real contest for office in Southern states took place in the Democratic primary, Negroes could be effectively eliminated from the decision-making process by keeping them out of the primary.

In a series of decisions involving various attempts to keep Negroes from voting in the Democratic primary in Texas, the Supreme Court in *Smith v. Allwright* held that the primary is a part of the election process and therefore suffrage qualifications that are in effect in the general elections also apply in primaries.[10]

Removal of legal impediments, alone, will not ensure wide participation of the Negro in the electoral process. Efforts by Negro leaders such as the late Martin Luther King to arouse Negroes to demand equal rights and to use the ballot box as a means of achieving recognition may do more than formal legislation to increase the Negro participation in elections. Recent legislation which authorizes the attorney general to appoint federal registrars in areas where Negroes are denied the right to register and more effective action by federal officers against state and local officials who deny civil rights to Negroes will also strengthen the Negro leaders' position as they seek to remove the fear that keeps Negroes from trying to exercise the right to vote.

REGISTRATION OF VOTERS

Concern over qualifications of voters would be useless if there were no means by which those legally disqualified could be kept from the polls without serious impediments to those who are qualified. Likewise, the idea of "one person, one vote" is meaningless unless a system can be devised which effectively

[9] 256 U.S. 232 (1921).
[10] 321 U.S. 651 (1944).

prevents persons from voting more than once without seriously discouraging the rank-and-file voting population. One means for ascertaining that all those who seek to vote are qualified and for reducing fraud in elections is a system of registration of voters. Briefly, a registration system provides that all persons who wish to vote on election day register beforehand. Registration performs two functions. It provides a period of time prior to election dates during which election officials can check the qualifications of those seeking to vote and eliminate those who are unqualified. In the second place it identifies each voter so that the record will show that he has voted and he can be prevented from voting a second time.

Substance of a Registration System

A typical registration system provides that all persons seeking to vote have their names registered a certain period of time prior to the date of the election. At the time of registration the voter supplies certain information needed to pass judgment on his qualifications and to identify him when he appears to vote on election day. The standard information includes date of birth, to determine age, place of birth or of naturalization to determine citizenship, and present address along with the date when the person moved to that address, in order to determine residence. Identification is usually established by signature, but physical characteristics and picture may be used.

Kinds of Registration Systems

Although there are many variations in registration systems from state to state and even in different areas of a single state, most of these may be classed as either periodic or permanent. In periodic registration the voter is required to register periodically, usually before each general election. A single registration serves for one general election and for all other elections until the next general election. Old registration lists are destroyed, and a new list is made for each general election. A permanent registration system permits a qualified voter to register once and that registration remains valid as long as he does not change residence and as long as he actually votes (usually once every four years).

Registration Administration

The officers responsible for the administration of elections are usually also the registration officials. Voters may go to the central office to register when they move to a new location or when they reach voting age. In many cases registration officials establish field stations at periodic intervals to encourage more persons to register. Card systems are now more commonly used than are registration books. Duplicate or triplicate cards may be used so that the loss of one set of cards would not be serious. One set can always be kept at central headquarters and another set can be sent to the precinct polling places on the dates of elections.

Registration is usually closed during a period of four or five weeks immediately preceding an election. During this period the officials check the accuracy of the lists. Clearing registration lists of names that no longer belong there can be a continuous job. Vital statistics can be used to cancel the names of deceased persons, and court records supply names of those who are disqualified by reason of crime. The biggest task is to remove the names of those who no longer live in the area. This may be done by mail. A double post card is mailed to each name on the list. One card, with instructions, is addressed to the registered voter, the other is addressed to the election office. If the voter still lives at the address, he signs the card and returns it to the office. Here the signature is compared with the original, and if it appears to be authentic, the name is included in the list for the coming election. Those names for which no card was returned are taken from the active list. In some cases, registered letters may be sent to persons from whom no reply was received before they are removed.

The personal canvass is widely used to check the accuracy of registration lists. Two clerks (usually of opposite political parties) are assigned a certain geographic area and supplied with the names and addresses of all persons registered from the area. The clerks are instructed to call at each address and to ascertain if the persons registered still live at the address shown. A single check at the manager's office of apartments and hotels may be sufficient. At all addresses where the clerks cannot verify that the persons registered from that address actually live there a notice is left. This notice instructs the registered voter that unless he visits the registration office by a certain date his name will be removed from the list. In some jurisdictions registration lists are made public along with notices that if anyone is interested, he can challenge the qualifications of any name on the list and the registration officials will make a check of all such names.

In those states where registration is not required in all areas, the cities are more likely to be the areas in which it is required. Since one purpose of registration is to provide an opportunity to check qualifications of voters prior to election day, this seems more important in cities where the election officials will not know voters personally and where the population is much more mobile. Many rural areas and small towns have only one polling place and nearly every eligible voter is known personally to one or more of the election officials; in such instances registration is looked upon as an unnecessary inconvenience.

ELECTION ADMINISTRATION

The electoral process is generally administered by local officials under procedures specified by state law. The major steps in the total voting process are (1) acceptance of names to be included on ballots, (2) printing of ballots or preparation of mechanical devices, (3) conduct of the election at precinct polling places, and (4) determining the final tally. Most of these functions are performed under the supervision of a local county or city clerk in the rural areas and small cities; in the large cities they are supervised by a commission or board with a staff of full-time workers. Registration and the maintenance of the voter lists are usually the responsibility of this same board or commission. In two-party states an equal number from each party serve on the commission. They may be elected, appointed by a local executive, or appointed by the Governor. The secretary of state serves as a general-election officer for the state. Candidates for statewide offices file their certificates of candidacy with him, he sends to local officers the names to be included on ballots, and he makes the final tally of votes for state offices. The same election officials administer both the direct primaries and the general elections.

The officials responsible for election administration map out the boundaries of precincts each of which will have a polling place, select judges and clerks to work at each polling place, supply each with a list of qualified voters, and deliver record books and ballots or machines to each polling place. Final records are delivered to the election commission at the close of election day, and an official tally is announced by the commission. Almost every election produces charges of irregularities in certain areas of large cities. Some of the problems related to the conduct of elections result from the kinds of clerks and judges that are recruited, and some result from a lack of supervision by the election commission. Judges and clerks are often persons very much interested in the final results of the elections, and some of them may be over-anxious to influence the result in their precinct. These officials are usually selected by the election commission from lists of names supplied by the party ward committeemen, and they are often precinct party workers. Election commissions generally do not have supervisors who can make spot checks to supervise the actual voting process or even to make spot checks when a specific report of irregularity is reported to them.

THE NOMINATION PROCESS

Before the use of official ballots, individuals supplied their own ballots or they were supplied by political parties; therefore, no formal official process for nominating candidates for office was required. Since the general adoption of the so-called Australian ballot system in this country, governmental officials prepare an official and uniform ballot. The preparation of such a ballot requires some established process for the nomination of candidates so that election officials will know whose names are to be printed under each office to be filled. In nonpartisan elections the nomination process is nothing more than a preelection in which the number of names for each office is reduced to two. For the first election anyone can have his name included as a candidate for office by filing a declaration of candidacy. The declaration may have to be accompanied by a cash payment or a petition signed by a certain number of supporters. Since no party labels appear on the ballot, the two candidates receiving the greatest number of votes for each office will be printed on the ballot to be used at the general election. This system is used widely in small and medium-sized cities.

The Direct Primary   Since Wisconsin adopted the direct primary on a statewide basis in 1903, it has become the most popular method of nominating candidates for office in both state and city elections. Under the system each party's list of candidates is selected directly by the voters, who go to their regular polling places and vote for the candidates they want to represent their party. This direct primary requires the preparation of what might be called an official primary ballot. For a candidate to get his name included on the primary ballot he is required to file a declaration of candidacy. Although there is wide variation from one state to another as to how he is required to validate his declaration, two plans are most often used. In one plan the candidate makes a cash payment, generally referred to as a filing fee. The amount of the fee is determined by the importance of the office sought, but it is assumed to be enough to discourage those who are not serious candidates. In many primaries the candidate must validate his declaration by filing with election officials the signatures of a certain number of qualified voters who will support him for the office. The number of signatures required is designated by law and is usually a certain percentage of the votes cast for the office in the last election, but in some cases a fixed number is required. Often a small filing fee may be required along with the signatures to petitions.

The Closed Primary   Where there is strong party competition for elective offices there will be strong sentiment for the closed direct primary. In such a primary only members of a party are permitted to vote to help select the candidates for the party; i.e., Democrats vote in the Democratic primary, Republicans vote in the Republican primary, and, supposedly, nonparty members do not vote at all. Since seldom will more than one independent file for any office, their names will be placed on the general-election ballot without a primary. The practical problem faced by election officers is how to limit each primary to party members. Since party membership in this country is very informal, some kind of test of party membership must be devised. In some states this is taken care of by registration. The voter is required to declare his party membership when he registers; then the judges at the polling place permit him to vote only for candidates of the party shown on his registration card. Many states, however, do not require that the voter indicate party preference at the time of registration. In these states the voter is required to tell the officials at the polling place which party ticket he wishes to vote. Ordinarily, the voter will be permitted to have the party ticket he asks for, but provisions are usually made whereby a voter who has always been a Republican can be challenged if he asks to vote in the Democratic primary. In case of such a challenge, the voter may be required to swear that he will support the candidates of the party whose ticket he has requested in the coming general election. There is, of course, no way by which he could be held to such an oath.

The Open Primaries   Although by far the most states permit the voter to have the ballot of only one party in the primary, some states have what is referred to as an open primary. Under an open-primary system, the voter is not required to divulge his party preference either at registration or at the polling place. In the limited or restricted open primary the voter receives the ballots of both political parties and in the secrecy of the voting booth he decides which he will use. He cannot, however, vote for some candidates on each party ballot. When he returns from the booth, he can deposit only one ballot in the box to be counted.

The state of Washington is the only one which uses the blanket primary. Under this system the voter receives a blanket ballot and is free to help nominate a candidate of one party for mayor and of the other party for councilman. In the blanket primary the party label of each candidate is shown, and the Republican with the greatest number of votes and the Democrat with the greatest number of votes are declared winners; their names will appear under the respective party labels on the general-election ballot. In the nonpartisan primary no party labels are shown either on the primary or on the general-election ballot; the two candidates with the greatest number of votes for each office are declared the winners, and their names are printed on the general-election ballot. Thus, the two candidates for mayor could both belong to the same party or they could both be independents.

Regardless of the formal system used to nominate candidates, much of the important decision making takes place before the voters cast their ballots. In cities with one or more strong party organizations, endorsement by party committeemen is, if not indispensable, very useful. Few will put the resources required for an effective campaign into it without assurances of support from some party influentials. Since most city organizations are not controlled by any single party figure or committee, each candidate may have support from some of the ward committeemen. The price a candidate must pay for a committeeman's support is hard to measure; some candidates could not get it at any price, others need only make a contribution to the party chest or promise some kind of patronage if they are elected.

EVALUATION OF PRIMARIES

In the beginning of the chapter the point was made that parties and candidates developed their strategies around the electoral machinery that is imposed upon them by law. Certainly the kind of campaign that might produce nomination in a delegate convention would not ensure victory in a direct primary. The politician who can work behind the scenes to dominate the process by which convention delegates are selected might be unable to control the direct primary, where the number of participants is multiplied many times. Candidates must have access to more money to conduct successful primary campaigns than is required to campaign for convention delegates. Since party funds are generally concentrated for the general-election fight, candidates in the primary must seek support outside regular party channels; therefore, the victors may have contracted political obligations outside the regular party which must be paid off after election. This means that outside forces will compete with party officials for the limited patronage available to the winning candidate.

Although evidence is limited, there is reason to believe that the mass media and nonparty organizations play a greater role in direct primaries than they do in the convention process. Delegates to nominating conventions may be classed as "pros"; they are usually chosen from among the party officials, regular party workers, or officeholders. These people are less likely to be influenced by editorials or news stories designed to affect election results. On the other hand the mass voters may have little commitment to any party candidate and may swing to one or the other on the basis of a publicity campaign sponsored outside party channels. Non-party-oriented civic leaders may play a more significant role in a city primary than they could possibly play in a party convention. The preliminary events that lead to the selection of convention delegates are fairly well guided by party officials, and few civic leaders are apt to play a leading role in this process, but in the mass primary campaign the endorsement of well-known business, educational, and religious leaders may constitute the balance of power in a close primary race.

In spite of the problems the direct primary poses for the party official, he may be willing to go along with it, but he will insist that it be closed. The open primary presents many unsatisfactory possibilities to the experienced party leader. He fears that if permitted by law to do so, independents and even members of the opposing party will enter his primary and saddle the party with candidates whom he and others like him do not want. He insists only that members of opposing parties stick to their own party primaries and that independents either not be admitted to primaries or be limited to voting for independent candidates. Political party leaders may formulate a successful strategy to deal with the closed primary, but they find it difficult to cope with one which allows outsiders, at will, to select the party's candidates for office.

GENERAL-ELECTION BALLOT FORMS

Ballot forms as used here refers to either the paper ballot which is handed to the voter and which he marks in the voting booth or the face of a voting machine which confronts the voter when he enters the booth. The general system of voting prevailing in most parts of the country conforms to what is often referred to as the Australian ballot. The ballot is official, having been prepared by the government, it is blanket in that it includes the names of all candidates that have met minimum requirements, it is available to the voter only after he enters the polling place, and the voter casts his vote in secret. But within this system, variations in the form of the ballot are possible. Although numerous variations are found, most ballots may be classed as being either the Massachusetts or office-bloc ballot or the Indiana or party-column ballot.

The office-bloc ballot groups all candidates under the title of the office they are seeking. Usually the party designation will be shown after the name, but nonpartisan ballots are also prepared in this form. On the party-column ballot, candidates of a single party are shown in a single-party column along with the office they are seeking. A common, but not universal, feature of this ballot is a voting box or circle at the top of the party column, which permits the voter to cast a straight party vote by marking a single X in the square or circle. The assumption is that the party-column ballot encourages straight party voting while the office-bloc ballot encourages the voter to cross party lines. Evidence to support these assumptions is scarce, but since party workers think the assumption is true, any attempt to switch to the office-bloc form produces a vigorous contest.

SPECIAL KINDS OF ELECTIONS

Although most city elections conform to the general pattern discussed above, some experimenting with different techniques has taken place, and some of these have a staunch, if generally small, body of followers. These experimental forms are sufficiently different from regular patterns that, if adopted widely, they would force existing groups to alter their strategies in order to maintain their present influence, and they might even alter the structure of group control in a city's politics.

Proportional Representation

Proportional representation has not found acceptance in this country, although it has been used widely in one form or another in Europe, particularly on the continent. The rationale or philosophy of proportional representation is simply that all groups organized for political purposes should be represented in a legislative body in proportion to their numbers; i.e., if in a given city there are four groups each composed of persons whose interests are sufficiently alike to cause them to stick together in an election and they constitute 40, 30, 20, and 10 percent respectively of the voting population, on a ten-man city council the first group should have four representatives and the others, in order, should have three, two, and one. This concept of group representation should not be confused with the movement to equalize the number of voters in legislative districts that has followed the Baker decision. Representation in this country has consistently been based on geographic districts; proportional representation is based on community of interest without regard to geography.[11]

[11] For a favorable discussion of proportional representation, see George H. Hallett, Jr., *Proportional Representation: The Key to Democracy*, National Municipal League, New York, 1940.

Two general forms or procedural systems have been used in an attempt to achieve the goal of proportional representation. The first is the *List System,* under which each group organized to support candidates for the legislature is permitted to nominate a list of candidates that it will support and these lists are printed on ballots under the name and symbol of the groups supporting them. In its simplest form, each voter merely indicates the list which he prefers and does not cast his vote for individual candidates. At the close of the election, the ballots are totaled for each group list. If, as in the example above, four groups have lists on the ballot and ten councilmen are to be elected, the number of representatives each group receives would be determined by the ratio of the number of votes it received to the total vote cast.

The Hare System   The few cities in the United States that have experimented with proportional representation have used what is known as the Hare system, which has been advocated by the Proportional Representation League and has been incorporated in the Model City Charter sponsored by the National Municipal League. The system is often referred to as proportional representation by the single transferable vote. This system is designed to produce the kinds of results described above—representation of groups in proportion to their voting strength—without requiring voters to choose from among groups or party lists. In fact, the support for proportional representation in this country has come from those who are oriented toward nonpartisan elections for city councilmen.

A major feature of the Hare system is preferential voting, which requires the voter to indicate his first, second, third, etc., choices from among the names on the official ballot. The ballot consists of a list of candidates whose names have been filed with election officials. Different filing procedures may be employed; some places require signatures to petitions, some have filing fees, and some may require an indication of group support. The order in which names are placed on the ballot must be specified by law, but alphabetic listing is considered to be an objective method. Some jurisdictions permit each candidate to list the name of the party or group which is sponsoring him, but others permit no indication of party or group support.

Each voter is permitted to mark his ballot for as many candidates as he wishes, but he must indicate by numbers his preference. The familiar use of an X to vote for a candidate is not adequate in the Hare system. Instructions on ballots usually instruct the voter to indicate preferences for as many candidates as there are places to be filled on the council. Since the transfer of ballots is a distinctive feature of vote counting in the system, the more preferences the voter indicates, the greater are the chances that his vote will actually help elect a councilman.[12]

EVALUATION OF PROPORTIONAL REPRESENTATION

Proportional representation has been used in some cities, notably New York and Cincinnati, which have used it to elect their city councils. The United States Supreme Court in its recent reapportionment decision may cause increased interest in the system. If decisions of the Court go no further than to require that representative districts contain approximately equal numbers of voters, there will be no increased interest in proportional representation. But if the Court goes further, as there is some indication that it will, and insists that groups with common interests must be afforded equal representation, proportional representation may be the only system that is able to produce equitable representation for all politically active groups.

Obviously, proportional representation requires the voter to reexamine the election process. The idea of winner-take-all so prevalent in present election processes is not applicable if the philosophy behind proportional representation is to be accepted. Political leaders who are influential in determining the way large numbers of voters cast their ballots will have to develop new techniques to maintain that position of control.

Some evidence indicates that the use of a proportional representative system does affect the makeup of a city council. Sayre and Kaufman report that prior to 1937 the Democrats dominated the New York City council. Between 1920 and 1935 the Democrats won 90 percent of the seats four times, 85 percent twice, and dropped to two-thirds only twice. In the first election under the Hare system in 1937, the Democrats won only 14 out of 25 seats, and in the next four elections their majority hovered around the two-thirds mark, but in the three elections after proportional representation was abandoned, the Democrats won 24, 23, and 24 respectively out of 25.[13] Other factors, such as a change in the size of the council and a change in terms of office, may have intervened to affect the results but proportional representation seems to be a major factor. Sayre and Kaufman conclude: "When the New York City Council was elected by proportional representation, some minority

[12] For a description of the method of counting votes in the Hare system, see *ibid.*
[13] Wallace Sayre and Herbert Kaufman, *Governing New York City*, Russell Sage Foundation, New York, 1960, p. 176.

groups obtained a forum and a degree of access to the city's governmental decision-making machinery that were less readily available to them when the city returned to a single-membered district system."[14] In fact the ability of two Communists to win council seats was used as a major argument by the Democrats to defeat the proportional representation system.[15]

Banfield and Wilson indicate that the use of the Hare system in Cincinnati increased minority representation on the council and made it possible for a Negro to be elected. This, they suggest, was one of the principal reasons why it was defeated after many years of use. They also report that its use in Worcester, Massachusetts, allowed "Jews and Yankees" to be represented in the council and that its proponents claimed that without it all councilmen would be Irish Catholics.[16]

Certain generalizations about the possible effects of proportional representation in city elections can be offered even though no specific studies are available to support them. Since fairly small well-organized groups can usually be assured of electing a representative, there is less pressure on them to join one of the large parties in the election campaign. Were such groups faced with the typical district type of election, they might offer to throw their strength to one of the other parties in return for patronage or support for some issue. This means that whatever coalitions that are formed would, in the single-member district system, be formed prior to the election, while in proportional representation they would have to be formed among council members after the election was over. This might have a tendency to weaken the old-line parties and encourage something similar to a multiparty system.

A conjecture may be made that proportional representation tends to encourage racial, religious, or nationality groups, that might not otherwise do so, to form cohesive political organizations to seek council representation. In a typical ward election such groups would not be able to dominate the election of a councilman who they themselves would name; rather they would choose the candidate selected by others who seemed least unfavorable to them. Proportional representation, however, would open the door for some of these groups to name their own councilman.

Proportional representation permits groups with common interests to be effective even though they are spatially scattered over a wide area of the city. Groups dispersed over the wide area will seldom be more than a small minority

---

[14] *Ibid.*, p. 107.
[15] *Ibid.*, p. 543.
[16] Banfield and Wilson, *op. cit.*, p. 97.

in a number of districts, but if they constitute one-tenth of the voting population, they can elect one member of a ten-member council regardless of how widely they are scattered.[17]

A variation of the winner-take-all system is used in Philadelphia. Of the seven councilmen elected at large, a voter can vote for only five, and a party can nominate only five; therefore the second strongest party is assured of two of the seven representatives. New York, beginning in 1963, introduced a plan which provides for the election of two councilmen from each borough, but since each party can nominate only one candidate and each voter can vote only one candidate, two-party representation is assured.[18]

PROPOSITION VOTING

At a typical city election in this country the voter will be given an opportunity to vote for candidates for a long list of offices, and in addition he will be asked to vote for or against numerous proposals that are usually listed on the ballot as propositions. These may include such items as a complete city charter, single amendments to the charter, the property tax rate, the issuance of bonds, approval or disapproval of ordinances relating to nearly any subject, and the retention or removal of a popularly elected officer before his regular term expires. A feature of local government that distinguishes it from federal and most state governments is the extent to which popular votes are required on many political issues. In most cases the results of the vote on such issues determine their fate, but in other instances the voters are asked only to express an opinion for the guidance of the council or some executive officer.

Initiation of Proposals

Propositions may be placed before the voters in a number of ways. A charter commission may present a new charter or a series of amendments to the existing charter, the city council may propose charter amendments or, on its own motion, submit proposed ordinances to the voters. Constitutions and

---

[17] For studies of proportionment in New York City and Cincinnati, see Belle Zeller and Hugh A. Bone, "The Repeal of P.R. in New York City: Ten Years in Retrospect," *American Political Science Review,* vol. 42, pp. 1127–1148, December, 1948; and Ralph A. Straetz, *P.R. Politics in Cincinnati,* New York University Press, New York, 1958.

[18] Banfield and Wilson, *op. cit.,* p. 78.

charters regularly require that tax rates and bond issues be submitted to the voters for approval before they become effective. In addition many city charters permit the qualified voters by petition to place proposals on the ballot; this process is usually referred to as the "initiative." The initiative may be used to secure a vote on the removal of a city officer, on a charter amendment, or on a proposed ordinance. The number of signatures required to place each kind of proposal on the ballot is specified in the city charter. Usually the number of signers for a recall election is quite high (as much as 25 percent), for charter amendments it may be as high as 10 percent, and for ordinances only from 3 to 8 percent are required. Percentages are usually based on the number of votes cast in the last election for mayor or on the number of registered voters. The number of signatures required is generally greater if a special election is called for than if the proposition is to go on the ballot at the next regular election.

Petitions seeking the enactment of an ordinance may be directed to the city council, and the charter may require that the council take a vote on the proposal without amendment. If the council adopts the ordinance, no election is necessary. If the council does not adopt the ordinance within a fixed time period, it is then placed on the ballot.

Referendum

Strictly speaking, a popular vote on any proposition is a referendum, regardless of the process by which it is placed on the ballot. Votes on tax levies, bond issues, and charter amendments may be classed as mandatory referenda since they must be submitted to popular vote. Propositions which are submitted merely to get a popular expression of opinion as a guide to the council are often called optional referenda. The referendum, however, is generally used to refer to elections on ordinances which have been passed by the council and have evoked organized opposition. If enough signatures can be obtained, the effective date of the ordinance is postponed until an election is held. The number of signatures required to refer an ordinance in this way is usually from 3 to 8 percent of the number of votes cast in the last election for mayor.

Simple majority votes are required for a decision on many propositions submitted to popular vote, but two-thirds majorities may be required for tax rates and bond issues. In some cases something more than a simple majority may be required to approve charter amendments.

EVALUATION OF INITIATIVE AND REFERENDUM

The adoption of the initiative and referendum may be traced to the decline in public confidence in legislatures, particularly during the latter part of the nineteenth and the early part of the twentieth centuries. Their introduction and widespread adoption as a regular part of the decision-making machinery of government was a part of the twentieth-century reform movement which has been referred to earlier. Most attempts to evaluate these institutions, which, in essence, confer legislative power directly on the voters, consist of listing advantages and disadvantages that have been used as debating arguments by proponents and opponents of these modes of increasing popular sovereignty. Proponents generally point to evidence indicating that legislatures are dominated by minority groups who think more of private than of public interests and that, therefore, these devices are necessary to protect the public interest. They also maintain that even if these devices are not widely used, they constitute a sort of "gun behind the door" to check legislatures.[19] Some suggest that popular interest is stimulated when voters have an opportunity to vote directly on important issues. The argument has been made that constitution makers are willing to limit the number of restrictions upon legislative bodies which so often clutter up these documents if the people have the kind of checks afforded by the popular initiative and referendum.

Opponents argue that confidence in legislatures and in the principle of representative government is lowered by these devices. They insist that legislative issues are so complex that voters are unable to make a rational decision about them, and that the features of the legislative process such as hearings, informal debate, and compromise are impossible in the initiative-and-referendum process.

The difficulty of evaluating these devices in terms of lists of advantages and disadvantages is that what appears to be an advantage to some is perceived to be a disadvantage by others. It is, likewise, difficult to use performance standards as a means of making a value judgment about such devices. There is no question but that many important issues have been both approved and rejected by popular vote. When a proposition which has been adopted by the legislature is defeated by a referendum, those who favor the proposal are likely to condemn the referendum, while those who oppose the proposition will praise it as a great protection against bad legislation.

[19] See J. G. LaPalombara and C. Hagen, "Direct Legislation: An Appraisal and a Suggestion," *American Political Science Review*, vol. 45, pp. 400–421, June, 1951.

The important question to be asked is, "In terms of legislative output do
these devices make any difference?" Evidence is available to indicate that
they do make a difference. Some significant measures passed by legislatures
have been defeated when submitted to a popular vote, and some important
issues have been enacted through the initiative procedure that legislatures
consistently refused to pass. This does not imply that the devices are either
good or bad, except in the eyes of those who have strong opinions about the
proposals themselves. The second question that should be raised is, "What
groups are likely to fare best when decisions are left solely to legislative
bodies, and what group interests are likely to have the best chance for victory
if they are decided at the election polls?"

Although there is insufficient evidence to provide firm answers to these
questions, more research should shed some light on them. Probably the most
significant observation to make here is that a legislature constitutes an arena
for decision making with a certain configuration of interests, and that the
electorate, acting through the initiative and referendum, constitutes another
decision-making arena with a different configuration of interests. If the mix
of interests in each arena is the same, the decisions flowing from each should
not be far different, but if the mix of interests is different, the outputs of the
two arenas are likely to be different. Under existing systems of representation,
few legislative bodies are likely to be true cross sections of the voting public.
The manner in which representative district lines are drawn, the inequality of
districts, and the overriding power of political leaders to control elections for
representatives produces legislatures that are not equally representative of
the electorate. A popular referendum which opens the decision-making process
to all voters who want to participate wipes out the inequalities in districts, permits interest groups to vote their full strength regardless of how they may
be spatially distributed over the city, and probably makes it impossible for
political leaders to influence as many votes as they do in the election of
officeholders.

One might suggest that regular political organizations, which are most
likely to dominate the process by which legislative districts are made, as well
as control the process of nomination and election of legislators, will find the
initiative and referendum a disadvantage to them. On the other hand, citizen
groups which organize to sponsor a single cause, as well as minority groups
whose members are widely dispersed over a city, may be able to get decisions
more favorable to them in the election arena than they can get in the
legislative arena.

VOTING BEHAVIOR

Probably no facet of politics has received as much attention from empirically oriented political scientists as has voting behavior. The facts available lend themselves especially well to the research techniques which have become the tools of the trade for a new breed of political researchers. Voting data are readily available, as are vast amounts of census data, e.g., on age, income, race, nationality, and residence. Sophisticated statistical techniques are available to determine correlations between census-type data and voting behavior. Research methods involving sampling, interviewing, questionnaires, indexing, and scaling have enabled researchers to generalize about large-scale voting behavior by studying intensively a selected sample of the total population.

Much of the research thus far has been concentrated on state and national elections, even though the areas studied have been in cities. Since city elections are held at different times from state and national elections and may involve different mixes of voters, generalizations developed from national and state election data may apply with less validity to local elections. The difference in voter turnout in city, national, and state elections taken alone may be enough to create doubt that voting patterns observable in national elections can be assumed to explain voting behavior in city elections. In most large cities in the United States the voter turnout in mayoral contests is well below the turnout in presidential elections.[20]

Nonvoting

One of the most obvious kinds of political behavior in this country is the high degree of nonvoting. Although this behavior pattern is clear enough in national elections, when participation is around 60 percent of the qualified voters, it is even more pronounced in local elections, when participation may not exceed 25 percent. Researchers who have sought to probe for an explanation for nonvoting have suggested that it may be accounted for, in part at least, by what is called political alienation, anomie, or apathy. Murray Levin, in his study of the 1959 election for mayor in Boston, describes what he calls alienation.

> Our analysis of this post-election survey has shown that a large proportion of the electorate feels politically powerless because it believes that the community is controlled by a small group of powerful and selfish individuals who use public office for personal gain. Many voters

[20] See Banfield and Wilson, op. cit., p. 225 (table).

assume that this power elite is irresponsible and unaffected by the outcome of elections. Those who embrace this view feel that voting is meaningless because they see the candidates as undesirable and the electoral process as a sham.[21]

The degree of alienation felt by potential voters is measured by responses to questions that probe their attitudes on whether the average voter can have any effect on public decision making. The assumption is that voters who are alienated, i.e., who feel they are powerless to influence public policies, are hostile to existing officeholders and the political system in general and that they express this hostility by staying away from the polls or, if they go to the polls, by casting negative votes. The implications of alienation are somewhat different from those of apathy as it is generally applied to nonvoting. The term "apathy" may be used to express mere lack of interest or concern; an apathetic potential voter might be one who would merely spend his time off work at the bowling alley rather than at the polls. The alienated voter is one whose attitudes are definitely negative because of his views about the political process, in general, and his inability to influence it, in particular.

Political alienation may be a useful concept to help explain a great deal of nonvoting, but it does not, in itself, identify all the specific kinds of potential voters who stay away from the polls on election day. Many qualified voters are simply not interested enough to register and vote; they are not involved enough to be alienated. These are the potential voters who may be persuaded to exercise their franchise only in terms of political crisis. When this group is lured to the polls, the "rascals" may be thrown out or a major change in political structure approved.

Voting Regularity

A number of studies have been made in recent years to throw more light upon the question of which groups in the society are most likely to go to the polls. Sufficient correlations have been found to justify some generalizations on the subject. Robert Dahl found in his New Haven study that the following relations existed: (1) people with higher incomes vote more than do those with lower incomes, (2) those with higher social standing were more regular voters than those with lower social standing, (3) those with more formal education participated more than those with less schooling, (4) businessmen, professionals, and white-collar workers turn out in elections more

[21] Murray B. Levin, *The Alienated Voter*, Holt, Rinehart and Winston, Inc., New York, 1960, p. 458. Copyright, Holt, Rinehart and Winston, Inc., 1960.

than do those in blue-collar working groups, and (5) persons in better residential areas have a higher percentage of voting than do those living in poorer residential areas.[22] Williams and Adrian found that in wards dominated by Democratic-labor groups the labor union members had superior voting participation records.[23]

Other studies have produced information about voter participation although they are not specifically related to city elections. A greater percentage of men vote than do women, more property owners vote than do non-property owners. Voting is higher among older people than among the younger ones. For example, twice as many vote at fifty-one as do at twenty-one.[24] Difference in participation in elections can probably be explained in terms of the images prospective voters have of the way they may be affected by the results.

How People Vote

If one can predict with assurance the groups that are most likely to vote in large numbers, he may be able to predict election results. This assumes, of course, that the factors which condition group voting can be ascertained and that there is consistency in voting behavior. Evidence available seems to assure that, "the pattern that appears in one local election tends to be repeated in all others so long as the electorate is essentially the same (i.e., barring large differences in turnout or changes in the composition of the population)."[25]

Although political party membership plays a major role in determining how people vote in national and state elections, it is much less significant in city elections. Sayre and Kaufman found that in New York party membership is "only loosely related to voting behavior."[26] This does not mean that parties do not affect election results. Voters may support regularly candidates of one party simply because they feel such candidates are, over a period of time, more likely to represent their point of view and that party workers may be able to get more people out to vote, thereby influencing results.

Certainly formal education, income, religion, ethnicity, and occupation are all factors influencing voting patterns. Banfield and Wilson maintain that these

[22] Robert Dahl, *Who Governs?*, University of Yale Press, New Haven, Conn., 1961, pp. 282–283.

[23] Oliver P. Williams and Charles R. Adrian, "The Insulation of Local Politics under the Nonpartisan Ballot," *American Political Science Review*, vol. 53, p. 1061, December, 1959.

[24] Adrian, *Governing Urban America*, 2d ed., McGraw-Hill Book Company, New York, 1961, p. 1061.

[25] Banfield and Wilson, *op. cit.*, p. 226.

[26] Sayre and Kaufman, *op. cit.*, p. 129.

factors are all associated and that it is not now possible to indicate the influence of each factor separately when others are held constant. Perhaps, these social class factors act through party preferences; i.e., political parties and their candidates make their appeals on this basis. Democratic candidates make a stronger appeal to Catholics, blue-collar workers, and those with less income and less formal education, while Republican candidates are more acceptable to professionals, businessmen, and upper-income groups.

Banfield and Wilson make a strong case for "difference in ethos" as an "explanatory principle" in understanding voting behavior. They suggest that one conception of politics, which they refer to as "public-regarding," is accepted by middle-class citizens and is Anglo-Saxon Protestant in its origin. Another conception of politics, which had its origins in lower-class immigrant culture, is "private-regarding." Many of the issues which are decided at the ballot box in city elections tend to align supporters and opponents in terms of whether they are public-regarding or private-regarding. On this basis they have developed a set of hypotheses:

(1) that in all social classes the proportion of voters who are decidedly public regarding is higher among Protestants than among other ethnic groups;
(2) that in all social classes the proportion who are private regarding is higher among those ethnic groups (e.g. Poles) whose conception of politics is, in the relevant respects, most opposed to the Protestant one;
(3) that people in the upper middle and upper classes are more public regarding than those in the lower middle class;
(4) that people who are decidedly private regarding on one matter tend to be so on all matters; and
(5) that decidedly public regarding and decidedly private regarding voters tend to be farther apart on all matters, including those which have no public-private dimension than are other voters.[27]

BIBLIOGRAPHY

Books

Adrian, Charles R.: *Governing Urban America*, 2d ed., McGraw-Hill Book Company, New York, 1961, chap. 4.
Banfield, Edward C., and James Q. Wilson: *City Politics*, Vintage Books, Random House, Inc., New York, 1963, chap. 16.

[27] Reprinted by permission of the publishers from Edward C. Banfield and James Q. Wilson, *City Politics*, copyright 1963, the President and Fellows of Harvard College and the Massachusetts Institute of Technology, p. 235.

Campbell, Angus, et al.: *The American Voter*, John Wiley & Sons, Inc., New York, 1960.

Childs, Richard S.: *Civic Victories*, Harper & Brothers, New York, 1952.

Hallett, George H.: *Proportional Representation: The Key to Democracy*, National Municipal League, New York, 1940.

Hermans, F. A.: *Democracy or Anarchy? A Study of Proportional Representation*, University of Notre Dame Press, Notre Dame, Ind., 1941.

Kornhauser, Arthur: *When Labor Votes*, University Books, Inc., New Hyde Park, N.Y., 1956.

Lazerfeld, P. S., et al.: *The People's Choice*, Columbia University Press, New York, 1948.

Levin, Murray B.: *The Alienated Voter*, Holt, Rinehart and Winston, Inc., New York, 1960.

Scammon, R. M.: *America Votes*, The Macmillan Company, New York, 1956.

Wilson, James Q.: *Negro Politics: The Search for Leadership*, The Free Press, Glencoe, Ill., 1960.

Articles

Cutright, Phillips, and Peter H. Rossi: "Party Organization in Primary Elections," *American Journal of Sociology*, vol. 64, pp. 262–269, November, 1958.

LaPalombara, J. G., and C. B. Hagen: "Direct Legislation: An Appraisal and a Suggestion," *American Political Science Review*, vol. 45, pp. 400–421, vol. 45, June, 1951.

Mott, R. G.: "Preferential Voting and How It Works," *National Municipal Review*, vol. 1, pp. 386–400, July, 1912.

Williams, Oliver P., and Charles R. Adrian: "The Insulation of Local Politics under the Nonpartisan Ballot," *American Political Science Review*, vol. 53, pp. 1052–1063, December, 1959.

Zeller, Belle, and Hugh A. Bone: "The Repeal of P. R. in New York City: Ten Years in Retrospect," *American Political Science Review*, vol. 42, pp. 1127–1148, December, 1948.

13

PARTY AND INTEREST-GROUP POLITICS

In an earlier chapter the point was made that it is difficult to discuss city courts since the judicial function in cities is primarily a state rather than a city function. The discussion of political parties in cities presents a similar difficulty. Political parties exist in most cities, even where elections are on a nonpartisan basis, but they often function primarily for state and national elections rather than in city contests. The existence of political parties in American politics and the fact that city party organizations constitute a part of the base upon which state and national parties rest are sufficient reasons for giving some attention to their structure, even when they play a relatively minor role in purely city politics. In some cities, however, the party plays a significant role in local elections and in the decision-making process at the local level. More often than not, where a political party functions as an effective instrument to determine city policies, there is no strong opposition party; i.e., in party-governed cities, the opposition party may put up slates of candidates, but its chances of winning on any regular basis are very small. The two-party system is not regularly found in the political life of American cities.

LEGAL NATURE OF PARTIES

Although national party structure is extralegal, i.e., determined by party custom and practice rather than by law, state party organization (and therefore, city organization) is provided for in considerable detail by state law. The organization of national party committees and conventions is determined by the parties themselves, but state central committees and city committees are creatures of state law. Names of party officers, the method of their selection, some of their duties, their terms of office, and to a certain extent the qualifications of members are spelled out at length in state statutes. The existence of legally recognized political party officers in a city, however, does not of itself prevent the existence of self-appointed party leaders in some city wards. In fact, unofficial party workers may exercise more influence in an election than do the legally constituted ward officers, but control of the legal machinery constitutes an advantage to party workers who really want to be influential in city politics. Politicians who seek to control local politics in modern cities will try to do so by capturing the legal party apparatus, rather than by relying on an extralegal machine type of structure.

PARTY ORGANIZATION

Since local party organization is determined by state law, there may well be 50 different varieties, but one can make some generalizations that are useful to the student who would like to examine in greater detail the structure in any particular state. Party organization is usually based on existing political units; seldom will one find a district created solely to furnish representation for party organization. The smallest unit which serves as a base for party organization is the precinct. This unit generally serves no governmental purpose except as a polling place either for registration of voters, for elections, or for both. In large cities the precinct may contain from 500 to 2,000 voters, depending on whether paper and pencil ballots or voting machines are used.[1] The next largest unit in party organization is the ward in large cities and the township in suburban and rural areas. The ward is usually a representative district from which a committeeman or alderman is chosen, and it may contain from a tenth to a fiftieth of the city's total population, depending on the size of the council. A township, in some areas, serves as a local government performing a limited number of local functions, but in other areas its chief purpose is to serve as a base for party organization. In large suburban areas the population of a township may compare favorably with that of a city ward, but in outlying areas they are much smaller. A significant fact is that

---

[1] For a discussion of the party worker at the precinct level see Sonya Forthal-Spiesman, "The Precinct Worker," *The Annals of the American Academy of Political and Social Science,* vol. 259, pp. 30–45, September, 1948.

township lines may not conform to municipal boundaries. In one area surrounding a large city, for example, parts of a city of over 50,000 are in three different townships and a single township contains either all or parts of a dozen municipal corporations. The point is that party organization based on townships aligned in this way does not constitute a viable organization for conducting city campaigns. Some states have provided another kind of representative district as a basis for local party organization. This district is usually the one used to select representatives to the county legislative body, but it is not any more likely to conform to municipal boundaries than are townships.

Some states start formal party organization at the precinct level; if so, a party committeeman (and usually a committeewoman) are chosen by each party for each precinct.[2] Although in many states the selection is made at the regular direct primary, in others the selection is made in mass meetings of party members. The committee people selected in the precincts, together, constitute the ward committee or the township committee, as the case may be. Other states start formal organization at the ward or township level; a committeeman and committeewoman are chosen by each party in each ward in large cities and in each township in other areas. Either the direct primary or the party mass meeting is used in the selection process. The ward and township committee people then appoint precinct captains in each of the precincts within their ward or township. These precinct captains may not be specifically provided for by statute, but their positions are well established in practice.

The city organization in large cities and the county organization in other areas is based on the ward or township organizations. In the case described above, in which the wards and townships have committees composed of precinct committee people, the chairman and vice chairman of each ward or township committee become members of the city central committee or the county central committee. In the second case, in which formal organization starts at the ward or township level, the ward committeeman and committeewoman automatically become members of the city or county committee. If a city has 20 wards, for example, the Democratic City Central Committee would consist of 40 members, usually equally divided between men and women; the Republican City Central Committee would be similar. In a suburban county with 20 townships, the county central committee for each party would be the

[2] For a more detailed account of formal organization see Russell Ross and Kenneth F. Millsap, *State and Local Government and Administration*, The Ronald Press Company, New York, 1966, pp. 205–212.

same size. This would be true even if as many as 50 municipal corporations function in the county. The cities within such a suburban county are unlikely to have any formal city central committee. This may account, in part, for the general acceptance of nonpartisan elections in many suburban cities.

Contact between the state party organization and city and county central committees is assured, since these local committees constitute the base upon which state central committees are built.

Functions of Party Officers

Since party committeemen and -women are provided for by state law, they are assigned some official duties. In most states, even where local and state officers are nominated by the direct primary system, there are conventions to write party platforms, to select delegates to national conventions, and to nominate state committeemen and -women to represent the state at national party committees. The arrangements for the series of meetings required to produce a state convention are the responsibility of party officers. In the event of a vacancy in any office on the party ballot between the date when nominations are made and the date of the general election, the appropriate party committee will name someone to fill the vacant spot on the ballot. In some states these party committees have an official role in nominating candidates for delegates to state constitutional conventions.

Most of the work of party officers is to maintain party organization, raise money, and help conduct election campaigns. These officials receive no salaries, and no public funds are allocated to them for their work; they must depend on contributions, money raised at social functions, and their personal funds to conduct the party's business. It is not uncommon for ward committeemen to ask for contributions from persons seeking the party's nomination for city offices in return for an endorsement. The assumption is that money received from such contributions will be used for party purposes.

The *modus operandi* of ward committeemen varies from city to city and from ward to ward in the same city, depending on the personality of the committeeman and the character of his ward.[3] These committeemen often constitute a liaison between the voter and city officials. Persons seeking to get on the welfare rolls, businessmen who seek a change in parking restrictions, real estate dealers who want a change in land-use zoning, and the father

[3] One of the best discussions of the activities of party workers at the local level is found in Frank Kent, *The Great Game of Politics*, Doubleday, Page and Co., Garden City, N.Y., 1923, chaps. 1, 4, 6, 7.

whose son has been picked up by the police all seek help from the precinct captain or the ward committeeman. Common mythology and newspaper reports about political influence combine to give the citizen the impression that the only way to get action from city officials is through political channels. Even though the myth may no longer be true, as long as many citizens think it is true, they will beat a path to the doors of party officials.

The complexity of government structure in a modern city may strengthen the position of the party committeeman. Many citizens will at one time or another have reason to deal with the city on some matter which to them is important. In most cases the average citizen does not know where to go or whom to see to discuss his problem. City workers, themselves, are often not very helpful. If the first officer contacted is not one who can deal with the problems, he may not know where to direct the citizen. It may well be that a party worker is more accessible to many citizens than is a city official. Even though the party worker contacted may have little or no influence in solving the problems involved, he may be able to get the citizen to the right place for its consideration.

The party, through its officers, may furnish a place where citizens can go for entertainment, to meet important people, and to unburden themselves of complaints about city hall. These local party headquarters often serve an important function in linking city officialdom and citizens who feel they are unable to cope with the complex procedures required by modern government.

Patronage Available to Party Officers

A ward leader's influence among voters in his ward will depend, in large measure, on his ability to give something of value to at least some of his constituents.[4] Prior to twentieth-century reforms in city government and public welfare programs, the local party leader had much to offer. He was allocated from the top a certain number of city jobs which would be filled on his recommendation, contractors in his ward would receive their share of city contracts, and in return they would employ workers recommended by the party leader. Law-enforcement officers could be persuaded to overlook illicit activities of those with proper contacts with the party, and city funds could be allocated for improvements desired by certain kinds of businesses. Although this kind of political patronage has been greatly reduced, it is by no means

[4] For an account of an early local party leader see William L. Riordon, Introduction by Roy V. Peel, *Plunkitt of Tammany Hall*, Alfred A. Knopf, Inc., New York, 1948.

entirely gone. Civil service, competitive bidding on contracts, and more professionalization in police departments have all taken their toll of things of value the party leader has to offer in return for support at the polls. Party gifts to needy families and aid to newly arriving immigrants which formed the basis for party control a half-century ago are no longer such useful tools. Public agencies which have assumed the welfare function are staffed by professional social workers who have been warned about the evils of mixing politics and welfare. Immigration has been reduced to a trickle, and public agencies are available to help new arrivals in the process of assimilation.

Personality, leadership qualities, and social attractions may have to take the place of things of value formerly available to party committeemen. There is no question but that older political leaders had a large following of voters who simply wanted to follow the leader even though they expected no kind of material reward. Political leaders today may have to develop this kind of charisma if they are to be effective in controlling large blocs of votes. This change may produce more political leaders who are also prominent officeholders than was true in the past. This kind of personal leadership is easier to develop and maintain if the leader is closely associated with issues and programs rather than with the kind of patronage described above.

Arrangement for regular meetings where citizens can gather in a social atmosphere and where discussion of issues of interest to them can be held may be a useful method of acquiring a position of leadership; obviously the character of the ward dictates the kind of appeal that is most effective. The changes that have taken place in patronage available to local party leaders may be a factor in the increased interest in modern political clubs.

Political Clubs

Banfield and Wilson maintain that by 1960 the Tammany organization in New York City had ceased to be a political machine and had become an alliance of clubs.[5] Although the local club was a feature of machine-type organization in the heyday of Pendergast, Murphy, and Crump, the character and functions of clubs have changed since that time. The club was, in the old days, the place where deals were made and patronage was dispensed; it was the place where the faithful could be greeted by the leader and rub

[5] Edward C. Banfield and James Q. Wilson, *City Politics*, Vintage Books, Random House, Inc., New York, 1963, p. 133; see also James Q. Wilson, *The Amateur Democrat: Club Politics in Three Cities*, The University of Chicago Press, Chicago, 1962; and Robert E. Lane, James D. Barber, and Fred I. Greenstein, *Introduction to Political Analysis*, Prentice-Hall, Inc., Englewood Cliffs, N.J., 1962, pp. 55–57.

elbows with the "boys." Generally, impetus for club organization comes from the local committeemen and -women, but, once started, the club may elect its own officers and arrange its own meetings and agenda. Although such clubs may be used by the local party chiefs to promote party candidates, the club may have as much effect on the committeeman as he has upon it. Although these clubs attract and hold members by sponsoring dances, fish fries, and other social functions, many of them sponsor meetings to discuss significant public issues. When clubs become institutionalized and have among their members persons who major interest is policy rather than patronage, new kinds of party leaders are needed to guide party organization, and often a kind of local independence is encouraged that tends to make control or dictation from the top more difficult. The local leader who has a viable club with him and who is looking for no private gain from his association with the central party machinery is apt to display a high degree of independence if he disagrees with central party leadership.

Incentives for Political Leaders

If one unfamiliar with party organizations were to observe some precinct captains and ward or township committeemen, he would be struck by the amount of time and effort they give to their job without any visible reward. The question of what they get out of it is often raised. Certainly, the rewards are not the same for all political leaders, and their own expectations vary from one committeeman to another. To some, the personal satisfaction they receive from the job and the contacts it creates for them are ample reward; to others, party office is looked upon as a stepping stone to government office. More and more party officers either hold some public office or seek such office once they have established a party following. Many of these leaders expect no monetary gain from their party position, and some of them actually spend their own money for party purposes.

The time has not arrived, however, when no party leaders use their position for personal profit. It would be difficult to describe a definite pattern by which party officers use their position in this way, but a few examples will indicate the avenues open to them. They may, of course, accept pay for any favors they may do for clients. This might apply to sellers and contractors who want to do business with the city, or it might apply to shady businesses whose owners feel they can buy, through party officials, protection from the police, laxity from city inspections, or special treatment for requests for licenses or permits. This kind of graft, no doubt, still exists in some areas, but it is safe to say that fewer and fewer political leaders can profit from it or would do so even if it were available to them.

The rewards that come to party leaders are, in modern cities, more likely to come in connection with their regular profession or business than from payments for political influence.[6] Many lawyers gravitate into political life, and some of them become ward committeemen. In this capacity they become well known to people living in the ward, to officeholders, and to those who deal with city government. Since party offices pay no salaries, these lawyers continue to practice law for a living. It is very possible that their legal practice is increased because of their party position. Many judges, particularly those in the lower courts, are still popularly elected on partisan ballots. Those judges who were successful in their campaigns had the open support of their ward committeeman, and most everyone knows it. Now, if a citizen has reason to go to court, he may feel that he has nothing to lose, and perhaps something to gain, by employing the committeeman as his attorney. Success in a case or two, even though deserved by the nature of the case, will create the impression that there is some relation between the attorney employed and the final result; therefore the attorney's stock rises rapidly.

Many real estate men find party politics interesting, and some of them become ward committeemen. They continue to operate in the real estate field, just as they did before, and under some conditions, their business may become more profitable. In the first place they become better known, and as a result more people go to them to list property for sale or to purchase property. The city government often must purchase real estate for parks, rights-of-way, and for the location of city structures. Although the city possesses the right of eminent domain, attempts to purchase usually precede the use of this power. Whether or not it is true, some property owners may feel that the party committeeman is their best agent in dealing with the city. In his position as party official the committeeman may learn of proposed city projects that, when completed, will add to the desirability of land surrounding the project. He may, if he wishes, secure options to real estate in the area and later make substantial profits. If, as is unlikely but still possible, the party official has influence with those who control land-use zoning, he may purchase land at the market price under prevailing zoning and then, if he can secure a zoning change, sell at a substantially higher price.[7]

Some party leaders are regular insurance agents or brokers. They represent established companies, and their prices are competitive; they do not cheat

[6] Frank Kent, *op. cit.*, chaps. 8, 22.
[7] See William L. Riordon, *op. cit.*, chap. 3.

anyone who deals with them. But the fact may be that they sell insurance to city employees, to contractors who depend on city contracts, and to those who sell to the city, which they might not be able to do if they did not occupy what is considered by outsiders to be a strategic party position. One need not assume that anyone is being dishonest or that graft is being dished out to reach the conclusion that some persons find party offices to be highly profitable.

City Machines

The city political machine has been a feature of American politics at least since Lord Bryce in 1889 described it as a party organization where the "source of power and the cohesive force is the desire for office and office as a means of gain."[8] The term "machine" might be applied to any political organization which time after time is able to achieve victory at the polls with the regularity of a smoothly running machine. But the term carries with it the connotation that the machine depends for its existence on what Banfield and Wilson call "material" rather than "nonmaterial" rewards.[9] That is, the dependence is upon money, jobs, and protection rather than upon such values as public service, pleasure in politics, or companionship. In some cases the public also equates graft, corruption at elections, and use of force and violence to quiet opposition with the machine's *modus operandi*.[10] Political machines formed their organizational structure before party organization was spelled out by law, but the structures they developed were not far different from the present legal party organization just described. In fact, the legislatures may have used existing machine structure as a pattern for the organization incorporated in law. The major differences are in the provision of regular procedures for popular participation in the selection of party officers, and the fact that these officers have fixed terms of office and some official duties to perform. Top leaders in the machine handpicked local ward and precinct leaders on the basis of their willingness to take orders and their ability to deliver their areas for machine-selected candidates, particularly in

[8] James A. Bryce, *The American Commonwealth*, Macmillan and Co., New York, 1889, vol. II, p. 111.

[9] Banfield and Wilson, *op. cit.*, p. 115.

[10] For literature on bosses see Harold Zink, *City Bosses in the United States*, The Duke University Press, Durham, N.C., 1930; H. F. Gosnell, *Machine Politics: Chicago Model*, The University of Chicago Press, Chicago, 1937; J. T. Salter, *Boss Rule: Portraits in City Politics*, McGraw-Hill Book Company, New York, 1935; Edward J. Flynn, *You're the Boss*, The Viking Press, Inc., New York, 1947.

the primary election. The machine loses if it cannot dictate the party's choice in the primary, even though the party may win in the general election.

Machine leaders were able to hold the organization together because they had something of value to offer in return for the efforts of its ward and precinct leaders, and these local leaders had something they could use as political currency to get out the vote of the faithful. To the ward and precinct leaders the machine leader (boss) could offer protection to businesses which operated on the fringes of legality, inside information about governmental decisions that might affect market values, influence in letting contracts and purchasing materials for those who had financial interests in businesses dealing with the city. The local leaders, in turn, could offer jobs, friendship, a place to socialize with those who wield power, and assistance for those who were in trouble with the police, who needed help in getting a license, or wanted the street in front of their house repaired.

Those at the top who kept the machines going received some satisfactions or they would not have expended the time and energy required to hold such an organization together. In some cities the boss owned or had a financial interest in businesses that contracted with or sold to the city. In other cases the boss expected payoffs from companies which sought his help when they needed zoning changes, special operating permits, lax enforcement of building codes, or freedom from police interference in operating taverns and handbooks. Machine leaders were, as a rule, uninterested in public policy issues. Officeholders, even though they owed their election to the machine, were left fairly free to deal with chambers of commerce, citizens' associations, and friends of city parks on policy questions, since party leaders depended more on material rewards than on policy decisions to pay off their workers. In fact, machine leaders were happy when city officers joined with interest groups to push through large public works projects, since they presented more opportunities for them to offer more jobs, contracts, and sales to the city. Some of the most elaborate public construction projects undertaken in cities have been sponsored under machine domination.[11]

Decline of the Machine

Evidence is unmistakable that the Pendergast, Crump, and Tammany type of machines have disappeared from the political scene. A number of factors have combined to account for their decline in power. Job patronage has been

[11] See Charles N. Glaab and Theodore Brown, A History of Urban America, The Macmillan Company, New York, 1967, pp. 222, 223.

substantially reduced by merit systems of civil service, competitive and open bidding on city contracts for construction and purchases have become common, immigration has been substantially reduced, tighter control over voter registration and election administration has reduced election irregularities, public welfare has been put on a professional basis, and more middle-class citizens have taken an active part in politics. In other words, when the sources of political power were withdrawn from machine leaders, they had nothing of sufficient value to buy the support they needed to maintain a viable organization. There is also some reason to believe that the level of morality acceptable to the average citizen has changed. The kind of graft that was accepted as a natural part of the political system sixty years ago is no longer an acceptable norm of conduct to new voters who treasure their right to participate in the political system. Crusading newspapers, leagues of women voters, and citizen reform groups have all played a role in raising the acceptable norms of political conduct.[12]

Although the city-wide political machine, for the time, seems to be on its way out, there are political organizations which still wield a powerful influence in city life. On a city-wide basis these are generally led not by a behind-the-scenes boss but by a powerful mayor. A number of cities have elected mayors whose victory can be attributed to their personal appeal and the programs they advocate. In some cases they built their own organization in opposition to the regular party organization and then took over the organization after being elected. A big-city mayor, in spite of the reforms that have weakened the boss, has a great deal of political patronage that he can use once he is elected.

Most cities have political leaders who are still referred to as bosses and organizations denounced as machines, but these are usually on a less than city-wide basis. A ward boss, a northside machine, or a Negro boss may still dominate elections in geographic areas of a city, but none of them, alone, can control an election at large. A mayor may find it necessary to make alliances with such local leaders and organizations in order to win a city-wide contest, but after the victory has been achieved, the local leaders maintain their independence. Sections of a large city where income level and formal education are low and the proportion of unskilled laborers is high are more likely to have a political leader who could be called a local boss.

[12] See Fred I. Greenstein, "The Changing Pattern of Urban Party Politics," *The Annals of the American Academy of Political and Social Science*, vol. 353, pp. 1–13, May, 1964.

CHANGES IN ORGANIZATIONAL POLITICS

The decline of the city political machine may have left a vacuum in city politics that it will take time to fill. A characteristic of most large cities is the plurality of interest it contains. Within its border are all ranges of income level, many racial and nationality groups, labor unions and management organizations, and a wide range of reform-oriented groups. This mixture spawns diversity and disunity, rather than consensus and community of interest. The machine, through the use of material rewards rather than ideology, was able to hold together an organization that could get things done. As the machine declines and ideology and issues become more important in holding a political organization together, politics becomes pluralistic and fractionated. In such a pluralistic system coalitions and compromises become the order of the day, and it may be much more difficult to secure positive action on public works projects, health and welfare programs, and educational efforts. Modern party structure may tend to produce negative action (maintenance of the status quo) rather than encourage bold new programs.

Political observers are interested in watching to see how the vacuum left by the demise of the machine will be filled. Political leadeship may, under new conditions, call for the kind of person who is a skilled broker who can put together a viable coalition of various groups, or it may call forth the charismatic type who by the attraction of his personality can sweep to victory. Unquestionably, the end of machine politics has reduced what reformers have condemned as vice, graft, and corruption in government and transplanted into the system middle-class norms of moral conduct, but something has been lost in the process.[13]

The decline of the well-disciplined city party has meant that city elections are likely to be won by alliances or organizations which Banfield and Wilson call "factions." They identify four classes of factions, according to "the nature of the inducements by which support is secured from voters and others."[14] Local *machines,* which are often remnants of older city-wide machines and which cohere around some colorful personality; *personal followings,* which support a local political figure because he represents the neighborhood rather than because of his principles or of any reward they make expect from such support; *interest* groupings, whose cohesion results from a community of interest such as lower property taxes, reform programs, or

[13] Banfield and Wilson, *op. cit.,* pp. 125–127.
[14] *Ibid.,* chap. 10.

higher wages for city employees; and the *club*, whose solidarity is accounted for by the personal satisfactions arising from membership in the club. The task of welding these organizations into a working alliance calls for different skills and probably different kinds of inducements from those required in the past to maintain a viable political machine. The widespread adoption of non-partisan elections has tended to weaken the city political party, which might have been the agency through which a workable alliance could have been achieved.

INTEREST-GROUP POLITICS

Many citizens with marginal interest in politics feel they can make the effort they are willing to expend count most by supporting a political party whose symbols appeal to them. These people can be counted on to vote regularly, support all or most of the party's candidates, and make small donations to the party campaign chest, but this is probably the maximum effort they will put out on political affairs. Other citizens will also make a commitment to a political party, but because of the diverse interests of its adherents, it cannot wage a vigorous campaign for specific policies; therefore they will join a more homogeneous group to fight for their favorite cause. Still other interested citizens will find no political party satisfactory and contribute all their political effort to some organization which is committed to policies that appeal to them. These organizations, other than political parties, which labor vigorously in the political arena for a wide variety of causes, are referred to as interest groups, or sometimes as pressure groups because of the tactics they employ.[15] Although generalizations that seek to identify interest groups and distinguish them from political parties are difficult, some identifying marks are recognizable.

Since political parties must make their appeal to a wide range of diverse groups of voters, they must adopt platforms that include policy planks on numerous subjects. Interest groups owe their cohesiveness to the fact that they limit their policy interest to a single issue or at least a very narrow range of policy issues.

[15] Perhaps the best discussion of interest groups is found in David B. Truman, *The Governmental Process*, Alfred A. Knopf, Inc., New York, 1951. See also D. C. Blaisdell, *American Democracy under Pressure*, The Ronald Press Company, New York, 1957; and "Unofficial Government: Pressure Groups and Lobbies," *The Annals of the American Academy of Political and Social Science*, vol. 319, September, 1958, entire issue.

Political parties with a wide range of policy issues to worry about must limit their position on each issue to broad generalizations in order not to alienate any section of party supporters. On the other hand, the appeal of the interest group to a limited clientele makes it possible for it to take a positive and clearly understood stand on the narrow range of political issues in which it is interested.

Political parties seldom have a formal type of membership. The voter, at his own option, chooses his party membership; he is required to go through no initiation ceremony, pay no dues, or even register his membership with any party officer or committee. Furthermore, he may leave the party at any time he chooses and elect to join another. No party in this country can supply a record of its membership. Interest-group membership is often, but not always, more formal. Most interest groups have a register of their members, collect dues, and often exercise some discipline over their members.

Political parties have as their chief or sole purpose for existence the control of the personnel and policies of government. If there were no way in which organized groups could participate in politics, there would be no use for parties. Many, but not all, interest groups exist for nonpolitical purposes but find that they can, because of their members and influence, affect policy decisions, and therefore they engage in politics. Labor unions, farm organizations, the American Medical Association, and the chambers of commerce are examples of organizations that perform nonpolitical functions as their first order of business, and they would continue to exist if they should decide to retire from the political arena.

The *modus operandi* of these two types of organizations are also different in significant ways. Political parties exert their influence through the process of nominating and electing candidates for political office under their own name, and they are willing to assume responsibility for conducting affairs of government. Interest groups, on the other hand, do not put up slates of candidates under their own name, and if they offer group support to candidates, the ones they select are usually running on a political party ticket. Interest groups are not asking to conduct governmental affairs and to assume group responsibility for the way these affairs are conducted. Some interest groups almost always support the candidates of one party, but they make a point of the fact that they do so on the basis of the candidate's record rather than because of his party affiliation. The student can find individual examples of interest groups that do not, in all respects, conform to the above definitions, but these generalizations will have some value in most cases.

Classification of Pressure Groups

A number of schemes might be devised to classify the interest groups found operating in big-city politics, but a useful one is to group them according to the nature of the policy programs they espouse.

Reform Groups   These are often called good-government groups, because the kinds of reforms they propose are defended as proposals to improve the governmental process. Many of these groups sponsor single reforms such as the short ballot, nonpartisan elections, or proportional representation. Others sponsor a wide range of improvements as do, for example, the National Municipal League and the League of Women Voters. Some reform groups are created to support a specific set of reform proposals at a given time, and when these proposals are either adopted or defeated, the group disbands. Other reform groups have a permanent existence and often are chartered under state law; if something they have supported is adopted, they transfer their support to another cause.

Professional and Occupational Groups   The nature of the issues that arise in city politics is such that the manner in which they are decided is of concern to professional and occupational groups; therefore these groups, although they steer clear of group affiliation with parties, exert considerable effort to affect public policy. A number of examples will indicate the kind of organizations referred to and the nature of their interests. Architects are interested in the procedures by which cities select the firms that design city buildings and other physical structures, and they are interested in physical planning from an aesthetic standpoint. Structural, electrical, and civil engineers are interested in building, electrical and plumbing codes, and in the qualifications of city inspectors who check on compliance with these codes. Doctors are interested in public health regulations, the operation of city hospitals, and such issues as compulsory immunization and fluoridation of water. Bricklayers, plumbers, electricians, and carpenters are interested in all kinds of codes related to construction in the city. Adoption of one type of provision may reduce the need for carpenters and increase the need for masonry workers. Construction workers often present the most formidable opposition to modernization of city building codes.

Business Groups   Most political issues related to traffic control, parking, street widening or relocation, and land-use planning vitally affect business interests. Like other groups which feel the impact of policy decisions, businessmen organize to exert maximum influence on the process by which these decisions are made. Only a few examples will be required to indicate the nature of the interests involved. Downtown businesses may be competitors in the marketplace, but they have a common interest in political decisions which tend to increase the number of potential customers that are brought into the downtown area. Therefore, the core-city merchants and bankers are interested in a downtown location for sports centers, civic and cultural centers, and municipal buildings. They favor better mass transit systems into the downtown area and ample parking for those who drive to shop. But there are neighborhood business organizations whose interests are often quite different. They favor the dispersion of facilities that attract large numbers of potential customers, on-street parking in shopping areas, and better lighting facilities and street maintenance in the outlying areas. Organizations of businessmen encourage city policies which stimulate business and seek to modify policies designed to be too restrictive in such matters as smoke control and water pollution. Since business interests often have internal conflicts, no single interest group can speak for all of them, but the chamber of commerce often represents a large segment of the business community on a wide range of issues. Most large cities will have a number of neighborhood organizations consisting of the businessmen in each important regional shopping center, organizations of real estate brokers, associations of parking-lot and garage owners, and many others.

Labor Groups   In many large cities labor unions constitute the most active political interest group in the city. In fact, some of these groups put more effort into political campaigns than do the regular party organizations. Unions often have full-time paid personnel whose chief work is in public affairs. These people organize study groups, support initiative petition campaigns, ring doorbells at election time, and carry out drives to get voters on the registration rolls. The numerous unions that exist in a large city are often represented on some kind of central labor council, and these councils try to coordinate labor's political activities. Although individual unions may determine their political position on local issues, the endorsement of the central labor council is sought on most major issues which go before the voters.

Special Elite Groups   The discussion of power structures will come later, but a word needs to be said here about elite groups that have appeared in a few large cities which seek to influence decisions made in the political arena. The Allegheny Conference in Pittsburgh and Civic Progress in St. Louis are representative of this kind of association. These organizations consist of community leaders whose names are well known in the city and are generally highly respected. Initiative for these organizations has come from business leaders who wanted to arrest the decay of downtown business areas. In the beginning a small group was invited to form the organization; later the remaining members chose new members to fill vacancies. These groups have in their membership the kind of names that are called upon to head community chest drives and to endorse symphony campaigns. Usually they include bankers, department store operators, and leading educators.

Although such groups give much attention to business development and the revitalization of certain areas of the city, they also endorse or oppose political issues that go before the voters. Civic Progress in St. Louis is given a large part of the credit for the successful campaign for the earnings tax and for the success of a major improvement bond campaign.

Citizen Committees   Mayors of a good many large cities have found it useful to appoint a number of citizen committees, not only to advise them in policy matters, but also to help put over programs sponsored by the administration. These committees are usually selected for a single purpose and go out of business when the purpose has been achieved. They may be created to campaign for a new charter or for charter amendments, for a new tax which requires popular approval, or for bond issues. In setting up these committees the mayor tries to persuade a representative from every major group in the city to serve. They are usually large groups and meet infrequently. They raise money, select public relations people to do the routine work, and their members make speeches when called upon. In bond-issue campaigns such a committee may be asked to screen a number of possible projects that might be supported by a bond issue, decide the total amount that voters should be asked to approve, and set up priorities for the various projects. As an incentive to voters, the mayor may announce publicly that if the bonds are approved, the committee will serve as a watchdog to decide when the bonds will be sold and to see that the money realized from the sale is properly spent.

Neighborhood Associations   In most large cities there are geographic sections that, although they are a part of the city politically, maintain a community solidarity that sets them apart from the rest of the city. This community of spirit may result from common nationality background or it may have a historic base. But every city has its Latin quarter, French quarter, or "the hill." Likewise, most cities contain areas which at one time were independent and had their own governmental machinery. Often these communities are organized into neighborhood associations that present a fairly united front to the city council and the mayor in demanding public improvements, better police service, or the relocation of major freeways.

Political Strategies of Interest Groups

The obvious ways in which interest groups seek to make their major impact are by influencing voters in elections and by lobbying with city legislators and administrators. In elections where the contest involves popular reaction to propositions rather than candidates for office, interest groups usually combine their efforts with others and work either with a citizens committee for the issue or with a committee against the issue. They will help raise money among their members, supply speakers, and take responsibility for a door-to-door or telephone campaign in a certain section of the city.

Somewhat more complicated strategy may be necessary if the interest group is to exert maximum influence through the election of candidates for office. If a city is predominantly a one-party city, as is often the case, a pressure group can exert maximum influence in the major party primary. Since nomination assures election, the interest group must secure the nomination of a candidate sympathetic to its cause or it is lost. If the majority party nominee is not sympathetic, the interest group usually is not strong enough to defeat him even if they could throw their total weight to the minority party ticket in the general election. This means that the group makes its major effort to secure at least one name on the majority party primary ballot that is acceptable, and then push for his nomination.

If a true two-party system should exist in a city, a different party strategy might be employed. The ideal goal would be to secure the nomination of a candidate on each party ballot who was sympathetic to the interest-group cause. The general election would, then, not be a serious matter, since both candidates would be acceptable. If, however, the interest-group candidates should be successful on one party ticket and be defeated on the other, the organization vote would be shifted in the general election to the party with the acceptable candidate.

Nonpartisan elections present different problems. Since there is no party choice involved, interest group support must be concentrated on the most acceptable candidate to give maximum assurance that he will be one of the two with the greatest number of votes. If their candidate's name is on the final ballot, maximum effort is made toward his election.

The strength of interest groups in elections is usually not that they have enough votes by themselves to nominate a candidate, but that they have enough votes to act as the balance of power and to swing the election to one or the other of two candidates, who otherwise would be fairly even. With this balance of power they are in a position to extract promises from a candidate in return for their support. Since there is usually a number of interest groups with sizable blocs of votes which to some degree are controlled by group leaders, victory may go to the candidate who can put together the support of more than one such group. One of the characteristics that distinguish interest groups from political parties makes it possible for a candidate to bid for the support of a number of groups without appearing inconsistent. The demands of a single interest group are limited in nature, involving only matters of direct interest to the group, and these demands may not be contrary to demands made by other groups. There is no inconsistency in a candidate's support of a union demand for higher pay for city employees and of a chamber of commerce demand for more rigid licensing of certain kinds of business activities. It is the willingness of interest groups to limit their demands upon officeholders and to leave them free to decide as they please on other issues that makes them effective politically.

This does not imply that interest groups are monolithic; it does, however, point up the fact that the more nearly they limit their demands to single issues, the more nearly they will be able to confront the candidate or city official with a united front. A taxpayers' league holds together because its members are interested in lowering taxes on real property, and as an organization, it lobbies on this single issue. Veterans' groups, business groups, and labor unions present united fronts only when the issue in question is limited to a subject closely related to the reason for their existence. On a wide range of issues, veterans take differing stands, as do business and labor organizations, and even though officers of these groups may take public stands on numerous issues, most observers know the rank and file will go their own ways.

Political Motivation

Adrian maintains that Americans participate in the political process according to their motivation and motivation depends upon the extent to which "the individuals' activities are well within the norm of society."[16] His hypothesis is that "the political activity of any group is proportionate to its stake in the marginal definition of legality and of law enforcement levels."[17] Thus, most professional men and middle-class businessmen are living well within the law so there is little possibility that decisions, particularly with respect to law enforcement, will affect them seriously; their motivation, if there is any,

---

[16] Charles R. Adrian, *Governing Urban America*, 2d ed., McGraw-Hill Book Co., New York, 1961, p. 124.
[17] *Ibid.*, p. 123.

for intense political activity must come from something other than self-interest. On the other hand, in any large city there are many whose livelihood comes from activities which are so near the edge of illegality that certain decisions about law enforcement can destroy them completely. A wide range of gambling operations already exist, or the potential for their existence is found, in every large city. Such operations are on the margin of acceptability in this country. The only way people involved in these activities can hope to operate is to be able to influence political decisions. Rooming-house operators, owners of rental property in low-rent areas, hotel owners whose facilities are available to prostitutes can stay in business and make a profit only if political decisions with respect to the laxity of law enforcement are satisfactory to them. These persons who operate in the gray area between acceptability and unacceptability must, to maintain their activities, seek to influence political decisions. The strategy employed by such groups must, of necessity, be different from that of interest groups described above. Their open endorsement of candidates would often be the kiss of death. Therefore, the payoff, under-the-table contributions to campaigns, and even threat of violence may prove to be their most effective methods of influence. The relations between marginal groups and the machine boss were probably closer than are relations between present-day politicians and these marginal types, but nearly every city has some wards in which there are alliances between the politician in the ward and those who operate in the shadows of the underworld.

NEWSPAPERS AND POLITICS

It is difficult to discuss in general terms the role played by newspapers in city politics. In the first place there are many kinds of newspapers; some are oriented toward the central city, others serve only specific sections of the urban fringe. Some seek to be national and international in their coverage, others concentrate on local readers. Many large-city papers are locally owned and operate as a single enterprise; others are under absentee ownership and operate as one of a large chain.

One characteristic that most newspapers have in common is that they try to influence public policy. There are, however, wide differences in the kinds of policies they seek to influence, in the values they seek to achieve, and the methods and intensity with which they seek to achieve their goal. There is also a great deal of difference in abilities of newspapers to achieve this end.

It is a common practice for city newspapers to provide editorial support for candidates for office both in primaries and in general elections. Most papers are always ready through editorials to instruct officeholders as to what the "general interest" requires of them, and they also instruct the voters on the proper way to vote on charter amendments, bond issues, tax rate proposals, and other propositions that appear on ballots at election time. Although some papers limit their efforts in these directions to the editorial page, others find ways of using their headlines and news stories to present their point of view in favorable light.

Generalizations about the forces which determine the values that newspapers will seek to achieve are very difficult to make; some papers are Republican, others Democratic, and still others independent politically. The political complexion of a newspaper nationally may mean little in explaining its position on local issues. Some common features about papers may help the student understand the general attitudes they take. They are all business enterprises and are expected to make money, or, at least, not lose any. They depend heavily on income from advertisers, and most big advertisers come from the business community. These factors precondition their managers to be favorable to propositions designed to create an environment favorable to business. Since as a business, newspaper management must deal on a regular basis with labor unions, just as other employers do, they may take an anti-union point of view locally. They may not oppose labor organizations on principle and they may support national legislation supported by labor, but at the same time, they may condemn local labor leaders and specific strikes that affect the image of the local community as a good environment to attract business.

Many large-city dailies are reform oriented as far as local government is concerned. Crusades for decency, good government, greater citizen participation, law enforcement, and the elimination of boss rule will in most cases enlist the support of newspapers. In fact, a paper may be instrumental in initiating such reforms by exposures of corruption or what is assumed to be undue pressure brought upon city officials to extend special favors. Newspaper influence is probably greater in influencing changes in governmental form and structure and in proposals submitted in a referendum than it is in the choice of government officials.

An interesting study of newspaper influence in an election on a major public issue was made by Scott Greer with the advice and assistance of Norton Long. In 1959 the voters of the City of St. Louis and St. Louis County defeated a proposed plan which would have created a single-district government with jurisdiction over the entire area with respect to certain major services. In sample interviews soon after the election, an attempt was made to learn something about what influenced voters to make up their minds how to vote. The two metropolitan dailies that serve the area, the *Post-Dispatch* and the *Globe-Democrat*, both took strong positions favoring the plan. Both carried a number of editorials urging voters to support the plan, their cartoons were favorable, and news stories that tended to be favorable outnumbered those that were negative. Their favorable position was emphasized by the fact that just before the date of the election they carried banner headlines in red ink, urging approval of the plan.

Results of the sample survey indicated that 57 percent in the city and 74 percent in the county had heard of the plan through the *Post-Dispatch* and 30 percent in the city and 47 percent in the county had heard of the plan through the *Globe-Democrat*. What is more interesting is that only 28 percent of the sample in the city and 49 percent in the county could accurately give the position taken by the *Post-Dispatch*.

The local newspapers which are primarily advertising sheets were solidly opposed to the plan. The survey indicated that 25 percent in the city and 50 percent in the county had heard of the plan through these community papers, and the percentage that knew the position of these papers was less than the percentage that knew the position of the *Post-Dispatch*. The researchers concluded, "Evidently a large proportion of the readers do not attend carefully enough to know the position taken—even by highly committed media."[18]

OTHER MASS MEDIA AND POLITICS

Radio and television constitute additional avenues for reaching voters and attempting to influence their decisions. These media have not in the past made as regular use of editorials as have the newspapers, but there is evidence that this policy is changing. Even some stations operated by the national networks are now presenting editorials on local issues. Editorials are clearly identified as such and usually accompanied by a statement that the station will award time for a responsible rebuttal. Radio and TV stations probably play a more important role in politics through the public affairs programs which they sponsor and by the sale of time to candidates and to organizations which wish to support or oppose some issue which is to be voted on than they do through editorials. In the Greer study referred to above, 57 percent of the respondents in the city and 70 percent in the county indicated they had heard of the district plan through television. This is practically the same as the percentage

[18] Scott Greer, *Metropolitics: A Study of Political Culture,* John Wiley & Sons, Inc., New York, 1963, p. 113.

that had heard of the plan through the *Post-Dispatch* and much greater than the percentage that had heard of it through either the community papers or the *Globe-Democrat*. Radio had not reached as many as had television; 26 percent in the city and 39 percent in the county had heard of the plan through this medium. This was not far different from the percentages for the *Globe-Democrat* and the community papers. Of those who had heard of the plan through radio and television, somewhat less than 20 percent did not know the position taken by these media.[19]

Radio and television managers tend to think of their role as educational and informative rather than propagandistic. Their public affairs broadcasts are often designed simply to provide more information about government and politics. When they arrange programs around controversial issues, they seek to balance the discussion by having diverse opinions represented. Both radio and television, but the latter in particular, tend to give visibility to office-holders, and this may add to their prestige with the public when they endorse public issues or when they seek reelection. Weekly programs in which re-porters quiz the mayor or the mayor simply talks to the listeners are fairly common. Although these are not necessarily designed to strengthen the mayor politically, they certainly give him an audience that he would not otherwise have.

EVALUATION OF MASS MEDIA IN POLITICS

There seems little doubt that newspapers, radio, and television are the most important sources by which voters get information about political issues and candidates, but the influence of these media in determining the reactions of voters is more difficult to measure. Newspapers are likely to be more widely read and to exercise greater influence among middle-class citizens than among those in lower economic brackets.[20] Therefore, newspaper influence is likely to be greater in suburbs than in central cities. The case study of the St. Louis area election indicated this clearly in the difference shown between the middle-class suburban county and the city with its large percentage of lower-income people. Within the city, upper- and middle-class wards more nearly followed the newspapers than did the central city slum and near-slum areas. It may well be that the values of newspaper editors simply are similar to those in the middle-class areas and that the fact that voters in these areas vote in accord

---

[19] *Ibid.*, p. 114.
[20] Banfield and Wilson, *op. cit.*, p. 324.

with newspaper policy reflects this similarity and does not supply evidence of newspaper influence.

The mass media are more likely to be influential in elections involving issues than in determining the choice of candidates for office. This is true, in part, because of the greater activity of parties and other politically organized groups in the election of officers, and in part because issues are so complicated that the voter seeks informed advice in making his choice. Because of the business character of most forms of mass media, they are likely to represent a moderately conservative point of view on issues affecting the local community. Although they may be reform-oriented in terms of honesty in government and efficiency in form and structure, on policy issues they are apt to reflect a conservative viewpoint.

City administrators make use of the mass media to carry their messages to the public and to create favorable images of themselves. On the other hand, administrators who are not acceptable to the press will find it a powerful institution to fight. There are numerous ways in which a mayor can be depicted in an unfavorable light. Zealous reporters can usually find some evidence of mismanagement or unethical conduct within any city administration to embarrass a mayor if they are instructed to do so. The mere fact that there are newspapers and radio and television stations ready to spread stories of graft, corruption, and mismanagement is, in itself, a constraint on the behavior of public officials.

BIBLIOGRAPHY

Books

Adrian, Charles R.: *Governing Urban America*, 2d ed., McGraw-Hill Book Company, New York, 1961, chaps. 5, 6.

Banfield, Edward C., and James Q. Wilson: *City Politics*, Vintage Books, Random House, Inc., New York, 1963, chaps. 9, 10.

Clark, Peter H.: *The Businessman as a Civic Leader*, The Free Press, Glencoe, Ill., 1960.

Flynn, Edward J.: *You're the Boss*, The Viking Press, Inc., New York, 1947.

Gosnell, H. F.: *Machine Politics: Chicago Model*, The University of Chicago Press, Chicago, 1937.

Greer, Scott: *Metropolitics: A Study of Political Culture*, John Wiley & Sons, Inc., New York, 1963, chaps. 4, 5.

Janowitz, Morris: *The Community Press in an Urban Setting*, The Free Press, Glencoe, Ill., 1952.

Kent, Frank: *The Great Game of Politics,* Doubleday, Page and Co., Garden City, N.Y., 1923.

McKean, D. D.: *The Boss: The Hague Machine in Action,* Houghton Mifflin Company, Boston, 1940.

Riordon, William L.: Introduction by Roy V. Peel, *Plunkitt of Tammany Hall,* Alfred A. Knopf, Inc., New York, 1948.

Ross, Russell, and Kenneth F. Millsap: *State and Local Government and Administration,* The Ronald Press Company, New York, 1966, chap. 8.

Salter, J. T.: *Boss Rule: Portraits in City Politics,* McGraw-Hill Book Company, New York, 1935.

Truman, David B.: *The Governmental Process,* Alfred A. Knopf, Inc., New York, 1951.

Zink, Harold: *City Bosses in the United States,* The Duke University Press, Durham, N.C., 1930.

Articles

The Annals of the American Academy of Political and Social Science, vol. 319, September, 1958, entire issue.

Forthal-Spiesman, Sonya: "The Precinct Worker," *The Annals of the American Academy of Political and Social Science,* vol. 259, pp. 30–45, September, 1948.

Greenstein, Fred I.: "The Changing Pattern of Urban Party Politics," *The Annals of the American Academy of Political and Social Science,* vol. 353, pp. 1–13, May, 1964.

LaGuardia, Fiorella H.: "Bosses Are the Bunk," *The Atlantic Monthly,* vol. 180, pp. 21–24, July, 1947.

Morian, Robert L.: "City Politics: Free Style," *National Municipal Review,* vol. 38, pp. 485–490, November, 1949.

14

THE STRUCTURE OF POWER AND INFLUENCE

The theme carried through this text is that the primary interest of the student of politics is to learn more about how the scarce resources within a community are distributed within the social system. Observation on a general level will reveal that there are many things that people want, that there are not sufficient quantities of these desirable things to satisfy the wants of everyone, and that some system exists within the social system to make decisions that determine how these scarce resources will be distributed. Obviously under the systems now in use not all people share equally in the distribution, nor do all people share equally in the decision-making process by which the allocations are made.

If jobs and occupations are considered to be of value, obviously some jobs have greater status and prestige value than others; and even though many persons desire the high-status jobs and occupations, only a few actually attain them. If wealth is considered a value to be greatly desired and vigorously pursued, cursory examination reveals that the existing system by which it is dispensed results in widespread differences in the amounts distributed to various groups in the society. Major city services regularly supplied by municipal corporations such as good streets, street lighting, playgrounds, and schools may be looked upon as desirable values, but few communities provide these services uniformly to all areas of the city. Examination of any large city will reveal that public schools in one part of the city have better physical facilities and better teachers than do those in other areas. In some sections of a city streets are dark, narrow, dirty, and not smoothly paved, while in other sections streets are well lighted, broad, clean, and well surfaced. Since decisions which produce these disparities are, in part at least, made in the political arena, the student of politics should be concerned about who makes the decisions.

Democratic theory discounts the notion that allocation of scarce resources is the result of natural forces and that man cannot intervene to alter existing distributive methods or decisions made within existing systems. To admit anything else would be to accept the philosophy that the political system is impotent to exert influence over the allocation process. Both politicians and political scientists agree that decisions made in the political arena have an important impact upon "who gets what, when and how." Acceptance of this notion that good things are distributed through the political process prompts the student to raise the question: Who or what groups within a community can make the authoritative decisions which determine how various segments of the community share in the resources that are available for allocation?

POWER-STRUCTURE STUDIES

Since Robert and Helen Lynd described the importance of the X family in *Middletown in Transition* and Floyd Hunter described the 40 powerful persons in Regional City, both sociologists and political scientists have given increased attention to the search for the powerful people who "call the shots" in American cities. Some of these studies seem to start with the assumption that there exists in the city a power structure which, within limits, can make the kinds of decisions that are of concern to students of politics; therefore the purpose of such particular studies is to discover and describe this structure.

No doubt researchers have been influenced by a rather large body of literature which has maintained that all large societies produce small ruling classes which dominate the nonruling class majorities. As representative of this literature, quotations from Mosca and Michels are included so that the student will have the flavor of this philosophy.

Gaetano Mosca, an Italian, organized his philosophy about "ruling class" in the last quarter of the nineteenth century.

In all societies—from societies that are very meagerly developed and have barely attained the dawning of civilization, down to the most advanced and powerful societies—two classes of people appear—a class that rules and a class that is ruled. The first class, always the less numerous performs all political functions, monopolizes power and enjoys the advantages that power brings, whereas the second, the more numerous class, is directed and controlled by the first, in a manner that is now more or less legal, now more or less arbitrary and violent, and supplies the first, in appearance at least, with material means of subsistence and with the instrumentalities that are essential to the vitality of the political organism. . . . On the other hand, granting that the discontent of the masses might succeed in deposing a ruling class, inevitably, as we shall later show, there would have to be another organized minority within the masses themselves to discharge the functions of a ruling class. Otherwise all organization and the whole social structure would be destroyed. . . . It follows that the larger the political community, the smaller will the proportion of the governing minority to the governed majority be, and the more difficult will it be for the majority to organize for reaction against the minority. . . . In other words, members of a ruling class minority regularly have some attribute, real or apparent, which is highly esteemed and very influential in the society in which they live.[1]

Robert Michels, writing with a similar philosophy, stated what is regularly referred to as his "iron law of oligarchy."

These phenomena would seem to prove beyond dispute that society cannot exist without a "Dominant" or "Political" class, and that the ruling class, while its elements are subject to a frequent partial renewal, nevertheless, constitutes the only factor of sufficient durable efficiency in the history of human development. According to this view, the government, or if the phrase be preferred, the state, cannot be anything other than the organization of the minority. . . . Reduced to its concise expression, the fundamental sociological law of political parties (the term "political" being here used in its most comprehensive significance) may be formulated in the following terms: "It is organization which gives birth to the domination of the elected over the electors, of the mandatories over the mandators, of the delegates over the delegators. Who says organization says oligarchy."[2]

Although Mosca and Michels were concerned with political activity and organization on a scale much larger than an American city, the extent to

[1] Gaetano Mosca, *The Ruling Class*, 4th ed., translated by Hannah D. Kohn, edited and revised by Arthur Livingston, McGraw-Hill Book Company, New York, 1939, pp. 50, 51, 53.

[2] Reprinted with permission of The Macmillan Company from *Political Parties: A Sociological Study of the Oligarchial Tendencies of Modern Democracies*, by Robert Michels, copyright 1962 by The Free Press, a division of The Macmillan Company, New York, 1962, pp. 353, 365.

which their works are quoted in modern discussions of power structures in American cities indicates that their philosophy has had a significant impact. For purposes of discussion one may assume that within the American city there is some pattern of power, i.e., there is some group, or combination of groups, that is more important in making decisions than is any other. Although some may profess to find no single power structure in a city, what they really mean is that they find no single group that can determine policy on all conflict issues that arise within the politics of the city.

The real issue that seems to make some power-structure studies different from others is not whether there is or is not a power structure, but whether the power structure is monolithic or pluralistic. Some studies profess to find a single power elite which pervades all areas of decision making, while others find no single power elite dominating the decision process in all conflict areas, but find one elite group which influences a single decision and another such group that controls a decision in another subject area. Although the pluralists find some overlapping of personnel among the various elite groups, the overlap is usually less than 50 percent. For purposes of discussion, power structures will be classed as either single elite structures or pluralitic structures. Agger, Goldrich, and Swanson present a typology based on four types of power structures.[3] Their four-cell model is based on two variables. The first considers the extent to which power is distributed broadly among the people (mass power structure) and the extent to which power is wielded by a few (elite power structure). The second variable considers the nature of the ideologic system in which decisions are made, i.e., the extent to which leadership is convergent and compatible (consensual) or divergent and conflicting (competitive). The four cells of the model are consensual mass power structure, consensual elite power structure, competitive mass power structure, and competitive elite power structure.

The discussion here will concentrate on the two types of power structures that researchers have described in various cities, the elite and the pluralistic. The elite or ruling elite system corresponds to Agger's consensual elite category, and the pluralistic is in his model the consensual mass category.

Elite Power Structure

The study *Middletown* by Robert and Helen Lynd sparked interest in the applicability of the idea of a ruling elite to a local community. The Lynds

---

[3] Robert E. Agger, Daniel Goldrich, and Bert E. Swanson, *The Rulers and the Ruled*, John Wiley & Sons, Inc., New York, 1964, p. 73.

found that practically all facets of life in the community (religion, politics, and education) were dominated by a single family. They further reported that the base of the power which this family possessed was economic; i.e., their ability to control the political decisions made in the community resulted from their ability to control jobs and other scarce economic values.[4] Peter Rossi contends that the Lynds did not start a tradition because "they were unable to communicate the techniques by which they singled out the 'X' family as the dominant center in Middletown."[5]

The work which did more than any other to set off a series of power studies was Floyd Hunter's study of Atlanta. Both the method used by Hunter and the conclusions he drew are worth serious study. Hunter describes power as "the ability of man to command the services of other men."[6] He makes clear that the term "power" has a neutral content as far as ideology is concerned, and no attempt is made in his study to pass judgment on whether power as used in "Regional City" is good or evil; he is interested primarily in identifying power holders, not judging them.

Hunter's methodology is generally referred to as the "reputational method" of studying power structures, because his list of top leaders was acquired by asking a selected group who they thought were community leaders. In other words, the men described by Hunter had reputations as leaders in Regional City; he does not in his study examine the specific actions of his leaders in the actual decision-making process of the city. In his search for the powerful men, Hunter secured a list of more than 175 names from the Community Council, the Chamber of Commerce, the League of Women Voters, newspaper editors, and civic leaders. Fourteen judges were used to give their opinions on who were the top leaders on the lists provided and to select by mutual choice the top 40 persons from the total list. Finally, 27 of the 40 were interviewed on the basis of a prepared schedule.[7]

On the basis of his study, Hunter concludes that power in Regional City is wielded by a few men, and the base of their power is economic position; "the dominant factor in political life is the personnel of economic interests . . . the structure of policy-determining committees and their tie-in with the other

[4] Robert S. Lynd and Helen M. Lynd, *Middletown*, Harcourt, Brace and Company, Inc., New York, 1937; also, by the same authors, *Middletown in Transition*, Harcourt, Brace and Company, Inc., New York, 1937.

[5] Peter H. Rossi, "Power and Community Structure," *Midwest Journal of Political Science*, vol. 4, p. 392, November, 1960.

[6] Floyd Hunter, *Community Power Structure: A Study of Decision Makers*, Anchor Books, Doubleday & Company, Inc., Garden City, N.Y., 1963, p. 4.

[7] *Ibid.*, p. 261.

powerful institutions and organizations of the community make government subservient to the interests of these combined groups."[8] The top leaders who make policy channel its execution through an understructure which forms a flexible bureaucracy. Various types of personnel operating in the power system are rated as follows:

> First rate: Industrial, commercial, financial owners and top executives of large enterprises.
> Second rate: Operating officials, bank vice-presidents, public relations men, small businessmen (owners), top-ranking public officials, corporation attorneys, contractors.
> Third rate: Civic organizational personnel, civic agency board personnel, newspaper columnists, radio commentators, petty public officials, selected organization executives.
> Fourth rate: Professionals such as ministers, teachers, social workers, personnel directors, and such persons as small business managers, higher paid accountants, and the like.[9]

The first two ratings are personnel who supposedly "set the line of policy;" the other two groups "hold the line."

The concept of a power elite as described by the Lynds and as found by a more rigorous research effort by Hunter is not far different from the elite structures described by C. Wright Mills:

> In every town and small city of America, an upper set of families stands above the middle classes and towers over the underlying population of clerks and wage workers. The members of this set possess more than do others of whatever there is locally to possess; they hold the keys to local decision; their names and faces are often printed in the local paper; in fact, they own the newspaper as well as the radio station; they also own the three important local plants and most of the commercial properties along the main street; they direct the banks. Mingling closely with one another, they are quite conscious of the fact that they belong to the leading class of the leading families. All their sons and daughters go to college, often after private school; then they marry one another, or other boys and girls from similar families in similar towns. After they are well married, they come to possess, to occupy, to decide. . . . So it has traditionally been, and it is today in the small towns of America.[10]

Some of the problems faced in trying to describe the nature of power elitism in American cities stem from the fact that no single definition has been

---

[8] *Ibid.,* pp. 100, 101.
[9] *Ibid.,* pp. 107, 108.
[10] C. Wright Mills, *The Power Elite,* Oxford University Press, New York, p. 20.

applied to the concept. If by "power elite" is meant nothing more than that a very small percentage of the total population participates actively in the decision-making process, there will be general agreement that this pattern can be found in most American cities. The studies summarized above, however, imply a more precise definition of "power elite" and therefore generate a considerable amount of opposition to their description of the ruling elite. Certainly as Presthus indicates, "We will assume that a power elite, if found, will constitute a very small proportion of the community, and that it will not be representative in social terms of the larger community," and that "Elitism connotes limited numbers, limited consultation with affected groups, disproportionate control of scarce resources of money, skill, and information, and a certain continuity and community of interest."[11] But the conclusions of the elite researchers seem to go further and to be more specific. Four characteristics can be identified with what is here referred to as an elite power structure.

1. A small number of top leaders make policy decisions in a city.

2. The power of the top leaders is derived from their economic position, which also establishes them in a high-status social position.

3. Power is so structured as to be continuous, with the few top leaders having an understructure upon which they can depend to supply the skill, time, and energy required to carry into effect the big decisions made at the top.

4. The power structure operates across the board for decision on all or most of the issues that are decided in the community.

Pluralist Power Structure

The concept of pluralism has been used historically almost as a synonym for democracy, in that it has been used to refer to a political system in which governing power is widely dispersed among the people who are governed. It has been used to identify a society in which power is shared among numerous private groups as well as by governmental officials. And it has been used to describe a governmental structure in which total governmental power is dispersed among many institutional centers by division of powers and separation of powers so that checks and balances can operate to prevent the concentration of power in the hands of any single group. Although some of these ideas have influenced the adoption of the concept of pluralism to describe the power structure in modern American cities, the term as now used

---

[11] Robert Presthus, *Men at the Top: A Study in Community Power,* Oxford University Press, New York, 1964, p. 26.

has more definite and limited meaning. The pluralist concept of the power system in a city implies that instead of one leadership group there are several top leadership groups in a community and that the same groups do not play an equal role in all kinds of decisions. When more than one group seeks to control a public decision on a specific issue, other groups may oppose them, and the final result must represent a compromise. Presthus sets forth five propositions as the basic tenets of contemporary pluralism.[12]

1. That competing centers and bases of power and influence exist within a political community. . . .

2. The opportunity for individual and organizational access into the political system [exists]. . . .

3. That individuals actively participate in and make their will felt through organizations of many kinds. . . .

4. That elections are a viable instrument of mass participation in political decisions, including those on specific issues. . . .

5. That a concensus exists on what may be called the "Democratic Creed."

If it can be assumed that the last four tenets are found in nearly any modern American city, the first tenet seems to be the critical one. If there are different groups within a community, each of which at one time or another seeks to control the community decision on a specific issue, and these groups have different bases of power, they are likely to have different interests. Therefore, any one group which seeks to exercise dominance on a single issue is likely to find opposition from at least one other group whose interest would be adversely affected. This idea of power in the political system is quite different from the elite concept, which implies that a single power group can dominate decision making on all community issues. The notion of group conflict is basic to pluralism, but it is difficult to accept in elitism.

One of the most important exponents of the pluralist model for understanding the way power is distributed in a community is Robert Dahl, whose study of New Haven produced conclusions quite different from those of Hunter. Dahl's method of study also represents an approach very different from the one used by Hunter. Hunter used what was referred to earlier as the reputational approach, which in effect identified leaders by their reputations as influential persons in the community. Dahl used what is commonly called the *decisional* approach. He selected what he considered to be significant decisions that had been made in New Haven, then sought information that would identify the persons who played a major role in the decision-

---

[12] *Ibid.*, pp. 22–24.

making process; i.e., he sought to identify leaders who actively tried to control action rather than to solicit opinions about who could control the decision-making process if they chose to do so.

In the New Haven study eight major decisions on redevelopment, eight on public education, and the nominations for elective office in both parties for seven elections were studied. Records, newspaper files, and interviews were used to reconstruct the historical events connected with the decisions studied. This study found no single group of "economic notables" that controlled the decisions in all three areas studied. Decisions resulted from coalitions of interested groups with some playing a greater role in one case and others predominating in other conflicts. He concludes that "the economic notables," far from being a ruling group, are simply one of many groups out of which individuals sporadically emerge to influence the politics and acts of city officials. Almost anything one might say about the influence of the economic notables could be said with equal justice about a half-dozen other groups in the New Haven community.[13] Dahl's conclusions about the power structure in New Haven differ from Hunter's conclusions about Atlanta in two important respects. In the first place, while Hunter found a monolithic power structure with a single group having power to determine policy in a wide area of issues, Dahl found a pluralistic power structure with power dispersed among a number of individuals and groups, none of which dominated policy making over a wide range of issues. In the second place, Hunter's monolithic power group consisted of top leaders in the economic life of the city; Dahl, on the other hand, found that the economic notables were no more powerful than were a number of other groups.

A number of other studies tend to support the conclusions of the New Haven study. Meyerson and Banfield, who have made intensive studies in Chicago, conclude that no single person or group controls decisions there. In their study in depth of public housing in Chicago, they found no evidence of a "top structure" which made policy.

> The public housing leaders seem to have supposed that the power structure of Chicago was something like that described by Hunter in "Regional City". . . .
> As the reader will see, we found no evidence that a "top structure" made policy respecting public housing. This may be because the top structure was so subtle and devious that we failed to discern its workings, because it was occupied with matters it considered more important

[13] Robert Dahl, *Who Governs?* Yale University Press, New Haven, Conn., 1960, p. 72.

than public housing, or, as we think most likely, because in Chicago, a city which is larger in population than any of 35 independent nations, there are so many "top" power-holders—and these have so little in common and so little in communication—that consciously concerted action by them is all but impossible. But even though concerted activity may not be feasible, some power-holders, as we show, exercise great influence in some spheres of activity.[14]

A number of studies such as those by Scoble of Bennington in Vermont, Freeman in Syracuse, Schulze in a Satellite City, and Mowitz and Wright in Detroit seem to support the pluralistic character of the power structure in American cities.[15]

A STUDY OF TWO CITIES

There seems to be some evidence to support the conclusion that the reputational method of studying power holders in a community tends to produce a monolithic or elite power structure, while a decisional approach results in a pluralistic model. The study made by Robert Presthus is, therefore, of special interest since he applied both methods to two cities in New York. In this study both the decisional and the reputational methods were applied to identify the power structure in the two communities.

In the decisional approach five important decisions were selected for study and they ranged over a ten-year period. Active participants in each decision, identified largely in terms of their role in initiating action, were named by others who were active participants. "A 'decision maker' in effect, was an individual nominated by another active participant as having been active in a given decision and who, when interviewed, also nominated himself as an active participant."[16] Interviews in depth were secured with each person identified as a decision maker.

To identify leaders by the reputational approach the researchers used a question similar to the one used by Hunter. "Suppose a major decision project

---

[14] Reprinted with permission of The Macmillan Company from *Politics, Planning and The Public Interest*, by Martin Meyerson and Edward C. Banfield, copyright 1955 by The Free Press, a division of The Macmillan Company, New York, p. 115.

[15] Harry M. Scoble, Jr., "Leadership Hierarchies and Political Issues," and Robert O. Schulze, "The Bifurcation of Power in a Satellite Community," in Morris Janowitz (ed.), *Community Political Systems*, The Free Press, Glencoe, Ill., 1961, pp. 19–80 and 117–145. Robert J. Mowitz and Deil S. Wright, *Profile of a Metropolis*, Wayne State University Press, Detroit, 1962. Linton C. Freeman and others, *Local Community Leadership*, University College, Syracuse, 1960.

[16] Presthus, *op. cit.*, p. 56.

were before the community, one that required decisions by a group of leaders whom nearly everyone would accept. Which persons would you choose to make up this group—regardless of whether or not you know them personally?''[17] In order for a person to be included as an influential he had to be nominated by 20 percent of the total nominations.

The study tries to supply evidence related to two questions: (1) Which of the two methods of research is the most useful in identifying community leaders; and (2) Is the leadership in the two cities studied an economic elite or is it pluralistic? The two methods were found to complement each other, and each tended to validate the other in some cases and supply new names to consider in other cases. The reputational method tended to identify men with command of resources who had potential power but who did not openly exercise it in specific decisions. The decisional method focused on behavior and identified persons who played an active role even though they did not occupy a position that included them in the reputational list.

In both communities "the powerful" constituted a relatively small number of persons. In Edgewood the power structure was dominated by economic elites; in Riverview political party leaders played a more dominant role.[18]

EVALUATION OF POWER-STRUCTURE STUDIES

The great number of power-structure studies that have been undertaken since the appearance of Hunter's report on Regional City is evidence of the current interest in the subject. These studies have used different methodologies, the kinds of cities studied have been different, and they have reached different conclusions. The two methods generally employed are the reputational, in which top leaders are identified because of the reputation for leadership which they have in the community, and the decisional, by which top leaders are selected because they have played an active role in specific decisions that have been made in the community. It is quite possible that differences in con- clusions resulting from various studies result from the different approaches used to identify power structures. Obviously, the reputational approach tends to select persons who because of their positions, prestige, and visibility in the community could be influential if they chose to be; it does not provide evidence to prove that they were actually powerful in any specific conflict that was decided in the community. In fact some potentially influential persons intentionally elect to avoid participation in community conflicts for business

[17] *Ibid.*, p. 57.
[18] *Ibid.*, p. 430.

reasons. Some corporations may restrain their top executives from becoming involved in local politics, while others may encourage participation. Some business leaders may try to draw a line between conflicts that they consider political and those that are nonpolitical and opt to avoid the former but participate actively in the latter. Reputational studies would most certainly discover such a person as a top leader, but decisional studies would find him an active leader only if the right conflict issues were selected for study.

No one can say for sure the extent to which behind-the-scenes influence plays a role in community decision making, but most students feel that such influence is often important. Only by interviews with persons who were actually involved in the decision-making process can this kind of influence be discovered and the behind-the-scenes operators be identified.

If the assumption is made that persons are likely to become highly involved in conflicts only when they have some interest in the outcome, some reputational leaders may not be discovered in a decisional study simply because they have no serious concern about the outcome. If they play any role at all, it may be only to permit their name to be used on a letterhead or in propaganda material.

There is no doubt that the Presthus study has demonstrated that each of the two methods commonly used to study power structures has its advantages and that each can be used to complement the other. No doubt, further studies will make use of both techniques, or at least if only one is employed, the researchers will make allowance for its weaknesses.

The cities which have been selected for study have been of different sizes and have been in widely separated areas. There is certainly no assurance that they have much in common except that they have been American municipal corporations. The nature of the economy, the kind of political structure, the formal decision-making machinery, and the social character of the cities may well have been so different that generalizations about power structures are impossible. Presthus indicated that in one of the two cities he studied the power structure included political leaders at the top level while the other did not. This result may simply be an indication that party strength may be an important variable in determining who top leaders are. Any attempt to generalize about power structure by comparing studies of small cities and of large cities may be like trying to average apples and oranges. The nature of the conflicts generated and the political and social systems may be so different that a completely different set of hypotheses would have to be constructed for cities of different sizes.

The consistency with which economic leaders appear in power structures, particularly when the influentials are identified by the reputational method, may simply be a reflection of cultural values which assign high status to executive positions in commerce and industry. If a study were to be conducted to determine the positions in a community which should be best paid and which parents would most prefer to have their sons achieve, it is not unlikely that the results would be the enumeration of the economic positions whose occupants would by the reputational method be identified as the top influential persons. And this might be true even if some of the persons involved purposely shied away from community conflicts.

The resources which individuals can bring to the battle may also be a factor in the structure of power and influence. Since money is a major resource required to carry on an extensive campaign, persons with access to money will be invariably persuaded to become involved in most major conflicts. The major contributors to the campaign fund raised to put over any major conflict issue might well turn out to be the same persons a postconflict study would reveal as the top leaders. The need for funds to carry on any major campaign may be one reason why certain professional groups fail to rate high on the power-structure scale when the reputational method is employed. The conclusion, supported by most power-structure studies, that skill, expertise, and know-how are not enough to ensure inclusion in the list of influential persons may be a result of the type of issues studied. Issues which are fought out in the political arena in modern times tend more and more to depend upon technical or professional know-how and upon such issues the public may give greater weight to the doctor, the engineer, or the scientist than they do to the corporation president. Such issues as water fluoridation, stream pollution, or compulsory immunization may bring to the top as decision influencers the professionals. This may be particularly true if there is a high degree of consensus among the professionals. The weakness of skill as a factor in determining influence is often due to the fact that issues are raised in the political system in such a way that the experts are divided, with equally competent professionals on each side. Although scientists may agree that there is a positive correlation between air pollution and lung diseases, they may not agree on policy issues which are raised by proposed means of controlling air pollution.

THE ROLE OF POLITICAL PARTIES

An interesting feature of most studies of power structures has been the absence of political party leaders among the power elite. This may be because, of the cities which have been selected for observation, none had strong party organizations; the selection of some other cities might well have produced different results. But it may well be that the political party does not play a major role in decision making in most American cities. It has been noted in Chapter 12 that party leaders in cities tend to be more interested in patronage and organization maintenance than in policy formulation. If this is true, the party leader may view policy as a threat only when it would reduce patronage available to him or be dysfunctional to party organization. Many of the policies which have been the chief concern of civic leaders during the period when the major power-structure studies were being made are not likely to be perceived as a threat by the party leaders. What Agger calls "community conservation" policies may actually appeal to the party leader, since they increase jobs and government spending; e.g., urban redevelopment, improved streets and highways, better public utility facilities offer the political party leader a chance to help distribute both job and economic patronage. Even if he is not an initiator of such projects, he is unlikely to lead any opposition against the civic leaders who sponsor them.

Since many of the major policy activities of cities in recent years have been oriented toward community conservation activities, the establishment of an elite group with a minimum of organized opposition has been possible. These policy goals have been framed in terms of the general interest and are, therefore, nonpolitical in character. To maintain this political impartiality and thereby attract into the effort certain business types, party involvement had to be deemphasized. This may be why party officers appeared so infrequently in power-structure studies. Peter Rossi hypothesizes that polylithic rather than monolithic power structures are likely to be found in cities where elections are on a party basis, and where party lines tend to coincide with class lines and the party favored by the lower class has some chance of being elected to office.[19]

POWER IN BIG CITIES

A major part of power-structure research has been concentrated in smaller cities, of under 100,000 population. Even if there were general agreement among existing studies on a model structure of power and influence in the cities involved, it would be dangerous to assume that such a model could be projected upon large cities. Banfield has indicated that Chicago would not

[19] Rossi, *op. cit.,* p. 399.

fit the elite model and that any attempt to identify the top leaders in Chicago without including the mayor would be unrealistic. Salisbury has indicated that in St. Louis the mayor has been able to attract an elite group of civic and economic leaders to support certain important policies, but one would certainly have to include the mayor himself as an important initiator of policies.[20] Agger has speculated on the possibility of projecting the findings of his group to the big cities, but he admits his discussion is purely speculative. The problem of trying to find a power structure in a typical metropolitan area is even more formidable, since in such areas there is no central political arena where issues can be decided; instead there are hundreds of small, sometimes competing arenas in which policies are regularly decided.

One observation about the location of power and influence in large cities seems plausible. The political party leaders are likely to play a more important role. They may not rank high as policy initiators, but the nature of politics in large cities may make their role as brokers of first-rate importance. The range of policy issues is apt to be wider, and the variety of points of view and of interest groups is greater in the large city. The party leaders may be the only avenues through which the majority required to adopt policy changes can be achieved.

The changing character of the large central cities may also produce changes in the nature of the power structures. The flight of the upper and upper-middle classes to the suburbs and the increase in the Negro population in the central city make it less likely that whatever power elite that emerges will be composed of top economic leaders. Labor leaders, Negro leaders, and party officials may be the source from which the influentials will be recruited.

The pluralistic concept of power and influence is more compatible with the thesis that the author has tried to maintain in this text. The single-elite concept tends to emphasize consensus and play down interest-group competition; the pluralist or multiple-elite concept is based on the existence of competing groups, each using whatever strategies it can devise and selecting the arena most congenial to it for gaining its goals. The political system in large cities may more nearly conform to a series of political games in which no single group has exclusive control, as described by Norton Long, than it does to the model proposed by the power elite studies.[21]

[20] Robert H. Salisbury, "Urban Politics: The New Convergence of Power," *Journal of Politics,* vol. 26, pp. 783, 784, December, 1964.
[21] Norton Long, "The Local Community as an Ecology of Games," *American Journal of Sociology,* vol. 64, pp. 251–261, November, 1958.

BIBLIOGRAPHY

Books

Agger, Robert E., Daniel Goldrich, and Bert E. Swanson: *The Rulers and the Ruled,* John Wiley & Sons, Inc., New York, 1964.

Banfield, Edward C., and James Q. Wilson: *City Politics,* Vintage Books, Random House, Inc., New York, 1963, chap. 17.

Dahl, Robert: *Who Governs?* Yale University Press, New Haven, Conn., 1960.

Freeman, Linton C.: *Patterns of Local Community Leadership,* The Bobbs-Merrill Company, Inc., Indianapolis, 1968.

Hawley, Willis D., and Fredrick M. Wirt: *The Search for Community Power,* Prentice-Hall, Inc., Englewood Cliffs, N.J., 1968.

Hunter, Floyd: *Community Power Structure: A Study of Decision Makers,* Anchor Books, Doubleday & Company, Inc., Garden City, N.Y., 1963.

Lynd, Robert S., and Helen M. Lynd: *Middletown,* Harcourt, Brace and Company, Inc., New York, 1929.

———— and ————: *Middletown in Transition,* Harcourt, Brace and Company, Inc., New York, 1937.

Michels, Robert: *Political Parties: A Sociological Study of the Oligarchial Tendencies of Modern Democracies,* The Free Press, New York, 1962.

Mills, C. Wright: *The Power Elite,* Oxford University Press, New York, 1956.

Mosca, Gaetano: *The Ruling Class,* 4th ed., translated by Hannah D. Kohn, edited and revised by Arthur Livingston, McGraw-Hill Book Company, New York, 1939.

Polsby, Nelson W.: *Community Power and Political Theory,* Yale University Press, New Haven, Conn., 1963.

Presthus, Robert: *Men at the Top: A Study in Community Power,* Oxford University Press, New York, 1964.

Janowitz, Morris (ed.): *Community Political Systems,* Nos. 1 and 3, The Free Press, Glencoe, Ill., 1961.

Articles

Ehrlich, Howard J.: "The Reputational Approach to the Study of Community Power," *American Sociological Review,* vol. 26, pp. 926–927, December, 1961.

Kaufman, Herbert, and Victor A. Jones: "The Mystery of Power," *Public Administration Review,* vol. 14, pp. 205–212, summer, 1954.

Long, Norton: "The Local Community as an Ecology of Games," *American Journal of Sociology,* vol. 64, pp. 251–261, November, 1958.

Polsby, Nelson: "How to Study Community Power, the Pluralist Alternative," *Journal of Politics,* vol. 22, pp. 474–484, August, 1960.

————: "Three Problems in the Analysis of Community Power," *American Sociological Review,* vol. 24, pp. 796–803, December, 1959.

Rossi, Peter: "Power and Community Structure," *Midwest Journal of Political Science*, vol. 4, pp. 390–401, November, 1960.

Salisbury, Robert H.: "Urban Politics: The New Convergence of Power," *Journal of Politics*, vol. 26, pp. 775–797, November, 1964.

Wolfinger, Raymond E.: "Reputation and Reality in the Study of Community Power," *American Sociological Review*, vol. 25, pp. 636–644, October, 1960.

PART 5
FUNCTIONS OF URBAN GOVERNMENT

15

TAXATION AND REVENUE

One of the important political issues that must be resolved through the political systems of cities relates to the sources from which revenue will be collected to meet the costs of city government. Although conflict may arise over the total amount of revenue a city should try to raise, the most serious disputes arise over the various sources that shall be tapped to produce revenue and the proportion of the total burden each source should share. Any single source of revenue that is available to cities falls in a different manner upon those who must share the city's financial burdens, or at least, people think the burden falls upon different classes unequally. For example, owners of real estate feel that a tax on property places the tax burden on them and relieves the apartment dweller who owns no real property of his fair share of the tax burden. Income taxes, which are not directly related to property ownership, distribute the tax burden among potential taxpayers in a different way. If the income tax is set as a fixed rate, regardless of size of income, taxpayers will be affected differently than if rates are graduated so that they increase as income rises. Taxes on liquors, cigarettes, theater tickets, and other so-called luxury items impose a burden directly only upon those who purchase the taxed items. The point is that although all groups accept the necessity for taxes, they disagree over the kinds of tax levies which should be assessed, because each type of levy falls differently on the members of the various groups. This is why any proposal to alter an existing tax structure must be understood as a political issue, and why the forces that interact to produce decisions on these issues are of the same kind as those involved in other substantive issues which must be resolved through the machinery of city government.

Attempts have been made to set forth "canons" of taxation which underlie good revenue programs. Such canons prescribe that taxes should be *equitable;* i.e., they should fall equally on those in the same class; *certain,* i.e., they should be objectively determined, not arbitrarily; *convenient,* i.e., the act of paying should not place an undue burden on the taxpayer; and *economical to collect,* i.e., the cost of collection should not reduce the total revenue substantially.[1] Although these factors may still have some weight in the political process by which kinds of taxes and tax rates are determined, other more political considerations are likely to play a more significant role.

RELATIONSHIP BETWEEN TAX PAYMENTS AND SERVICE RECEIVED

Mosher and Poland, in discussing public attitudes toward taxes, make the following observation:

> An inherent obstacle to the understanding of public finance arises from the obvious fact that with regard to most governmental activities there is no direct, visible relationship between what one pays, as an individual or a member of an organization, and what he receives. There is lacking the clear and unmistakable *quid pro quo* that one enjoys when he exchanges his money according to a fixed price for a loaf of bread or a car or a house. In most public finances the convenient index of price, to which we are so accustomed in our private economic transactions, is denied us. The money which we spend on government comes to be looked upon as a compulsory contribution with little if any return.[2]

This attitude helps explain a wide range of political behavior with respect to issues related to the problems associated with financing governmental ser-

[1] For a discussion of Adam Smith's canons, see Jewell Cass Phillips, *Municipal Government and Administration in America,* The Macmillan Company, New York, 1960, pp. 423–424. See also G. Theodore Mitau, *State and Local Government: Politics and Processes,* Charles Scribner's Sons, New York, 1966, p. 585.

[2] Reprinted by permission of Dodd, Mead and Company, Inc., from Fredrick C. Mosher and Orville F. Poland, *The Costs of American Government: Facts, Trends, Myths,* p. 6. Copyright c. 1964 by Dodd, Mead & Company, Inc., New York.

vices. Since the results to be achieved from tax increases are not likely to be very visible to the taxpayer and the improvements are not clearly related in his mind to the tax increase, politicians avoid, like the plague, proposals to increase taxes. On the other hand, they must be sensitive to the ever-increasing demands of their constituents for more and improved governmental services. The incompatibility of these attitudes pushes the political leader toward the use of revenue measures which in a more direct way relate collections to services. The use of revenue bonds which are funded by direct charges for use of the facility constructed are less unpopular than are general revenue bonds which are funded through regular taxes. Voter approval for the construction of a new bridge is easier to achieve if the bonds required for its construction are to be paid off from tolls charged users of the bridge than if the bridge is to be toll-free and the bonds are to be paid off from general taxes. The use of special or earmarked taxes for such facilities as zoos, libraries, and parks results from the desire of those who sponsor these services to relate the service and the tax more directly than would be the case if they were supported out of general tax revenues. The common practice of cities which own and operate their water, electric, and natural gas distribution systems to charge the consumer on the basis of the amount used rather than to support these services by general taxation is, in large part, an attempt to relate services and costs as directly as possible.

Mosher and Poland also cite the illusion of "consumer-sovereignty" as a factor in determining political behavior in tax matters.[3] The widespread use of general taxes to support public services allows the consumer no opportunity to exercise any choice to vary his costs by altering his use of the service. Conservation activities may be given greater public support if costs are to be paid from income derived from the sale of hunting and fishing licenses, since this system permits the potential user to avoid the costs by abstaining from fishing or hunting. For the same reason there is strong public support for making art museums, zoos, swimming pools, and skating rinks self-sufficient by charging for their use.

TAXING ACCORDING TO ABILITY TO PAY

Another attitude toward taxes that has sufficient acceptance in this country to influence political behavior is the idea that the tax system should fall upon

[3] Ibid., p. 62.

citizens roughly according to their ability to pay. This attitude seems to be opposed to the idea of relating charges and service use; yet they are not necessarily inconsistent. Those who maintain that the tax structure should be based on ability to pay are generally applying this principle to what might be called the general revenue, as distinguished from special-revenue accounts which are more closely related to specific services. Such well-established city services as police protection, fire protection, maintenance of streets, public health, and sanitation are so generally maintained out of regular tax revenue that there is little support for proposals to alter the system. In fact, one would find it difficult to devise a workable scheme whereby citizens could pay for these services in direct relation to the extent of use. On the other hand, utility services such as transportation, electricity, and water can be furnished at a fixed cost per unit used.

NEED FOR SERVICE AND ABILITY TO PAY

Another factor that enters into the process of decision making with regard to sources of revenue is that there is often a negative correlation between ability to pay and the need for certain kinds of government services that are traditionally supported out of general tax revenue rather than by service charges. Needs for specialized and often costly educational services are greatest among the underprivileged with low incomes and often large families. Need for welfare services, health programs, and sanitary services is concentrated in those areas of the city inhabited by those least able to pay for them. To a lesser extent the greatest demands for police and fire protection are also in the lower-income sections of the city. This negative relationship between need and ability to pay precludes any possibility of the use of service charges to support such public services. But even though this assumption is generally accepted, there is ample room for political conflict in determining the kinds of general taxes that will be used to support these services. It is obvious that the kind of tax adopted will determine how the load is distributed among the population, and one can predict that groups will either oppose or support tax schemes according to the way they perceive their interests to be affected.

SOURCES OF MUNICIPAL REVENUE

Table 15.1 shows the sources of revenue for municipalities for 1957 and 1962.

TABLE 15.1   National Summary of Municipal Revenues, 1957 and 1962
(amounts in millions of dollars)

Item	1957	1962	Percent change
Total revenue	12,047	16,794	39
General revenue	9,285	13,127	41
Intergovernmental revenue	1,756	2,686	52
From state government only	1,489	2,128	43
General revenue from own sources	7,529	10,459	39
Taxes	5,908	7,940	34
Property	4,297	5,812	35
Sales and gross receipts	934	1,303	40
General	602	866	44
Selective	332	437	32
Other	676*	824	22*
Charges and miscellaneous	1,621	2,519	55
Current charges	954*	1,511	58*
Interest earnings	112	164	46
Special assessments	217	268	24
Sale of property	44	97	120
Other and unallocable	294	479	63
Utility revenue	2,378	3,136	32
Water supply	1,079	1,453	35
Electric power	810	1,114	38
Transit	375	399	6
Gas supply	114	170	49
Liquor stores revenue	60	77	28
Insurance trust revenue	323	454	41
Employment retirement	317	446	41
Unemployment compensation (Washington, D.C.)	6	8	33

* A change in classification of on-street parking revenue was made.

Source: U.S. Bureau of the Census, *Census of Governments,* Washington, 1962, vol. 4, p. 11.

THE GENERAL PROPERTY TAX

The general property tax dates as far back as colonial times and has over the years been a major revenue producer, particularly at the local level. Provisions of the United States Constitution made it practically impossible for the federal government to use the property tax, but it became the generally accepted method of raising revenue at the state and local levels. At the turn of the century half of all state revenues came from this source, and 89 percent of the revenue for all local units of government was derived from it.[4] During the current century, states have practically abandoned the general property tax as a major source of revenue; it was producing only 3 percent of total state revenues in 1962. Local units of government have continued to rely heavily on this form of taxation; it was producing 88 percent of total local tax revenue in 1962, almost the same as in 1902.[5] The high percentage figure shown for local governments is due, in part, to the fact that school districts and other special-service districts are forced by law to rely almost wholly on the property tax for revenue purposes. Cities, which have somewhat greater freedom than special districts, have adopted other forms of taxes, but in 1964 the property tax accounted for approximately 60 percent of the total revenue for all cities. Considerable variation exists among large cities in the extent to which they depend on the property tax. For example, in 1963–1964 the property tax accounted for 86 percent of Houston's tax revenue, but only 46 percent of Philadelphia's tax income was from this source. These percentage figures are based on total tax revenue; if total city income, including grants from states and the federal government, is used as the base, the percentage share derived from property would be less.

Nature of Property Taxes

General property taxes are levies made by a governmental unit upon owners of property which is located within their jurisdiction. For tax purposes property is usually classified as *real* or *personal*. Real property includes land and buildings. Personal property includes *tangible* property such as machinery, livestock, household furnishings, jewelry, automobiles, and *intangible* property such as stocks, bonds, notes, and other evidences of ownership of things of value.

In order to levy property taxes it is necessary to give an assessed valuation to all property to be taxed and to identify its owner. This is the function of an officer usually called the assessor. Since all deeds which transfer ownership of land must be recorded, there is no great difficulty involved in identifying landowners. The more difficult job is that of assigning a value for tax purposes to each piece of real estate; these problems will be discussed later. Tangible personal property is also fairly easy to identify but is equally difficult to evaluate equitably. In some instances the individual taxpayer may be asked

[4] *Ibid.*, pp. 69, 70.
[5] *Ibid.*, pp. 69, 70.

to assign a value to his property, particularly household furnishings. Standardized tables of values may be used to assess automobiles, livestock, and machinery for tax purposes.

Taxation of intangible property presents a different problem. In the first place an individual may possess notes, stocks, and bonds and have them deposited where they would never be found by an assessor if the owner chooses not to declare them. In general, real property is taxed in the governmental jurisdiction where it is located, regardless of the residence of the owner, while personal property is taxed in the area of residence of the owner, regardless of the location of the property.

After property has been assessed, the legislative body, by law or ordinance, sets the rate at which it shall be taxed. Rates are expressed on a percentage of assessed value, as so many mills on the dollar, as so many dollars on the $100, or as so many dollars on the $1,000 of assessed valuation; payment is required either on an annual or a semiannual basis.

Problems of the Property Tax

States which for many years depended heavily on property taxes have either lessened their reliance upon this source of revenue or have abandoned it entirely. Local governments have been forced to rely on property taxes for a large part of their income, but there are consistent demands from city political leaders for authority to tap other sources of revenue in order to relieve their dependence on the property tax. A number of problems related to this tax account for the shift to other revenue sources.

The property tax is generally unpopular. This unpopularity is due, in part, to the fact that the total amount assessed against each taxpayer comes due once a year and usually must be paid in full in order to avoid penalty. Withholding of income taxes from regular paychecks tends to lessen the impact of this tax, and sales taxes are collected by the retailer in relatively small amounts, but the homeowner may find that he must pay around $400 at the end of the year in a lump sum or be faced with deliquency penalties. Politicians are sensitive to the unpopularity of the property tax, and they are slow to suggest tax increases, even when it is obvious that additional revenue is required to maintain adequate services.

Assessment of property for tax purposes has, in practice, presented many serious problems. In the first place it is difficult to arrive at agreement on a basis for fixing the value of property for tax purposes. Market value is difficult to determine for kinds of property that are not regularly on the market;

and even for kinds of property which do sell regularly, there are wide fluc-
tuations in selling prices. Laws recognize these difficulties and usually stipulate that, for tax purposes, property shall be taxed at *true value* or *real value*.
These terms imply something different from market value, but no one has
ever determined exactly what they mean.

Officers whose duty it is to set the value on property are called assessors,
and in many instances they are popularly elected on a local basis. Although
some cities will have their own assessor, the value of property in cities is
generally determined by an officer of the county in which the city is located.
The unpopularity of the property tax forces assessing officers, who depend on
votes for their jobs, to underassess property; i.e., they assess all property
at a certain percentage of what they think it is actually worth. In some cases
this may be as low as 20 percent of true value, while in others it may go as
high as 75 percent. There is also widespread feeling on the part of taxpayers
that some pieces of property are assessed at a greater proportion of their real
value than are other parcels. This disparity is often attributed to political
influence exerted by some property owners.

The property tax is alleged to be inequitable. There may have been a time
in American history when property ownership was a fair indicator of ability
to pay. Today there is evidence to suggest that there may be little correlation
between property ownership and ability to pay. Many young families prefer
to purchase homes rather than to live in rented apartments, but they are able
to make only a small down payment and must pay off a mortgage over a long
period of time. It is difficult to see how a homeowner with only a very small
equity in his home is any better able to pay taxes than is a person who rents
an apartment, if they both have equal incomes. Certainly property taxes cannot, as can some other kinds of taxes, take into account such factors as
income, number of dependents, and cost incurred because of sickness.

The lack of uniformity of tax rates on property produces inequities for
owners of similar kinds of property and generates competition among taxing
units for certain kinds of development. Tax rates are established by the legislative bodies of cities, school districts, and other governmental units which
possess legal taxing power. Tax rates on two apartment buildings of the same
size, age, and type of construction may be quite different if they are on
opposite sides of a line that marks the boundary between two cities. Certain
kinds of property, such as large apartment houses that appeal to families
with few children, large office buildings, and modern warehouse facilities, produce no great demands for expensive government services, but they constitute
an attractive tax base for a local community. Although such property is owned

by people who do not live where it is located and is used by people living in numerous surrounding cities, the total tax payments of owners and renters go to the single political subdivision in which the property is located. As a result, a small city which serves as a county seat will attract high-rise office buildings, and their location within the county seat town means that the city can secure large revenues with relatively low tax rates. It is quite possible to find in a large metropolitan area a city with the lowest property tax rate spending the largest amount per person for public services.

Heavy reliance on the general property tax by large cities tends to defeat attempts at prevention of blight and at rehabilitation of older sections and also tends to weaken the economy by driving commerce and industry to lower tax areas. Since improvement of property increases its real value, it also increases the tax assessment. This results in a higher total tax bill, often without compensating increases in rents. The federal government has recognized this problem in its urban renewal programs by requiring certain tax exemptions for renewal projects. Competition among outstate cities for location of industrial plants is keen, and since tax rates in these cities are often lower than in metropolitan areas, large cities are losing important industrial plants.

Exemption of certain kinds of property from taxes places a heavy burden on property that is subject to taxes. Since the United States Supreme Court ruled that states (and therefore cities) cannot tax the instrumentalities of the federal government, federal property has been exempt from local taxes.[6] The expansion of federal government facilities in recent years has made this exemption a serious matter for cities and school districts. Almost every large city has a federal court building, an office building, one or more post offices, and in many cases some kind of ordinance facility. As far as city services are concerned, these facilities place on the local government the same service responsibility as if they were privately owned, yet they pay no taxes.

The same kind of exemption has been given to property owned by the state, schools, churches, and charitable organizations. A city may find that as much as 20 percent of its total property is covered by this tax exemption. In some instances this exemption extends to commercial properties which have been deeded to universities but which continue to be used just as if they were privately owned.

The difficulties involved in locating and assessing tangible and intangible property for tax purposes have produced special criticism of the application of tax rates to this kind of property. Since evidence of ownership of in-

[6] *McCollouch v. Maryland,* 4 Wheaton 316 (1819).

tangible property (notes, stocks, bonds, etc.) can be hidden away in bank vaults, they may never be placed on the tax rolls. The temptation to hide this kind of property is great, since existing tax rates often would be equal to the income it produces. If a bond bears 5 percent interest, the income it produces would be practically the same as the tax would be in an average city if it were assessed at face value. Many states have either abandoned the property tax on intangible personal property or have fixed the rate of tax as a percentage of income produced rather than as a percentage of property value. Costs of assessing and collecting tangible property taxes are so high in relation to revenue yield that many tax officials are advocating the abandonment of this tax except on automobiles. The property tax on automobiles is relatively easy to enforce since the owner of a vehicle can be forced to show a receipt for the tax before a license to operate it will be issued.

Limitations on Property Tax Rates

All but seven states have some kind of legal limitation on the amount of property taxes that can be levied by local governments. The typical limitation is in terms of the rate that can be levied against assessed value of property. Such restrictions may be expressed as so many dollars per thousand dollars of evaluation, or as cents on the one dollar evaluation. A few states express their limitation as a percentage by which the tax levy for one year can exceed the levy for the proceeding year, and other states have their restrictions in terms of absolute dollar amounts or per capita amounts. Although limitations on property tax rates date back to 1870, the great depression of the 1930s brought increased pressure to either lower or hold the line on property taxes.[7]

Although states impose legal limitations on the property tax rates that can be levied by local governments, some of them permit local units to exceed these limits by popular vote. In some cases greater than a simple majority is required for approval of such increases. A local legislative body may be authorized to levy a tax of $1 on each $100 of assessed valuation without a vote, increase the levy to $2 by a simple majority vote, and go beyond $2 by a two-thirds majority vote.

Some of the tax limitations which were imposed many years ago are unrealistic today, and cities have devised ways of increasing the total revenue

[7] A complete discussion of these restrictions is found in Advisory Commission on Intergovernmental Relations, *State Constitutional and Statutory Restrictions on Local Taxing Power,* Washington, 1962.

produced by the property tax without violating legal restrictions.[8] The simplest method is to increase the evaluation of property for tax purposes. Since assessed values are usually determined locally rather than by the state, this can be accomplished in a single taxing jurisdiction without affecting the state at large. Seldom are assessed values of property for tax purposes anywhere near actual or market value; hence there is ample room for increases without going beyond market value. If property has been assessed at 25 percent of its real value, raising assessments to 35 percent would produce an increase of 10 percent in revenue without any rate increase. A number of factors, however, operate to limit increases in assessments. Property owners are often organized to bring political pressure to defeat such proposals, local assessors are often popularly elected and they fear defeat at the poll if they raise assessments, and there is a certain amount of competition among local taxing jurisdictions to keep assessments low in order either to attract new industry or to hold what they have.

Another method used to circumvent legal tax limits is to create new taxing units. Since legal limits generally apply to specific governmental units rather than to geographic areas, two or more taxing units may exist within the same area. Suppose, for example, that a city has reached its maximum tax level but wants to initiate an extensive air pollution control program. Since the city cannot increase tax rates to cover the costs of the new program, a special air pollution control district can be created whose boundaries are the same as those of the city. The newly created district may be able to levy property taxes to cover its costs of operation, and although the taxes paid by property owners in the city have been increased, the legal limitations have not been violated. There is no doubt that unrealistic legal tax restrictions have accounted for many of the special taxing districts that exist in metropolitan areas today.

Assessment Equalization

Since assessment of property for tax purposes has traditionally been the job of local officers, wide variations from one part of the state to another exist in the ratio of assessed value to actual value. Within each assessment unit (usually the county) there is a board of equalization to which an individual property owner can appeal if he feels his property is assessed at a higher ratio than is other similar property in the area, but the boards are without power to equalize assessments among different assessing units. If a large city

[8] See *Ibid.*, pp. 60–67.

is within two counties, two different assessors will be evaluating property within different areas of the city, and considerable variations may exist. Some states have a state tax commission or state board of equalization to equalize assessments among counties. Such boards usually do not deal with individual complaints, but they may establish a ratio of assessed value to actual value that all counties must follow. If the state commission decides that all property in the state shall be assessed at 35 percent of actual value and it finds that in some counties property is assessed at only 25 percent of actual value, it can order assessors in these counties to increase all assessments by 10 percent. Statewide equalization is most significant in states where there is a state property tax with a uniform rate over the whole state. Since the state rate will be the same in all counties, persons owning land in a county with low assessments would be paying less tax than would those owning land of equal market value in counties with higher assessed valuations. A similar problem exists in metropolitan areas where there is no single assessment office to fix property values for tax purposes in all the taxing jurisdictions in the area.

TAXES ON INCOME

The federal government has for years depended on personal and corporate income taxes as its chief source of revenue by adopting some kind of income tax. Wisconsin was the first state to adopt a personal income tax in 1911, and by 1965, 36 states had adopted some form of individual income tax. Such taxes have, however, been relatively low; the total of income tax collections by all states was only 7.7 percent of the amount collected by the federal government from this source in the previous year.[9]

The extensive use of the income tax by the federal government and its partial use by states have operated to discourage the use of such taxes for local revenue purposes. In only five states (Kentucky, Michigan, Missouri, Ohio, and Pennsylvania) are income taxes a significant source of revenue. Of the 43 largest cities in the United States (with populations over 300,000), 10 use the income tax, and 32 with populations of 50,000 or more have some kind of income tax. Philadelphia was the first city to tap this source of revenue in 1939, Toledo imposed an income tax in 1946, St. Louis in 1964, and Kansas City in 1963.[10]

[9] Advisory Commission on Intergovernmental Relations, *Federal-State Coordination of Personal Income Taxes,* Washington, October, 1965, p. 62.
[10] *Ibid.,* pp. 69–73.

Factors Affecting Support for or Opposition to Local Income Taxes

One reason for city political leaders to urge a tax on income was the pressing need for more money to support city services and the feeling that higher property taxes would affect the city adversely. Increased urbanization following World War II has produced demands upon cities to undertake new services and improve established ones, but existing sources of income have been insufficient to meet the demands. The large core cities were already suffering from the decentralization policies of large corporations and the flight to the suburbs of upper- and middle-class families. Increased taxes on property threatened to accelerate this trend. Therefore, those most interested in maintaining and rebuilding downtown areas turned to the income tax as a large revenue producer which would not deter business growth.

There was also a feeling among leaders in the large cities that suburban dwellers who worked in the city should help support the city's costs of operation. Since the city could not levy taxes on property outside the city limits, the income tax seemed the easiest means of reaching those who live outside the limits but depend on the city for their incomes.

There are also indications that the income tax is relatively elastic; i.e., the income from the tax will rise and fall with the rise and fall of economic activity as measured by gross national product. As business activity expands, incomes increase and taxes rise without any change in tax rate.[11] Since property assessments are relatively stable, taxes on property are not likely to increase as fast as costs of governmental services.

Some support for greater use of income taxes comes from groups which seek to reduce the tax burden on low-income classes and shift a greater burden to those in higher-income brackets. The rates of property and sales taxes remain the same regardless of the size of the tax base; i.e., the property tax rate is the same for the owner of a small home as it is for the owner of a million dollars worth of property, and the same is true for sales taxes, since there is no increase in tax rate as the amount purchased rises. Income taxes are easily graduated so that tax rates increase as size of income goes up. This has not been characteristic of present municipal income taxes, but one may predict from federal and state experience that if greater use of such taxes for city purposes is made, rates will be graduated. With increased concern for elimination of poverty, particularly in large cities, there may be greater pres-

---

[11] See Advisory Commission on Intergovernmental Relations, Federal-State Coordination of Personal Income Taxes, Washington, October, 1965, table on p. 42, for comparative elasticity of taxes.

sure for the use of income taxes to support increasing costs of local government since this kind of tax is easily adjusted to lower the tax load on those least able to pay. Tax exemptions can be made of all income below a fixed amount, and additional exemptions can be made for dependents. The income tax is particularly well adapted to use as an instrument in a broad-gauged war on poverty.

SALES TAXES

Taxes on sales of certain commodities have been used by states for many years. The most commonly used sales tax has been levied on motor fuel and was adopted by most states to finance state highway systems. The general retail sales tax came into common use by states during the Depression, when income from property taxes dropped sharply and increased burdens of welfare programs fell upon the states. By 1962 all but 13 states had general sales taxes and about 25 percent of all state revenues were derived from this source. About one-third of all state revenue is derived from selective sales taxes and gross receipts on motor fuel, tobacco, alcoholic beverages, insurance, public utilities, and gambling.[12] Since these sources have been good revenue producers at the state level, cities have tried to tap them to meet their financial needs. Total city revenues from sales and gross receipts taxes increased from $685,000 in 1953 to $1,438,000 in 1963; this represented an increase of 110 percent.[13] Although sales taxes on special commodities such as tobacco, motor fuel, and liquors are more common, general retail sales taxes are increasing in popularity. Some state laws encourage cities to levy sales taxes by authorizing the state's regular sales tax machinery to collect such taxes within any city which levies the tax; collections are then returned to the city for local use. In these cases the amount of the levy is limited and usually it must be approved by a popular vote.

One of the strongest arguments for general sales taxes is that they are good revenue producers at a minimum collection cost. Opposition comes from groups which maintain that such taxes are regressive, i.e., the rate is the same for all income groups and therefore does not reflect the ability-to-pay principle. The present movement to wage war against poverty may retard

[12] Reprinted by permission of Dodd, Mead and Company, Inc., from *The Costs of American Government* by Fredrick C. Mosher and Orville F. Poland. Copyright c. 1964 by Dodd, Mead and Company, Inc., New York, pp. 99, 100.
[13] International City Managers Association, *The Municipal Year Book*, Chicago, 1965, p. 243.

attempts to place greater reliance on general sales taxes to support local government, since the burden of such taxes falls harder on low-income groups. Some of the opposition might be removed if foods and medicines were exempt from the levies.

OTHER SOURCES OF REVENUE

Total revenue of cities from all sources was $18.1 billion in 1963. Approximately $3.6 billion of this was derived from sales by municipally owned utilities and liquor stores. Approximately 3 percent, $498 million, was income derived from insurance-trust funds and is not available for spending except for annuity payments. The amount received from municipally owned public utilities is gross income, and most, if not all of it is used for maintenance costs or reserved for future capital expenditures. The largest sources of general revenue are the taxes discussed above, grants-in-aid from the federal government and the state, and charges made for municipal services such as garbage collections and recreational facilities. Small amounts of revenue are received from fines, delinquent tax penalties, and interest on city funds, which are either kept on deposit in banks or invested in government securities.

MEASURES OF TAX CAPACITY AND TAX EFFORT

Cities have for years received substantial grants-in-aid from the federal government for planning, housing, urban renewal, and war against poverty, and Congress is constantly receiving pleas for more financial aid, particularly to meet the problems of air pollution and mass transportation. As the demands for aid exceed the funds which decision makers feel should be allocated to meet them, there arise some serious questions: Are the cities doing all they can, or should, to finance their own projects? Are the states doing all they can, or should, to help their cities meet the demands made upon them? In fact, considerable criticism has been leveled at state decision makers; it is asserted that they have done very little to come to the aid of large cities that constantly face financial difficulties. Some federal aid programs already require that there be evidence of local or state effort before financial assistance becomes available.

The whole set of problems connected with intergovernmental payments, particularly when such payments are designed to equalize, in part at least, public service among various jurisdictions, raises the question of how to measure the relative financial capacities and the tax efforts of various governmental units.[14] In other words, how can the ability of a city to pay and its willingness to pay be measured so that these factors may be taken into consideration in grant-in-aid programs? Answers to this question must be found if equalization of public services among various governmental units becomes a more important factor in determining how grants will be allocated.

EVALUATION OF TAX SOURCES

The fact that cities must raise revenue in order to finance municipal services is generally admitted and is, therefore, not a political question. Political issues arise, however, over the sources from which city revenue shall be derived and the amount that shall be raised for public purposes. A basic conflict arises over the extent to which services shall be financed on the basis of quantity of service used or by general taxation where there is no relation between tax payments and service benefits. But even where agreement is reached that certain public services can never be financed by service charges, there is ample room for conflict over the kinds of taxes that should be levied to pay for the services. Since each kind of tax that is available to cities falls upon different groups in different ways, existing taxing systems are the results of compromises that have been worked out through group interaction in the governmental decision-making arena. The degree of freedom cities have to make decisions about tax sources is often circumscribed by state laws, but these state restrictions also represent the play of group conflict in the state arena. As the voice of cities is given increased weight at state capitals, these restrictions may be relaxed. But as the cities receive greater discretion in the kinds of taxes they can levy, conflict with the city political arena will be intensified. As long as a city cannot legally levy an income tax, for example, those who would be most directly affected by such a tax have no need to organize opposition to it. If, however, the state permits the city to levy an income tax, this potential opposition will become active.

The pressures for greater state and federal aid for city services may be viewed in the same way. Since each level of government has its own tax system, the tax burdens of each level fall in different ways on different groups. For example, organized property owners may seek more aid from the federal and state governments, since they do not raise their revenue from property

---

[14] For a discussion of this problem, see The Advisory Commission on Intergovernmental Relations, *Measures of State and Local Fiscal Capacity and Ability to Pay*, Washington, 1962.

taxes. Non-property owners, on the other hand, may be more willing to raise local property taxes to support increased city services.

The significant variations in the tax system of state and cities furnish evidence of the differences in the mixes of political forces that control state and local decisions. It is interesting to notice that the states where the most cities levy income taxes (Pennsylvania, Ohio, and Michigan) are highly industrialized. It would be an interesting project to study a few cities which have adopted general sales taxes and compare their political characteristics with those of other cities which can legally use the sales tax but have not opted to do so.

DEBT MANAGEMENT

The regular day-to-day expenses of operating cities are generally met by annual revenue from service charges, taxes, and intergovernmental payments. Ordinarily cities are not permitted to operate with deficits. An exception to this is the practice engaged in by some cities of selling notes or borrowing from banks in anticipation of revenue to be received. Since cities depend heavily on property taxes and since such taxes are paid at a specific time in the year, the city treasury may be depleted before taxes are received; tax anticipation notes may be sold to meet regular payrolls and other expenses, then paid off when the taxes are received. For the construction of physical facilities and the purchasing of land, cities may contract debt to be paid off on a long-term basis.

Bonds

Cities usually contract long-term debt by the issuance of bonds which constitute legal obligations against the city. Different kinds of bonds may be issued by a city; the choice often depends on the nature of the improvement contemplated. *General-obligation* bonds constitute an obligation upon all taxable property within the city. When such bonds are offered for sale, the purchaser is assured that a specific tax levy against property within the city will be made and the proceeds dedicated to the payment of interest and principle on the bonds. General-obligation bonds are regularly used to finance public improvements which are for general public use and for which no special use charge is to be made. Schools, city halls, public hospitals, and major streets are usually financed by the sale of general-revenue bonds.

Cities often use *revenue* bonds to finance improvements for which use charges will be made. For example, toll bridges, opera houses, swimming pools, and water plants may be financed through the sale of revenue bonds. These bonds are redeemed from the tolls or charges made for the use of the facilities constructed, and they do not constitute a general obligation against the taxable property within the city. Purchasers of such bonds know that they cannot be paid off out of general taxation, therefore they must be convinced of the feasibility of the project before they are willing to bid on them. Whereas only those who own property within the city help redeem general-obligation bonds, users of the facilities regardless of where they live help pay off revenue bonds. Because of the greater element of risk involved, revenue bonds usually carry higher rates of interest.

Size of Local Debt

The total debt of all cities in the United States had risen from $13,558,000 in 1953 to $28,743,000 in 1963; this is an increase of 112 percent.[15] Such gross figures of city debt have little meaning unless they are studied in comparison with other kinds of measures. In 1963 the total national debt in current dollars was $305.9 billion, a rise from $269.4 billion in 1946. The total public debt of federal, state, and local governments in current dollars was $375 billion in 1962, a rise from $285 billion in 1946. The increases in public debt of all levels of government appear to be great when measured in current dollars, but a different impression is made if the debts are measured in constant dollars or as a percentage of gross national product.

Mosher and Poland have provided some interesting figures on the total public debt in this country.

> The total public debt in constant (1961) dollars declined from $440 billion in 1946 to $375 billion in 1962.
> Per capita debt in constant (1961) dollars declined from $3,099 in 1946 to $2,012 in 1962.
> The gross public debt declined from 135 per cent of Gross National Product in 1946 to 68 per cent in 1962.
> Debt was five times general receipts in 1946; in 1962 it was only two-and-one-half times receipts.
> The net debt of governmental agencies declined from 61 per cent to 33 per cent of total public and private debt.[16]

[15] International City Managers Association, *op. cit.*, p. 245.
[16] Mosher and Poland, *op. cit.*, pp. 99, 100.

These figures, which show relative declines in public debt even though in absolute terms the debt is increasing, simply means that everything else has increased faster than has public debt.

As shown in Table 15.2, the federal government debt accounted for 94 percent of the total public debt in 1946 but for only 79 percent in 1962. State debt was only 1 percent of total public debt in 1946 but was 6 percent in 1962. Local governments accounted for 5 percent of the total public debt in 1946 and for 15 percent in 1962. These figures demonstrate that, relatively, state and local debts have increased at a greater rate than has the federal debt from 1946 to 1962.

Some observations are necessary when efforts to compare debts of various governments are made. National government debt simply reflects excess of expenditures over revenues and is not directly related to specific physical facilities. State and local debt, on the other hand, is almost always related to specific facilities which account for the debt incurred. Likewise, state and local debts are funded either by specific service charges which are committed to that purpose or by special tax levies that can be used for no other purpose; the national government debt is funded from regular tax revenues as Congress authorizes their use for that purpose. Local and state debts are not only incurred for specific purposes but usually must be approved by popular vote; federal debt requires only action by Congress and the administration.

It is interesting that state and local government debt generally runs counter-cyclically to national debt. National debt shows marked increases in times of

TABLE 15.2   Percentage of Gross Governmental Debt, by Level of Government

Spending level	1946	1962	1962 as a percentage of 1946 (in adjusted dollars)
Federal	94	79	111
State	1	6	934
Local	5	15	436
All levels	100	100	133

Source: Reprinted by permission of Dodd, Mead & Company, Inc., from *The Costs of American Government* by Fredrick C. Mosher and Orville F. Poland, copyright c. 1964 by Dodd, Mead & Company, Inc., New York, p. 100.

depression and in times of war; state and local debt go down in times of economic distress and in times of war and increase in peacetime, when materials become more available, and in periods of prosperity, when voters are willing to pay the costs of expansion of facilities.[17]

Evidence of a trend toward financing municipal services through service charges is evident in municipal debt management. In 1953 only 23 percent of all long-term city debt was in the form of nonguaranteed obligations (revenue-type bonds), i.e., 77 percent of the debt represented general obligations against the city's taxable base. In the next ten years general-obligation bonds rose by only 68 percent, while revenue-type indebtedness had increased by 233 percent. At the close of 1963, 37 percent of all long-term city indebtedness was nonguaranteed.[18] Some of the increase in the use of revenue-type bonds may be explained by the fact that such bonds can in some states be issued under restrictions less severe than those imposed for the issuance of general-obligation bonds. Figure 15.1 shows graphically long-term debt of municipalities by type of obligation and purpose of issue.

State Limitations on Local Debt

Legal authority for cities to issue bonds, of course, comes from the state, and most states either by statute or constitution place limitations on this authority. The most common limitation relates to the amount of bonded debt a city may have at any given time. These restrictions are generally expressed as percentages of total assessed value of property. A typical restriction might be one that limits the total municipal debt to 10 or 15 percent of total assessed value of property. Many states, however, deal separately with general-obligation bonds and bonds to be funded from specified service charges. In some instances a limit on bonded debt for general purposes will be specified in the constitution, but cities will be authorized to issue bonds for special purposes (e.g., street construction or sewer systems) beyond the limit specified for general purposes. Just as was indicated in the discussion of state limitations on property tax rates, local governments often find ways of circumventing restrictions on bond issues. Since limits are based on property assessments, the actual dollar amount of bonds that can be sold will be increased if the assessing authority can be persuaded to raise all assessments by a fixed percentage. Tax bills could still remain the same for other purposes if the

[17] *Ibid.*, p. 97.
[18] International City Managers Association, *op. cit.*, p. 246.

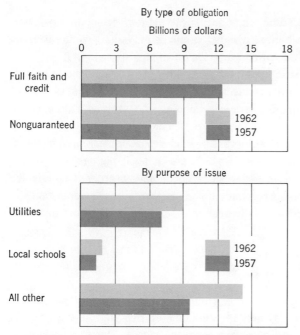

By type of obligation

Billions of dollars

Full faith and credit

Nonguaranteed

1962
1957

By purpose of issue

Utilities

Local schools

1962
1957

All other

Figure 15.1   Long-term debt of municipal governments by type and by purpose of issue, 1957 and 1962. (Source: U.S. Bureau of the Census, *Census of Governments*, Washington, 1962, vol. 4, p. 9)

regular tax rate is reduced. The limitations apply separately to governmental jurisdictions, even though more than one jurisdiction exists within a given area. Therefore, if a city has reached the limit of its bonding authority and still wants to sell bonds to construct a sewer system, it can create a special sewer district and sell the bonds under the bonding authority allocated to special districts.

Other state limitations relate to procedures and techniques for the issuance of bonds. A common requirement is that bond issues must be approved in a popular election. In some states only a simple majority vote is required for approval; in others a two-thirds majority is needed. Often a greater majority will be required to approve general-obligation bonds than is required for revenue bonds.

Some states do not permit cities to issue bonds for unlimited periods; i.e., all bonds must be sold to come due in not more than twenty years, and only serial-type bonds can be issued by cities under some state laws. To ensure prompt payment of city bonds, the ordinance authorizing the sale must include the authorization of a tax sufficient to meet interest and principal payments, or, in the case of revenue bonds, it must contain a provision which earmarks certain income for bond-redemption purposes only.

In addition to legal restrictions on city bonded debt, economic considerations are a factor in determining the size of city debt. Bonds must be sold in the regular financial market. Brokers who handle bond sales and prospective buyers examine the credit rating and debt structure of a city before they decide to bid on a bond issue. If a city goes beyond a reasonable limit, it may find that no one will buy its bonds or that bids are at such high rate of return that the issue is not feasible. In general, city bonds have been in demand since interest received by the holders is not subject to the federal income tax. For this reason municipal bonds usually bear interest rates well below the rates on corporate bonds.

INTERGOVERNMENTAL PAYMENTS

All statistical sources which collate revenue for cities carry an income item called "intergovernmental payments." Included in this item are grants to cities from the federal government and from the states. These are generally in the form of grants-in-aid, which were discussed in Chapters 4 and 5. Reference, however, should be made here to a movement which has found favor with big-city mayors to alter the nature of these intergovernmental payments. The term "tax sharing" may be used to cover the various kinds of such grants that have been suggested. The idea of these plans is to let the federal and state governments use the tax sources available to them and their centralized collection institutions to collect more revenue than they expect to use and to return, under some predetermined formula, a portion of this money to the cities. This type of sharing of income gets its support from those who seek to shift part of the tax burden from general property taxes and from those who prefer to remove federal and state limitations on the purposes for which aid can be spent as well as to lessen existing controls over the administration of activities supported by the grants. Some support also comes from persons who want to reduce the size of the federal bureaucracy. Their point is that an elaborate administrative organization is now required to oversee grants-in-aid. If money were rebated to cities on a formula basis, the only administrative problem would be one of accounting.

The political issues involved are not difficult to see. The sharing plan would place the decision-making power over use of the shared income within the political arenas of the various cities. The present plan ensures that at least the major decisions relating to allocation of resources for the various purposes will be at the national or state level. This political reality leads to the prediction that those who now possess the power to allocate these scarce resources are unlikely to give it up voluntarily.

SUMMARY

One of the most pressing problems facing modern American cities is how to secure revenue sufficient to meet the increasing demands made upon them. This problem is particularly serious in the older core cities where boundaries have remained fairly stable as industries and upper-class residents have migrated to the suburbs. Existing tax bases in these cities are woefully inadequate to meet current needs if property taxes are to continue to be the chief source of revenue. But since changes in revenue sources alter the proportion of revenue that will be taken from various groups, proposals for tax reform always produce heated political conflict. The winners in such conflicts are often determined by the political arena in which the conflict is resolved. Since the federal government and the states are in positions to tap the tax resources that are likely to produce the most revenue with the least political opposition, they may find it necessary to carry a more significant part of the burden for financing the costs of government services in the large central cities than they are currently carrying.

BIBLIOGRAPHY

Books

Adrian, Charles R.: *Governing Urban America*, 2d ed., McGraw-Hill Book Company, New York, 1961, chap. 15.
Advisory Commission on Intergovernmental Relations: *Coordination of Personal Income Taxes*, Washington, October, 1965.
————: *Measures of State and Local Fiscal Capacity and Tax Effort*, Washington, October, 1962.
————: *State Constitutional and Statutory Restrictions on Local Taxing Powers*, Washington, October, 1962.
Bird, F. L.: *The General Property Tax: Findings of the 1957 Census of Governments*, Public Administration, Chicago, 1960.
Chatters, Carl H., and Albert M. Hillhouse: *Local Government Debt Administration*, Prentice-Hall, Inc., Englewood Cliffs, N.J., 1939.

Committee for Economic Development: *A Fiscal Program for a Balanced Federation*, New York, June, 1967.

Mosher, Fredrick C., and Orville F. Poland: *The Costs of American Government: Facts, Trends, Myths*, Dodd, Mead & Company, Inc., New York, 1964, chaps. 1, 4, 6.

Sigafoos, R. A.: *The Municipal Income Tax: Its History and Problems*, Public Administration Service, Chicago, 1957.

Articles

Brazer, Harvey E.: "The Role of Major Metropolitan Centers in State and Local Finance," *American Economic Review*, vol. 48, pp. 305–316, May, 1958.

Egger, Rowland: "Nature over Art: No More Local Finance," *American Political Science Association*, vol. 47, pp. 461–477, June, 1953.

Salisbury, Robert H.: "St. Louis Politics: Relationship among Interests, Parties, and Government Structure," *Western Political Quarterly*, vol. 13, pp. 498–507, June, 1960.

If the political intensity of decisions which face public officials is measured in terms of the amount of conflict they generate, decisions which determine government expenditures must rank as high-intensity issues. Although there can be found in any governmental jurisdiction some opposition to every kind of expenditure, there can also be found some support for every expenditure. There is some reality in the old slogan that the way for a legislator to be consistently elected to office is to vote for every expenditure bill and against every measure to increase taxes, but it fails to take into account that although there are always groups lobbying for new or increased expenditures, there are also groups opposing overall increases in expenditures as well as specific budgetary items.

The basis of the conflict over proposed expenditures lies in the fact that the total resources available for spending are never sufficient to meet all the demands made upon these resources and attempts to increase tax income always generate strong public opposition. Since the "lump of wealth" is never big enough to go around, decision makers know that if they do not oppose certain expenditure proposals, there will not be enough of the lump left to finance their own pet projects. One may conjecture that public expenditures will rise sharply in periods when the total resources available for allocation increases sharply without alterations in tax rates or tax structure. In other words, if a governmental unit receives most of its revenues from income taxes, its total income will rise rapidly during periods when personal and corporate incomes are high even though there is no change in the rate structure. Pressures for spending can, therefore, be more easily met without fear of reprisals from those who oppose tax increases. Expenditures, particularly of local governments, are likely to rise sharply in times of rising prices, wages, and property values, simply because there is more available to spend under existing revenue structures.

The economist with a special concern for public finance is interested in understanding the effects of government spending on the total economy of the area involved. He, therefore, seeks to learn how expenditures for certain purposes affect personal incomes, retail trade, and imports into and exports from the community. This kind of information may be useful for political scientists, but their primary interest is to observe the manner in which persons group themselves in order to either support or oppose government expenditures. Once the patterns of political organization are discovered, the search for motivation can proceed. The key to understanding how groups react to expenditure proposals is to discover the image they have about how the expenditure will affect their own interests. This image, for some, may have been formed by studying the economic impact of the proposed expenditure, but for most persons it will have been formed by emotion, snap judgment, or a politician's speech, with little or no study of its actual social or economic consequences.

THE NATURE OF CITY EXPENDITURES

Municipal expenditures may be grouped into two broad categories, those for what are considered to be general or regular governmental purposes and those which are looked upon by citizens as business expenditures. This broad classification is significant for political purposes because the two types generally produce different reactions among the voters. The first class includes expenditures for police and fire protection, streets and sewers, public health and welfare, parks and recreation, and in some areas education. These are the public activities which must be supported out of general tax revenues and which compete with one another for a share of the always limited amount of general revenue available. For example, one group may feel compelled to oppose increases in expenditures for major street improvements, not because its members are against such improvements, but because the proposed expenditure will not leave enough in the general revenue fund to support parks and recreation programs in which they have a primary interest.

So-called nongovernmental expenditures generally arouse less political conflict, since they come from special public funds which are legally earmarked for particular purposes. Three kinds of expenditures constitute the major allocations in this class. Perhaps the largest includes expenditures for improvement, maintenance, and operation of public utilities such as electric generating and distributing facilities, water plants, natural gas systems, and mass-transit facilities. The significant feature of expenditures for these services is that they come from charges for specific services, and even if the money in the utility funds were not spent for improvement and operations, it might not legally be allocated for typically governmental services. There is, therefore, less incentive on the part of lobbying groups to oppose proposals for expenditures to maintain utilities. Another nongovernmental expenditure is operation of stores or sales agencies. The operation of liquor stores constitutes the largest item of expenditure in this group, since in some places the sale of intoxicating liquors is a public monopoly. If the income from the operation of stores is used to purchase new stock, and profit is used to improve, maintain, and operate the stores, little public conflict is generated. Only when part of the income from these operations is transferred into general revenue accounts does it become a pawn in the total conflict over resource allocation. Expenditures from insurance trust funds is another major item in the nongovernmental class. Most cities, particularly the larger ones, have health and pension plans for their employees. These plans are financed by contributions from employees and from the city. Income derived from these contributions is deposited in trust funds which can be used only to pay out benefits to employees and to pay administrative costs of the plan. Although fairly large amounts of money are involved, these expenditures produce little political conflict, since they are largely determined by a formula contained in the ordinance which established the health and pension plan. Conflicts that develop arise over the contents of the ordinance that defines contributions and benefits, not over specific annual expenditures to meet the costs of benefits provided.

EXPENDITURE TRENDS

Evidence is clear to show that total public expenditures in this country have risen sharply, whether they are measured in current dollars, constant dollars, or as a percentage of gross national product. Figure 16.1 represents graphically per capita public expenditures in selected years from 1902 to 1962

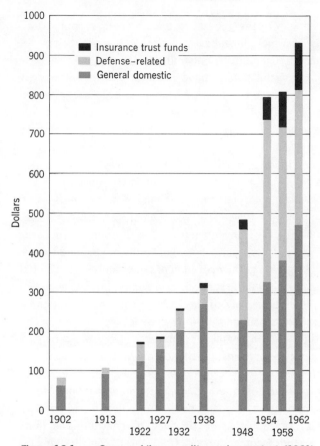

Figure 16.1   Gross public expenditures, in constant (1961) dollars, per capita for selected years, from 1902 to 1962. (Reprinted by permission of Dodd, Mead & Company, Inc., from *The Costs of American Government: Facts, Trends, Myths*, by Frederick C. Mosher and Orville F. Poland, copyright c. 1964 by Dodd, Mead & Company, Inc., New York, p. 22)

measured in 1961 constant dollars, and Figure 16.2 compares total expenditures as a percentage of GNP for three categories of expenditures. The years selected were peacetime years; war years would have shown far greater expenditures. The student will note that per capita expenditures in 1961 constant dollars increased from $84 in 1902 to $254 in 1932, the depression period, and continued to increase, reaching $933 in 1962. In the sixty-year period from 1902 to 1962 the per capita growth averaged 4.1 percent a year.

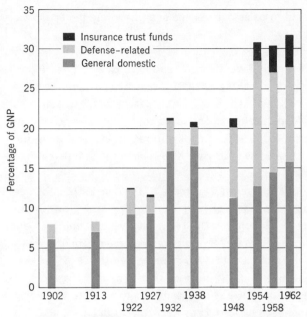

Figure 16.2   Gross public expenditures as a percentage of gross national product for selected years from 1902 to 1962. (Reprinted by permission of Dodd, Mead & Company, Inc., from *The Costs of American Government: Facts, Trends, Myths*, by Frederick C. Mosher and Orville F. Poland, copyright *c*. 1964 by Dodd, Mead & Company, Inc., New York, p. 24)

The growth rate from 1902 to 1932 was 3.8 percent a year, not much less than the 4.47 annual increase after 1932.[1]

In terms of a percentage of GNP, gross public expenditures rose from 7.7 percent in 1902 to 21.3 percent in 1932 and were at 31.7 percent in 1962. Mosher and Poland conclude that in the five noncrisis periods of the twentieth century, general expenditures (not including insurance trust funds) have remained surprisingly stable in terms of percentages of GNP. The general tendency has been for defense-related expenditures to rise sharply during war periods, then decline after war periods but remain at a higher plane than before the war period. General domestic spending has tended to move in the opposite direction; i.e., downward during war periods and upward following

[1] Fredrick C. Mosher and Orville Poland, *The Costs of America's Government: Facts, Trends, Myths*, Dodd, Mead & Company, Inc., New York, 1964, pp. 21, 23.

such periods. Nonwar expenditures also increased sharply during the economic depression of the 1930s.[2]

The trends just described are for expenditures of all units of government. It is interesting to see how nearly federal, state, and local expenditures follow the same trends. In terms of percentage of GNP, federal expenditures have risen most, but much of the increase is accounted for by defense activities and insurance-type trust funds. Total expenditures rose from 2.6 percent of GNP in 1902 to 20.4 percent in 1962. If expenditures for general domestic activities are considered separately, the rise has been from 0.4 percent of GNP in 1902 to 2 percent in 1962.

State expenditures were at a level of 1 percent of GNP in 1902 and rose to 7 percent in 1962. Local expenditures have experienced less growth than have either federal or state expenditures. In 1902 they were running at the rate of 4.5 percent of GNP, and by 1962 they were at 8 percent. The increases for the federal government amounted to 17.8 percent, for states 6 percent, and for local governments 3.5 percent. It must be kept in mind, however, that some of the federal expenditures were for grants-in-aid to state and local governments and that some state expenditures were for aid to local units.

If expenditures for grants-in-aid are eliminated and only direct expenditures are included, Table 16.1 shows the percentages of total public expenditures accounted for by the three levels of government for selected years from 1902 to 1962.

While the federal government's share of total expenditures was rising from 34 percent in 1902 to 58 percent in 1962, and the states' share was growing from 8 percent in 1902 to 14 percent in 1962, the expenditures of local units of government were decreasing from 58 percent of the total to 28 percent.

[2] *Ibid.,* pp. 44, 45.

TABLE 16.1 Percentages of Direct General Expenditures by Level of Government for Selected Years from 1902–1962

Spending level	1902	1913	1922	1927	1938	1948	1954	1962
Federal	34	30	40	31	44	62	67	58
State	8	9	11	12	16	13	11	14
Local	58	61	49	57	40	25	22	28
Total	100	100	100	100	100	100	100	100

Source: Reprinted by permission of Dodd, Mead & Company, Inc., from *The Costs of American Government: Facts, Trends, Myths,* by Fredrick C. Mosher and Orville F. Poland, copyright c. 1964 by Dodd, Mead & Company, Inc., New York, p. 44.

These figures are somewhat misleading, since they include the large expenditures connected with war and national defense activities. Table 16.2 gives the same type of information for direct general expenditures for domestic purposes only.

The same general trend is evident, even if not quite so drastic. Federal domestic expenditures were 17 percent of the total in 1902 and had risen to 27 percent in 1962. State expenditures for domestic purposes were rising from 10 percent in 1902 to 24 percent in 1962. But expenditures of local units were declining from 73 percent of total expenditures in 1902 to 49 percent in 1962. Even though in terms of percentage of total expenditures local government expenditures have declined, these units were still spending almost as much as the national and state governments combined for domestic purposes in 1962.[3]

The significant point which these comparative statistics make is that over a period of sixty years, the part of total governmental expenditures that has been accounted for by local units of governments has been declining, while the parts accounted for by the federal government and the state have been increasing. This is true even if national defense—related expenditures are disregarded and only domestic spending is considered. This does not mean that since larger parts of total expenditures are now made by federal and state governments, the type of spending is better or worse than it would have been if the reverse were true. One may conclude, however, that Congress and state legislatures allocated money for different purposes than city councils or county boards of supervisors would have. The kinds of interest pressures which influence decisions at these three levels are different, and the mix of interest representation varies greatly in the three kinds of legislative bodies.

[3] This information is summarized from *ibid.*, pp. 19–60.

TABLE 16-2   Percentages of Direct General Expenditures for Domestic Purposes by Level of Government for Selected Years from 1902–1962

Spending level	1902	1913	1922	1927	1938	1948	1954	1962
Federal	17	18	18	15	36	23	26	27
State	10	11	15	15	19	26	24	24
Local	73	71	67	70	45	51	50	49
Total	100	100	100	100	100	100	100	100

Source: Reprinted by permission of Dodd, Mead & Company, Inc., from *The Costs of American Government: Facts, Trends, Myths,* by Fredrick C. Mosher and Orville F. Poland, copyright c. 1964 by Dodd, Mead & Company, Inc., New York, p. 45.

It may well be that the dissatisfaction of some interest groups with local decisions for allocations of resources has led them to support greater domestic spending by federal and state governments in the belief that they could secure decisions in these areas for allocation of funds more nearly in line with their interests and values.

REASONS FOR INCREASED EXPENDITURES

In the late nineteenth century Adolph Wagner attempted, by historical analysis, to generalize about government spending over periods of time. On the basis of his study he concluded that with advances in social progress there is an expansion of government activities and consequently a rise in public expenditures. He concludes that public expenditures increase at a rate faster than the growth of the economy as a whole. Wagner accounted for the relative increase in government spending by the need for greater expenditures to maintain law and order in an advancing society, increased state participation in productive enterprises which had previously been left to private activity, and increased demands from a culturally progressive society for more and better services.[4] Certainly, these factors are operating today to push public expenditures upward.

Some of the factors operating in modern American culture which affect expenditures in the public sector have a special impact on spending at the municipal level. (1) The trends in population are clearly away from rural areas and into metropolitan areas. Since the costs of many public services are dependent on the number of persons to be served, increases in the populations of cities and their suburbs result in greater expenditures by local governments. (2) The nature of the migration into the large cities places financial burdens on the large core cities. A great number of migrants from rural areas are moving into metropolitan areas. Many of these newcomers are poorly educated, have no skills with which to find jobs, and are not familiar with city living. These people often congregate in low-rent districts and constitute a heavy drain on the city treasury for police and fire service and for health and welfare activities. (3) Cities tend to operate under conditions of increasing costs.[5] Generally economists expect that in private industry, costs per unit

---

[4] Adolph Wagner, *Grundlegung der politischen Oekonomie*, 3d ed., C. F. Winter'sche Verlagshandlung, Leipzig, 1893, p. 893, as quoted in Mosher and Poland, *op. cit.*, pp. 20, 21.

[5] See Jewell Cass Phillips, *Municipal Government and Administration in America*, The Macmillan Company, New York, 1960, pp. 437, 438.

decrease as the number of units of production increases. If this rule held true for cities, per capita costs of city government would decline as the population of cities increased. Just the opposite is true. Examination of per capita expenditures for various sizes of cities in the United States reveals that there is an increase in each class as the population increases. This is largely because the costs of city services increase as people live in more densely populated areas. Waste collection and removal, fire protection, health and welfare services must be performed at a more intense level than is required when people live far apart. (4) Public demand for services increases as the cultural pattern of living progresses. Demands for swimming pools, educational "frills," better streets, faster transit, and quicker snow removal are constantly increasing, and candidates for office must announce support for better public services in order to be elected. All these increased activities call for greater public expenditures. (5) Generally rising prices of labor and materials increase governmental costs even if services are maintained at a constant level. Careful examination will reveal that the only items for which tax money is spent are personal services and the purchase of materials. When salaries and wages go up, expenditures will also rise, since about 50 percent of all public expenditures are for this purpose. When wages, cement, gasoline, bricks, lumber, and drugs increase in price, the costs of government will follow, since the city government is probably the largest single purchaser of supplies and employer of labor in any metropolitan area.

PURPOSES OF CITY SPENDING

Expenditures of cities may be analyzed in terms of their character and the object for which they are made or on a per capita basis.

Expenditure by Character and Object

The last two censuses of governments were taken in 1957 and 1962; therefore comparative figures given here are for these two years. Only sample surveys are made for other years. Table 16.3 shows total expenditures for all municipalities in terms of the character of expenditure.

Total direct expenditures in 1962 amounted to $17,136 million, compared with $12,565 million in 1957, an increase of 36 percent. Current operations accounted for approximately $11.25 billion, which was an increase of 39 percent over 1957. Capital outlays amounted to about $4.1 billion, of which

TABLE 16.3   Municipal Expenditures by Character in 1957 and 1962
(in millions of dollars)

Character of expenditure	1957	1962	Percent increase
Current operation	8,100	11,273	39
Capital outlay	3,253	4,127	27
Assistance payments	344	408	19
Interest on debt	516	804	56
Insurance benefits and repayments	352	524	49
Total direct expenditures	12,565	17,136	36
Intergovernmental expenditures	274*	193	−30*
Total	12,839	17,329	35

* Includes a nonrecurrent item of $138 million, paid by Long Beach to the State of California.

Source: From U.S. Census Bureau, *Census of Governments.* Washington, 1962, vol. 4, p 11.

construction was by far the largest single item; purchase of equipment and acquisition of real estate accounted for the remainder. Assistance payments were over $400 million, interest on debt amounted to over $800 million, and insurance benefits and repayments were $5.25 million. Intergovernmental expenditures were just under $200 million in 1962. It is interesting to note that while total direct expenditures increased by 36 percent from 1957 to 1962, capital outlays for land and existing structures increased by 73 percent, interest by 56 percent, and insurance benefits by 49 percent. The total of expenditures for personal services was $7.676 million, an increase of 38 percent over 1957.

Expenditures by Character and Functions

Table 16.4 shows total municipal expenditures for 1962 compared with 1957, organized by standardized functional categories.

Total general expenditures increased from $9,692 million in 1957 to $13,475 million in 1962, an increase of 39 percent. Expenditures for education, highways, and police protection were each over the billion dollar mark in 1962. The total cost of fire protection and sewerage collection and disposal are each just under the billion mark. General expenditures exclude expenditures of utilities, liquor stores, and insurance trusts. These together account for $3,854 million.

TABLE 16.4   Municipal Expenditures by Function for 1957 and 1962
(in millions of dollars)

Function	1957	1962	Percent change
General expenditures:			
Education	1,474	1,952	38
Highways	1,328	1,701	29
Public welfare	496	710	43
Hospitals	537	699	30
Health	166	191	15
Police protection	1,041	1,475	42
Fire protection	709	988	39
Sewerage	652	875	34
Sanitation other than sewerage	504	626	24
Parks and recreation	459	640	39
Housing and urban renewal	247	642	160
Airports	105	193	84
Water transport and terminals	47	77	64
Parking facilities	88	68	−23
Libraries	145	211	46
Financial administration ⎫		248	
General control ⎭	512	401	27
General public buildings	157	206	31
Interest on general debt	309	512	66
Other and unallocable	715*	1,059	48*
Total general expenditure	9,692	13,475	39
Utility expenditure:			
Water supply	1,305	1,567	20
Electric power	844	1,016	20
Transit	487	533	9
Gas supply	110	149	35
Total utility expenditure	2,746	3,265	19
Liquor store expenditure	50	65	30
Insurance trust expenditure	352	524	49
Total	12,839	17,329	35

* Includes a recurring payment of $138 million paid by San Diego to the State of California.

Source: From U.S. Bureau of the Census, *Census of Governments*, vol. 4, 1962, pp. 11, 12.

PER CAPITA EXPENDITURES

Figure 16.3 shows the average per capita expenditure of municipalities for cities of various sizes, classified by selected functional categories, for 1962. Total general expenditures for all municipalities averaged $115.87 per person. As previously noted, per capita costs increase as the size of cities in-

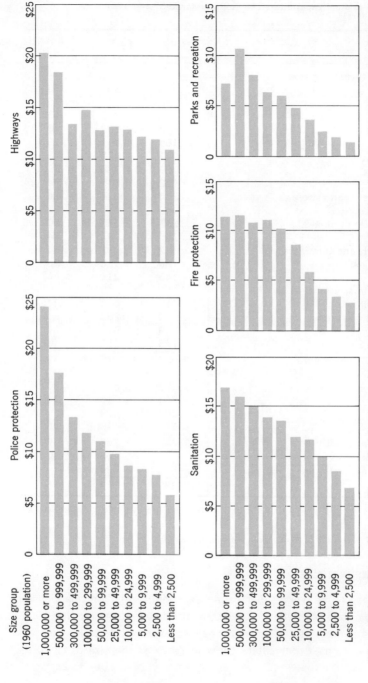

Figure 16.3   Per capita expenditures of various groups of municipalities for selected functions. (Source: U.S. Bureau of the Census, Washington, Census of Governments, 1962, vol. 4, p. 9)

crease. The per capita cost in cities with populations between 50,000 and 100,000 averaged $111.46, while it was $219.12, almost double, in cities over a million.

All indicators point to an increase in city expenditures. Such increases occur because of political pressures that exert influence on those who are in a position to determine expenditures. The chief activity of many interest groups which try to influence local decision makers is to increase the level of spending for some specific service. Very few interest groups are organized primarily to reduce total public spending. Some may seek to reduce expenditures for certain purposes to which they object, but they are not chiefly concerned with reduction of total spending. Indirectly, groups who lobby to reduce taxes are trying to lower general expense levels, but they may not be as much interested in lower spending as they are in changing the sources from which expenditures are to be supported.

This constant pressure, as urbanization increases, for services, which require greater expenditures, gives assurance that all available revenue will be spent. In fact, if one compares the spending levels of a number of city governments which have varying levels of income, he is likely to conclude that those who have more spend more. Therefore, level of expenditure probably depends more on the tax base which determines availability of revenue than on any other factor. One of the major problems which faces metropolitan areas today is the fact that municipalities which have the greatest need for high levels of public spending are the ones with the lowest tax bases, and therefore they are the least able to raise the revenue required to sustain high levels of expenditure.

The political facts of life are that expenditures are likely to be made not according to some objective basis of need but rather because of the play of interest groups which bring pressure at important decision points in the formal process by which allocations are made. In order to observe and understand the tactics of pressure groups as they seek to influence the allocation of revenues, one should become familiar with the process in city government by which these decisions are made and the points in the process where influence might be effective.

THE BUDGET PROCESS

Since the federal budget was established by the Budget and Accounting Act in 1921, practically all governmental units have adopted some kind of formal budgeting procedure, and some states now require that all local governments prepare some kind of formal budget. Cities have been in the forefront of the budget movement, and city managers, in particular, have considered budgetary procedures to be a part of sound financial administration.

In simple terms, a budget is a financial document which projects the amount of revenue expected during a fiscal period and includes recommendations for the expenditure of that revenue. The budget process includes the procedures by which revenue estimates are made, the procedure by which decisions relative to allocations are made, and the manner in which final decisions on recommendations are arrived at. In substance, the term budget or budget process means financial planning prior to the period in which expenditures are to be made.

Budgets are often classified according to the agency which is given formal authority to prepare the budget document that contains the revenue estimates and the spending recommendations. Since the power to authorize spending of tax revenue has traditionally been a legislative function in this country, early budgets were prepared by legislative committees. Some city budgets are still prepared by a committee of the council or board of aldermen; these documents are generally referred to as legislative budgets. In other cities a board or commission which is composed of some members of the council and some administrators is responsible for preparation of the budget. Although the board or commission as a budget agency has lost favor in cities as the movement toward strong mayors and city managers has gained popularity, the board of estimates in the City of New York[6] and in St. Louis still plays a significant role in budgeting.

The Executive Budget

The movement to strengthen the position of the chief executive at both the state and city level has dominated governmental reform efforts since the beginning of the twentieth century. The popularity of the strong-mayor—council and the council-manager plans of city government was due in large part to the desire for more leadership, both at the policy and at the administrative management levels. If those who were planning structural reform in city government wanted to increase the role of the chief executive in policy decisions, one way to do so was to give him a strong voice in determining how revenues of the city would be allocated for various city services. This can be accom-

---

[6] Wallace Sayre and Herbert Kaufman, Governing New York City, Russell Sage Foundation, New York, 1960, pp. 368, 369.

plished by creating what is called an executive budget. In principle, this type of budget means that first decisions as to the amount of money that shall be spent for various activities of the city government will be made by the mayor or the city manager. Legally the city charter simply provides that the chief executive shall prepare a budget and transmit it to the legislative body; institutionally, the office of budget director is either assigned to the central office of the chief executive or made a part of a department whose head is appointed by and responsible to the chief executive. But whatever the specific administrative arrangement, the mayor or manager makes or directly influences decisions on such matters as the total expenditure to be recommended and the manner in which this total expenditure shall be distributed among the various service functions that the city must finance. This means that those who seek to exercise influence in the first budget-making step of the total financial process must do so through the chief executive and his budget officers. Pressures on the chief executive come from heads of administrative departments, citizen committees which are closely connected with certain types of public services (e.g., citizens' committee for support of the zoo), and regular interest organizations, discussed in another chapter.

Budget Procedure

The steps which constitute a typical budget-making process are as follows:

Executive Budget Instructions   At a time specified by the budget calendar the budget officer will send to all agencies of the city which spend public revenue the forms and schedules which they are to use in submitting and justifying their requests for money to carry on their work during the next fiscal year. Along with this material will go general instructions from the chief executive. These instructions are to serve as guides to the spending agencies in preparing their requests for funds. These guidelines are usually in broad general terms and are intended to convey impressions about the general state of the city's finances. The manager, for example, may feel that income prospects are good and that the services of the city need to be improved; therefore he may suggest that department heads decide how they can raise their level of services and that they estimate total cost including the new service levels. On the other hand, the manager may foresee significant reductions in revenues and may in his budget instructions insist on cutbacks in service levels. Instructions may be more selective in nature. The manager may feel that some specific service activity needs to make a great leap forward; in order to finance improvements in the one area, other spending agencies must be advised to either hold the line or even cut back on expenditures. The point is that the executive budget gives to the chief executive power to issue such instructions with the assurance that his position as chief administrator will carry weight with department heads who owe their appointment to him.

Departmental Estimates   Most large departments have within their organizational structure a planning group whose function it is to assist the department in planning ahead for departmental responsibilities. This group may be assigned the task of preparing estimates of the financial needs of the department for the year ahead. Estimates will be based on recommendations from division heads, requirements of law, predictions of prices and wages, and instructions from the chief executive. When estimates are satisfactory to the department head, they are set forth on forms supplied by the central budget office. Some oral consultations between the department head and the budget director or the chief executive may take place before the estimates leave the department.

It is impossible to know all the considerations that go into the process by which departmental budget estimates are made. Certainly there are pressures within the department to be considered. Employees want increases in salaries and wages, division heads want to improve and expand services, clientele groups associated with the services rendered insist on more support for the kind of work the department is doing. Even a councilman may take a special interest in the estimates of a department whose activities are concentrated in his ward. The fact is that most pressures which are exerted at this level of budget making are for increasing, not decreasing, expenditures. If there is any pressure operating to restrain budget estimates, it is from the budget office or the chief executive. With the knowledge that estimates, as a matter of practice, are generally reduced before the final budget is approved, department heads are likely to ask for more than they expect to get. A department head scores some points with his own workers and clientele groups if they feel he is exerting every effort to get as much for them as possible.

Negotiations with the Budget Office   After departmental estimates, along with information justifying the estimates, have reached the budget office, they are summarized on forms designed to give an overview of what the budget would look like if all departmental requests were approved. Normally the totals at this stage turn out to be considerably in excess of what the mayor or manager plans to submit to the city council. Some reductions can be made by the budget director where departments have obviously failed to comply with instructions, and in some instances the budget officer may be persuasive enough to secure reductions by personal conferences with department heads.

But in many instances intervention by the chief executive with department heads will be required to bring estimates within policy guidelines.

Presentation to the Council   After the chief executive has either reached agreements with spending agencies or has made a final decision on estimates without agreement, the budget document is prepared for presentation to the council. The various forms that this document may take will be discussed later, but, regardless of form, it will contain in summary and in detail the anticipated surplus to be available for future use, the income expected from all revenue sources, and the expenditures recommended by the mayor or manager for each agency authorized to spend money. The document will be accompanied by charts, graphs, and explanatory material to justify the recommendations it contains. The chief executive may simply send the budget material to the council for consideration, or he may personally deliver a budget message explaining the rationale upon which the recommendations are made.

Legislative Consideration   If the city council or board of aldermen functions with regular standing committees, as most large ones do, the budget will be referred to the appropriate committee for consideration. This consideration may include the appearance of department heads to explain their needs and presentation by representatives of interested groups in support of or opposition to sections of the budget. Many charters now require that the public be given an opportunity to see the budget and that a date, place, and time be announced for a public hearing on its contents. At such a hearing, under rules provided by the council, any interested persons may express their opinions about the budget.

Official action may be taken on the budget either by an ordinance to adopt the budget or by appropriation ordinances which incorporate the recommendations contained in the budget. City charters differ on the legal competence of the council to alter the budget. In some cases there are no limitations on the council's authority to increase, decrease, or delete items contained in the budget, or to add completely new items. Numerous specific limitations, designed primarily to protect the solvency of the city, have been written into city charters. The assumption seems to be that chief executives are more likely to keep income and expenditures in balance than are councils, unless the councils are legally checked. The simplest kind of restriction provides that budget items for payment of interest and principal on the public debt cannot be altered. In some cases total expenditures cannot be approved that exceed the total revenue estimates contained in the budget plus the surplus carried over from previous years. Some charters merely say that if the council authorizes expenditures in excess of anticipated revenue, it shall at the same time authorize new sources of revenue equal to the increases approved.

Other charter provisions operate to restrict the freedom of action of the council in dealing with the budget. Very few large cities have what might be called a unified financial system, i.e., a system in which all revenues from whatever source go into a single general revenue fund from which all expenditures are authorized. There are always certain revenue sources that, when approved, were committed for specific purposes. For example, certain sources of income are for the maintenance of a zoo, other sources for parks, education, or similar functions. Since revenues from these earmarked sources cannot be used for any other purposes, they represent limits to the council's freedom of choice in spending.

Executive Action on Appropriations   As has been previously noted, modern chief executives have extensive veto power, particularly with respect to appropriation ordinances. This power may range from the power to veto only entire ordinances to the power to reduce specific items and sign them into law with the reduced amounts. In some instances executive vetoes may be overridden by the council, but the time element and the special majority vote required make this unlikely.

Most charters have some kind of provision which takes care of a situation in which the council might fail to take any action on the budget by the beginning of a new fiscal year. A common provision stipulates that if the council has taken no action on the tax rate and on appropriations by a specified date just prior to the beginning of a fiscal year, the tax rate and budget as recommended by the chief executive shall become effective as if they had been approved by the legislature.

Allocation of Appropriations   After the council has either adopted the budget by ordinance or has passed separate appropriation acts to authorize spending for the next fiscal year, accounts are set up for each spending agency showing the amounts authorized for each purpose by the appropriation ordinance. The general interpretation is that the amounts authorized for spending agencies are not available to them until they have received allotments from the chief executive through the budget officer. Appropriation amounts are for a fiscal year, which is usually twelve months. If there were no administrative controls over departmental spending, some departments might exhaust their total appropriations before the end of the year. Most city charters stipulate that the chief executive shall control rates of expenditures by making periodic allotments to all agencies, either on a monthly or quarterly basis. In case the mayor or manager feels that the total amount appropriated for the year is greater than the revenue expected, he can make allotments of less than one-fourth of total appropriations for the first quarter to assure that available revenue will last through the entire year. If later it appears that total revenue will be available to meet all appropriations, allocations may be increased.

In certain instances the mayor or city manager can authorize a spending agency to make transfers from one appropriation account to another. This depends to a considerable extent on the degree of detail used in the appropriation ordinance. If appropriations are so detailed that for a specific office there are separate items for supplies and equipment, transfers from one to the other could be approved, but it is unlikely that transfers will be permitted from one general purpose to another, i.e., from control of communicable diseases to inspection of places which sell food. Certainly, transfer from one department to another will not be possible unless approved by ordinance of the council.

Budgeting for Capital Expenditures

Normally, budgets are prepared for one fiscal period, which in cities is one year, and appropriations are for one year only. This type of annual budgeting presents problems in the process of planning for major construction programs. Construction of buildings, major streets, bridges, and utility plants must be spread over fairly long periods, and redemption of construction bonds takes many years. Long-range planning for capital expenditures is now a fairly regular practice in cities. Under general direction of the chief executive the budget officer works with the planning office to determine construction needs over a period of time. Priorities are established for the projects, and in cooperation with the department of public works cost estimates are developed. This information is organized in what is usually called a capital budget, which includes recommended capital spending for a period of from five to ten years. City councils are asked to debate and approve with modification the capital budget as a long-range spending guide.

The capital budget does not of itself authorize spending. Using this budget as a guide, the chief executive includes in each annual budget the items for capital expenditures required to meet each year's obligations under the long-range capital-expenditure program.

Budget Forms and Systems

Governmental budgeting is relatively new in this country. The first federal budget was prepared in 1923, and although there was some literature on the subject as well as some local budgeting before that date, the adoption of budgeting at the national level stimulated greater interest among states and cities. The advantages of public budgeting have become generally accepted, but there has been considerable experimenting to find a system that produces the kinds of results its advocates claim for it. The general purpose of budgeting has remained pretty much the same; it is a process for systematically relating the expenditure of funds to the accomplishment of planned objectives. The differences in various budget systems which have been proposed from time to time have been in the degree of emphasis given to various factors involved in the process of relating expenditure to objectives.

The form and structure which a budget takes is dependent on the budget philosophy adopted; i.e., on the purpose which the budget is expected to perform. Historical examination of public budgeting in this country reveals three major phases in budget development, and each phase was marked by a concentration on a different goal which the budget was expected to achieve. Any attempt to relate expenditures to objectives will include the processes of planning, management, and control; the differences in systems lie in the emphasis which each system gives to these three processes.[7]

Budgeting for Purposes of Control   Since public budgeting came into existence as one of the many twentieth-century reform measures, it was viewed as a means for the executive to control the expenditure of public funds to ensure that they would be expended honestly, efficiently, and for the specific purpose designated by the legislature. Although there is evidence in the literature and even in the practice of budgeting from 1920 to 1935 that advocates of public budgeting hoped it would improve financial planning and strengthen the management area of the executive, for practical purposes budgets were designed and used primarily as instruments of control over public spending.[8] If the budget system is expected to be used primarily as an instrument of control, its form and structure will be designed to serve this end.

This control philosophy dictated that authorizations to spend clearly indicate the agency being authorized to spend and the manner in which the allocation could be lawfully spent. Therefore, early budgets were organized around administrative units, each of which constituted a spending agency. Budget authorizations were made specifically to individual departments, boards, commissions, and agencies, which together constituted the total

[7] The following discussion is based upon Allen Schick, "The Road to PPB: The Stages of Budget Reform," *Public Administration Review*, vol. 26, pp. 243–258, December, 1966.

[8] See A. E. Buck, *Public Budgeting*, Harper & Brothers, New York, 1929, pp. 181–188.

administrative branch of the state or city. But spending authority was not extended in lump-sum amounts, since such authorizations would not be conducive to detailed control of the expenditures of these agencies. The accepted pattern was to itemize in detail the amounts that could be spent for various purposes. A typical budget document therefore authorized expenditures for each department by object, and within each object it specified individual items of expenditure. An object classification might include personal services, supplies, equipment, fixed charges, and capital outlays. Within the equipment classifications would be included the specific items to be purchased, e.g., desks, business machines, or file cabinets. This form of budget made it easy to set up a series of accounts for each department and for each object of expenditure, and through a preapproval and preaudit procedure to ensure that expenditures would be made within the limits authorized and for the purposes listed.

This general system, with modifications, probably is still dominant in municipal budgeting, and there is no intention to say that control is the only function it performs. A certain amount of planning is required to prepare a budget in which proposed expenditures must be classified by object and item, but the planning tends to concentrate on material or services to be purchased rather than on public functions to be performed. Likewise, this type of budget serves to some extent as a management tool. But the concept of management is restricted to supervision of spending activities to assure that total expenditures will be within the income and that specific expenditures will be in accord with legislative authorizations. This philosophy is in complete accord with the theory which supported the movement for a strong executive. The need for the strong executive was to exercise continuous supervision over departments and agencies to see that graft and corruption were eliminated and that all public funds were properly accounted for.

Budgeting as a Management Tool   As the battle against graft and corruption in the handling of public funds appeared to be won, reformers turned their attention from the negative control philosophy to a more positive concept of management as a tool for initiative and innovation, to improve the level of services administered by government. New recruiting techniques, more objective methods of evaluating candidates for jobs, and better salaries raised the prestige level of public service and brought into the service persons who needed fewer external controls to assure honesty and integrity. When the fear that public funds would be converted to private use had lessened, fewer restrictions were needed upon the expenditure of funds allocated to departments. Administrators were willing to assume that department heads and their division heads knew best how to use resources made available to them to achieve the purposes of the department. Lump-sum appropriation began to replace line-item budgets in cities with professional managers and in strong-mayor cities.

The tremendous increases in total government spending, the rise in number of persons involved in administration, and the increase in the number of services undertaken combined to produce criticism of the typical line-item type of budget. Although it maximized central control over spending, it did not constitute an effective management tool. In fact, expansion of government renewed demands for greater unity in administration to prevent duplication and overlapping of activities. The answer seemed to be to strengthen the position of the chief executive so that he could more effectively manage the administrative branch. Reorganization of administrative structure, with all activities being grouped into a small number of single-headed unifunctional departments, was a part of this struggle for more effective executive management.

Direct control of the entire budget process seemed to be another means by which the chief executive could exercise direct influence over all governmental agencies, since they would have to appeal to the budget agency to defend their spending requests and depend on budget allotments to carry out their work. At the federal level the transfer of the Bureau of the Budget from the Treasury Department to the Executive Office of the President in 1939 was concrete evidence of the move to give the chief executive the budget system as an instrument of management. If management rather than audit-type control of expenditures was to be the function of the budget system, the form and structure of the budget document would need to be reexamined. The chief executive becomes interested more in the purposes for which money is requested and spent and is less interested in specific objects which are purchased.

The first Hoover Commission reports dealing with administrative reorganization recognized the usefulness of the budget system as a management tool and recommended what has become known as the *performance* type of budget. This recommendation was received with approval in the federal administration, and Little Hoover Commissions in many states included similar suggestions in their reports. Management-oriented city managers and professional budget officers soon adopted the idea of performance budgeting at the city level.[9]

---

[9] See Commission on Organization of the Executive Branch, *Budgeting and Accounting*, Washington, 1949; Fredrick C. Mosher, *Program Budgeting: Theory and Practice*, Public Administration Service, Chicago, 1954; Gladys Kammerer, *Program Budgeting: An Aid to Understanding*, University of Florida Press, Gainesville, 1959.

The move involved a basic change in budget philosophy and necessitated drastic changes in the forms used by spending agencies to submit their requests for funds and in the organization of the final budget document. Interest was concentrated on programs to be carried out or functions to be performed, rather than on persons to be paid or objects to be purchased. All spending agencies were asked to identify each program or function they expected to carry out during the year, to devise a system for estimating the unit costs involved in each program, and to request budget approval by programs rather than for objects and items of expenditure.

The innovations involved in performance budgeting can be illustrated by an oversimplified example of budgeting in a department of health. Under a typical object-item type of budget, the department would in its budget estimates ask for (1) money to pay salaries and wages, the total amount being determined by the number of employees expected and salary levels to be paid, (2) money for certain fixed costs such as insurance, utilities, and rent, (3) money for general operating costs, including supplies and equipment, and (4) money for capital expenditures such as building repair, new buildings, or expensive hospital equipment. Although the department would relate these proposed expenditures to its overall public health function, there was no attempt to break the public health function down into specific programs to be undertaken and to show unit costs of each program.

Performance budgeting would concentrate attention on specific health programs, either required by law or included in broad assignments of power to the department. For example, the department might decide that some of its major functions are (1) contagious disease control, (2) operating a TB hospital, (3) inspection of water supplies, and (4) testing dairy herds from which the city milk supply is received. Such programs would constitute the bases for requests for funds. If the department proposes, as a part of its contagious disease—control program, to immunize each child in the public school, it computes the unit cost of vaccinating one child; then all that is needed to arrive at program costs is the number of pupils in the schools to be immunized. This kind of presentation seems to supply more pertinent information to the chief executive and the council than does a request based on wages and other objects and items of expenditure.

The idea of performance budgeting has received widespread approval in cities, and most city budgets show evidence of its influence even though the conversion has not been complete. Major difficulties faced by performance-budget advocates were related to computing unit costs of services and programs. Most governmental agencies have avoided complicated systems of cost accounting. Since governments do not produce and sell commodities which have to be priced to show a profit, there has been little pressure to use cost accounting. Computation of unit costs for performance budgeting requires considerable adjustment in the traditional accounting systems found in most governmental agencies.

Budgeting as a Planning Tool   Most of the literature dealing with public budgeting that has appeared in the last five years is related to what is referred to as *Program Planning Budget Systems* (PPBS).[10] Some authors have considered the changes in the approach to budgeting that have taken place at the federal level, particularly in the Department of Defense, as merely an extension of the performance-budget idea promulgated by the Hoover Commission. Those closer to the federal budget process, however, are convinced that PPBS represents a different philosophy of budgeting, requires a different approach to the functions that a budget system should perform, and a difference in the preparation of budget documents. Some of the forces or circumstances that brought PPBS into federal budgetary practice in certain departments may be so peculiar to the federal government that the new philosophy will not filter down to the local level.

Schick suggests that program budgeting has been brought into the federal government by three forces:

(1) The acceptance of the economic fact that government taxing and spending policy can be used effectively to influence the general economy of the nation.
(2) The development of systems analysis and operations research to the point where, in certain areas at least, the costs and benefits of alternative courses of action can be arrived at scientifically.
(3) Government planning in terms of goals to be achieved and budgetary planning in terms of revenues and expenditures have drawn closer together operationally.[11]

The rationale for PPBS is that budgetary systems are useful primarily for the purpose of planning the courses of action government should take. It assumes that the purpose of government can be articulated in sufficiently definite terms that a choice of alternatives can be made objectively if the costs and benefits of each alternative are subject to scientific determination. Considerable success has been achieved in applying this kind of analysis to problems of determining the mix of manpower, weapons, and material that will achieve maximum defense objectives, in deciding the best location of military

[10] For a discussion of PPBS see a series of six articles in a symposium on the subject: *Public Administration Review*, vol. 26, December, 1966.
[11] *Ibid.*, pp. 253–256.

bases and of strategic weapons, and in making maximum use of expenditures for water-resource development.

The more complicated government becomes in terms of the number of demands for service that are made upon it, and the more technical problems associated with performing these services become, the more the planning function will consume the time and attention of decision makers. The most significant phase of planning comprises the determination of goals and the allocation of resources to achieve these goals. Since desirable goals are always beyond the resources immediately available, decision makers will welcome any system which defines for them the relative costs and benefits of the various alternative choices available to them. If PPBS appears to supply such information, its growth is assured. But if costs of various alternatives as shown by budget analysts include only economic costs without taking into consideration political costs, which are much more difficult to quantify, cost benefit analysis will be of only limited use to the decision maker who is required to operate in a political environment.[12]

EVALUATION OF BUDGET PROCEDURES

"To budget or not to budget" is no longer the question. The battle for public budgeting has been won; the questions now are how to budget and what function the budget system should maximize. Most observers are ready to admit that adequate constraints exist to ensure a fairly high degree of honesty and integrity in the handling of public funds and that therefore the budget system need no longer be used to serve primarily a control function. The issues relative to changes in budgetary systems seem now to revolve around the use of budgeting as primarily a management tool or as a planning tool.

Although the student of politics must be concerned with *how* decisions are made, he may agree that the more important concern is about *what* decisions are made. If there is no relationship between the nature of the budget system and the kinds of decisions coming from the political system, debate over types of budgets loses much of its interest. If, on the other hand, the behavior of those who make decisions in the political system is conditioned by the nature of the budget system, the nature of the system becomes crucial for the student of politics. Schick's position is stated clearly:

[12] For a criticism of cost-benefit analysis in budget making, see Aaron Wildavsky, "The Political Economy of Efficiency: Cost-Benefit Analysis, Systems Analysis, and Program Budgeting," in *The Politics of the Budgetary Process*, Little Brown and Company, Boston, 1964, pp. 292–310.

The case of PPB rests on the assumption that the form in which information is classified and used governs the actions of budget makers,
and conversely, that alterations in form will produce desired changes in
behavior. Take away the assumption that behavior follows form, and the
movement for PPB is reduced to a trivial manipulation of techniques—
form for form's sake without any significant bearing on the conduct of
budgetary affairs.[13]

The reader will be aware by now that the author accepts the assumption that
form, structure, and procedures do affect behavior and that decisions ground
out by political institutions are affected by the nature of the institutions themselves. Therefore, a discussion of budget systems is very relevant to the
study of politics.

The total budget process supplies reliable information to political decision
makers about the total resources that are available for distribution. This information may be nothing more than educated estimates of anticipated surpluses and expected revenue from existing tax and other income sources, but
it may also include estimates of what total revenue might be if various
alternative revenue sources were tapped. If it goes no further than this, the
revenue side of the budget provides for more informed decisions in adopting
tax and revenue ordinances. More crucial, however, is reliable information
about how alternative revenue measures would affect the economy of the area.
To the extent that tax policies become tools for manipulating the economy as
a whole, the political implications of the revenue side of budget become more
important. This means, probably, that cost-benefit analysis as applied to
revenue structure is more important at the federal level, but it is by no means
useless for large cities. Competition among cities for industry and the ability
of residents to go outside the city in which they live to make purchases are
factors which political decision makers must take into consideration in
determining costs and benefits of various sources of revenue.

It is on the expenditure side that budget form may have its most important
impact. The nature of the budget systems may play a significant role in
deciding where in the political system decisions will be made and the kind
of data, if not the value premises, which will be brought to bear on the
decision makers. Both the line-item budget and the performance type of
budget start with the assumption that existing functions and services will be
continued; debate over objectives or goals is likely to occur only when the
budget contains requests for funds to finance new activities or expand older
ones. Although the performance budget may furnish the legislator with more

[13] Schick, *op. cit.,* p. 257.

information about what governmental service he is buying with appropriation dollars, its chief use is for the executive who takes his general-management duties seriously.

The political implications of program budgeting as it is conceived by its proponents in the federal government seem to be far more significant. Since goals and objects of government are not assumed as "givens," but are to be determined by complex cost-benefit analysis of alternatives, decisions about what should be done may gravitate further from the legislature to the executive than they have already. This may be good or bad, depending on one's values, but it is a difference that must be taken into account. For one who tends to analyze public decisions in terms of a pluralistic political model, the case for program budgeting seems to give too great emphasis to justifying the choice of one alternative rather than others in terms of *economic* costs. The choice of one high dam over the alternate of a series of low dams may very well be justified in economic terms, i.e., in terms of specific benefits in relation to costs. But there may be many other factors which are important to the politician and which were not figured into the cost-benefit analysis. Support for a series of small dams spreads the construction over a wider area and pleases certain groups who do not want to see their land inundated. In fact, by his support for the low dams, a legislator may have bought support for a public service wholly unrelated to water resources. Who can say with certainty what all the costs and benefits of any alternative choice are?

One may concede that the more data relative to cost-benefit relationship the better, but such data must not be limited to the range of economic costs. Economic cost-benefit analysis may provide relevant data to supply to decision makers, and such data may be a factor affecting final decisions, but as long as representative bodies reflect as wide a range of interest groups as they now do, many political considerations unrelated to economic efficiency will also operate to determine political behavior.

BIBLIOGRAPHY

Books

Adrian, Charles R.: *Governing Urban America,* 2d ed., McGraw-Hill Book Company, New York, 1961, chap. 15.
Buck, A. E.: *Public Budgeting,* Harper & Brothers, New York, 1929.
Burkhead, Jesse: *Government Budgeting,* John Wiley & Sons, Inc., New York, 1965.

Isard, Walter, and Robert Coughlin: *Municipal Costs and Revenue Resulting from Community Growth,* Chandler-Davis Publishing Co., Wellesley, Mass., 1957.

Kammerer, Gladys: *Program Budgeting: An Aid to Understanding,* University of Florida Press, Gainesville, 1959.

Mosher, Fredrick C.: *Program Budgeting: Theory and Practice,* Public Administration Service, Chicago, 1954, chaps. 1, 2, 7.

————— and Orville Poland: *The Costs of American Government: Facts, Trends, Myths,* Dodd, Mead & Company, Inc., New York, 1964.

Wildavsky, Aaron: *The Politics of the Budgetary Process,* Little, Brown and Company, Boston, 1964.

Articles

Lindbloom, Charles E.: "The Science of Muddling Through," *Public Administration Review,* vol. 19, pp. 79–88, spring, 1959.

Tiebout, Charles: "The Pure Theory of Local Government Expenditures," *Journal of Political Economy,* vol. 64, October, 1956.

"Planning-Program-Budgeting System: A Symposium": Allen Schick, "The Road to PPB: The Stages of Budget Reform;" Werner Z. Hirsch, "Toward Federal Program Budgeting;" Samuel M. Greenhouse, "The Planning-Program-Budgeting System: Rationale, Language, and Idea-Relationship;" Francis E. McGilvery, "A Management Accounts Structure;" Robert L. Banks and Arnold Kotz, "The Program Budget and Interest Rate for Public Investment;" Aaron Wildavsky, "The Political Economy of Efficiency: Cost-Benefit Analysis, Systems Analysis, and Program Budgeting," *Public Administration Review,* vol. 26, December, 1966.

PLANNING AND LAND-USE CONTROL

Planning is an accepted part of all organized activities. In its broadest sense, planning means simply the acceptance of certain goals as desirable, searching for alternative means which might lead to the achievement of these goals, and selecting the means that appear likely to produce the greatest benefits (in terms of goal achievement) with the fewest costs. Every large business corporation has as a major goal the realization of profits, and its officers plan their sales, production, and personnel policies with a view to achieving this profit goal. They are not unmindful, however, that there are other goals which cannot be overlooked in the planning process. The drive to maximize profits cannot be permitted to undermine the health of workers, to alienate the public, or to produce hostile reactions from governmental authorities. Although planning in nonprofit organizations such as labor unions, farm organizations, and large charitable associations proceeds from a different central goal, a cost-benefit analysis would be a useful scheme for understanding the rationale of their planning decisions.

In governments, planning in certain specific areas is fairly well known and generally accepted. Financial planning through the budget process is nearly universal in cities; planning for specific public improvements (e.g., the construction of a bridge or the reclamation of a swamp for park purposes) is essential if the necessary financing is to be secured. Engineering plans must be put in final form, and the exact schedule of repayments must be legalized before bonds can be put on the market.

A discussion of planning in cities might include almost every facet of municipal government, but the purpose of this chapter is to center attention on one phase of planning that relates to the physical development of cities, or more specifically, to the way land will be used. One of the most scarce resources in large cities is land, and the manner in which it is used will determine what cities will look like and, to a large extent, how the people will live. In general, land in a city may be used for residential, commercial, industrial, recreational, religious, governmental, and aesthetic purposes, and the nature of living within any given city will be affected by the relative ratios of land used for these various purposes.

If there is no public agency whose business it is to make authoritative decisions as to the purpose for which land areas are to be used, the decisions will be made by the play of economic forces in the marketplace. Organizations that need land for legitimate activities will select sites according to their desirability to meet organizational needs, the costs of making them usable, their availability in terms of the real estate market, the availability of capital for development in the location, and the price of the land. These factors in combination have, in large measure, determined the physical character of most American cities. This means that corporation officers, real estate men, land developers, and bankers have participated most directly in decisions as to how land has been used.[1] In many instances social consequences likely to result from these land-use decisions were overlooked or given relatively little consideration.

With the introduction of land-use planning as an acceptable function of city governments, a new factor has been added to land-use decision making which plays an important role in city development. Although city planning in the sense of determining the use to which land can be put is now legally within the power of city officials, economic forces continue to play a significant role. A city plan may specify that a certain area shall be used only for a specific purpose, but such an ordinance cannot assure that the area will be so used. If the use specified in the ordinance is not economically or socially feasible, the land may simply remain unused until planning decisions are changed to conform more nearly to economic and social realities. That is, the legal power to plan and zone may be more negative than positive in its impact on actual

---

[1] See Charles R. Adrian, *Governing Urban America*, 2d ed., McGraw-Hill Book Company, New York, 1961, pp. 457–458.

land development; ordinances may authoritatively determine what will not happen to land, but it may be more difficult to legislate what will actually happen.

THE PHILOSOPHY OF LAND-USE PLANNING

Action of city officials to affect the land-use pattern in cities through powers of government was not simply an attempt on their part to grab more power to satisfy personal ambition; it was a positive response of officials who were sensitive to demands from citizens for changes in specific land-use practices that they disliked. In other words, nonplanned land use resulted in developments which some influential citizens found objectionable, and they decided that the most appropriate remedy for the problems they perceived was for the power of government to be brought to bear on land-development policies.

Obviously, when the power of government is used to proclaim that certain land areas can be used only for specifically designated purposes, that decision limits the freedom of the owners of the land to use it as they please, and it may well set limits to the price at which they can dispose of their holdings. Acceptance of such limits on economic freedom in this country must be justified by fairly substantial evidence that the action is for the "common good," the "general welfare," or the "general interest." As has been discussed earlier, what this really means is that those who are in positions to determine governmental policy will decide, according to their own value systems and the organizational pressures that impinge on them, the land-use pattern they perceive to be in the general interest.

In more specific terms, urban planning as discussed here involves the superimposing of public authority to control land use in the interest of what may be called the public welfare, as distinguished from land-use patterns that would develop if only economic and social determinants of land use were permitted to have free play. In terms of economics, land is just another commodity to be traded in the marketplace, and purchasers offer prices determined by the returns that the land will produce. Since returns will depend on the use to which land can be put, highest prices will be paid for land adopted for uses which offer greatest returns. With no other forces operating, the free play of the market will produce "the highest and best use of the land."[2] But economic forces are not the only ones that play a role in determining how

[2] See Stuart Chapin, Jr., *Urban Land Use Planning*, Harper & Row, Publishers, Incorporated, New York, 1957, chaps. 1 to 3, particularly pp. 40, 41. By permission of Harper & Row, Publishers, Incorporated.

land will be used in urban areas. "Socially rooted" determinants, or ecologic forces, operate to produce important patterns of land use. Chapin identifies these social determinants as (1) dominance, gradient, and segregation, (2) centralization and decentralization, and (3) invasion and succession.[3]

"Dominance" is a term used to express a tendency for a given land-use pattern to influence land uses in the surrounding areas. As one moves away from the dominant center, its influence on land use diminishes; the term "gradient" is used to refer to this receding dominance as one moves farther from the center. "Segregation" expresses a tendency for similar land uses to cluster within a large urban area. Even without governmental interference, large department stores cluster in the downtown area, used-car lots seem to stretch for blocks, one adjacent to another, along certain streets, and apartment buildings apparently spawn other apartment buildings. Taken together, these ecologic forces tend to explain the sector and multinuclei models of development discussed in Chapter 2.

Chapin describes centralization as, "the congregation of people and urban functions in a particular urban center or its functional use areas in the pursuit of certain economic, cultural or social satisfaction."[4] "Decentralization," on the other hand, refers to the breaking down of urban centers, accompanied by movements of population to new satellite areas. Religion, race, nationality, fashion, or similarity of values may be factors which influence centralization. The point is that these socially rooted values are important in determining land use.

"Invasion" is used to refer to the process that takes place when one population group or kind of land use penetrates into another area which differs economically, socially, or culturally. Succession occurs when the new group or land use displaces the original population group or land use. Such terms as "invasion" and "block busting" are used when a minority racial group moves into and displaces an existing majority group.

When government, by official acts, intervenes to guide or alter the economic and social forces which otherwise would determine urban land development, the process is called "planning." The intervention is justified by its supporters on the grounds that there is a public interest in how land-use patterns develop that transcends any private interest and that the political process can produce a better plan. This does not mean that economic and cultural values will cease to play a role in land-use planning, but these values will be considered

[3] See ibid., p. 20.
[4] Ibid., p. 25.

along with other sets of values to provide a rational growth plan for the area involved. This attempt of governmental jurisdictions to intervene to provide a land-development pattern in a predetermined way, rather than to let the development proceed as it otherwise would if uncoordinated economic and social forces were permitted to operate uninhibited by public controls, will constitute the theme for this chapter.

HISTORICAL BACKGROUND

There is no way to set a time or a single event that can be identified as the beginning of city planning. Certainly Europe furnishes many evidences of city planning that predate any evidences to be found in the United States. William Penn's layout for Philadelphia and l'Enfant's plan for the nation's capital are well known, but these plans were primarily street designs, with some indication of location of public facilities. The "City Beautiful" exhibit at the 1893 Chicago World's Fair stimulated popular interest in plans to beautify American cities, and early city planning focused largely on the assumption that the primary goal of planning was aesthetic.

A more significant step in planning development was the convening of the first national planning conference, called by the U.S. Department of Commerce. This conference gave city planning a broader emphasis than was contained in the city-beautiful concept, since representatives from many city reform—oriented groups attended. In 1917 The American City Planning Institute was created as a technical organization of the National Conference on City Planning.[5] The New Deal, as a part of its drive to pull the nation out of the Depression, gave encouragement to city planning, and by 1940 the number of planning agencies in this country was estimated at 1,600. Federal grant-in-aid programs have encouraged and in some cases required city-planning agencies as a condition for grants.

Many early planning agencies were, at best, only semiofficial; i.e., they were created with the blessing of government but were not clothed with governmental powers. Whatever plans they made were guides which private and governmental agencies could use or choose to avoid. Much so-called metropolitan-wide planning is still at this stage. Any plans made for the entire area are promulgated by semipublic commissions or by ad hoc committees composed of officers of cities and counties within the area serving in an ex officio

[5] Donald H. Webster, *Urban Planning and Municipal Policy,* Harper & Brothers, New York, 1958, pp. 10, 11.

capacity. Approval of these agencies may be required before certain federal support is available, but they have no power to impose their will within individual cities. The official municipal or county planning agency which is an integral part of the governmental structure of a single city or county is now fairly common. The 1963 *Municipal Year Book* reported that 1,262 cities with populations over 10,000 had such agencies.[6]

LEGAL STATUS OF PLANNING

Insofar as planning includes only the development of principles of land use and master-plan maps as guides to the city council and administrators in meeting their policy-making responsibilities, no serious legal problems are involved. When, however, ordinances are enacted which are designed to use the power of government to force property owners to use their land in conformance with the plan, the question of interference with property rights arises. The right of the government to take private property for public use after just compensation has been recognized since the nation was formed, but this right of eminent domain does not extend to the right of the government to determine the use to which a private owner can put his property. Traditionally, the only limits on private property use were those which acknowledged the right of government to prevent nuisances. When a land use was clearly detrimental to nearby residents, governmental action to abate the nuisance was generally upheld.

City ordinances establishing land-use districts, prescribing the height of buildings and the area of the lot they can occupy, were challenged as denials of property rights under the Fourteenth Amendment. The power which a city has to limit private use of land must come as a grant from the state; this may be in the form of a constitutional or statutory grant. Since the state can confer upon cities only powers which it legally possesses, the source of the state's power to interfere with private rights needs to be identified. The legal theory is that states possess what courts have called "police powers," which are defined broadly to include the right to limit personal and property rights of citizens provided the limitations are reasonable attempts to protect the public health, safety, morals, and welfare of its inhabitants. Many restrictive measures which are imposed to make city planning effective are upheld under this police-power doctrine. Since the most significant legal issues arise directly from restrictions imposed by zoning ordinances, they will be discussed later.

[6] International City Managers Association, *The Municipal Year Book*, Chicago, 1963, p. 324.

THE MASTER PLAN

A great deal of city planning is done on a piecemeal basis; i.e., individual agencies prepare their own plans for administering their policy programs. The fire department may prepare a long-range plan for the construction of new station houses, the replacement of old equipment, and the purchase of new types of equipment. These plans may provide for the financing of capital improvements as well as recruitment and training of new personnel. Similar plans may be prepared by departments of public works, police, parks, and welfare departments. These, however, are not "master" or "general" plans in the terms of reference of city-planning literature and actual practice.

Adequate definitions of city planning are difficult to find, since professional planners are not always in agreement as to the comprehensiveness of the term. The discussion here will be somewhat more limited than some students of the subject would prefer, since it will concentrate on what might be called physical planning. The master plan is designed to concentrate on the physical development of the city, and its purpose is to make the city a more desirable place for citizens to live, work, and play in. Planning, therefore, requires that choices be made as to what decision makers want the city to look like in the future, and these choices must be implemented through authoritative decisions about how land is to be used. A master land-use or development plan must, therefore, be comprehensive and long-range in character.

If planned development is to be effective, the planning must include all land area within the jurisdiction of the planning authority, whether it is privately or publicly owned, and guidelines for construction of physical facilities on the land must apply to both public and private construction. The legal authority made available to cities by state law places limits on the comprehensiveness of city planning. Cities cannot exercise freely authoritative control over the development of property by the federal government, the state, special school districts, or religious congregations, but if the city has a respectable master plan, these independent agencies can often be persuaded to make their development programs conform to it.

Master plans are designed to furnish guidelines for development over a long period of time. The preparation of a comprehensive land-use plan usually involves judgments looking at least twenty years into the future. Therefore, attention is not confined alone to existing undeveloped areas. Areas with older structures and those that are considered underdeveloped at the present time are considered to be eligible for change within the time range covered by the plan. Obviously, human vision is not perfect, and regular review is essential if the plan is to be viable. Changes in technology, construction methods, economic values of land, and even changes in social and aesthetic values upon which the plan was originally based will dictate changes from time to time.

The Status of a Master Plan

A master plan should be looked upon as a set of general statements about how future development will proceed, rather than as a control instrument which establishes legally permitted uses for specific parcels of land. The plan is usually in the form of a document that sets forth certain goals which the planners have set for the city to achieve, statements about existing uses of land, and general statements about the kinds of development recommended within roughly defined spatial areas of the city. Often, specific means for achieving the development goals will be included, but these are better considered as tools for plan implementation than as integral parts of the plan itself. For purposes of clarity and emphasis, the general statements in the plan are expressed graphically by a map or maps which show the existing land-use pattern along with the new development recommendations. It should be emphasized that these maps showing desired development are not meant to be precise in the sense that the proposed development areas conform with existing ownership of specific parcels of land. Where a superhighway, a railroad, a river, or any major natural barrier is shown as an area boundary, the boundary may be considered to be discrete, but in most cases the exact line of demarcation between different land-use patterns must be spelled out in detail later by zoning ordinances.

Although a master plan may be given official status through its formal adoption by action of the council, it is not generally considered a legal definition of land-use patterns; the zoning ordinance serves this function. The plan, once adopted, becomes a guide to decision makers when they are faced with specific development decisions.[7] If an organized group demands a city park in a particular area, reference to the master plan will reveal whether or not the demand conforms with long-range development decisions. In many cities the legal structure is so designed that the city council, before making any decision that involves the physical development of the city, must submit the proposal to a planning authority and get a judgment as to whether or not the proposal conforms with the long-range master plan.

[7] See T. J. Kent, *The Urban General Plan,* Chandler Publishing Company, San Francisco, 1964, p. 34.

Making the Master Plan

Master plans are generally prepared by a number of persons working together on an intensive basis for a limited period of time, usually one to two years. Once a plan is adopted, it is subject to regular review as important development decisions are made, both in the public and private sector, that affect it, and revisions are made when found necessary. At intervals (fifteen to twenty years) a more comprehensive study is made to revise the existing plan or to produce a completely new one.

STRUCTURAL ORGANIZATION FOR PLANNING

If administrative structure is organized rationally (which it often is not), the place of planning in the total administrative structure will be determined by those it is designed to serve. If the plan is intended to serve the general public and organized interest groups who are concerned with city development and who wish to use it as a means of circumscribing the freedom of choice of the executive and the legislature in making decisions directly affecting land use, then the natural choice is to entrust planning to an agency with a high degree of autonomy. If the plan is prepared primarily for use of the mayor or manager as a guide for drafting policy recommendations to the council, reason would dictate that the planning agency occupy a place in the bureaucracy directly responsible to the chief executive. If, on the other hand, the master plan is created as a guide to the city council in order to assist it in its deliberations on policy issues involving the city's physical development, then the planning agency should be closely associated with the council.[8] Kent suggests three ways in which the planning function may be incorporated into the total governmental complex of a city.[9] Figure 17.1 represents these three patterns of organization.

Planning as an Independent Activity of a City Planning Commission

This structural arrangement includes a semiautonomous planning commission which can make decisions outside the mainstream of city political conflict. The assumption is that decisions with respect to land use can be made in an atmosphere where only issues directly related to land development

[8] *Ibid.*, pp. 22, 23.
[9] *Ibid.*, pp. 13–18.

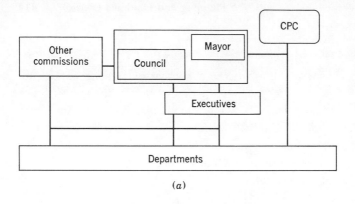

(a)

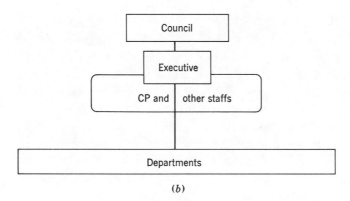

(b)

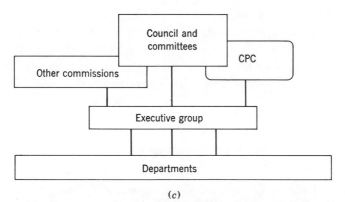

(c)

Figure 17.1   Location of planning function in city administrative organization: (a) an independent activity of the city planning commission; (b) a staff aide to the chief executive; (c) a policy-making activity of the city council. (Source: T. J. Kent, Jr., *The Urban General Plan*, Chandler Publishing Company, Inc., San Francisco, 1964, p. 14)

418

would be relevant and other issues which arise regularly in council deliberations would not impinge upon planning decisions. Since city planning got its start during the first quarter of the twentieth century, it was influenced by the general reform mood of the time. Both city executives and legislators were suspect, and efforts were made to assign authority to decision makers who could exercise discretion independently of regular political officeholders. Perhaps the specific step that was most influential in determining the place of planning in the total governmental structure was the preparation of the 1928 Standard City Planning Enabling Act by a committee of nine working through the Department of Commerce.[10] This act provided for a commission with independent status whose members would not be subject to regular political influences. The standard act was adopted by many state legislatures, and the independent planning commission was firmly entrenched in city government until World War II. Professionals selected by the planning commission and employed to assist in the planning process made their reports and rendered technical advice to the commission. Legislative power, however, was not conferred upon the independent commissions. Recommendations which required ordinances to make them effective had to be transmitted to city councils, but very often such recommendations carried great weight and were enacted into law.

Planning as a Staff Aide to the Chief Executive

As the trend toward stronger executives made more headway under the influence of the new public administration movement, demands were made for the inclusion of the planning function as an arm of the chief executive, since planning may be looked upon as a management tool useful to the executive in coordinating all administrative activities. Furthermore, legislatures were looking more and more to the executive for the initiation of policy, for budget recommendations, and for overall policy coordination. The growth of the professional manager plan in city government gave added impetus to the movement to put planning under the executive's control.

Kent credits the work of Robert A. Walker in 1941 as being a factor in speeding up the move toward abolition of the independent status of planning commissions. Walker's work was a critical evaluation of planning commissions in 37 cities, and he clearly came out in favor of making planning an executive

[10] *Ibid.*, pp. 13, 32–59, and Edward C. Banfield and James Q. Wilson, *City Politics*, Anchor Books, Doubleday & Company, Inc., Garden City, N.Y., 1963, pp. 188–190.

function. Although Kent uses the term "staff aide" to the executive, he states, "the planning director is a full-fledged department head who reports to the chief executive."[11] Actually, the professional planner could be a staff officer assigned to the executive office of the mayor or manager, or he could be an auxiliary department head appointed by the executive. In either case, professional planning work would be done for the executive, who would transmit reports and findings to the council. Legislative power would still remain with the council, and specific land-use policies would be determined by ordinance.

Planning as a Policy-making Activity of the City Council

Kent's own words express the rationale of this concept of planning organization: "The third concept holds that the city council is the primary client of the city-planning agency because it is the final policy-making authority in municipal government. This is my belief, and it is upon this concept that I base my definition of the primary uses of the general plan. At present, a minority of the city-planning profession holds this view."[12] This concept calls for a citizen planning commission with professional staff, but the commission is viewed as an advisory body, reporting its recommendations directly to the council. The professional planning staff supplies the commission with the research studies and the technical know-how upon which their recommendations are based, and in Kent's view, the director presents the commission's reports to the council. He recognizes that the chief executive also needs advice on planning matters, and he assumes that the planning agency would serve his needs as well as those of the council, but the planning director would not report to the council through the chief executive.

This arrangement emphasizes the role of the council in policy matters and accepts the idea that the planning commission, although it may serve the executive in an advisory capacity, is not subordinate to him. Kent takes the position: "After the commission and the executive have considered all proposals, there is no reason why they should not submit opposing points of view and recommendations for them to consider."[13] This structural pattern would certainly place decisions about land use directly in the mainstream of city politics, and they might easily become issues to intensify the struggle for power between the council and the executive which is so much a regular part of city policy making.

[11] Kent, *op. cit.*, p. 15.
[12] *Ibid.*, p. 16.
[13] *Ibid.*, p. 18.

ESTABLISHING PLANNING GOALS

Public control of land use and the physical development of cities through an official planning structure are now generally accepted. Present-day conflicts that arise over planning are not over the issue "to plan or not to plan;" the real issue develops when planning officials are facing specific decisions about permitted land use within various areas of the city. These conflicts arise largely because the goals which city planning is designed to achieve are not clearly defined and uniformly accepted as valid. If goals could be expressed objectively and be popularly approved, the means of achieving these pre-determined goals might be left pretty much to the professionals. But the goals themselves are usually either so subjective that consensus is difficult or so nonspecific that broad value judgments are involved at the implementing stages. Concern over the lack of agreement on clearly stated objective planning goals accounts, in part, for the popular demand for a citizen commission to pass upon decisions that alter existing land-use patterns.

Chapin maintains: "Land goes into use as a consequence of a myriad of individual and group actions. Motivated by values, ideals, and resultant articulated attitudes held by the various organized and unorganized segments of the urban population, these actions follow a defined behavioral sequence that culminates in land-use changes."[14] He suggests that the values which are the determinants of land use may be grouped into three categories: (1) profit-making values, (2) socially rooted values, and (3) public-interest values. The behavior pattern of individuals and groups which seek to influence land-use patterns is influenced by the one of these sets of values which is of most concern to them, and the final consequences of decisions on development result from the interplay of these three groups of values (see Figure 17.2 for a graphic presentation of this model). The economic values which motivate landowners to seek land-use patterns to maximize profits are fairly well understood, and they exert strong pressure on those who are charged with the responsibility for making authoritative decisions on land use. Socially rooted values refer to those forces which prompt individuals to maintain existing land-use regulations in order to preserve social structures or to support changes in land use in order to break down existing patterns that preserve segregation. Both the economic and social values operate to determine land-use development in the free market without any governmentally imposed controls, but they continue to operate to influence decision makers even when land-use controls are legally delegated to some kind of planning authority.

[14] Chapin, *op. cit.*, p. 66, 67. By permission of Harper & Row, Publishers, Incorporated.

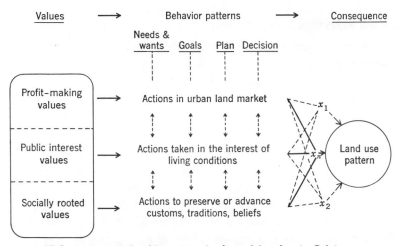

Figure 17.2   Interrelationships among land-use determinants. Points x_1, x_2, . . ., x_n represent points where all side effects of actions seeking changes in land use reach equilibrium, with a consequence of 1, 2, . . ., n changes occurring in the land-use pattern. (Source: F. Stuart Chapin, Jr., *Urban Land Use Planning,* Harper & Row, Publishers, Incorporated, New York, 1957, p. 68. By permission of Harper & Row, Publishers, Incorporated)

Public-interest values may play only a minor role in determining land use in a free market, but they may become a dominant force when planning is accepted as a legitimate function of city government. The legal base upon which public control of land use rests is that such control is designed to protect public health, safety, morals, and welfare. The imposing task of the planner is to convert these widely accepted generalities into operational guide-lines which are sufficiently objective to be useful. Chapin defines the task of the planner as that of developing "a land use scheme fitted to the needs and sensitive to the wants of the urbanite, both economic and social, but also to harmonize the considerations with the public interest in a plan that maximizes livability in the city and insures sound development for the community as a whole." He then defines *livability* as referring "broadly to those qualities in the physical environment of the urban area which tend to induce in citizens a feeling of mental, physical, and social well-being according to the extent to which their fundamental day-to-day living needs and wants are satisfied."[15]

Some of these public-interest values can be specifically identified and, per-haps, objective standards can be made applicable to them, but the area in which the play of value judgments and human discretion will still be im-portant variables in land-use decisions is very broad indeed. Objective stan-

[15] *Ibid.,* p. 41.

dards to protect against accident hazards, noise, and atmospheric pollution and to ensure adequate sunshine, privacy, and protection against criminal activities may be devised, but the concepts of beauty, amenity, and pleasantness are so individual in nature that they cannot be formulated in sufficiently objective terms that they can be left to administrative determination.

The existence of what are referred to as professional planners, who either serve cities on a full-time basis or are employed in a consulting capacity to prepare comprehensive plans, raises the question of the role they play in the total planning process. Few cities today would enter the process of preparing a comprehensive plan without seeking the assistance of someone who considers himself a professional planner. What does the professional have to contribute to the total planning process? Certainly he is not as expert at financial planning as is the city budget officer, he is not as qualified to produce a long-range plan for police protection, fire protection, and health and welfare as are the men who head these functional departments. The role of the professional planner must be that of the generalist who can examine the proposed plans of the specialist planners and try to give them unity, i.e., make sure that, together, the specialty plans contribute to the overall goals and that they do not work at cross purposes. Altshuler finds that comprehensive planners claim that their most important functions are "(1) to create a master plan to guide the deliberations of specialist planners, (2) to evaluate the proposals of specialist planners in the light of the master plan, and (3) to coordinate the planning of specialist agencies so as to insure that their proposals reinforce each other to further the public interest."[16] The assumption is that the "public interest" as used here means the goals supposed to be achieved by general plans. Altshuler then continues:

> Each of these functions requires for ideal performance that the comprehensive planners (a) understand the overall public interest, at least in connection with the subject matter of the plans, and (b) that they possess casual knowledge which enables them to gauge the approximate net effect of proposed actions on the public interest. . . . Every government planner of integrity, no matter how specialized, must be guided by some conception of the public interest. And since plans are proposals of concerted action to achieve goals, each must express his conception as a goal or series of goals for his community.[17]

[16] Alan A. Altshuler, *The City Planning Process: A Political Analysis,* Cornell University Press, Ithaca, N.Y., 1965, p. 299. Copyright c. 1965 by Cornell University. Used by permission of Cornell University Press.
[17] *Ibid.,* pp. 399, 400.

Lay members of citizen commissions, city councils, and city chief executives may be excused if they ask why a professional planner is more competent to decide goals for their city's development than they are. It is very difficult to defend the position that knowledge or technical competence qualifies a person to lay down values for others or to determine what their goals should be. This does not mean that the professional planner serves no useful purpose, but it does imply that the useful role he can play is more circumscribed than many who are working in the field are willing to admit. The professional can make studies of existing land-use patterns and assess the social and economic pressure that will determine future development in the open market if no public-interest controls are initiated. Out of his experience he may produce several alternative proposals for future city development and, with some assurance, predict the consequences that might follow from the adoption of each alternative. He can bring to bear upon the alternative finally chosen his technical competence to present the plan in the form of a series of reports and maps so that it is within the comprehension of those who have an interest in it. With the benefit of the assistance rendered by professionals, the responsible decision makers are in a better position to exercise the power entrusted to them by the public. Another of Altshuler's observation is pertinent at this point: "A sensible view, however, would appear to be that the potential threat to pluralism and democratic control of goal-generalist evaluation and innovative thinking is not that the planners may be sly, stupid, or unwise, but that the laymen responsible for public decisions may accept their proposals uncritically."[18]

CONTENT OF A GENERAL PLAN

If the general plan is to serve a useful purpose in guiding decision makers as they are faced with specific issues which affect the city's development, it should contain certain essential elements. The presentation here will follow fairly closely the suggestions made by Kent but will be somewhat less inclusive.[19]

1. An introductory section should describe existing land-use patterns in the city and as a matter of historical record seek to identify the factors and forces that have shaped past physical development. The political structure which shows the interrelation of decision centers and points of political responsibility may also be included, along with some statements that will explain how the plan is to be used.

[18] *Ibid.*, p. 350.
[19] Kent, *op. cit.*, chap. 5.

2. The value premises upon which the plan is based or the goals which it is designed to achieve should be outlined as specifically as possible, and some attempt should be made to show how the major design elements of the plan relate to these goals. This may be the most difficult part to prepare, but it may also be the most rewarding in terms of achieving public acceptance. The very least that can be expected is evidence as to whether the plan envisages the development of a balanced community, fairly self-sufficient, with some specific features to give it an identity of its own, whether it is to be basically a residential community filled with residents who plan to work, shop, and recreate in surrounding areas, or whether it is to be primarily an industrial and commercial community with a minimum emphasis on the amenities demanded by upper-middle-class residents.

3. The "basic physical elements of the urban environment"—land use, circulation, and community facilities—constitute the body of the plan.[20]

"Land use" includes the delineation, in a general way, of the uses to which private land is to be put. It shows where people will live, work, shop, and seek recreation. The plan may go so far as to indicate general areas for single-family living, apartment living, major shopping areas, specialty shopping areas, heavy industry, and light warehousing. It does not, however, seek to identify these separate areas sharply enough that lines between them can be identified as boundaries separating independently owned land parcels.

"Circulation" relates to street and highway layout and the routes and stations to be used by mass-transit systems. The existing circulation system is shown in relation to new construction, street widening, and resurfacing contemplated.

"Community facilities" refers to the location of public facilities such as schools, parks, playgrounds, community centers, city halls, and other physical facilities planned for public use. This section of a plan may also include plans for future growth of electric, water, and gas utilities as well as for storm drainage and sanitary sewers.

OFFICIAL ADOPTION OF A MASTER PLAN

Under organizational forms and procedures in most American cities the general plan is prepared by professional planners working closely with a citizen planning commission. Decisions on policy matter required in the preparation stage are made by the Commission with the advice of the professional staff. The commission decides what should be included in the plan and how it will be presented in the form of a written document along with maps, tables, and charts, but ordinarily the commission does not have legal authority to adopt

[20] *Ibid.*, p. 18.

the plan as a guide for city development. The commission presents the finished product to the city council and recommends that it be adopted. It is common practice for the council to hold public hearing on the plan after it has been presented to them. At these hearings interested persons and groups are given an opportunity to express their approval or disapproval of the plan in general or of specific sections in particular.

After public hearings, the council may ask the commission to review certain parts of the plan in view of opinions expressed, or it may adopt or reject the plan. There is often misunderstanding as to the meaning attached to council action when it officially adopts or approves a master or general plan. Some interpret such an adoption as equivalent to zoning and assume that the areas of land use described in the plan are by its adoption legally zoned for the use indicated. This is not a correct interpretation of the use of a master plan. Although areas of land use are indicated on plan maps, they are to be construed as generalized statements without legal meaning as far as use of any specific land parcel is concerned. The proposals for land use are designed as guides to be used in preparing a comprehensive zoning ordinance which will legally control the specific use of all parcels of land covered by the plan.

Procedurally, what formal adoption of the plan means is that every proposal affecting the development of the city which comes before the council must be considered in relation to the approved plan. This is usually accomplished by requiring that before the council acts on such proposals they be transmitted to the planning department or commission for study and recommendation. Thus, new street construction, acquisition of park land, expansion of city buildings, or changes in zoning ordinances would be submitted to the planning agency, which would examine the proposal, determine if it conforms with the plan, and make specific recommendations to the council. The power to take effective action rests with the council, rather than with the planning agency, but recommendations from the agency carry a great deal of weight in most cities. Persons who agree to serve on planning commissions are often citizens with some prestige in the community, and they often have the confidence of the mass media. Council actions which do not conform with recommendations from the commission are interpreted to the public as politically motivated to please "selfish interests" rather than to protect the general interests of the public. Citizens who give their time to serve on these commissions are not likely to continue as members of such a commission if councils consistently reject their judgments on matters submitted to them.

MAKING PLANS EFFECTIVE

Emphasis has been placed on the broad general character of master plans and on the necessity for more specific action to make its goals effective. Many actions of the council affect the plan in a peripheral way but are not so directly related that they become matters for planning commission action. Speed limits, street parking restrictions, and health regulations may have some effects on developmental aspects of the city but they do not usually fall under the surveillance of the planning agency. Some of the most important and direct means by which elements of a master plan are implemented and which are matters of concern to the planning commission are (1) land-use zoning, (2) subdivision control, (3) public improvements, and (4) building and construction controls.

Land-use Zoning

In order to implement the land-use development provided for in a general way in the master plan, the council by ordinance creates zoning districts and designates the acceptable land use in each district. Since land developers are legally bound by the zoning ordinance, it must be very specific with respect to both the boundaries of each zoning district and the approved uses in each. The zoning ordinance applies to the development of privately owned land only; the use of municipally owned land is determined by the city's public improvement program. Historically, cities established zoning districts along a scale of intensity of land use; single-family residences constituted the least-intense use, and heavy industrial was considered the most intense use. Any use was permitted in a district which was not more intense than the use legally designated for the district; i.e., in a multifamily-use district, single-family residences were permitted, and in a commercial-use district, single-family and multifamily uses were also permitted. In recent years zoning ordinances have tended to prescribe a single use for a district and to prohibit any other use even though it is of less intensity.

Three basic land-use patterns are generally designated: (1) residential, (2) commercial, and (3) industrial. Within each of these three broad categories, subdivisions are usually defined. Although many variations exist, the following classes of land use are fairly common:

I. Residential
   A. Single family

     B. Two family
     C. Medium-density apartments
     D. High-density apartments (including high-rise)
 II. Commercial
     A. Service type, including office buildings, medical centers, barber and beauty shops, eating places, and banks
     B. Shopping centers
         1. Regional shopping centers
         2. Community shopping centers
         3. Neighborhood shopping centers
 III. Industrial
     A. Light industrial, as represented by warehousing and industrial parks
     B. Heavy industrial, including large manufacturing plants

Only large cities are likely to have areas including all these land uses; the use most often not found in small suburban cities is the industrial category.

Special Permits   Some types of land use present special problems relating to traffic congestion, noise, or sanitation and even though they fall within one of the classifications of the zoning ordinance, they are permitted only after an application for a special permit is approved. Automobile agencies, service stations, drive-in sandwich shops, taverns, and places of amusement often fall within the special-permit category. If, for example, an oil company wants to erect a service station within a commercially zoned district, it can do so only after a special permit has been issued. Application for a special permit may be made to the council or to the planning agency. If the request is made to the council, it must be referred to the planning agency for recommendation. The planning agency evaluates the impact of such use on traffic and related matters and makes its recommendation to the council. The council, after a public hearing, may deny the request or pass an ordinance granting the permit. Often such permits are granted only under clearly stated conditions. These conditions may include landscaping requirements, fencing, hours of operation, and traffic-flow patterns on parking lots.

The special-permit practice is praised by those who want to give city officials maximum control over the kind of establishments that will be permitted in the city. The practice is criticized by those who see in it a device through which city officials can exercise arbitrary control or even discriminate against certain developers. The basis for legal authority to judge certain specific applications for land use rather than rely on the general zoning classes to control such use is that certain kinds of uses present peculiar problems that are difficult to control by general ordinance. Although courts are willing to uphold the special-permit procedure in these cases, they will not hestitate to protect the landowner if evidence that the procedure is used to discriminate against him for reasons that bear no relation to legitimate land-use concerns is presented to them.

Changes in Zoning Ordinances   As reviews of the master plan of a city are made in due course and alterations are made, amendments to the comprehensive zoning ordinance will have to be made to reflect these changes. Requests for more specific changes, however, are received regularly by the council and the planning authority. The request may be simply to move the boundary separating two districts to enable a developer to increase the area he plans to develop. For example, an apartment developer may feel that a well-planned project requires more land than he owns in the properly zoned district; he therefore requests that adjoining land in the single-family area be rezoned so that he can develop the entire area. Other requests are made to change the zoning of a specific tract of land lying in the heart of a district to a different land use. A landowner may request that his holdings be rezoned from single-family to multifamily use without changing established zoning boundaries. This type of request is generally referred to as spot zoning. In most cities these requests for zoning changes can be acted upon by the council only after they have been submitted to the planning agency for recommendation and after a public hearing.

Variances   Strict application of zoning laws may produce a serious hardship for an individual landowner. The boundaries of districts may be drawn in such a way, because of special topographic problems, that his property is very difficult to develop economically if the provisions of the zoning code are rigidly adhered to. Most city charters or zoning ordinances provide for a board of zoning review or board of adjustment to which a landowner can appeal when he feels that he has a hardship case. If the board is convinced of the justice of the appeal, it issues a variance, which in effect alters the application of the zoning law to his property. The building commissioner is then instructed to grant a permit in conformance with the variance authorized. Appeals to the courts are open to those whose requests for variances have been denied.

Nonconforming Uses   When zoning ordinances are adopted, they always include in land-use districts areas that are already developed. In some cases the existing use of land does not conform to the use permitted in the ordinance. Zoning ordinances are not retroactive; therefore existing nonconforming uses are permitted to continue. The general rule is that a nonconforming use cannot expand the scope of its present operations, nor can it be changed to another nonconforming use, and abandonment of such use for a specified time ends the right to nonconform.[21]

Subdivision Controls

Most land development in modern cities is by developers who assemble large tracts of land and plan to develop them either as a residential area, a shopping center, or an industrial park. Even though the general land-use pattern contemplated conforms with the zoning ordinance, the developer is required to comply with regulations applying to subdivisions. Such regulations relate to width and construction of streets and walkways, sewer layout, easements for utilities, lot area for each building, yard areas, and the way buildings face in relation to streets. Subdividers are required to submit detailed plats of proposed subdivisions to the planning agency for review. When the planning agency is assured that the plat conforms to all facets of the ordinance, approval of the plat is forwarded to the council. An ordinance approving the subdivision is required before the developer can proceed. In very large developments the overall plans may be approved in general, but when actual work is ready to begin on a section of the total development, it must be presented in detail for review and approval.

Building and Construction Controls

Building construction is fairly rigidly controlled in cities with comprehensive land-use ordinances. These controls include the type of building construction permitted, the kind of electrical service permitted, and the nature of approved plumbing installations. Cities either write their own building, electrical, and plumbing codes, or they adopt by reference codes drafted by national associations. In order to develop some degree of uniformity within an urbanized areas, cities are often urged to adopt standard codes, and many of them do so.

The building commissioner is the administrative officer directly charged with responsibility for enforcing these construction codes. When a builder is ready to start construction, he submits detailed plans showing the location of the building on the lot, complete architectural drawings, and specifications, and asks for a building permit. Before issuing the permit, the building commissioner checks to see that the construction is within a properly zoned area

[21] Webster, *op. cit.*, pp. 404–412.

and that the plans comply with the building code in all respects. Separate permits are generally required for electrical and plumbing work. At regular times, as the construction progresses, inspectors from the building commissioner's office make on-the-spot checks to see that the actual construction conforms with plans upon which the permit was issued.

Occupancy Permits

A final check on land use is made before any new construction is occupied. Before newly constructed physical facilities can be used, an occupancy permit must be secured from the building commissioner's office. If, for example, a builder received a building permit for construction of a single-family home, whoever buys or rents the home must secure a permit to occupy it. This is to ensure that it will not be occupied by more than one family or by someone who wants to put it to a commercial use. The occupancy permit may be required each time that occupancy changes.

Control for Aesthetics

Many cities are seeking to extend land-use controls in order to beautify the city as well as to achieve other objectives. The method widely used is to create a board of architectural conformity or a design and review board and require that all plans for new construction be submitted to such a board for approval as to conformity with aesthetic standards. These boards, often composed of architects and engineers, review plans only in terms of their effects on the beauty of the community. They look at such matters as physical design, conformity with existing structures, and proposed landscaping. The extent to which city power can be used to force compliance with restrictions that are justified only by reason of aesthetics has never been established clearly by courts. Early cases tend not to include such restrictions within the police power, but more recent decisions have placed a broader interpretation on what can be covered by the concept of general welfare.[22] Even though there may be a legal question about the power of a city to control land for purposes of beauty, as a practical matter it can exercise considerable influence even without clear legal sanctions. Many builders and developers plan to confine their activities within a fairly narrow geographic range and therefore will be regularly dealing with the same control agencies. They have no desire to create

[22] See *State ex rel. Carter v. Hayes,* 182 Wis. 148 (1923), and *Berman v. Parker,* 348 U.S. 26 (1954).

unfriendly relations with the people to whom they must go for approval of subdivisions and building and occupancy permits. Furthermore, members of control boards are usually reasonable, and their recommendations may be welcomed by developers. In the exceptional case in which a builder feels that he is being forced to make substantial alterations solely for the sake of conformity, the courts are open to him and he can seek judicial relief.

PUBLIC IMPROVEMENTS

A major effort to guide the development of the city as a good place to live in can be made by the city itself through its duly constituted officers. The character of city office and court buildings, community centers, street design, and park system will to a great extent set a pattern for the character of private development that will be attracted to the city. Scarcity of land in urban areas is forcing city officials to move quickly to acquire sites for public use while they are still available at reasonable prices. Land-acquisition programs require long-range planning to develop need for public facilities and proper spatial distribution of these facilities. The element of a master plan that describes the kinds and locations of public-use facilities may be the most important part of the plan as far as the city voters are concerned.

Although the enumeration of public improvements contemplated and their projected locations are important parts of the public-improvements section of a master plan, the proposals designed to finance such facilities may be of even greater concern to the citizens. The plan itself will do little more than indicate a rough timetable for the acquisition of sites and the construction of facilities, but it may also suggest whether financing should be through general-obligation bonds, revenue bonds, or tax revenue on a pay-as-you-go basis.

Implementation of the public-improvements section will be through capital budgeting, which is primarily an administrative device. Capital budgets are generally developed for a five-year period to show expenditures that will result for the public-improvements program and the methods proposed to finance them. The expenditure required each year to fund these projects is included in the annual operating budget and used by the council to set annual tax rates.

METROPOLITAN-WIDE PLANNING

Planning as it has been described is based on the reasonable exercise of the police power by a recognized governmental authority, in this case the city. The problems of planning the development of a large metropolitan area are far more complex, since there is no single governmental unit that can exercise such power over the entire area. Each city can plan within its borders, and counties can plan for the development of unincorporated areas within the limits of the county, but no authoritative agency exists to plan for the entire area or even coordinate the individual plans drafted by local authorities. If the time ever comes when a single government is organized with metropolitan-wide jurisdiction, that government might well be delegated sole planning powers in the area. Until that time arrives, makeshift schemes will have to be used to seek some kind of overall order.

The kinds of planning likely to be tried under the present multiple-government structure may be described as functional rather than comprehensive. Such functional services as highways, sewers, control of air and water pollution, mass transit, and perhaps industrial development cannot be planned by 100 or more separate authorities; therefore quasigovernmental commissions have been created to prepare plans in one or more of these functional areas. In some cases state laws may provide some legal sanctions to support such commissions; in others, grants-in-aid from federal and state governments may be withheld until evidences of metropolitan-wide planning are present. The practical difficulty faced by semipublic commissions is that they must depend on consensus-type decisions, since they have little or no enforcement power. The withdrawal of some of the governmental units represented on the commission could very well destroy its effectiveness. Another problem in the creation of such commissions is the question of representation. In order to secure cooperation of individual cities, each demands equal representation, and as a result, a majority vote of the commission may represent a very small minority of the total population of the area.

The system of planning now found in metropolitan areas means that the least controversial issues, and therefore often the least important ones, are likely to be dealt with effectively. The parochial interests of representatives from the autonomous governments will block consensus when they feel their own small area will be affected adversely. Given the nature of politics in metropolitan areas today, one may predict that area-wide planning will most likely come from pressures brought to bear by the federal and state governments, rather than from initiative on the part of local city officials.

EVALUATION: THE POLITICS OF PLANNING

It is easy for one to study the legal basis, the organizational structure, and the methodology of planning and conclude that technical expertise is all that is required to produce ideal cities. The facts are that professionals cannot work in a politically neutral environment to produce master plans for city development. Decisions concerning land use are matters of dollars and cents to those who own land and those who want to develop it. At the same time such decisions determine the nature of the environment of residents who live near undeveloped land areas. Since the stakes are high, the pressures on decision makers are great. The legal authority for city officials to mark out specific land areas and control their use is clearly established, but many forces other than their own values determine how they will use this authority. Recommendations supported by reasoned arguments will be an important factor, but the play of political forces will produce significant adjustments in what appears to the politically isolated professional planner as the rational decision to be made.

Some planning commissioners and councilmen are closely associated in their business dealings with real estate men and land developers, and although they may not be directly pressured by representatives of these interests, they easily see and tend to be sympathetic with their point of view. Other decision makers are isolated from such interests and see more clearly the viewpoint of the individual landowner, and others are so committed to the value of accepting expert advice that they are willing to buck political forces and follow the recommendations of professionals.

A fact of life that weighs against development along politically determined lines is the play of economic forces in the land market. If the planning decisions are so unrealistic in terms of the market that no developer will risk capital to follow the plan, the land will lie idle. Suggestions will be made that almost any development is better than no development at all, and pressures will mount for changes in zoning. These pressures will be strengthened when some developer publicizes a specific scheme for developing the area which offers substantial increases in the tax base but does not conform to the master plan and existing zoning. Zorbaugh suggests:

> Whatever we think such evidence indicates, certainly it is apparent that city planning and zoning, which attempt to control the growth of the city, can only be economical and successful where they recognize the natural organization of the city, the natural groupings of the city's population, the natural processes of the city's growth. An ideal city is not likely to be the mold for a real city.[23]

[23] In George A. Theodorson (ed.), *Urban Ecology*, Harper & Row, Publishers, Incorporated, New York, 1961, p. 49.

One cannot escape the conclusion that decisions about land use are political decisions and that the nature of the process by which land-use decisions are made is not different from the way other issues are settled in the political arena. The pluralistic nature of the democratic process produces compromise decisions which take into consideration all the group interests involved and give to no single group complete dominance. Because of variables affecting land use that are not entirely clear to many citizens, the advice of professionals may play a more important role in planning and zoning decisions than is true in some other public conflicts, but the professionals will be effectively challenged when vital issues are at stake. It is probably true that planning decisions simply reveal the "power distribution in the community at that particular time," as Mowitz and Wright said was true in Detroit.[24] Recognition of the political nature of planning decisions accounts for the insistence of many students of local government that the planning authorities be in the mainstream of politics, not isolated in an autonomous body that is insulated from the influences that make pluralistic democracies viable. There is no question but that there is a growing tendency to make the planning function a part of the chief executive's responsibility by placing it within a regular administrative department.

[24] Robert J. Mowitz and Deil S. Wright, *Profile of a Metropolis, A Case Book,* Wayne State University Press, Detroit, 1962, p. 135.

BIBLIOGRAPHY

Books

Adrian, Charles R.: *Governing Urban America,* 2d ed., McGraw-Hill Book Company, New York, 1961, chap. 20.
Altshuler, Alan F.: *The City Planning Process: A Political Analysis,* Cornell University Press, Ithaca, N.Y., 1965.
Aschman, Frederick T., and Richard L. Nelson: *Real Estate and City Planning,* Prentice-Hall, Inc., Englewood Cliffs, N.J., 1957.
Banfield, Edward C., and James Q. Wilson: *City Politics,* Anchor Books, Doubleday & Company, Inc., Garden City, N.Y., 1963, chap. 14.
Black, Russell V.: *Planning for the Small American City,* Public Administrative Service, Chicago, 1944.
Chapin, F. Stuart: *Urban Land Use Planning,* Harper & Brothers, New York, 1957.
Delafons, John: *Land-use Controls in the United States,* Joint Center for Urban Studies of the Massachusetts Institute of Technology and Harvard University, Cambridge, 1962.

International City Managers Association: *Local Planning Administration*, 3d ed., Chicago, 1959.

Kent, T. J.: *The Urban General Plan*, Chandler Publishing Company, San Francisco, 1964.

Lauter, H. W.: *Subdivision Regulations*, Public Administration, Chicago, 1941.

Makielski, Stanislaw J., Jr.: *The Politics of Zoning*, Columbia University Press, New York, 1966.

Mumford, Lewis: *The City in History*, Harcourt, Brace & World, Inc., New York, 1961.

Spreiregen, Paul D.: *Urban Design: The Architect of Towns and Cities*, McGraw-Hill Book Company, New York, 1965.

Walker, Robert: *The Planning Function in Urban Government*, 2d ed., The University of Chicago Press, Chicago, 1950.

Webster, Donald H.: *Urban Planning and Municipal Public Policy*, Harper & Brothers, New York, 1958.

Articles

Blessing, Charles A.: "Perception in Planning," *Journal of the American Institute of Planners*, vol. 26, pp. 2–4, February, 1960.

Churchill, Henry S.: "Planning in a Free Society," *Journal of the American Institute of Planners*, vol. 20, pp. 189–191, autumn, 1954.

Meyerson, Martin: "How to Bring Planning and Policy Together," in Edward C. Banfield (ed.), *Urban Government: A Reader in Administration and Politics*, The Free Press, Glencoe, Ill., 1961, pp. 488–497.

Mitchell, Robert B.: "The New Frontier in Metropolitan Planning," *Journal of the American Institute of Planners*, vol. 27, pp. 169–175, August, 1961.

It is extremely difficult to discuss line activities of city governments in a general way. Although the total service activities in which American cities are involved are very similar, the manner in which these activities are grouped within administrative departments differs from one city to another, and there are considerable differences among cities in the degree of emphasis they give to each service area.

PUBLIC WORKS

Every city government engages in activities which involve construction, maintenance, and operation of physical facilities. Such activities may be considered together as public works. One requirement they have in common is that engineering competence is essential for top management people in the administration of such activities. Another significant characteristic of public works activities is that politically oriented groups like to have a voice in public works decisions because they offer extensive opportunities for political patronage. Probably the greatest number of nonprofessional city jobs are in the work crews required in public works activities. Perhaps even more important is the fact that such politically charged issues as the location of streets, bridges, airports, and other physical facilities, the methods of financing new construction, and public versus private construction are involved in public works decisions.

Streets and Public Ways

One of the most expensive activities in which cities engage is the construction and maintenance of public ways, including streets, bridges, tunnels, and other roadways for automobiles, buses, and trucks. As has been indicated earlier, the overall layout and location of the various kinds of roadways, from private residential streets to multilane throughways, is a physical planning function. Although public works administrators play a major role in this part of the total planning process, their chief concern is with the implementation of the circulation element of the general plan.

In a typical large city the roadways in the circulation system may be grouped into at least three broad classes based on the public agency which is responsible for their maintenance. Multilane, limited-access throughways are generally constructed and often maintained by the state, using state and federal funds. Certain major streets are important arteries for traffic from one part of the county to another, and the county may be the agency responsible for their construction and maintenance, even of those sections located within municipal corporations. Remaining city streets constitute a majority of the total mileage of roadways located in cities and are the responsibility of the cities themselves. Although some grant-in-aid money may be available to help construct such streets, management and maintenance are generally left to the city.

The portion of a state highway system that is within the limits of a city raises few issues that are resolved within the city's decision-making machinery. The issues that are raised produce significant local conflict, but since decisions are made elsewhere, the city government may be little more than another interest group seeking to influence state decision makers. Location of such highways and the number and location of entrance and exit points are likely to produce the most heated conflicts. Since final decisions on these matters rests with a state authority, access of competing groups at the state level may mean more than access to city hall. Each set of participants, however, is anxious to persuade high city officials to lobby for their cause, since the voice of city political leaders is not without influence at the state level.

Obviously, certain kinds of private interests are vitally concerned with the location of these throughways, and they use all the lobbying techniques available to press their point of view upon state officials. Homeowners fear the effect of traffic noise on their property values or the livability of their areas. Hotels, motels, theaters, and restaurants are often affected by the ease of access to these establishments from major highways; hence owners of these kinds of businesses seek to influence highway decisions. But cities as institutions also have a vital stake in the development of such traffic generators as a state highway. City officials who are trying to implement physical development plans know that the location of and access to such highways will affect many parts of their general plan. A new free bridge alongside a city toll span on which bonds are still outstanding is a case in point. City recreational centers which include a large stadium for baseball and football and smaller structures for indoor sports may be either advantaged or disadvantaged by the location of major trafficways in relation to them. In some cases proposed locations of such superhighways may intersect existing or proposed park land, and in such cases the city has a vital interest in the decision which determines final location.

Highways, often controlled by a county government, which are primarily used for interarea communication raise numerous political issues. Since superhighways have limited access and are often fenced to keep local traffic and pedestrians off the right-of-way, issues of local safety are not serious. The local throughways, however, without limits to their accessibility, present real problems to local decision makers. These problems relate to speed limits, parking controls, stop signs, and pedestrian crossings, particularly in school areas. The county engineer is interested in efficient movement of traffic over the wider county area; officials of small municipalities and school districts are primarily concerned with traffic within their own territorial boundaries. Demands for more stop signals and low speed limits made by local city officials conflict with the county's desire to use the streets in question to facilitate countywide traffic movement. These issues always elicit discussion about where legal power to control traffic resides and they produce the typical arguments about area-wide government versus government by numerous small cities.

Local streets which are used primarily to feed traffic from smaller communities into the major arterial trafficways are generally constructed and maintained by the cities in which they are located. Some degree of intercity cooperation is arranged on an informal basis to handle problems of maintenance on streets which constitute boundary lines between cities and those which carry fairly heavy traffic through two or more cities.

Construction, widening, and resurfacing of local streets are the responsibility of the municipalities in which they are located.[1] Larger cities may maintain street work crews and do much of their own construction work, but smaller cities award contracts to private individuals or companies for both street construction and maintenance. Although annual income in these cities is sufficient to finance routine repair and maintenance work, major construction costs usually must be met in some other manner. Conflicts arising over the method to be used in financing this construction work often are the most serious issues faced by small-city decision makers. One method is to sell general-obligation bonds and amortize them over a period of years from general property tax levies. If this method is used, all property in the city will share in the cost of the improvement, regardless of its location in relation to the site of the improvement. At the other extreme, the entire cost of the project can be assessed against the owners of property that abut the street which is being improved. The rationale for such assessments is that the market value of the adjoining property will be increased by the improvement; therefore those owning the abutting properties will receive the most benefit from the improvement. The kind of compromise often adopted is one that assesses part of the costs against adjoining property and part against all taxable property in the city. The proportion assessed against abutting property often depends on the extent to which the street is used for through traffic.

Two methods are generally available to cities which elect to assess all or part of the costs of public improvements against property most directly served by an improvement. One is to offer for sale special assessment bonds to be funded by a special tax levy against all property designated by ordinance as lying within the improvement district. The other is to issue special tax bills against property within the improvement district. The total amount to be raised by the tax bills is determined and then prorated among property owners, usually on a front-foot basis for streets and a square foot basis for sewers. These tax bills constitute obligations against the property owners affected, and they are issued to the contractor to pay him for his work. The bills are drawn so that they bear rather attractive rates of interest and can be paid over a fixed period of years. The contractor may keep the bills and receive payments as they come due, but the more common practice is to sell them to a finance company which specializes in this type of investment. These bills, if unpaid, become liens against the property involved, in the same manner as do delinquent taxes.

---

[1] For more information about street construction see International City Managers Association, *Municipal Public Works Administration,* 5th ed., Chicago, 1957, chap. 2; Harold F. Alderfer, *American Local Government and Administration,* The Macmillan Company, New York, 1956, pp. 546–552.

Since contractors may have to discount tax bills when they sell them, they often bid higher on construction work to be funded in this fashion. Many cities build up what they call a public improvement fund and then pay for construction work out of this fund. In these cases the city makes its own collection of the tax bills issued for improvements to replenish the improvement fund.

Street Lighting

Increasing crime rates in modern cities and the rapid change to night shopping have caused city officials to give greater attention to lighting plans.[2] Adequate lighting is now a general requirement before city approval is given to new shopping centers or major renewal programs. New technology in area lighting has made it necessary for cities to secure competent consultants in order to achieve maximum service at minimum cost. The chief political issues which arise with respect to lighting involve financing and method of installation and maintenance. Major installations involving large areas of the city require bond issues, which must be approved in popular elections. Long-range programs which call for improvement of small areas at a time can be financed out of general revenues on a year-to-year basis. Construction may be let to private contractors on the basis of competitive bids, or it may be contracted for with the electric utility company that serves the city. Considerable pressure is exerted by contractors' associations and labor unions to let construction work to independent contractors. Service contracts for general maintenance are usually made with the electric company, but in very large cities private electric contractors may bid on maintenance contracts and the electric utility company is paid only for current consumed.

Traffic Control

Traffic enforcement is a responsibility of the police department and the municipal courts after other city decision makers have devised traffic codes. Most large cities now employ traffic engineers to plan overall traffic patterns which are designed to move traffic expeditiously. The department in which the chief traffic officer is located may be authorized to issue traffic regulations which go into effect for a specified period of time without council approval. At the end of the trial period, these regulations may become a regular part of the code unless the council takes positive action to void them. Other cities require that recommendations from the traffic office go directly to the council,

[2] See International City Managers Association, *op. cit.*, chap. 4; Alderfer, *op. cit.*, pp. 552–553.

and a change in the traffic ordinance is necessary before the recommendations can be enforced.

Conflicts with respect to traffic controls arise because different groups seek to achieve different purposes through traffic regulations. Not all persons are equally motivated by the desire to move cars along the streets as fast as possible. For some, the protection of pedestrian movement takes first priority; for others, on-street parking is of first importance. Easy access from side streets into primary streets conflicts with free movement of traffic along these primary arteries, and the location of stop signs and traffic lights along these through streets becomes a matter of heated debate.

Many traffic experts are stressing the need to move people, rather than automobiles, in modern cities and are urging measures to give priority to buses over private cars in overall traffic codes. Measured in terms of numbers of persons transported, a good case can be made for traffic controls that encourage people to use mass-transit facilities, but the popularity of the private automobile is a force sufficiently effective in the political arena that traffic codes are likely to favor this kind of traffic. Vast expenditures for super-highways into the downtown areas, rather than for better mass-transit facilities, reflect the value and political strength of present commuters in our large cities.

Parking

If one asks a businessman, a city officer, or an ordinary citizen of a large city what the most urgent problem the city faces is, the answer is apt to be parking.[3] The intensity of the parking problems in older parts of the city has prompted the adoption of policies designed to prevent such problems in newly developed areas. Subdivision and building codes now establish parking requirements for each major kind of land use. Even in the absence of strict legal requirements, new commercial developers recognize the economic necessity for large parking areas around shopping centers.

The major problems are in areas which are already developed, where vacant land for parking is not available, and where demolition of existing structures is too expensive. In land clearance and urban renewal projects, plans for parking may be included, but new parking facilities may be necessary to prevent many areas from becoming blighted to the extent that they will require redevelopment. Increasing need for traffic relief has brought pressure to

[3] See Charles R. Adrian, Governing Urban America, 2d ed., McGraw-Hill Book Company, New York, 1961, pp. 427–429.

cease using the two outside lanes of streets as parking lots in order to keep them open to traffic. As "No parking" signs go up along more and more streets, increased demands for off-street parking facilities are made. Many cities are supplementing private parking facilities by constructing underground and high-rise parking garages. These facilities are financed by the sale of revenue bonds to be funded from fees charged for their use.

The use of perimeter parking areas around the major downtown shopping centers has been suggested as a means of relieving traffic congestion.[4] Pedestrian malls and shuttle bus service are planned for shoppers who use the new parking areas. Engineering and technical problems related to vehicle parking can be solved; the major conflicts arise because of personal preferences of vehicle users who insist on driving downtown and parking close to their work or their shopping destination, and the possible effects on business in areas not adequately served with adjacent parking areas.

Public Building Construction and Maintenance

All cities own and maintain some kind of public buildings. In small cities a city hall may be the only existing public facility, but in larger cities building construction and maintenance include large office buildings, city court buildings, auditoriums, convention centers and mart buildings, wharves and docks, and public markets.[5] The maintenance of such facilities may appear at first glance to be nothing more than a management problem to be handled as any big business takes care of its building-maintenance problems. To a certain extent this is true, but this type of work requires the employment of a large number of unskilled and semiskilled workers and, therefore, can be used very effectively by political party leaders as job patronage. Highly skilled and professional jobs in the public service are not particularly useful in building party strength, but building maintenance jobs can be filled by those living in the low-income wards, and party leaders want to be able to offer them in return for votes.

The policy adopted by a city relating to insurance of buildings against fire and storm damage often produces significant political conflict. Many suggest that a large city should not purchase insurance on its buildings since they are often scattered over a wide area and loss at any one time would constitute only a small percentage of total investment. Furthermore, the city through its

---

[4] See C. E. Stonier, "Metropolitan Traffic Crisis," *Traffic Quarterly*, vol. 11, pp. 214–231, April, 1957.

[5] See International City Managers Association, *op. cit.*, chap. 9.

bonding power can raise money to construct a new building and spread the cost over a long period. That is, a single fire or storm loss would not seriously disturb the city's financial position. There are, however, agents who are anxious to sell insurance contracts to cities, and they often have strong political contacts. Some cities have created insurance boards or commissions to make a study of insurance needs, and often a pool of companies is created to write the kinds of contracts recommended.

Sewers and Sewage Disposal

One of the most expensive construction projects facing cities is the construction of storm and sanitary sewers and sewage treatment plants.[6] Many cities took advantage of federal programs during the 1930s to complete expensive sewer installations. The designing and construction of sewer systems is an engineering job, and technology in this field is well developed. The problems faced by city officials are not primarily technical in nature, but instead are political. These problems relate to the cooperation of the numerous city governments that exist in a single watershed and which need to use the same watercourse to carry away liquid wastes, to the methods of financing construction, and to the kind of charges that can be assessed for upkeep and maintenance.

Some metropolitan areas have been able to provide area-wide sewer management even though efforts to consolidate other functional services have failed.[7] Where consolidation has not been achieved, cooperative arrangements have been made among cities to achieve some kind of unified sewer system. Original construction costs of main trunk sewers are often assessed against all property within the government jurisdiction, under the assumption that the system of main sewers serves all areas. Separate districts are then created to finance sewer lines which serve a small watershed, and assessments are made only against property owners in the district. Lateral sewer lines which serve individual homes are usually assessed directly against the property owners on a square foot basis.

Administrative costs and general maintenance can be financed either by a general property tax against all property at a uniform rate or by service charges against users. When service charges are made, they generally are

---

[6] *Ibid.*, chap. 6.

[7] The Metropolitan St. Louis Sewer District, which includes all of the City of St. Louis and most of the heavily populated areas of St. Louis County, is an example.

based on the quantity of water used by a property owner, under the assumption that all the water used by a customer finally finds its way into the sewer system. The latter method is particularly useful for cities which already levy their constitutional maximum tax rate to support other services. A combination of the two methods may also be used.

Cities try to extend their trunk sewers to creeks, rivers, lakes, or oceans and let these natural watercourses carry away the city's liquid wastes. Smaller cities, often because of their location, are required to construct lagoons into which their sewers empty. Increasing concern over water pollution in this country has focused attention on the need for sewage treatment plants. The purpose of these plants is to remove pollutants in sewage before it is turned into the main watercourse. The problem has interstate implications, since many of the streams into which sewage is dumped are under jurisdiction of the federal government; therefore Congress and federal administrative agencies have taken notice of the problem of water pollution. Some cities have been given notice by the federal government that they must provide acceptable treatment plants or cease using the navigable watercourse as a dumping ground.

The design and construction of sewage treatment plants, like that of most public works facilities, constitute an engineering problem; the political problems involve decisions as to methods of paying for the facilities and what government or combination of governments shall share in the project. Where an area-wide sewer authority exists, such an authority can plan, construct, and operate the required facilities and determine how the cost will be allocated. Where a number of cities operate their own sewer systems which reach a major river by connecting with the sewer system of another city, the problem is more complicated. Once the problem of allocating costs is solved, either revenue bonds to be funded by service charges or general-obligation bonds to be funded by property tax levies can be used to finance treatment plants.

Garbage and Rubbish Removal

Tons of solid wastes (garbage and rubbish) are found on the premises of private homes and business places in modern cities.[8] Private property owners cannot be expected on their own to dispose of these solid wastes; therefore cities are required to provide a collection service and to find ways of disposing of what is collected. Collection can be accomplished by a fleet of city-owned

[8] International City Managers Association, *op. cit.*, chap. 5.

trucks operated by city employees or by contracting with an entrepreneur who owns his own vehicles and employs his own crews. Smaller cities tend to contract with private sanitation companies, while large cities more often make this a regular city function.

Many small cities pay for collection by assessing service charges against home and apartment owners; they require commercial and industrial concerns to arrange for their collection and disposal. Larger cities usually support this service out of general tax revenues. The problem of solid-waste disposal is becoming more and more serious. Open dumping and burning are prohibited in most urban areas; therefore either sanitary landfills or specially designed incinerators must be used. Although both methods of disposal are technically satisfactory, cities are finding it politically difficult to secure a location for these facilities. Everyone recognizes the need for such facilities, but no one wants them located in the area in which they live. Some of the most heated public hearings that take place in city halls are those dealing with the location of a proposed incinerator. Often bonds for construction of such plants are defeated simply because residents fear the incinerator might be located in their residential areas.

Enforcement Activities

Not only are public works departments required to administer numerous functions performed by city governments; they are also charged with the responsibility of enforcing rules and regulations contained in zoning ordinances and building codes. One of the most important of these enforcement activities relates to the issuance of building permits and approval of subdivision construction.

If a builder seeks a permit to construct a single building on a platted lot, the procedure is very simple. He submits a set of working drawings for the building and a sketch showing the location of the building on the lot. The public works department, before issuing the permit, checks to see that the project conforms with zoning ordinances and construction codes.

After required permits are issued and actual construction begins, inspectors must make periodic on-the-spot checks to see that all phases of construction conform to the plans as approved. The job of the building commissioner is not finished when all construction is completed. City ordinances often contain what are referred to as performance requirements relating to noise, smoke, and odors that may result from operation of commercial and industrial facilities. Regular inspections must be made to check compliance, and special checks are necessary when specific complaints are received. In cases of flagrant violations, the commissioner may take steps to either secure compliance or close the operations.

Most large cities have ordinances regulating rooming house operations and requiring certain standards of maintenance for rental property. The inspections required to check for noncompliance and the legal steps to secure compliance often fall to the building commissioner's office. When structures are judged to be health hazards, legal steps must be initiated to have them condemned and either rebuilt or torn down. Although these enforcement activities seem to be purely ministerial in nature, not requiring a great amount of discretion, in practice they present many difficulties. Altering existing uses or condemning property forces the evacuation of families which are able to pay only small rents, and they may be unable to secure housing elsewhere. In fact, one of the most politically sensitive offices in the administrative branch of the city is the one which is responsible for these enforcement functions.

Airport Facilities

The importance of air travel to the economic life of American cities has forced city governments to go into the airport business.[9] As larger planes are placed into service, longer runways are required and more land is needed to meet these requirements. One of the most pressing problems cities face in their attempt to meet demands for improved airport facilities is that of location. Pressure to keep air terminals close to the downtown areas comes from those interests which are keyed to the maintenance of the central city as the heart of the economic and recreational life of the urban area. But lack of adequate space, problems of noise, and safety considerations tend to force cities to seek locations away from congested areas, particularly those with tall buildings. This means, in many cases, that the city must either extend its boundaries by annexation or operate airport facilities outside its limits. Some cities have found little difficulty in annexing areas needed for this purpose, but others have been forced to purchase land outside their boundaries and occupy it very much as a private owner would. This means that the city is without police power in the airport area and that its regular fire protection does not extend to facilities on airport land. Problems of location have led many who are vitally interested in the development of air travel to suggest that terminal facilities in large urban centers should be handled by a county

[9] *Ibid.*, chap. 8.

government or a metropolitan-wide airport authority, rather than by a core city. The New York Port Authority has been given responsibility for management of major airports in the New York area.[10]

The problem of distance from downtown facilities may be solved in part by strategic location of helicopter landing places, by superhighways from airport to central district areas, or by monorail systems. The dispersion of authority among dozens of autonomous governmental agencies in metropolitan areas makes planning for adequate terminals, travel between terminals, and travel from terminals to activity centers extremely difficult.

Large cities usually operate airports independently of other regular services. Instead of placing airport management in a department of public works, a semi-independent airport commission is created to perform the management function. Airport financing is not a regular part of the city's general revenue budget. Construction is generally financed by revenue bonds together with grants from the state and federal governments. Funds for bond retirement and for operating expenses are derived from revenue produced by airport facilities. Airlines lease space under a contract with the airport commission, and these leases produce a major part of total operating revenues. Facilities are also rented to flight training schools, maintenance shops, and in some cases airplane manufacturing plants. Location of major airports outside the central business area has resulted in severe parking problems around main terminals. Parking lots and multilevel garages are being constructed to meet these needs, and parking fees from such facilities add to total airport revenue.

PUBLIC UTILITIES

No sharp line can be drawn to separate public works from public utilities. In general, one may class as public works those activities which are almost universally publicly owned and operated, and as public utilities those activities which are public services but are very often owned and operated by private corporations on a profit basis. Perhaps the best way is to simply enumerate the service activities that are generally considered to be public utilities: electric light and power generation and distribution, natural gas storage and distribution, water purification and distribution, mass transit by bus or rail,

[10] For a discussion of the politics involved in this transfer, see Herbert Kaufman, "Gotham in the Air Age," in Harold Stein (ed.), *Public Administration and Policy Development, A Case Book,* Harcourt, Brace and Company, New York, 1952, pp. 145–197.

telephone service, and steam generation and distribution. These differ from purely private business because they are basic service needs and are generally available to the user from a single source. Food distribution is a basic public service but, because of the nature of the business, the shopper can select from a number of sources available to him. The assumption is that as far as price is concerned the consumer is protected by the free play of competition. Such is not the case with the services just listed. Only one source of electricity, natural gas, water, telephone, or public transit is available to the consumer, and he is forced to pay the schedule of rates charged by the single supplier.

Because of the distinctive nature of public utilities, governments have considered that they are "so affected with the public interest" that their operations should be controlled by law. The alternative to private ownership under governmental regulation is public ownership and operation. American commitment to private enterprise economy has been a major factor operating to slow down attempts of cities to operate public utilities as public works projects. Proponents of public ownership maintain that certain economies can be realized under government ownership that are not possible under private ownership. In the first place, no profit margin would be expected under public ownership. In the second place, since interest on city bonds is not subject to federal income tax, they will bear lower rates than private corporations would have to pay for financing. Taxes on corporate income applicable to private utility companies could be saved, since such income taxes do not apply to governmental income. The assumption is that these economies could be passed on to consumers in the form of reduced rates. Opposing arguments are well known. The general belief is that private business is more efficient than publicly managed businesses, and therefore, any economies inherent in public ownership would be wiped out by inefficient management. Government operation is so tied up with politics that public utilities would be used as bases for party patronage by the party in power. It is difficult to assess the strength of these opposing arguments, since they are based on generalizations that do not hold up in all cases. Although some cities may be able to sell bonds at lower rates of interest than can private utility companies, the credit rating of other cities may be so bad that buyers will require unusually high rates. Not all city utility operations are grossly inefficient, nor are all private companies equally efficient. Judgments about economy and efficiency will have to be made in individual cases when the issue of public versus private ownership arises. It is quite possible that philosophic attitudes about the proper role of government will be more important than issues of relative economy in deciding the issue.

Another set of considerations may very well decide the future trend with respect to some types of utility services. As long as private ownership is maintained, service charges will be set at levels high enough to meet operating costs and provide a margin of profit on investment. The city may, however, desire to increase public use of utilities to achieve other goals. Public transit service is a case in point. If a city wants to make a concerted effort to relieve traffic on city streets and to reduce strain on downtown parking facilities, one means available is to make public transit so attractive that many persons will foresake their cars and use public transit vehicles. Experience indicates that economic pressures force private utilities to raise rates, reduce the number of runs, and take routes out of service when they do not pay their way. All these actions tend to put more private cars on the streets and further complicate the traffic and parking problem. Public ownership would permit management decisions designed to achieve ends other than that of making the service financially self-sufficient. A city government may rationally decide that a transit system loss of a million dollars annually could be offset by savings achieved from decreased automobile traffic and reduced pressure for parking facilities in the downtown area. Opposition to public ownership based on the myth of public inefficiency may be met by transferring operational management, under contract, to a private management company.

Public Regulation of Utilities

The principle is now well established that private corporations which supply utility-type services will be subject to government control and regulation. The political issues that arise are concerned with (1) what governmental agency will exercise control and (2) the nature and severity of regulation. When regulation first became a common practice, cities in which utilities were permitted to operate regulated their activities. In recent times regulation has tended to be shifted to the state and in some matters to the federal government. If a utility service were supplied by a private corporation with home offices, generation plants, and distribution facilities wholly within a single city, regulation by the city would be simple enough. Most modern utility corporations, however, operate on an intercity or interstate basis, and cities find it difficult to exercise effective controls under existing legal systems. If regulation is made a state function, cities become interested parties, appearing before state commissions to influence the kind of decisions made. Regardless of where the regulatory function is located, the kinds of issues are pretty much the same.

Rate Regulation   Since public utility companies operate as monopolies in their service areas, consumers cannot depend on competition to hold rates to reasonable levels; therefore, approval of rate schedules is an important part of the regulatory function. The principle on which rate regulation rests is fairly simple, and it produces little conflict. Utility rates should be set at levels which will permit the company a "reasonable rate of return" on the "value of capital used in rendering the service." Regulatory laws and ordinances do not usually freeze a specific rate of return in the law; they delegate to the administrative agency charged with enforcement of the law the power to determine what is a reasonable rate of return under changing market conditions. Usually the rate set by a regulatory commission remains relatively stable even though interest rates and profit margins of nonutility companies fluctuate widely. Rates of return permitted by various commissions vary from place to place, but 6 percent is about average.

Conflicts may develop over rate schedules even though total income and profits of the company will not be affected. The changes may simply alter the manner in which total utility costs are shared by different classes of users. If schedules increase the rates of large commercial and industrial users and lower rates to homeowners, opposing sides are easy to identify. But often changes fall the other way. In order for an electric utility to make electricity compete favorably with natural gas as an industrial fuel, very attractive rates must be offered to get plants to install electric furnaces in new construction or to convert old installations. Any losses sustained during the conversion period may be made up by nonindustrial users. The relative charges among different classes of users may produce greater conflicts than does a request for a small change in the total income to the company.

Regulations to Ensure Safety   Many utility operations, by their nature, involve questions of public safety. High-voltage electric lines and gas mains constitute safety hazards unless adequate precautions are taken. One purpose of public regulation is to develop adequate safety standards for utility operation and to exercise sufficient supervision to ensure compliance with these standards. Standards of safety for old established service systems have been worked out and tested by years of experience, but reevaluation is required as new techniques are developed. For example, the application of atomic energy to generate electricity poses new problems of safety; the public will accept such change only under the assumption that some government authority will have sufficient know-how and power to deny change until adequate safety precautions are assured.

Regulation of Service   Since the public is dependent on a single source for utility services, regulatory agencies are usually empowered to require that a utility be willing to serve all customers within a given area and be capable of supplying the total requirements of area customers. Homeowners, hospitals, and business places have become so dependent on electricity, for example, that interruption of the flow of adequate current when demands are made can result in catastrophe. One of the most serious conflicts that arises over regulation of service levels relates to public transportation systems. The regulatory agency is placed in the position of mediator between extreme demands of the public for bus service every five minutes and company insistence on adjusting service in terms of economic demands.

Quality of Regulation

The theory that government as the representative of the interests of the consuming public has a responsibility to exercise some control over the rates, safety, and service levels of utility companies which supply essential services on a monopoly basis is not contested by either the companies involved or consumer spokesmen. But issues have arisen over the quality of regulation that has resulted from existing public service or public utility commissions. Some observers have complained that members of regulatory commissions become so closely involved with company personnel and so aware of the problems involved in operating a large utility company that their decisions more nearly reflect the interests of the company than those of the consuming public. Senator Paul H. Douglas of Illinois commented that there is a

> ... tendency of independent regulatory agencies to surrender their regulatory zeal as they age, and to become more and more the protagonist of a clientele industry, and less and less the vigilant defenders of the welfare of the consumers or the general public. All too often, those who are supposedly being regulated, actually regulate their nominal regulators.[11]

Commission members are often appointed for long terms of office, and their reappointment is not directly related to public approval or disapproval. Companies, on the other hand, claim that decisions of regulatory commissions are arbitrary and unreasonable, and they often ask the courts to intervene in their behalf.

[11] Paul H. Douglas, "Improvement of Ethical Standards in the Federal Government," *Annals of the American Academy of Political and Social Science*, vol. 280, p. 154, March, 1952.

City officials, reflecting attitudes of their constituents, are often strong critics of regulatory practices of state commissions. Since state governments have generally assumed the regulatory function, the power of cities to control rates and service levels has been relatively ineffective. The best that cities can do is to appear as a complaining party before the commission and present their case. The complaint is often made that members of regulatory commissions are residents of outstate areas and are, therefore, unfamiliar with the relations between utility management and the major public users of their products in the large cities.

Utility Franchises

The one control tool retained by most cities is the right to grant or withhold a utility franchise. The franchise is essentially a right or license for a utility to do business in the city.[12] The right to operate in the city usually means that no competitor will be permitted to operate in the same area, and it usually includes the right to use city property for service facilities and in some cases the right to use eminent domain to take private property which is required to provide adequate service. Although franchises are awarded for fairly long periods (often twenty years), they do run out and the company is dependent upon the city for a renewal. In many states, long-term franchises must be approved by a popular vote; therefore public satisfaction is of concern to utility management.

Probably of more direct concern to the private utility company is the fact that a city can, if it chooses, decide to own and operate its own utility system. As long as service furnished by a private company is satisfactory, public support for government operation is hard to get, but if dissatisfaction becomes widespread, voters can be persuaded to desert their natural affinity for private enterprise and accept city ownership.

ORGANIZATION FOR PUBLIC WORKS AND PUBLIC UTILITIES

No single model can present a picture of typical organizational structure for administering these functions. A truly integrated plan would provide for a single department of public works and utilities, with a single director appointed by the mayor or city manager. Major divisions within the department

[12] See John Bauer, *The Public Utility Franchise*, Public Administration Service, Chicago, 1948.

would reflect the separate functions just discussed.[13] These could include (1) division of streets, to handle street construction and maintenance, street lighting, traffic control, and parking facilities; (2) division of building construction and maintenance, to handle construction and maintenance of city-owned properties, to grant subdivision and building permits to private developers and occupancy permits to users of property, and to make inspections of boarding house; (3) division of sewers, to construct and maintain sewer lines and disposal facilities; (4) division of garbage and rubbish removal, responsible for collection of garbage and refuse and for all disposal facilities or for letting contracts for this work to sanitary companies and for supervising their performance; (5) division of motor pool and garage, to handle the purchase and management of all motor equipment for all city departments; and (6) division of airport management, to operate city air terminals. If no public utilities are owned and operated by the city, an additional department could handle problems of franchising and inspecting private utility operations.

Each public utility function which a city undertakes to operate is likely to be set up in the organizational structure as a semiautonomous operation; i.e., the water system will be operated separately from the electric power and light system and the gas distribution system. Each utility function is generally expected to pay its own way by setting service charges sufficiently high to meet operating costs. Each of these operating functions is likely to have a citizen board to determine questions of policy, and a full-time director to handle day-to-day management functions. Each utility function generally enjoys financial independence, i.e., it accounts for its own revenues, authorizes its own expenditures, and often contracts its own debts. The regular accounting controls of the city may apply to utility operations, but utilities often arrange for an annual audit by outside firms. Some utility operations are permitted to carry over surplus funds from year to year, but in many cities surpluses revert to the general revenue fund.

As officials and citizens of complex metropolitan areas become aware of the problems of handling public works and utility-type functions on an individual city basis, demands for area-wide machinery will increase. Sewer systems and treatment plants, mass-transit facilities, and airports have already been transferred to area-wide authorities in many metropolitan areas, and major streets and traffic control will probably follow the same pattern soon. Every indication is that federal agencies, through their grant-in-aid programs, intend to force an intensification of the trend to area-wide administration.

[13] See Thomas H. Reed, *Municipal Management,* McGraw-Hill Book Company, New York, 1941, pp. 557–567.

BIBLIOGRAPHY

Books

Adrian, Charles R.: *Governing Urban America*, 2d ed., McGraw-Hill Book Company, New York, 1961, chap. 18.

American Public Works Association: *Public Works for the Future: A Report on Research Needs and the Transfer of Knowledge*, Chicago, 1963.

———: *Street and Urban Road Maintenance*, Chicago, 1963.

Bauer, John: *Transferring Public Utility Regulation*, Harper & Brothers, New York, 1955.

———: *The Public Utility Franchise: Its Functions and Terms under State Regulation*, Public Administration Service, Chicago, 1948.

Burger, Robert D.: *Solid Wastes Research Needs*, American Public Works Association, Chicago, 1962.

Caywood, Russell E.: *Electric Utility Rate Economics*, McGraw-Hill Book Company, New York, 1957.

International City Managers Association: *Municipal Public Works Administration*, 5th ed., Chicago, 1957.

Ostrom, Vincent: *Water and Politics*, Haynes Foundation, Los Angeles, 1956.

Owen, Wilfred: *The Metropolitan Transportation Problem*, The Brookings Institution, Washington, 1956.

Phillips, Charles F., Jr., and Richard D. Irwin: *The Economics of Regulation*, Irwin, Inc., Homewood, Ill., 1965.

Public Administration Service: *Better Transportation for Your City*, Chicago, 1958.

Reed, T. H.: *Municipal Management*, McGraw-Hill Book Company, New York, 1941, chaps. 23, 24.

Seburn, Thomas J., and Bernard L. Marsh: *Urban Transportation Administration*, Yale University Press, New Haven, Conn., 1959.

Van Scoyoc, Melwood W.: *Factors in Determining Municipal Utility Rates*, Municipal Finance Officers Association, Chicago, 1965.

Welch, Francis X.: *Cases and Text on Public Utility Regulation*, Public Utilities Reports, Inc., Washington, 1961.

Articles

Bauer, John: "The Crisis in Urban Transit," *Public Management*, vol. 34, pp. 176–178, August, 1952.

Burns, James M.: "The Crazy Politics of Fluorine," *New Republic*, vol. 128, pp. 14–15, July 13, 1953.

Moynihan, Daniel P.: "New Roads and Urban Chaos," *The Reporter*, vol. 24, pp. 13–20, Mar. 30, 1961.

Simpson, H. S.: "Mass Transit Can Be Saved," *Public Management*, vol. 35, pp. 77–81, April, 1953.

Stonier, C. E.: "Metropolitan Traffic Crisis," *Traffic Quarterly*, vol. 11, pp. 214–231, April, 1957.

PUBLIC HEALTH, WELFARE, AND HOUSING

The nature of interrelationships along public health, welfare, and recreation justifies their treatment together, since emphasis is to be placed on conflicts that arise in their performance rather than on professional and technical aspects involved in their administration. Certainly many welfare cases are linked directly to health problems of family members, and, conversely, physical and mental health problems are related to inadequate diets and lack of medical attention. A joint approach to case work which recognizes these relationships and combines the skills of the welfare worker and the public health nurse, for example, seems to make sense. In many cities those who are served by public health and welfare departments occupy the poorest housing facilities in the city, and the problem of better housing may have to be solved before substantial improvements in health can be achieved.

Many of the arguments that have been used to justify keeping schools out of politics are used with equal force to secure political independence for public health and welfare services. Professionals working in these areas often complain that their effectiveness is impaired by political involvements. Welfare activities have in the past been undertaken on a fairly large scale by political party organizations, and complete separation of welfare from party involvement has not been easy. From the party point of view, aid to those in need constituted a direct link between the party leadership and the voter, and many local party leaders built their position of strength in the very-low-income wards by selective dispensing of welfare. As governments assumed the welfare function, party leaders sought to establish control over its administration, just as they had when their efforts were dependent on private resources. From the point of view of welfare recipients, they were not too unhappy with the kind of personal relations they had with party representatives. They received a certain amount of aid, with few questions asked; they paid off in terms of votes at election time, and party leaders expected no more.[1]

The bureaucratization of public health and welfare has replaced the local party functionary with the professional social worker and the public health nurse. Their goals and values are quite different, and an entirely new set of relationships between the dispenser of assistance and the recipient has developed. More questions are asked before assistance is given, more checks are made on how such assistance is used, and changes in life styles are often demanded. Few believe that the massive programs now financed by state and local health and welfare departments could ever again be handled on a private basis, but the political observer cannot overlook the impact the change has had on local party organization and the relations between local party workers and the voters in the poorer areas of large American cities.

There can be no question but that the professional health and welfare workers have won the battle for independence. Although the departments that administer these functions are generally parts of the regular administrative structure of the city government, rather than independent governmental units as are school districts, they operate with more freedom from internal city political struggles than do other departments. This is partly because of the dependence of local health and welfare activities on federal grants-in-aid. Federal restrictions on aid in health and welfare are particularly stringent and designed to prevent any political party from controlling expenditures in such a way as to build up its local political power. The nature of these restrictions has operated to strengthen the position of the professional vis-à-vis the layman and the politician. Health and welfare administrators as well as field workers must be selected under a merit system which places a high premium on special formal training and experience and devalues past and present political activity.[2] It would have to be a strong mayor indeed who could make

[1] For a colorful description of activities of machine leaders, see William L. Riordan, *Plunkitt of Tammany Hall*, Alfred A. Knopf, Inc., New York, pp. 33–38.
[2] See Clifford H. Greve and Josephine Campbell, *Organizing and Staffing for Full-time Health Services*, U.S. Public Health Service, Washington, 1957.

any great changes in the pattern of health and welfare activities in his city. Although legally he might cut from the local budget the city's share of the costs of such services, the threat of loss of federal aid would produce pressures which few mayors could withstand. In fact, issues related to health and welfare seldom are raised in city political campaigns, and the major conflict issues which arise in the administration of these services are fought out among the professionals. Often the nonprofessionals become involved simply because each side seeks outside support for its position.

Housing, particularly public housing, has remained a more active issue in the general political arena than have health and welfare. In general, governmental activities in the health and welfare field at the local level have posed no serious threat to organized groups able to throw their weight around in the political arena. It is true that public welfare was a threat to local party functionaries in some city areas, but other segments of party leadership were quite willing to see these leaders dethroned. Public housing, on the other hand, not only runs counter to the traditions of most private economy—minded Americans but poses a direct threat to property owners, particularly those engaged in the rental business. There is no powerful professional group or association to support public housing, as there is with health and welfare to lobby for its independence from the forces of politics.[3]

One faces a major difficulty in organizing a discussion about public health, welfare, and housing as city or local functions, since what local units of government do in these areas is intertwined with activities of the national and state governments. A case could be made for the assumption that much of the city's health, welfare, and housing work has been initiated in Washington and a large share of it financed out of national revenues. Although some states take a very active role in these service areas, others do little more than is necessary to qualify for federal aid, and delegate actual administration to local governments.

PUBLIC HEALTH

In general, matters of health have become public functions not because the condition of the health of individuals was of public concern but rather because certain kinds of ill health among some individuals create a threat to the health of others. Quarantine laws, which confined families to their own homes when one member was diseased, and public contagious disease centers were de-

[3] See Martin Meyerson and Edward C. Banfield, *Politics Planning and the Public Interest*, The Free Press, Glencoe, Ill., 1955, particularly chap. 4.

signed to protect the healthy more than they were to heal the sick. Confinement centers for the mentally disturbed were often called lunatic or insane asylums, and their chief function was to confine dangerous patients rather than to treat their mental illness.

Changes in public health services have resulted from breakthroughs in medical science and from a revolution in the public attitude with regard to the public obligation to render assistance to the members of society that desperately need help. Probably the discovery of methods of immunization against the more serious germ and virus diseases has done as much as any single scientific achievement to mark out the direction of public health efforts. When it became possible to stamp out smallpox, diphtheria, and poliomyelitis, it was not difficult to secure sufficient public support for either compulsory or extensive free immunization programs. As more effective means of treating mental illness are developed, the philosophy of the detention house or asylum is likely to be replaced by a positive program of outpatient treatment to make institutional detention less necessary.

Discovery of animal carriers of disease has led to entirely new public health programs designed to eliminate mosquitoes, rats, and other known disease carriers. Likewise, recent research that links water pollution, cigarette smoking, and air pollution to specific human illnesses will most certainly spark new advances in public health efforts.

Changes in philosophy are probably just as significant in the development of public health programs as are scientific advances. The older idea that aid to the sick was the responsibility of the family, church, or private association has been replaced by an ethos that regards individual health as a matter of concern of the whole society. The well-being of a community is dependent on the health of its individual members, and therefore, public health expenditures may be viewed as justifiable public expenditures. But the humane element in modern health philosophy must not be overlooked. Although this is not universally true, more and more citizens are becoming sensitive to the physical and mental suffering of their fellow citizens and are more willing to discharge what they feel is a personal obligation by supporting governmental health programs.

Public Health Functions

If one is to get a general image of the multitude of services carried on by governments under the rubric of public health, some classification scheme is necessary. The following categories, which include most of the activities of a large city health department, are adaptations of recommendations of the American Public Health Association.[4]

Collection and Maintenance of Vital Statistics   This may be administered centrally by a state health agency or by local city or county departments. Essentially the governmental unit involved in record keeping requires reports of birth, deaths (along with causes), and of certain kinds of diseases. Not only are these records useful for legal purposes, but they supply an essential source in studying incidence of certain kinds of diseases, the kinds of persons most often involved, and the cyclical character of the diseases.

Communicable-Disease Control   Some of the most serious diseases that have afflicted human beings have been practically eliminated through the application of discoveries in the field of medical science to enlightened public health work. Through the control of carriers of disease, immunization, and early detection procedures, such diseases as typhus, typhoid fever, smallpox, diphtheria, and poliomyelitis have been practically eliminated from our cities. Tuberculosis has been checked by diagnostic roentgenograms, clinical treatment, and special hospitals. Attempts to put knowledge now available to work to eradicate venereal disease are being made throughout the country, but social connotations connected with the venereal diseases make them much more difficult to conquer.

Environmental and Community Sanitation   A host of activities may be covered under this class title. Activities designed to assure safe food and water supplies include dairy and milk inspection and pasteurization requirements, regular testing of water supplies, health inspections for food processors and handlers, inspection and rating of public eating places, and inspection of meats and other foods which are known to be possible disease carriers. Programs to detect and destroy rabies-carrying animals, mosquitoes, and rats are regular parts of most city health department activities. Certain kinds of industrial controls may also be included in this category. Factories and mines where there are dangers from noxious fumes and dust particles in the air are required to provide minimum conditions to ensure the health of their workers, and health departments make regular inspections to check compliance with standards.

Present-day efforts to reduce air and water pollution are examples of problems faced by public health officers in their efforts to control health hazards when the control processes require costly alterations in existing industrial

---

[4] See "Local Health Department, Services and Responsibilities," *American Journal of Public Health,* vol. 41, pp. 302–307, March, 1951. This is the official statement of the American Public Health Association adopted Nov. 1, 1950.

equipment. Health hazards which result from air pollution caused by emissions from motor vehicles and industrial smoke stacks are well known, but political action required to reduce pollution to safe levels is difficult to achieve. In many cases local coal resources cannot be used because of their high sulphur content, or expensive new installations will be required in industrial plants. Therefore, control measures become matters of political conflict, with very influential forces lined up against solutions proposed by professional public health officers. The difficulty is compounded in the typical metropolitan area because of the multiplicity of political jurisdictions. Elected officials in the political entity in which large industrial complexes are located hesitate to place what they consider undue burdens on their industries, and surrounding areas affected by pollution are without legal authority to attack the problem. This may be a political issue with enough intensity of conflict to generate popular support for the creation of a single political authority large enough to cope with the problem, just as administration of sewers has been centralized in some metropolitan areas.

Health Research and Laboratory Facilities   Many of the larger public health departments are recognizing a responsibility to conduct research into major health problems. Some of these which are located near university centers enter into cooperative arrangements for joint research efforts into public health problems. Since laboratory facilities must be maintained for operational purposes, they can also become effective research institutions. Public health laboratories serve doctors and other governmental agencies by making a wide variety of tests. Some tests are made on a regularly scheduled basis; e.g., tests of the city's milk supply and the public water supply. Other tests are made on request; e.g., tests of animals for rabies, tests of samples submitted by physicians to determine if certain diseases are present, and tests of citizens for TB, diabetes, and other diseases. Many of these testing programs are carried on in cooperation with public school districts.

Family Health Services   Many health departments have a public health nursing program with visiting nurses who make regular visits to families that are unable to provide medical care through regular private sources. In conjunction with the nursing service, health care centers are located in the areas of greatest need, where physicians from the public health service or volunteers from the ranks of private practitioners provide medical service to low-income families. Often these services are concentrated in the fields of maternal and child welfare.

Hospitals   Most large cities maintain at least one public hospital. Although these institutions are maintained primarily to render hospital services to persons in financial need, they often accept patients on a paying basis, with charges based on ability to pay. These hospitals maintain emergency services for persons brought in by police who have been injured in wrecks, fires, and other kinds of accidents. Either the police department or the health department maintains emergency ambulance service to transport injured persons to the city hospitals.

Health Education   Preventive medicine places great emphasis on health education designed to inform people of ways to prevent disease and to encourage regular tests to discover trouble while it is in a treatable stage. Much of the health education program is arranged with school districts, but attempts are made to reach adults through all available means. Special programs are usually designed to check the spread of venereal disease, to encourage regular checks for TB and cancer, and to change the public attitude toward mental illness.

The Politics of Public Health

Since much public health work is technical in character and requires the skills of qualified professionals, one might assume that political conflict is reduced to a minimum in this area. But closer observation of the activities of top administrators in these departments will reveal that they are faced with hard decisions, and they are required to enter the political arena to fight for both moral and financial support for their programs. Few departments can depend on special earmarked taxes to support their efforts; therefore the head of the health department must enter the regular budget process and compete with all other spending agencies for a share of available revenues. Within the department, professionals have strong opinions about what efforts should be given priority and how departmental resources should be allocated. Decisions on these matters are political in character, and some means must be established to make them and still maintain unity among the competing program directors. To add to the difficulty in making such decisions, the directors of various programs often have citizen committees and clientele groups to support their particular demands for resources.

Aside from the types of internal conflicts that are common to all departments, some public health issues precipitate fairly intense public conflict. Mention has already been made of the conflicts inherent in attempts to curb air pollution. The problem of water pollution presents similar controversies. Proposals by health officials to fluoridate the public water supply have produced some of the hottest political conflicts some cities have seen for years.

Attempts to introduce programs of sex education into public schools in order to control the spread of veneral disease have often been met with strong and well-organized resistance. Inherent in all public health programs is the issue generally raised as "socialized medicine." Attempts of health departments to supply medical care to any except those clearly unable to pay for it are apt to meet resistance from medical societies, which have developed very effective techniques of influencing legislators.

Organization of Health Departments

The United States Public Health Service classifies the units of government which provide local health services as follows:[5]

1. *Single County Units.*   These county units serve the unincorporated areas of the county and municipalities which have no health department of their own.
2. *City Health Departments.*   These exist in the larger cities and serve the area within the incorporated limits. Where city and county boundaries are coterminous, the city department serves as the county unit as well.
3. *Local Health Districts.*   In areas of sparse population, a special health district may be formed to serve two or more counties.
4. *State Health Units.*   The state department may render certain kinds of health services directly, e.g., mental care in local care centers and specialized hospital care. But in most cases the state provides supervisory and advisory services to local health agencies.

No standard organizational pattern exists for all local health departments. The public health function may be performed by a division of a larger department of public health and welfare, but more often it will be performed by a separate department. A director of public health is generally the chief executive officer, and he is quite often required to be a medical doctor, often with special training and experience in public health work. This position may be a tenure one, covered within the city's merit system. Departments are usually subdivided along functional lines, with a division chief over each division. The functions discussed above are indicative of the kind of divisions likely to be found in a city health department.

Attached to many health departments is a lay board or commission. These boards are usually composed of fairly prominent citizens who can lend prestige and public acceptance to departmental programs. In some cases these boards make general policy and exercise supervision over departmental administration, and the board appoints the department director who becomes its chief

[5] Public Health Service, *Organization and Staff for Local Health Service*, P.H.S. Publication No. 682, Washington, 1961, p. 1.

executive officer. This organizational arrangement gives a high degree of independence to the health function, since the health director is not responsible directly to the mayor or manager. In other cities the director of the department is an appointee of the mayor or manager and the board serves only in an advisory capacity. Although such a board has no supervisory authority, its members may enjoy high prestige in the community, and the departmental director will find their support very useful in securing public acceptance for major health programs.

PUBLIC WELFARE

To a certain extent many activities of public health departments have welfare overtones. Family health centers and city hospitals generally have as their clients persons from low-income families who are economically unable to secure required medical service through regular private sources. Since the 1930s when the federal government assumed a responsibility for financing welfare services, the states have constituted the major dispenser of such services. In fact a number of important welfare services are handled directly by state departments through regional field offices. Other welfare services are administered by local governments with state grants-in-aid and a certain amount of administrative supervision.

If the term "public welfare" is used in its broadest sense, it would include government-sponsored insurance-type programs which are generally applicable to all citizens and for which no "means test" is required for participation in benefits. This would include the Old Age and Survivors Insurance program and Medicare. This program is administered wholly by the federal government and is financed by federally levied and collected payroll charges against employees and employers. It would also include employment compensation programs which are administered by the states but financed from federal payroll taxes assessed against employers. The federal financing feature makes it possible for the federal government to set minimum requirements which states must meet in order to receive federal payments. This program is intended to keep workers from going on the rolls of other welfare agencies when they are unemployed.

Social Security and Employment Compensation programs do not by any means cover the needs of all those who for one reason or another are unable to provide for themselves and for those who are dependent upon them. Many persons are, for physical or mental reasons, unemployable, some do not have the skills required to fill jobs that are available, and a great number of older persons have no social security benefits or have only minimum payments. Many children without parents have no means of support, and a great number of women with dependent children are unable to provide home care for them if they are forced to work full time to make a living. These are what are usually referred to as welfare cases.

Through federal, state, and local cooperative efforts, a wide range of welfare programs has been developed to meet the needs of these people. The primary role of the federal government has been to help finance the programs and to establish minimum standards of eligibility for individual payments, and of administrative competence. Some states have elected to administer welfare programs from a state department through local field offices; others have delegated administrative responsibility to cities and counties under state supervision.

The character of the population of our large core cities has made them the areas in greatest need of welfare services. The older housing facilities and lower rents found in the central city have attracted families with the lowest incomes. These are also the people with least education and the lowest level of trade skills. Many central-city dwellers have moved into core-city areas from marginal farms and from rural areas where they have been unable to make a decent living. These persons are the last to find employment, the lowest paid, and the first to be laid off. Thousands of people in every large city in America are dependent on private and religious charities or public assistance for the necessities of life. At the same time the central cities are often least able to support these welfare needs. Industries have moved from the central city, and the wealthiest taxpayers have established homes in the suburban municipalities.

Although the states and the federal government have come to the aid of cities in their welfare programs, available resources are often inadequate to meet the needs. The problem is not so much that there are insufficient programs to cover the kinds of needs found in cities, but that the amount of assistance that is available in each specific case is insufficient to meet even minimum levels of adequacy.

Kinds of Welfare Programs

A common method of classifying public welfare programs distinguishes between *indoor* and *outdoor* assistance. Indoor assistance refers to types of institutionalized care which in earlier periods constituted the major kinds of assistance available to the needy. Poor farms and almshouses with minimum-care facilities were available to those who had given up hope of ever being able to care for themselves. Today homes for the aged, the chronically ill, the mentally ill, and homeless children constitute the major kinds of public indoor assistance.

Outdoor assistance refers to programs designed to help people remain in the community, in their own homes when possible, with the hope that assistance will be only temporary and that recipients will be able to go on their own after the aid period is over. Children without parents may be placed in foster homes and their care paid for out of public funds. Direct relief payments will be made to families in which the breadwinner is without employment. "Categorical" assistance refers to welfare aid granted to persons who qualify under specified legal categories. These usually are older citizens, dependent children, and the blind. "General" assistance applies to all those who are dependent on the public for life's necessities and who do not fall within a specially designated category. General assistance may be in the form of specific commodities including foods, medicine, and clothing, in the form of direct money payments, or in reduced prices for certain commodities that are in surplus supply.

New programs sponsored by the federal government in its "war on poverty" and administered locally include training and retraining of workers for the kinds of jobs that are available to those with proper skills and "head-start" programs to help underprivileged children achieve better results in the regular public schools. An interesting feature of some of the poverty programs is the use of nongovernmental organizations as the local agencies to receive federal aid and to administer the program locally. Such organizations as the Urban League and neighborhood associations have assumed responsibility for some of these programs. Another feature of these programs has been the conscious effort of the federal officials administering them to require the inclusion of some of the poor people in the policy-making machinery at the local level.

Welfare officials at both the national and local levels are, as a result of the programs to alleviate poverty in the core areas of large cities, aware of the close relationship between welfare work and the public school systems. A great deal of poverty results from the fact that the heads of families cannot find regular employment at wages sufficient to maintain a family above poverty-level standards. This inability is often due directly to the fact that the family head has insufficient education to acquire the kind of skills required in the present economic system. Poverty in the next generation may be substantially reduced if children of the poor of this generation are kept in school and if the school system meets their specific needs. The problem is complicated by the fact that social conditions in the homes are not such as to encourage young children to strive for an education or to assist them in their learning efforts. For this reason children from homes where the parents have very little education, where there are no books or magazines, and where diets are inadequate for growing children need special assistance if they are to be successful in regular school programs, which are generally designed for children from upper- and middle-class environments. Welfare programs which fail to give major emphasis to helping underprivileged children succeed in the early years of school and encouraging their continuance in school will fail to make a long-range impact on poverty in our large cities. Basic revisions in some school programs may be necessary to meet the needs of pupils who are sure to fail if they are forced into curricula for which they are not equipped.

If welfare programs are to be effective in materially reducing poverty on a long-range basis, programs must be aimed toward attacking the economic and cultural causes of poverty as well as alleviating existing suffering. This may mean greater expenditures for research into basic factors which have made large cities the centers of very low-income and culturally deprived people and to seek some long-range solutions which attack the causes rather than the symptoms of poverty. Whether or not the reverse income tax or the guaranteed annual income for families will be the answer one cannot say, but certainly Americans are going to hear a lot more about programs of this kind if the many different welfare programs now in existence do no better than they have in the past in eliminating poverty.

HOUSING

Very little imagination is required to see the interrelationships between health, welfare, and housing. Since families with the lowest incomes by necessity are forced to seek living quarters in the lowest-rent areas, low educational level and need for public health and welfare services tend to concentrate in the areas of the city with the poorest housing facilities. Because rents are low and because of the type of tenant that low-rent housing attracts, landlords make little effort to keep property in good repair or to make it comply with minimum standards of decency. In commenting on the endurance of slums in American cities, Daniel Seligman observed:

> In the second decade of postwar prosperity, in a time of steadily advancing living standards, the slum problem of our great cities is worsen-

ing. Today some 17 million Americans live in dwellings that are beyond rehabilitation—decayed, dirty, rat infested, without decent heat or light or plumbing. The problem afflicts all our metropolitan areas (i.e. those in the Census Bureau's 168 standard metropolitan areas) but it is most severe in the biggest, richest, most industrialized cities. . . . Block by block, the slums are spilling out into once respectable neighborhoods as the middle class leaves for suburbia.[6]

The areas of cities that are referred to as slums and blighted residential areas are largely inhabited by older people whose incomes make it difficult for them to afford the rentals found in better areas, racial minority groups (particularly Negroes), and migrants from small towns and rural areas who are employable in only the most unskilled types of jobs. To many of these migrants even low-level slum property supplies better housing than they were accustomed to in the rural areas from which they fled.

Any attempt to deal effectively with the problem of adequate housing for present slum dwellers must take cognizance of the multifaceted nature of slums and blighted areas. The nature of living conditions in any given area is determined by the physical character of the housing properties, the economic potential of the residents, and the sociopsychologic characteristics of those who are likely to be found in the poorest housing areas. Scott Greer has called attention to the problem of defining the words "slum" and "blight," since they are value-loaded terms.[7] Often "blight" is used as the broader term and is applied to areas, regardless of the existing land-use patterns, where buildings are deteriorating and in a poor state of repair, where sanitary facilities are inadequate, and where utilities and sewage facilities are below standard. A slum is simply a blighted area where the land-use pattern is predominantly residential. Greer points out that, operationally, areas are designated as blighted when they are wanted for some higher use; i.e., there may be areas in a city where physical properties are very poor, rents are low, and utility and public services are minimal, but since no one wants the land in the area in order to convert it to a higher use, it is not declared blighted. Higher use generally means more profitable use. Better buildings are to be constructed, rental values will increase, more taxes will be returned to the city, and therefore, a better class of tenants and residents will be attracted. As Greer puts it, "The definition of blight is, simply, that 'this land is too good for these

[6] Daniel Seligman, "The Enduring Slums," Editors of Fortune, *The Exploding Metropolis*, Anchor Books, Doubleday & Company, Inc., Garden City, N.Y., 1958, p. 92.

[7] Scott Greer, *Urban Renewal and American Cities*, The Bobbs-Merrill Company, Inc., Indianapolis, 1965, pp. 20–27.

people.' "[8] The idea of higher use becomes a question of value, and any given use of property in a given area might be considered inadequate by someone who would like to convert it to a different use pattern.

Residential blighted areas or slums may be more easily identified, but here also the dividing line between standard and substandard housing is not entirely objective, and there is plenty of room for differences of opinion about the requirements that should be specified for standard housing units. Most large cities have elaborate housing and construction codes to control new building ventures, and many of them have codes designed to ensure minimum standards of housing in older rental units. Successful enforcement of these standard housing codes, however, has proved to be very difficult. The fact that substandard housing facilities are occupied indicates that there are no other housing units available at the rents these occupants can afford, that transportation to their jobs from other locations is difficult, or that the residents are not too much dissatisfied with existing conditions. If city officials make a determined effort to enforce housing codes, the results will be the displacement of families who have no other place to go. As long as the notion persists that housing is to be determined by personal choice of renters in the economic open market, city officials will find code enforcement very difficult.

But slums are not merely substandard physical properties, they are dwelling places for people, and the way of life of those who are either attracted to these areas or are forced by economic conditions to live in them determines to some extent the character of life style found there.[9] Without reference to the nature of physical structures, slum areas may be identified by the presence of unkempt lawns, streets littered with cans, broken bottles, and trash and rubbish of every description. "Social indicators of blight include presence of abnormally high rates of juvenile delinquency, venereal disease, and similar results from other health and welfare indices; and economic indicators include concentrations of tax delinquent and tax title properties, declining property values, and presence of an abnormally large number of building vacancies."[10] This is not to say that slums create delinquency and crime. As Seligman puts it, "It is now recognized that housing is far from decisive in the making of good citizens. Very few students of the subject now believe that the slums create crime and vice and disease; it is now considered more likely

---

[8] *Ibid.,* p. 31.
[9] F. Stuart Chapin, *Urban Land Use Planning,* Harper & Row, Publishers, Incorporated, New York, 1957.
[10] *Ibid.,* p. 232.

that the slums simply attract problem families. And their problems will not be erased by putting these families in public housing projects."[11]

Recognition of the fact that conditions in areas which are recognized as slums result not alone because of the physical condition of housing units but also because of the low level of aspirations of those who live there is certainly no reason for lack of concern or for failure to take public action to improve housing and life styles in the slum areas. The fact is that governmental efforts designed to cope with the housing problems may prove costly and ineffective if such attempts are not accompanied by vigorous efforts to meet the economic, social, and psychologic needs of those who gravitate to the slums because they see no other choice open to them. There is sufficient experience with massive housing projects that have been constructed to replace slums to demonstrate that the problems of urban blight cannot be attacked simply as a problem involving physical structures; effective programs must be devised to deal with the personal problems of those who have known no other life style than that of the slums.

Housing Programs

The federal government entered the housing field in the early years of the depression of the 1930s through the Emergency Relief and Construction Act, the National Industrial Recovery Act, and the Public Works Administration of the Department of Interior, but major federal activity to stimulate the construction of more housing dates from the passage of the National Housing Act of 1937. Under this act local communities were encouraged to create independent special-purpose housing authorities to construct and manage housing. State action was required to permit local communities to create housing authorities and to clothe them with the power of eminent domain and to extend tax relief for new housing projects. A major purpose of the act was slum clearance, rather than an increase in the housing supply. In fact, for each new housing unit constructed a slum unit had to be torn down. Legal approval for slum clearance and housing authorities was based on the doctrine

---

[11] Seligman, op. cit., p. 106. Seligman comments on the idea that housing change alone will change life style: "The new criticism reflects in part the disillusionment of liberals, who expected too much of the public housing. 'Once upon a time,' says a close student of New York's slums, 'we thought that if we could only get our problem families out of those dreadful slums, then papa would stop taking dope, mama would stop chasing around, and junior would stop carrying a knife. Well, we've got them in a nice new apartment with modern kitchens and a recreational center. And they're the same bunch of bastards they always were.' "

of police powers under the assumption that elimination of slums and construction of low-rent housing units would protect the health, safety, morals, and welfare of the people. During the Second World War the federal government entered the housing field to provide units for employees required in war plants. These projects were also managed by local authorities.

Increased federal involvement in housing was provided in the Housing Act of 1949 which was sponsored by Senators Taft and Ellender and had bipartisan support. The act encouraged private redevelopment of blighted areas through federal aid in the form of expanded loans and subsidies to local housing authorities for construction of low-rent units. A majority of urban redevelopment programs designed to revitalize declining areas of central cities and large public housing projects have been developed under this act and amendments added in 1954 and 1961.[12]

EVALUATION OF HOUSING PROGRAMS

There is no question but that most large American cities can point to extensive urban renewal projects which have replaced badly blighted areas (generally in downtown areas) with new apartments and commercial structures and to massive high-rise low-rent public housing projects. As integral parts of these projects streets have been widened and repaved, and lighting has been greatly improved. There is also much evidence to indicate that life styles of residents in the public housing projects have not been significantly improved, that serious maladjustments resulted as residents of renewal areas were forced to give up their flats and seek homes elsewhere, and that other fairly stable areas were blighted by the changes resulting from the influx of families from the renewal areas. Serious political issues have accompanied the public housing program, and some of them persist to vex the local authorities that now manage public housing projects.

In the early stages of public housing, efforts were made to fill housing developments with families that would be compatible; this really meant racial segregation. Recent attacks on racial segregation in schools and jobs have carried over into public housing. The issue of private versus public initiative has persisted throughout the debates on local projects, and strong opposition is voiced against tax exemptions awarded to urban renewal projects. Perhaps the best that can be said is that all public housing is not as bad as its

[12] For a more extended discussion of federal involvement in the housing field see Scott Greer, *Urban Renewal and American Cities*, The Bobbs-Merrill Company, Inc., Indianapolis, 1965, especially chaps. 1, 2.

opponents claimed it would be nor as good as its supporters expected. The most serious fallacy was in the acceptance of the myth that the social evils so generally associated with slum populations were due to bad housing and that improving housing facilities alone would cure these social evils. John P. Dean makes this point clearly:

> Social reformers hoped that USHA would introduce a new way of life for the slum family. They believed that many personal and social maladjustments would wither away in the new life of the community. But they failed to appreciate the problems of rehousing. . . . Those who are well trained in community organization and leadership have never thought of clearing the slums and providing in their place decent, safe and sanitary homes as the whole public housing job. But the vast bulk of housing officials are not well trained in the arts of organization and leadership. . . . Until housing officials frankly face the rehousing of families as a *social* experiment in relocation and adjust policies and procedures accordingly, large-scale rehousing operations will frequently be accompanied by conditions falling far short of current objectives of social welfare.[13]

Political issues that affect the amount of housing that is available in cities arise at a number of points in the political process. Decisions must be made to designate certain areas as blighted and ready for a renewal project, tax abatement must be granted to encourage capital investment, bond issues must be approved for street improvement, for better lighting, and for the city's share of costs. Questions as to the adequacy of police and fire protection in housing areas, the proximity of schools to homes, and adequacy of garbage and refuse collection come regularly before city officials. In areas where attempts are being made to arrest blight, to rehabilitate substandard structures, and to encourage the repair and maintenance of existing housing, questions as to the adequacy of the city's housing code and the rigidity of its enforcement are matters to be decided in the political arena. A specific issue which has produced heated political debate in the legislatures of some cities and will surely be carried into the judicial arena has arisen from attempts to force landlords to maintain their rental properties at legally fixed standards. The tool used is the city's right to condemn property for human habitation and its right to take private property for public use. City ordinances may authorize the building commissioner to give adequate warning to a landlord to make specific repairs to his buildings. If the facilities are not brought up to required standards within a specified time, the city may take over the

[13] John P. Dean, "The Myths of Housing Reform," *American Sociological Review*, vol. 14, pp. 283, 287, 288, April, 1949.

property, make the necessary repairs, and levy the charges against the owner. The only way by which the owner can redeem his property is to repay the city in an amount equal to its expenditures. Enforcement of these kinds of ordinances faces the same type of problems that cities face in enforcing all kinds of building codes. A host of inspectors is required to canvass all properties, and a sizable bureaucracy is required to handle the work involved in taking over property and contracting for its repair. Few city councils are willing to vote sufficient funds to support a bureaucracy big enough to do the job adequately.

RECREATIONAL FACILITIES

Most cities have for years maintained some kind of public park. In some cases these consist primarily of open land maintained for relaxation and picnicing, but in the larger cities public parks include zoos, museums, gardens, and fields for numerous competitive sports. In keeping with programs to improve the life styles of lower-income groups, neighborhood recreational areas and community centers have been developed where organized and supervised activities can be encouraged. In many cases these facilities are designed to appeal to residents of all ages from the preschool children to those of retirement age. School playgrounds are generally not in use during the summer months; therefore arrangements may be made with the independent school district to permit use of their facilities by the city. As cities acquire land for recreational purposes there is good reason to seek to select parcels adjoining or near school playgrounds so they can be used jointly by the schools and the city.

City parks have often been administered by a semi-independent board or commission. Although park operation is not usually delegated to a special district or authority, the city park board may function with as much independence as if it were an agency separate from the city government. In fact park maintenance is often supported by a special tax levied by a direct popular vote, and the council is without power to lower this rate or to decide the purposes for which the income will be spent. Additional revenue may be available from charges for concessions, and for use of certain park facilities such as golf courses, tennis courts, swimming pools, and admission charges to zoos, planetaria, and gardens.

The isolation of park boards from the mainstream of city politics may produce considerable political conflict if the city recreational program is assigned to the park board for administration. The goals of a recreational program supported from city revenues may be viewed quite differently by a park board and by a department of health and welfare, and therefore the question of how to allocate available resources between large open-space areas and smaller neighborhood play fields may depend on who has power to make the decisions. Persons primarily interested in using recreational facilities as a social resource to improve the life style of the underprivileged will insist on major outlays for better-equipped and supervised facilities in the low-income areas, while this kind of allocation may not be acceptable to those who see large central parks as major cultural resources of the city. One may speculate that the neighborhood playground supporters will fare better if allocations are made by a city council which has representation from all areas of the city than they would before a semi-independent park board whose members are appointed on a nonpolitical basis and who enjoy fairly long overlapping terms.

BIBLIOGRAPHY

Books

Adrian, Charles R.: *Governing Urban America*, 2d ed., McGraw-Hill Book Company, New York, 1962, chaps. 19, 21.

Agger, Robert E., Daniel Goldrich, and Bert E. Swanson: *The Rulers and the Ruled*, John Wiley & Sons, Inc., New York, 1964, chap. 13.

American Public Health Association: *Local Health Units for the Nation*, The Commonwealth Fund, New York, 1946.

Banfield, Edward D., and Morton Grodzins: *Government and Housing*, McGraw-Hill Book Company, New York, 1952.

Greer, Scott: *Urban Renewal and American Cities*, The Bobbs-Merrill Company, Inc., Indianapolis, 1965.

Hanlon, I. J.: *Principles of Public Health Administration*, 4th ed., C. V. Mosby Company, St. Louis, 1964.

Jacobs, Jane: *The Death and Life of Great American Cities*, Random House, Inc., New York, 1961.

Kaplan, Harold: *Urban Renewal Politics: Slum Clearance in Newark*, Columbia University Press, New York, 1963.

Meyerson, Martin, and Edward C. Banfield: *Politics, Planning and the Public Interest*, The Free Press, Glencoe, Ill., 1955.

Paul, B. J. (ed.): *Health, Culture and Community*, Russell Sage Foundation, New York, 1955.

Rossi, Peter, and Robert Dentler: *The Politics of Urban Renewal*, The Free Press, Glencoe, Ill.: 1961.

Vernon, Raymond: *Metropolis 1985*, Anchor Books, Doubleday & Company, Inc., Garden City, N.Y., 1960, chaps. 9, 10.

Weaver, Robert C.: *The Urban Complex*, Anchor Books, Doubleday & Company, Inc., Garden City, N.Y., 1966.

Articles

American Public Health Association: "Local Health Department Services and Responsibilities," *American Journal of Public Health*, vol. 41, pp. 302–309, March, 1951.

Bauer, Catherine: "The Dreary Deadlock in Public Housing," *Architectural Forum*, vol. 106, pp. 140–142, 219–222, May, 1967.

Crabtree, James A.: "Plans for Tomorrow's Needs in Local Public Health Administration," *American Journal of Public Health*, vol. 53, pp. 1175–1182, August, 1963.

Duggar, George S.: "The Relation of Local Government Structure to Urban Renewal," *Law and Contemporary Problems*, vol. 26, pp. 49–69, Winter, 1961.

Foard, Ashley A., and Hilbert Fefferman: "Federal Urban Renewal Legislation," *Law and Contemporary Politics*, vol. 25, pp. 635–684, Autumn, 1960.

Gans, Herbert: "The Human Implications of Current Redevelopment and Relocation Planning," *Journal of the American Institute of Planners*, vol. 25, pp. 17–18, February, 1959.

Levine, Sal, Paul E. White, and Benjamin D. Paul: "Community Interorganizational Problems in Providing Medical Care and Social Services," *American Journal of Public Health*, vol. 53, pp. 1183–1195, August, 1963.

Mulrooney, Keith: "Community Responsibility for Mental Health," *Public Management*, vol. 44, pp. 127–130, June, 1962.

Schreibers, Lee, John J. Grove, and Herbert R. Domke: "Air Pollution Control in Urban Planning," *American Journal of Public Health*, vol. 51, pp. 174–181, February, 1961.

SUBJECT INDEX

NAME INDEX